Provonsha

GOLDEN TREASURY

OF

BIBLE STORIES

GOLDEN TREASURY
of
BIBLE STORIES

Two Hundred and Three Bible Stories From Genesis to Revelation

By
Arthur Whitefield Spalding

Author of "Christian Storytelling and Stories"
and many other storybooks

Paintings by
Clyde N. Provonsha and Robert Temple Ayres

SOUTHERN PUBLISHING ASSOCIATION, NASHVILLE, TENNESSEE
PRINTED IN U.S.A.

Seventh Printing

This Book
Is Lovingly Presented to

by

TO PARENTS AND TEACHERS

We need to fill our children's minds with the Holy Scriptures. They are a shield against error and evil. Children in God-fearing homes may be led to treasure the Bible as the greatest of all books; but there are many, many children who do not have that privilege.

In the English language the most favored translation of the Bible is the Authorized Version of 1611. It is indeed a masterpiece of literature, and probably will never be equaled in felicity of phrasing and in grace and majesty of speech. But, like all living languages, English speech has changed much in these three and a half centuries, and the archaic style and phraseology of this version are perplexing and often unintelligible to the modern reader, especially to the child who is not from infancy fed upon it. Even those who are most highly favored will find a version in modern speech enlightening and pleasing.

There have been a number of modern translations, especially of the New Testament but some also of the Old, which have the merit of making clearer the meaning of the Bible. In this book of Bible stories I have made use of some of these, without cumbering the text for children by the specific references which would be expected in a book for adults. Whenever the quotation seems unfamiliar, it may generally be referred to some one of these newer versions, and especially to the Old Testament translation edited by J. M. Powis Smith and the New Testament translation by Edgar Goodspeed.

I have sometimes turned the phrasing of the quotation, from whatever source, into more childlike language, taking care to preserve the meaning. In some instances facts gained from non-Biblical sources have been included to make the setting clearer. The plain sense of the Bible text has been followed, without any attempt at indoctrination or sectarian interpretation. May this book be blessed of our Father in heaven to interest the children more deeply in the Bible and to make its meaning clear.

A. W. Spalding.

7

DEAR BOYS AND GIRLS

Let me introduce you to the Bible. Or, if you are already acquainted, let me suggest a longer visit. Forty centuries would be about right, don't you think?

The Bible is the grandest book in the world. It was written by a great many men, some of whom lived hundreds and hundreds of years apart, but all of whom were inspired by God. It tells of the beginning of the world and of the end of the world and of the beginning of a new earth which will be free from sin and suffering and death. Almost at the very last it says: "And God shall wipe away all tears from their eyes; and there shall be no more death, neither sorrow, nor crying, neither shall there be any more pain; for the former things are passed away. And He that sat upon the throne said, Behold, I make all things new." Revelation 21:4, 5.

That is the way God made things in the first place, and that is the way He meant them always to be. How there came to be sin and suffering and sorrow and death is one of the first things the Bible tells us. All the way between that first story, of six thousand years ago, and the last story, which will soon be, is what the Bible covers.

Moses, the first man who wrote any of the Bible story, lived about 2,500 years after the earth was created; but God told him how to write the story of those 2,500 years. Then there were about 1,500 more years from Moses to the last writer of the Bible, John. So you see the Bible covers 4,000 years, or forty centuries.

Since then there have been nearly 2,000 more years. But you know, the Bible foretold the main things that would happen in these 2,000 years; and in its prophecies it tells, not in story but in figures and numbers, what would happen even down to our own time, and beyond to that happy day when all tears shall be wiped away.

More than that, it tells how God made a plan to do away with sin and to save a people out of the trouble that sin brings. The stories tell this tale, and the poems and songs and prophecies of the Bible are bright with the promise. There is no other book in the world that does this, though we who love the Bible may tell it over again, at least in part, as this book does. This book tells only some of the stories that are in the Bible, the most important ones. If it should tell them all, it would make so big a book you could not hold it in your two hands. It will be a good thing for you to read all the Bible stories in the Bible itself. And if I were you, I would read all the texts that are listed at the top of every story in this book, for they are where the story comes from.

The reason that children need a book which tells the whole story over is that some of the language of the Bible is suited to big folks but is too hard for children to understand, and they need to have it made simple. But still, children can grow to understand even the difficult parts of the Bible. And so all I want to do is to make you better acquainted with the Bible.

I hope you have a Bible of your own. Anyway, there is a Bible in your house which you can read, maybe a big family Bible. That is the kind of Bible I first learned to read in my childhood home seventy years ago. And you know, that's how I came to own a Bible of my own, my very first Bible. For the Sunday school superintendent came in one day and saw the little boy poring over the big family Bible. And what did he do? Why, on the next Christmas tree he put a beautiful, fat little Bible just for me! I wouldn't be surprised at all if somebody big sees you, Buster Bill, or Bitsy Beth, reading the big family Bible, and finds you haven't any right-sized Bible of your own, he'll see to it, come Christmas, that you do have one.

And I hope you'll love that Bible and read that Bible till it wears out, just as I did. For it's the greatest book in the world, and "able to make thee wise unto salvation, through faith which is in Christ Jesus." 2 Timothy 3:15.

God loves you, dear children, as I love you truly.

Your old friend,

A. W. Spalding.

9

THE BLACK-AND-WHITE PICTURES WERE DRAWN BY THE FOLLOWING ARTISTS:

Bernard Barton

Norman Anderson

Joseph Camana

Clem Gretter

Georgette Delattre

Don Sibley

Gil Evans

Herb Tauss

Dorothy Burke

Hal Frater

Anthony Billotto

Bernard Safran

Maxwell Schwartz

Harry Bernie

Annabelle Forsch

CONTENTS

Stories of the Ancients

Stories of the Patriarchs

Stories of the Exodus

Stories of the Judges

Stories of the Kings

Stories of the Prophets

Stories of the Remnant

The In-between

Stories About Jesus

Stories Jesus Told

Stories About the Apostles

List of Paintings

Adam and Eve in Their Garden Home

God performed the first wedding ever to be held on the earth, and gave the Garden of Eden to Adam and Eve to be their first home. Adam was to love and protect Eve and treat her as an equal, and she was to be a helper for him. Together they could have been perfectly happy in their beautiful home.

CLYDE N. PROVONSHA, ARTIST

STORIES OF THE ANCIENTS

Adam to Abraham

"In the Beginning"

Genesis 1:1-25

IN THE BEGINNING of this world there wasn't any boy and there wasn't any girl. And there wasn't any father or any mother. There just wasn't anybody at all upon the earth. Not in the beginning.

And there weren't any animals. There wasn't any kitten to frisk about, or any doggie to run and bark, or any pony, or any cows, or any lambs. And there wasn't a single bird, not a canary, or a mockingbird, or a bluebird, or a crow. And there weren't any chickens. Not back there in the beginning.

More than that, there wasn't any sun, or any moon, or any star. You couldn't see a thing. And there wasn't anything to see. No grass, no flowers, and no trees. There weren't even any stones, or any ground, or rivers, or lakes. There just wasn't anything at all, in the beginning.

But up in heaven, and everywhere, there was God. God is the maker of all things, and nobody made God. For God has always been living and always will be living. Of course we can't understand that, but it is true. From eternity to eternity, there is God.

God made the angels in heaven. Heaven is a wonderful place. It is God's home, more beautiful than you can think. And there the angels were. But the angels went everywhere, wherever God sent them on errands. And God went everywhere. He is everywhere at once.

So God came down with His angels to where this world was to be. And that was the beginning.

In the beginning God created the heavens and the earth.

All was dark, and there was nothing that had any shape.

Then God sang because He was happy for what He was going to do. And the angels sang with Him.

And God spoke. He said, "Let there be light."

And suddenly there was light, so that you could see whatever there was to see. But there was nothing to see, only a great lot of water, all mixed up.

Then God set that water to whirling, so that it made a great ball, which is this earth. While it was turned toward the light, everything was light. And God called that the Day. But when it was turned away from the light, everything was dark. God called that the Night. It

19

took quite a while to go around once. It took twenty-four hours of light and darkness. That made the first day of the beginning of creation.

So the next day God said, "Let there be air, to make the sky. And let the sky be between the water on the earth and the water above the sky." And it was so. And the earth kept on turning, out of the light into the dark and back to the light again. And the evening and the morning were the second day.

Then the next day God said, "Let the waters on the earth be gathered together in one place, and let the dry land appear."

All at once there was dry land, and it rose above the waters. God called the dry land Earth. And the waters He called Sea.

And yet there was nothing on the earth but bare ground. Then God said, "Let the earth bring forth grass, and plants bearing seed, and fruit trees bearing good fruit."

All of a sudden the earth was a garden. The grass sprang up, and the plants came up, with beautiful flowers on them. And the trees grew and grew—why, you could see them grow, with branches and little twigs and leaves on them to make shade, and flowers to make fruit. Oh, it was a beautiful garden indeed! And that was the third day.

Then the earth turned on, away from the daylight into the darkness of the night. And it went around all the way, until it came to the light again. And now God said: "Let there be lights in the heavens, a great light to rule the day, and a lesser light to rule the night, and many, many little lights to sprinkle the sky in the night."

Suddenly there was the sun shining in its might, making the light of day. And as the earth rolled around into the night, there was the moon to shed its soft light on the earth. And there were the stars, many, many, many of them, to light up the sky in the night. And the earth rolled around to the sun and the light again. And that was the fourth day.

But as yet there was no creature on all the earth, not a bird, or a fish, or a four-footed animal. If you had been there, you wouldn't have heard a sound except the soft swish of the water, and you wouldn't have seen anything move except the grass and the leaves on the trees as the wind ran through. Still! So still in the great garden God had made of this earth.

Then God said: "Let there be fishes in the sea. Let there be creatures in both sea and land. Let there be birds in the air." And it was so. All the waters swarmed with fishes that could swim. And out of the water came the frogs and the toads and the newts and the salamanders. And on the land and on the water and in the air came the birds with wings, some that flew low, and some that flew middling high, and some that soared away in the blue, blue sky. The fishes swam, and the toads hopped, and the frogs leaped, and the birds flew; so there was motion everywhere. And the little peeping frogs twittered, and the big bullfrogs croaked, and the chickens cackled, and the blue-birds and larks and orioles sang, and the eagles whistled away up in the sky. So there were motion and music everywhere. And that was the fifth day.

Then came the sixth day. And God said: "Let there be living creatures on the earth, four-footed creatures, such as cattle and horses and sheep and goats. Let there be creeping things, like caterpillars and worms and all sorts of creatures, little and great." And it was so. There were the little cats and the big cats, and the mice and the elephants, and the rabbits and the horses, and ever and ever and ever so many animals, all in the great park that God had made the earth to be.

And now it was the middle of the sixth day, but creation was not yet finished. For there was no one to rule over all the earth, over the fishes and the frogs and the birds and the animals. There wasn't any man or any woman or any boy or any girl, not anyone.

There was a hush, while everything waited for what God would do next.

And that is the next story.

Did you ever hear how the world was made?
    Listen! I'll tell you the story:
In the golden light and the purple shade,
By morn and by night, each day was made,
    By God, the Lord of glory.

For God came down in power and might,
    While the angel choir stood singing;
And He took the day right out of the night;
For the day was born when God said: "Light!"
    And the sky with praise was ringing.

So one by one the thoughts of God
    Came forth in flowers and birdies,
Till the fair earth stood, from sky to sod,
An open book of the thoughts of God,
    To show what the Lord God's word is.

God's Children

Genesis 1:26-31; 2:7, 18, 21-25

ALL was still. It was the middle of the sixth day. And God had made everything beautiful in its place. There was the green earth, with its grass and its flowers and its trees. And there was the blue sea, with its little waves lapping on the shore. There were the rivers and the brooks and the springs, sparkling in the sunlight. And in the sea and the rivers and the lakes were the finny fishes. Overhead and in the trees and on the ground and even on the water were the feathered birds. And on the earth were the sheep and the cows and the horses and all the four-footed animals.

Up until now, on this sixth day, there were motion and music: the fishes swimming, and the birds flying, and all the animals going about and talking in their own ways. But now it was noon, and everything hushed and waited for what God was going to do. For as yet there was no one to be the head of everything in the world. And all the fishes and birds and animals knew that God was going to give them someone to love them and guide them and rule over them.

Then in the silence God spoke: "Let us make man and woman in our image, to be like us. And let them rule over the fish of the sea, and over the birds of the air, and over the cattle, and over all the earth." And He did.

But, you know, this first man and woman in the world were never babies at all. Everybody since then has started out as a baby. You did, and I did, and daddy and mother did, and uncle and auntie, and grandmother and granddaddy, and kings and queens and newsboys. Every one of us and every one of them was a baby once. And then we grew, or are growing, into men and women.

But it wasn't that way with this first man and woman, Adam and Eve. They were children of God, made in His image. I suppose God said, "Let us start them out full grown, for there will not be any father and mother to take care of them as babies."

So God took some dust of the ground and shaped it into the form of a man. It's very much like your making mud pies. Or like the doll maker's making a doll out of fine clay, and painting it, until your dolly looks just like a sure-enough baby. Only you can't make your mud pies live. And the doll maker can't make the dolly live. But that's what God did.

There lay the man, all perfect: hands and feet, with fingers and toes and arms and legs and body and head, with eyes and nose and ears and hair, just beautiful! But not alive.

Then, seems to me, God stooped down to kiss this lovely child of His. And He breathed into man's nostrils the breath of life. And, what! Man became a living soul.

When he opened his eyes and looked on the world, his beautiful home, Adam knew right away what it was. For he was full grown. He didn't have to learn to walk, for he could walk. And he didn't have to learn to talk, for he could talk. He didn't have to start eating by taking milk. In fact, there wasn't any milk to take. But there were wonderful fruits all around: strawberries and grapes and apples and oranges, besides wheat and corn, and beans and coconuts, and more foods than you could name. And birds to sing, and fish to swim, and animals to play and work. And blue sky and green earth, and sun and moon and stars to shine. So Adam was very happy. There was just one thing he didn't have, and that was someone to talk to and work with and love.

Then God said, "It is not good that the man should be alone. I will make a good helper for him."

So God put Adam to sleep. And while he slept, God took a piece of him, a rib from right over his heart, and healed the place all up again. Then out of the rib He made a woman, just as He had made the man out of dust. She was more beautiful, in a way, than Adam was. And God breathed into her the breath of life, and she too became a living soul.

When Adam woke up, there was the woman right by his side. And she said, "What's your name?"

And he said, "Adam. What's yours?"

And she said, "I don't believe I have any name. I've just waked up."

So he said, "I'll give you a name. Your name is Eve. Come, Eve, let's go out and look all around, and in and through our beautiful home."

"All right," she said, "let's do!" And they did. That's how human life began on this earth.

And that was the end of the sixth day. God's work was finished.

Then all the angels sang and shouted for joy. And God sang with them. And Adam and Eve, listening, joined in. And everybody and everything sang and were happy. For the world was made.

The First Sabbath

Genesis 2:1-3; Exodus 20:8-11

IN SIX DAYS God made the heavens and the earth, and then came the seventh day. For the week is made up of seven days. But why? This is why:

On the first day God created. On the second day He created. On the third day, and the fourth day, and the fifth day He created. And on the sixth day He created, and man was the crown of His creation. Thus the heavens and the earth were finished, and all the host of the things in them. And on the seventh day God had ended all the work which He had made; so He rested on the seventh day from all His work, and looked it over, and rejoiced in it. And God blessed the seventh day, and made it holy, because on it He had ceased from all His work, in doing which He had brought about creation. And this seventh day He called the Sabbath day. For Sabbath means "rest."

What a wonderful day was that first Sabbath! There was a great gathering and a great meeting on that Sabbath day. God came first, and He was the teacher. The angels came next, and they were the choir. And down in the body of the house of God, which was this earth, were the worshipers. And how many do you think there were? Just two: Adam and Eve! Unless you count the animals, too, and the birds and the fishes and everything. I suppose they were worshiping, too, in their way, because they were thankful and happy, and God spoke to them and through them. Maybe they made the orchestra.

But let's stay with Adam and Eve. When they woke up that Sabbath morning, they wakened to the first full day of their lives. For they were only one day old! But they weren't babies. Adam was a big man, and Eve was a grand woman. They were taller than we are, and far more beautiful, I'm sure. For they never had sinned, and sin is what has made sickness and ugliness and runtiness and disfigurement.

What a wonderful thing to have your first day a Sabbath! And the very first Sabbath there ever was! No one but Adam and Eve could have that experience; and I'm glad for Adam and Eve, aren't you? Well, when they waked up that first Sabbath morning, they saw the angels coming to Sabbath service, singing. Oh, how the hearts of Adam and Eve bowed down in worship!

24

Then, when they had watched and listened to the choir, then they saw—and He had been there all the while—they saw their heavenly Father, God. You might call Him the Preacher, but He was more than that. He was their Teacher. For on this Sabbath day they didn't just sit and listen to a sermon. Their Father, God, came and took them by the hand and led them out through the garden, the beautiful, wonderful home He had made for them. It was His first inspection of this world He had made, and He shared it with His children.

It would take us all day to tell of the things He showed them and taught them: the flowers with all the colors of the rainbow, and the trees with their leafy branches waving a welcome in the breeze, and the brooklets dancing their ripples over the precious stones of their beds—the diamonds and rubies and sapphires and emeralds, and the gold and silver ledges. And the birds singing, and the fishes leaping, flinging the pearly waterdrops from their shining coats of mail. And the animals walking and running and leaping, or grazing quietly in the meadows by the river and the sea. And the blue waters lapping with low sounds on the shore. And the heavenly odors that they smelled, and the many luscious fruits borne on the trees, and the mosses and the shells and the jewel-encrusted rocks.

Why, this was a Sabbath school, the very first Sabbath school that ever was held, with God and the angels and all creation. And I suppose they didn't just walk with solemn steps all the way. They were not afraid of God; for they were His children, and they loved Him. And the angels loved them, and they loved the angels, too. So sometimes, I suppose, just like children today, they took the hands of the angels and ran and laughed with them. And when they came to the brooks or to the seashore, they waded right in with their bare feet and laughed at the waters rippling over them. They climbed the green hills and swung on the long vines and played with all the animals and had the happiest time.

Then, again, they sat down at the feet of their Father, God, while He told them stories. Don't you suppose they liked to listen to His stories of creation?—how one day light sprang up, and another day land and green things started growing, and on and on and on to the very moment they were created. And then God told them about the Sabbath, and why He had made it a rest day for them forever.

And I think, don't you, that when the sun went down on that first Sabbath day, Adam and Eve said to their Father, God: "Oh, it's been such a happy Sabbath day! Thank you, dear heavenly Father, for all You've done for us. Let's have many Sabbaths. Shall we?"

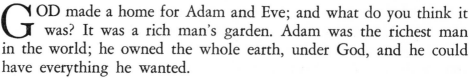

The Garden Home

Genesis 2:8-15, 19, 20

GOD made a home for Adam and Eve; and what do you think it was? It was a rich man's garden. Adam was the richest man in the world; he owned the whole earth, under God, and he could have everything he wanted.

Of course all the earth was a garden, in a way, because everything was beautiful, and there was nothing ugly in it. The hills and mountains were crowned with trees, the valleys and meadows were covered with grass and flowers, the brooks and rivers ran with clear, sparkling water, the sky was blue and the sun shone, and at night the moon and the stars came out. The animals were gentle, the birds were tame, the fishes would swim into your hand. There was food for the taking for man and beast and bird and fish. And everything was just lovely.

But still God made a garden, eastward in Eden, and He put the man and the woman in it. And He told them: "This is your special home. Keep it carefully. Plant the seed that will grow food for you. Train the vines to make houses for you. Space the trees that will give you fruit. Listen to the birds sing. Talk to the animals. Go hand in hand wherever you are. Work together and play together and talk together and sing together. And when I come down in the cool of the evening, come and tell Me what you have learned that day."

So Adam and Eve went out to do what God told them to do. When the birds sang, they sang back. When the animals talked, they talked back; for though the animals did not use human speech, Adam and Eve could understand them. And when the flowers smiled at them, they smiled. When the vines curled their tendrils around their fingers, they lifted them up and trained them into bowers. When the trees softly rustled in the breezes, Adam and Eve listened, and they said, "God is whispering to us through the voices of the trees."

And I think God said to them: "Now this is your schoolroom, and all you see are your schoolbooks—plant and flower, and vine and tree, and insect and fish and frog and bird and animal, and sun and moon and star. Even though you may not see Me with you sometimes, all these things I have written on the face of nature will tell you more and more of Me."

26

Then pretty soon God gave Adam an examination. It was just as much an examination for Eve; because mostly what he knew was what she knew, and what she knew was what he knew.

Well, this was the examination: God brought the creatures one by one before Adam, and He asked him what each one was. How could Adam know? Why, because he could read God's thoughts written on nature. When God spoke and made an animal or anything, that animal or other thing looked just like what God said. So since Adam could read God's thought, when he saw the animal he called it just what God had said when He made it.

So suppose God brought a horse and said, "Adam, what is this?" Why, Adam said right off, "Horse." Only he didn't say "horse," because that's a word in the English language, and there wasn't any English language then. But Adam said in the language of God just what the horse was. And God said, "Right!" Then, say, He brought a dove and said, "Adam, what's this?" And Adam said, "Dove," or whatever it was in God's language. And he was right again.

So Adam went through the whole list, and he was perfect! And Eve was perfect too. That examination was just fun, for they never gave a wrong answer. So they went to school in the Garden of Eden, right there at home. And the angels came and taught them. And God Himself came down in the cool of the evening and walked and talked with them and taught them. What a perfectly perfect school!

"These are lessons that our children need to learn. To the little child, not yet capable of learning from the printed page or of being introduced to the routine of the schoolroom, nature presents an unfailing source of instruction and delight. The heart not yet hardened by contact with evil is quick to recognize the Presence that pervades all created things. The ear as yet undulled by the world's clamor is attentive to the Voice that speaks through nature's utterances. And for those of older years, needing continually the silent reminders of the spiritual and eternal, nature's teaching will be no less a source of pleasure and instruction. As the dwellers in Eden learned from nature's pages, as Moses discerned God's handwriting on the Arabian plains and mountains, and the Child Jesus on the hillsides of Nazareth, so the children of today may learn of Him. The unseen is illustrated by the seen. On everything upon the earth, from the loftiest tree of the forest to the lichen that clings to the rock, from the boundless ocean to the tiniest shell on the shore, they may behold the image and superscription of God."—*Selected.*

The River and Tree of Life

Genesis 2:8-10; Ezekiel 47:1-12; Revelation 22:1, 2

THERE are three persons in the Bible who tell of the river of life and the tree of life. The first one is Moses, in Genesis 2, when God made the world. The second is Ezekiel, in his forty-seventh chapter, when he saw a vision of God's kingdom. The third is John, in Revelation 22, who tells of the new earth and the river and tree of life within it. Moses and Ezekiel call it just the river, but John calls it the river of life. Moses and John call the tree the tree of life, but Ezekiel, though he tells what it is and does, just as John does, only calls it "trees." But putting these ideas all together, we see that the three of them are talking about the same river and the same tree of life.

Now this river God made for the Garden of Eden and for the whole earth. It seems it started in the Garden, and when it had flowed outside it became parted into four rivers, which went everywhere, I suppose in smaller and smaller streams, and maybe lakes, and maybe sinking into the earth and coming up in springs, to water the ground. For you know there wasn't any rain back there. The way God watered the earth was sort of an irrigation system. There were little rills of water under the ground, and overhead there was a dew at night. That gave enough moisture to water the rich soil. And it all came from streams of the river of life.

John tells that the river comes from the throne of God; and because God is the source of all life, I suppose that's why it is called the river of life. Of course John is telling of the river in the new earth, but that is very much like the Garden of Eden, and before we get through these stories we shall find out they are the same. So I suppose that in the Garden, where the river started, there was a seat, perhaps of marble or some other white stone, where God often sat when He came to visit Adam and Eve, and before which they sat down before Him on the shining floor, to listen to His words of life.

Ezekiel says the river is little at the beginning, only ankle-deep, but a few rods along it has grown bigger, so that you would have to wade to cross it. That's the way it is with the life of God: it starts little, like a seed, but it grows greater and greater, like the plant or the tree growing from the seed, and at last it gives fruit to many.

The tree of life was in the midst of the Garden, on either side of the river. It was a wonderful tree, bearing its fruit every month, each time a different kind of fruit. Maybe there were twelve varieties, just as we have that many and more varieties of apple tree, each one bearing a different fruit and ripening at different times.

But the tree of life was different from every other tree in the Garden; because while their fruit gave strength to those who ate it, this tree of life gave life more abundantly. Whoever ate it right along would not die, but have everlasting life. It must have been a beautiful tree, perhaps with shining green leaves like orange or rhododendron or magnolia, its fruit gleaming amidst its leaves like silver and gold and all the colors of the rainbow.

Adam and Eve often sat under the shade of this tree while they listened to their heavenly Father giving them the words of life. They saw God, and they heard His voice. And in the flowers of the tree they smelled the fragrance of His life. And in the fruit of the tree they tasted His goodness. And the feel of it in their hands was like velvet and ivory and silk and gold. How they loved the tree of life!

It is in the plan of God to give the tree of life again to us. Isn't it pretty wonderful that the Bible starts out with the tree of life and ends with the tree of life? You read about it in the second chapter of Genesis and in the last chapter of Revelation. And there is a lesson for us to read in that. We do not now see the tree of life; it is far away, but it is not dead or lost. We have wandered away from it, but God still sends some of its life to us.

It's a little like getting the fruit of the orange tree. Perhaps, if we are in a northern clime, the orange trees are away down south, and we can't see them or touch them or take the fruit off them. But still we get oranges; they are shipped up to us. And we get orange juice because it is prepared and frozen and sent to us. We do not get so much as if we owned the trees because, maybe, we are not rich enough to buy all we want; but we get some. Just so, although we are far away from the tree of life and its fruit, God sends it to us in the words of the Bible and the good gifts of life. The more we open our hearts to His truth, the more fruit of the tree of life we get.

29

The Tree of Death

Genesis 2:9, 17; 3:1-6; 1 Timothy 2:13, 14

BUT there was another tree in the Garden, a very different tree. It was beautiful too, and its fruit looked very inviting, but it was a tree of death. The Bible calls it the "tree of the knowledge of good and evil." God told Adam and Eve that they should not eat of it or touch it; for if they should, they would surely die.

Of course Adam and Eve could not know what it meant to die; for they saw that God had given life to all things, but He had never taken life away. And that was death. God gave them this tree to test them, to see whether they would obey Him or not. If He had not given them such a test, they would always have been just like babies, who cannot choose for themselves, but have to be guarded and cared for all the time. It would have been a very sad thing, wouldn't it, for Adam and Eve always to be like babies.

So God gives us tests today. For instance, He tells us what is good to eat and what is bad to eat. If we use what is bad, like whisky and tobacco, which are poisons, it will bring death to us. And every boy and every girl and every man and every woman who knows what God says must do His commandments, or they will be eating of the fruit of the tree of death.

So Adam and Eve went about their work in the Garden. And maybe it was many days and many months that they kept God's commandment. The Bible does not tell us how long it was, but they must have been good and happy for quite a while. And Adam probably said to Eve, "Stay right with me, and don't go near the tree of death; for there is danger there."

Now Eve did not mean to leave Adam; but she got so interested in tending a bed of flowers and watching the hummingbirds and the bees visiting them and then flying away that she forgot, and kept following them until suddenly she found that Adam was not with her. And when she looked around, what should she discover but that she was right under the tree of the knowledge of good and evil!

"Well," she thought, "I'll just look at it. That will not hurt anything." But as she looked, she thought she saw that it was a very fine tree, as pleasant to her eyes, maybe, as the tree of life. And then there was fruit on it that looked very good to eat. And she never thought to stop and call Adam. She just kept on looking, and wondering why God had told them not to eat the fruit when it seemed so good.

And then, suddenly, she was startled by a smooth voice coming from amid the branches of the tree. She looked and she looked, and what did she see? Why, there was the most beautiful creature that God had made, next to man. It had a beautiful body that gleamed like gold. It had great gauzy wings that enabled it to fly like the birds. Adam and Eve had often seen it, and perhaps it had come to them and they had petted it. Of course all the animals loved to be near Adam and Eve, and sometimes to be petted; but none of them, not even this beautiful and wise creature, could ever talk to them in human speech.

That beautiful creature was the serpent; not like the snake we know today, but altogether different, the highest next to man. And now that serpent was talking to Eve. "Why!" thought Eve, "however did he learn to talk?"

The serpent said, "Has God told you you could not eat of any tree in the Garden?"

"Oh, no," said Eve. "We may eat of the fruit of every tree except this one; but God has said we should not eat of it, lest we die."

And the serpent said, "You shall not die. God knows that the minute you eat of it, your eyes will be opened, and you shall be like God, knowing good and evil. Just see! I have eaten of it, and now I can talk, like you. You are very beautiful, Eve; but wouldn't you like to be very wise, too? Just eat of this fruit, and you will be like God."

Poor Eve! The serpent deceived her, and she fell. She put out her hand and took the fruit the serpent picked for her. It felt good. She smelled it, and it smelled good. Then she took just a little bite, and it tasted good.

"Now," said the serpent, "see! You have eaten of it, and you are not dead. Eat some more."

"Oh," said Eve, "I must take it to my husband." And she ran with some of the fruit in her hands, and found Adam. "See!" she cried, "I have eaten of the fruit of the tree of knowledge, and I didn't die. Adam, the serpent can talk because he has eaten of it. He says that if we eat it, we shall be like God, knowing good and evil."

Adam was stricken to the heart. He knew that what God had said was true. But here was Eve, his lovely wife, who had disobeyed and eaten of the forbidden fruit. He made up his mind that he would die with her if she must die. So he took the fruit and ate it. Together they ate the fruit of the tree of death. And they must die!

31

Cast Out

Genesis 3:7-24; Matthew 17:1, 2; Revelation 19:8

AT FIRST, after they had eaten of the fruit of the tree of death, Adam and Eve thought they felt better. But in a few moments they began to feel bad. They had been clothed in garments of soft light, which John in Revelation calls the righteousness of the saints. Because in the beginning they had been innocent and good and righteous, their faces and their bodies shone with the light of God, more beautiful than any garments that man can make. But now it was slowly disappearing, because they had lost the righteousness. More and more it faded, until they found themselves naked, without any covering.

In terrible fear they ran into a thicket, and plucking some leaves from a fig tree, they fastened them together by their stems, and made aprons for themselves. But, oh, how changed they were! No longer happy looks, but anxious faces. No longer the soft light of God clothing them, but draggled aprons of wilted leaves. The day moved on to the evening, and the air was chill.

Soon they heard the voice of God in the Garden, calling, calling. How happy had they been before to hear that lovely voice! But now they shrank in fear, and hid. And God called, "Where are you?"

Seeing they could not be hid from the eye of God, they crept forth, and Adam answered, "I heard your voice in the Garden, and I was afraid, because I was naked, and I hid myself."

And God said, "Naked! Who told you you were naked? Have you eaten of the tree of which I told you that you should not eat?"

Adam trembled. Now his terrible sin was before him, and he could not face it. He said, "The woman You gave me, she gave me of the tree, and I ate."

"What is this you have done?" God asked Eve.

And Eve, like Adam, tried to throw the blame on someone else. She said, "The serpent deceived me, and I ate."

Then God said to the serpent: "Because you have done this, you are cursed above every other creature. No longer shall you fly, but you shall crawl on the ground. And the woman and her children shall hate you, and bruise your head, while you shall bruise their heels."

There was more in that sentence than any of them understood,

32

The Lamb of God

Adam shrank with anguish from shedding the blood of the first sacrifice. He must take life, but he could not restore it. Successive sacrifices were commanded by God to continually remind man of the dark character of sin and to cause him to acknowledge and be sorrowful for the transgression that caused them.

CLYDE N. PROVONSHA, ARTIST

but it was to be made clear as the years and ages went on. And that will be partly told in our next story.

Then God said to Eve, "You shall have much sorrow. And you shall depend on your husband, and he shall rule over you."

And He said to Adam: "Because you have disobeyed, the ground which has brought forth food for you is cursed. Thorns and thistles it will bring forth. In the sweat of your face you shall eat bread, till you return to the ground. For out of the dust you were made, and to dust you shall return. Dying, you shall die."

So the Lord God sent the man and the woman out of their Garden home, and probably the serpent with them. God shut the gates of Eden, and placed there cherubim, or angels, with a flaming sword which turned every way, to keep the way of the tree of life, so that no man might come to it any more.

Sorrowful, sorrowful were Adam and Eve as they left the Garden and went out on the earth. How changed it was! While still more beautiful than anything we see today, it had the seeds of death in everything. The leaves faded and fell. The birds and the animals fought among themselves. Some of them grew very wild, and turned upon their kind and killed and ate them. And the plants themselves fought for first and highest place. Some of them made thorns and thistles, and all of them struggled against the others.

Adam and Eve tried to help the good ones. They kept the seeds of the good plants and sowed them and cultivated their little gardens. And they took care of the good beasts, and defended them against their enemies. They were very sorry for the wrong they had done. They did not die at once, but they knew that death awaited them. How could any good come out of all this evil? Oh, God was good, and He made a way.

They made a wee garden, did Adam and Eve,
In place of the Garden they'd had to leave.
They dug and they planted; they hoed and they sweat,
But little potatoes were all they could get.
The roses grew thorns, the apple trees spurs,
The thistles had prickles, the clovers had burs.
Said Adam and Eve: "Our sin is the curse.
But the earth still is fruitful; it might be worse.
To work is a blessing, to fill the day;
Tonight, at the altar, we'll kneel and pray."

33

The Lamb-- Promise of God

Genesis 4:2, 4; 22:7, 8; Isaiah 53; John 1:35, 36; 3:16; 1 John 4:16; Isaiah 14:12-17; Revelation 12:7-9; 13:8.

GOD is love. Everything that He does is done in love, because that is His nature. Satan, the devil, is hatred. Everything he does is done in hate, because that is his nature.

Love will conquer hate, and in the end there will be nothing but love. But it takes a long time to do this. It has taken six thousand years so far; but the time is almost finished that hatred shall rule in the world. God made a plan to conquer hate as soon as sin and death came into the world through Adam and Eve. Indeed, He made the plan even before that, from the foundation of the world; for God is never caught unready. He knows all things beforehand and is always ready to meet them. Now He asks you and me to help Him in this war, through the love He gives to us.

Satan was not always Satan. God created him pure and good, before He made this world. His name was Lucifer, which means "light bearer." He was the highest angel in heaven, the brightest and the wisest and the most beautiful. But sin started with him. He became proud because of his beauty. Then he thought he should be as high as God and the Son of God. He got some of the angels to side with him, and they rebelled against God.

So there was war in heaven; but Lucifer with all his angels was cast out, and his name became Satan, which means "enemy." And he was also named the devil, which means "the evil one." He made up his mind to conquer this world as soon as it was made. And this he did by capturing Adam and Eve.

First he captured the serpent, which yielded itself to him. When the serpent tempted Eve, it was the devil in the serpent that did it. So ever since then the serpent has been the sign of Satan, and sometimes he is called that old serpent, and the dragon. The dragon was a kind of serpent. When God condemned the serpent to lose his wings and to crawl on the ground, his wings were only gradually lost. Finally they were all lost, so that now there is no winged serpent, but only snakes. But for a while the serpent kept some stubby wings, though they could not lift him above the ground. And one kind of serpent,

34

the most dreadful kind, was the dragon, which had a heavy body and stubby wings, and sometimes is said to have had more than one head. So, though long ago the dragon and all winged serpents were destroyed in the Flood, the dragon remained in men's stories, and the devil is called the dragon and the great red dragon.

But the sign of God is something very different. It is a lamb. The lamb is the baby of the sheep, and nothing can be more mild and peaceable and good than a lamb. We would hardly expect a lamb to conquer a dragon, would we? And so we might think, too, that love, which is so sweet and good, could not conquer hate, which is so fierce and bad. But love will conquer hate, and the Lamb will conquer the dragon.

Love gives everything. Your father and your mother love you, and they give you all the good gifts they can. They feed you and clothe you and teach you and hold you close in their arms of love. And that is just what our heavenly Father does; and what the Comforter, who is the Holy Spirit, does; and what the Saviour, who is the Son of God, does. God is three persons in one: the Father, the Comforter, and the Son. And God so loved His children, even after they had sinned, that He poured out more of His love to save them.

The plan God made to save the world was that when the right time should come, the Son of God would leave His throne in heaven, and be born as the baby of a woman. He would grow up without sin in this sinful world, and He would show the love of God by healing the sick and comforting the sorrowing, by feeding the hungry, clothing the naked, and doing good to all. And so He would show the love of God. At last He would lay down His life to save from eternal death those who believe in Him.

And to be the sign of this coming Saviour, God told Adam and Eve to take a lamb, to slay it, and to offer it up as a burnt offering on the altar before which they prayed. It seemed to them a dreadful thing to take the life of an innocent lamb; but it taught them a little of the dreadful thing it was to sin and so cause the death of the Son of God. So the lamb became the sign of the coming Saviour, the Lamb of God.

They built their altar of stones before the gates of Eden. That still was home to them. They were like travelers on the road through life. Every day that went by and every night that passed meant that they were a little nearer the end. They must pass through death, but God told them that through His plan of salvation they would at last come back to their Eden home.

35

Brothers Good and Bad

Genesis 4:1-15; Hebrews 11:4; 1 John 3:11, 12

ADAM and Eve were very sad and very sorrowful after they had to leave their beautiful home in the Garden of Eden. They knew it was because they had sinned, and they were very sorry for that. The whole creation suffered with them, and this they knew was all their fault. No wonder they were sad.

But God loved them still, though they had done wrong, and to comfort their hearts He began to give them children, whom they would love, and so partly forget their sorrow.

God said: "I love My children of earth, oh, very, very much. That's why I made them. For love is life, and what we make live, we love. Now they are My children, and they will love too. So I must see that they have children to love."

So there was born to them their first child, a boy. Oh, how they loved him! They called him Cain. In a little while, perhaps only a year or two, God gave them another baby, and they named him Abel. Cain and Abel grew up together as brothers, but they were very different from each other. While their parents taught them alike, and loved them alike, Cain grew to be cross at times, and sulky. He blamed his father and mother for losing their home in the Garden and for making the earth less fruitful. Cain liked to work in the garden, though; and he might have learned many lessons there.

Abel, on the other hand, was a good-tempered boy, who listened to his father and mother and helped them all he could. He felt very sorry for them, because they were often sad, remembering what they had done. And when they told the boys of God's plan, that He loved them so much He would die for them, Abel believed. He kept the sheep, and when the time for sacrifice came, he willingly gave a lamb from his flock, though he loved the lambs. Though they could not go into the Garden of Eden, they could come to its gate, where the cherubim with the flaming sword kept the way. There they built their altar, and there they offered their sacrifice week by week.

When the boys had come to manhood, they were each to bring the offering of a lamb, to show they believed in the coming Saviour, the Lamb of God. But Cain would not do it. Instead, he brought some fruit and vegetables. I suppose he said, "These are much better than to kill a lamb. God ought to be pleased with this sweet offering." But his offering showed he did not believe in God's plan, and that he thought he was doing God a favor by offering fruits from his garden.

Abel brought a lamb, and offered it as God had told them to. God accepted Abel's offering, but He did not accept Cain's. Then Cain was angry and spoke cross words to his brother Abel. Abel tried to show him where he was wrong, but it only made Cain more angry.

Finally, when they were out in the field together, Cain became so angry that he rose up and struck his brother Abel dead. Oh, what a terrible thing for Adam and Eve to bear! Their first-born, whom they had loved so much, had become a murderer.

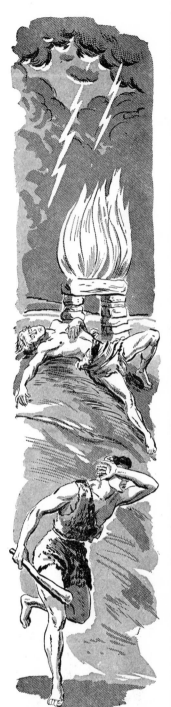

God said to Cain, "Where is Abel, your brother?"

And Cain said, "I don't know. Am I my brother's keeper?"

God said to him: "What have you done? Your brother's blood cries to Me from the ground. And now you are cursed from the earth which you have tilled. Hereafter it will not yield its strength to you. And you shall be a wanderer, afraid for your life."

So Cain went out from the presence of the Lord. And since he now hated the soil which he once had loved, as soon as he had married and had some children, he built a city and lived in it, letting others farm. Some of his children became very skilled in making instruments of music and farming and war; but they grew very wicked too.

Adam and Eve had other children, girls and boys. The next son they had took the place of Abel. His name was Seth. And Seth grew up to be like Abel. He was good and true; and when he had married and had children, he taught them to love God and to obey His commands.

So there were two families or tribes of men in the world—the children of Cain, who were mostly wicked, and the children of Seth, who were at the first mostly good. And the earth began to be filled with people. Men lived a long time then, hundreds of years, because sin had not yet taken so much of their strength. Adam lived to be 930 years old, and nearly all his children and their children and their children lived to be more than 900 years old. Six generations of his children saw Adam before he died, and by that time there were thousands and thousands of them. Just think what it would be like if you could see your great-great-great-great-great-grandfather! Adam tried to teach them all the right way and to love God, and some of them did as he taught them. The last man who saw him and was taught by him was a man who never died.

A Man Who Never Died

Genesis 5:21-23; Hebrews 11:5; Jude 14

THERE are two and one-half billion, or twenty-five hundred million people living on this earth now. That is more than ever have lived in one generation before. But when you try to count up the number of people who have lived through all the more than one hundred and fifty generations, it becomes so many that no one could count them. And yet among all these hundreds of billions of people, there are just two men who have never died.

Two men who have never died? Yes. Why, where are they then? Can we see them? Does anybody ever visit them? Do they ever visit us? They must look awfully old. Who are they? And where are they?

Well, they do not look awfully old, but even more fresh and young than anyone now living on this earth. No, we can't see them or visit them. I am not sure that they never visit us, but if they do, it is in some disguise, so that we would not know them. Where are they? They are in heaven.

I will tell you their names. They are Enoch and Elijah. God took them each one to heaven without ever seeing death. Elijah lived on earth about 2,800 years ago; but Enoch lived long before that, over 5,000 years back. So Elijah is now nearly 3,000 years old, and Enoch is over 5,000; but they are as young as they ever were, and I am sure they look younger, for they have eternal life.

Now Enoch was of the line of Seth. His father Jared's father was Mahalaleel, who was the son of Cainan, who was the son of Enos, whose father was Seth, the son of Adam. All these men lived nearly a thousand years each; but Methuselah, Enoch's son, lived the longest, 969 years. Only he didn't live as long as his father, who is still living.

Enoch loved the Lord, and he did right. His son was born when Enoch was sixty-five years old, and for three hundred years after that Enoch walked with God. The world was growing very wicked; but Enoch tried to stop the tide of evil and to lead men to obey God. He told them that God loved them and wanted to make them happy, but if they broke His commandments they would get only death. He told them that the Lord was coming sometime, with ten thousand of His saints, to judge the world. That seemed very silly to the wicked men of that generation. They knew that the story Adam and Enoch told, of the creation and the Garden of Eden and the sin that drove them out, was true; for there was the Garden and the gate guarded by the flaming sword right before their eyes, and they could see it. But nevertheless they went on as they pleased, overeating, and being drunken, and living lives of wicked pleasure, as though there were no God. But some of them believed and turned away from evil. And especially were there righteous ones of the descendants of Seth, of whom Enoch was one, and his son, and his son's son, and Noah and all his family.

Enoch often went up into the mountains and forests to talk with God and have God talk with him. Then when he was filled with the Spirit he would come down and labor with the world, both the bad people and the few good ones. At last, one day, as he spoke to a crowd, they saw his face begin to shine with the glory of God; and slowly, gently, he was lifted up in their sight and carried away.

They thought that perhaps God had taken him to some other part of the country. And for days and weeks they searched for him where they thought he might be, but to no avail. He was not found, for God had taken him to heaven.

Enoch was a good man, as perfect as a king;
You never heard or saw him do a single wicked thing.
He walked with God all day, and when evening came along,
He knelt beside his bed and prayed for God to keep him strong.

And that, I say, is quite the thing for you and me to do;
A pleasant thing it is to walk with God, and Enoch too.
I shouldn't wonder if sometimes, when we are studying flowers,
They both come down and spend with us some very happy hours.

I'd like to hear dear Enoch say, "My boy, this lily cup
Is God's first steppingstone to heaven. I hope you're coming up."
And then I'd say, "Why, Enoch, yes! Please teach me how to climb.
I know you did, and now in heaven you're happy all the time."

I guess the way that Enoch walked and talked with God all day,
He learned to read God's thoughts in flowers and birds and stars
   alway.
And I believe that I can learn, if God will teach me how,
And just as much as Enoch then, may walk with God right now.

39

God Sends Forth Noah

Genesis 6; Ezekiel 14:14; Hebrews 11:7

GOD looked down on the earth and the men He had made, and it grieved Him to His heart to see that almost everyone had become evil. The earth was still fair and beautiful, though it was under two curses. First, because of Adam's sin it brought forth weeds and thorns and thistles amid its good plants. And second, because of Cain's crime it did not yield its full strength, at least to Cain and his sons.

But men had become very evil. They knew that God had created the earth and them. There was the Garden of Eden, the outside of which was always before their eyes. But the other god, Satan, offered them so much pleasure, like eating the fruit of the tree of the knowledge of good and evil, that they chose to follow him. Some of them even worshiped the serpent, or the dragon, which Satan had used to make Adam and Eve sin.

There was great wealth at their hand; for the silver and gold and iron and other metals were not then buried in the earth, but were right at hand, in plain sight. They used these treasures, with precious wood of the noble trees, to make themselves palaces and temples and groves and gardens. And there they feasted and drank and broke every law of God. God saw that every thought and intent of their hearts was only evil continually.

Yet there were some good men. The sons of Seth were taught the good way, and they kept it. As the people of Cain pressed into the valleys and fruitful plains, the sons of Seth fell back before them and went to live in the mountains. But gradually some of Seth's descendants fell into the ways of the Cainites, and more and more the love and truth of God were lost. Enoch was in the seventh generation, and he taught his son Methuselah and some others. Methuselah taught his son Lamech, and they both taught their son and grandson Noah. But by that time there were few who really loved God and kept His commandments.

So the Lord took Noah, who was as righteous a man as Enoch, and sent him forth with a message to the world. Noah preached that unless men would turn from their wickedness and folly, God would send a flood of waters on the earth which would destroy them all.

There were giants in the earth at that time, and they ruled over weaker people and made slaves of them, and killed and murdered as they pleased. There came to be great beasts, like giants among the animals, which the giants trained to fight and destroy weaker men and their homes and farms. Even in our day the bones of some of these giant animals are found buried in the earth, which show us how terrible were things in Noah's time.

Noah had three sons, Japheth, Shem, and Ham. And as these sons grew up, their father and mother taught them diligently the ways of God, and they too kept the truth. Noah went everywhere, giving the message of God. For 120 years he preached the end of the world to the poor weak peoples and the mighty giants and to all men. Perhaps sometimes in the later years he took Japheth, or Shem, or Ham with him to take part in his mission. But the giants only laughed at him, or threatened him and drove him away.

Meanwhile, by God's order, Noah and his sons and perhaps some hired workmen were building an ark, a great ship, as a refuge when the Flood should come. The ark was three hundred cubits long, fifty cubits wide, and thirty cubits high, with three floors or decks, a door in the side, and a window in the top. A cubit is as long as from the elbow to the tip of the longest finger; and as men then were bigger than now, the cubit may have been two or three feet long; we do not know exactly. But it was a very great ship. It was made of the hardest wood, almost like iron. So it took many years to build.

The men of that time thought Noah was very foolish to build a great ship like that on dry land. Besides, it had never rained, and they did not know what rain was. Their great men, their leaders and teachers, said it was impossible for water to fall down from the skies and drown them all. There were some of the people who believed Noah at first; but as the years went on and their great men made fun of Noah, and the pleasures of the world called to them, they fell away. Though the poor people were wretched and their masters were cruel, all of them finally joined in making fun of Noah and his family. They said they were poor fools, who didn't know anything. And who wanted to be fools like them?

So at last there were left as believers in God's word only Noah and his wife and his three sons and their wives. Noah's father, Lamech, died five years before the Flood came, and his grandfather, Methuselah, died the very year of the Flood. Noah and his family preached and pleaded to the very last, but only they were ready when God's judgment fell.

There Came the Flood

Genesis 7; 8:1-5; Matthew 24:37-39; 2 Peter 3:3-7

THEY stood around the great ship, the ark that Noah had built on dry ground, all the people from the countryside, and the near-by cities, and some from far away. They laughed and they joked about foolish old Noah, now shut up in the ark.

"How long do you think he'll stay in there?" they asked one another.

And they said, "It must be awfully dull in there, without anything going on."

"Oh, they have to feed the animals, you know," another said.

"It was queer, though, how the animals came marching in there a week ago, nobody driving them or calling them," one remarked.

"Yes, and then that flash of light when the door slammed shut. What do you suppose did that?"

"Well, no doubt Noah is a great magician; he made it shut somehow. But he can't make the water come down from the sky."

So they talked, and they laughed, and they put away their fears, as they danced and drank and feasted and ridiculed old Noah, who had taken his family into the ark a week ago. God had made the animals come, as of their own will, and enter the ark. And when Noah and his family had gone in, God came in blinding light and shut the door. Seven days had now gone by since then.

Pitter-patter! Pitter-patter! What's that? The people looked up anxiously; for the sun had disappeared right in the middle of the day. Dark, angry clouds, such as they had never seen before, covered the sky. Pitter-patter! Pitter-patter! Whoosh! Drum, drum, drum! It was rain! And it had never rained before!

Now the people were scared. Some of them ran to the ark and pounded on the door, but God had shut it, and no man could open it. Others ran for their homes. But the water came down faster and faster, and the roads became mud up to their knees. It stopped them.

Then the ground heaved up, and great torrents of water shot into the air. The level plains became a sea. Some of the people got to the hills and climbed them. But the water followed them. Some bound their children on great beasts, like oxen and elephants and even bears;

42

for they knew these animals would climb for their lives. All the people who could got up to the highest mountains. But still the water climbed faster and faster, and it swept them all away.

Oh, how the poor people cried and wailed then! "If we had only listened to Noah," they said. "It's too late, too late!"

And it was too late. The water came down from the sky in torrents. The water gushed up from the ground in rivers. Men, women, children, beasts, birds—all were drowned in the terrible Flood.

The ark, with its precious freight of eight people and many beasts, birds, and creeping things, rose with the waters. The wind blew hard, the waves dashed high, the fountains of the great deep leaped up like waterfalls upside down. The ark shook and swayed and plunged and wrenched. But God sent angels down, who steadied it with their hands. For the storm was so terrible not even the stout ship that Noah had built could withstand it, only as the angels kept it.

All the wicked people were drowned. All the evil beasts, the winged serpents, the terrible dragons, the great overgrown lizards, which had threatened the lives of mankind, yes, even all the beasts and birds and land reptiles which had not gone into the ark were drowned; and there was no life outside the ark, except some of the creatures that lived in the water.

For forty days and forty nights the rain came down and the flood came up. Then the rain stopped. But all the earth was under water, and the ark alone floated on its surface. For five months the waters covered the highest mountains, and the ark floated on a shoreless sea. In the seventh month the ark came to rest in the mountains of Ararat. Down, down sank the waters, until the tenth month. And there came the eleventh month, and the twelfth month, and the first two months of the next year, before the Lord opened the ark, and let all that were in it come out.

But where, do you think, in all this wild welter of waters, was the beautiful Garden of Eden, with the river of life and the tree of life in it? Did God let it be whelmed by the Flood, as all the rest of the world was? I think not. While the Garden was on earth, in the years and centuries before the Flood, its gate was kept by the cherubim with the flaming sword. Nothing impure and sinful could enter there. True, the first sin of Eve and Adam was in the Garden; but that was right by the tree of death. They never got to the tree of life after that.

Now in the last chapter in the Bible, John tells of seeing the river of life and the tree of life in heaven. And what so right and natural as that God, before the waters of the Flood came, should take the Garden

of Eden to heaven? How did He take it? I do not know. He could have taken it up whole, as on a carpet, or just as you would take a toy house from your play on the living room floor and carry it upstairs to the nursery. And maybe He did. But I think perhaps He did it as He will take people to heaven.

If you or I should die right now, loving the Lord, our bodies would go to dust; but when the Lord comes in glory, He would raise us to life again, give us our bodies as before, and take us, all in glory, to heaven. God the Creator can make things out of nothing, He can turn them again to nothing, and He can bring them back to what they were before. That is the way He will make the new earth. And perhaps that is the way He did with the Garden of Eden.

Anyway, there is the river of life and there is the tree of life in the New Jerusalem. And when we get to the end of the book, we will talk some more about it.

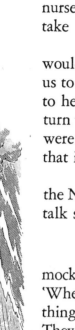

"To begin with, you know that mockers will come with their mockeries in the last days, men who go by their own passions, asking, 'Where is His promised advent? Since the day our fathers fell asleep, things remain exactly as they were from the beginning of creation.' They wilfully ignore the fact that heavens existed long ago, and an earth which the word of God formed of water and by water. By water the then existing world was deluged and destroyed, but the present heavens and earth are treasured up by the same word for fire, reserved for the day when the impious are doomed and destroyed." 2 Peter 3:3-7, Moffatt.

"For just as it was in the time of Noah, it will be at the coming of the Son of Man. For just as in those days before the flood people were eating and drinking, marrying and being married, until the very day Noah entered the ark, and knew nothing about it until the flood came and destroyed them all, so it will be at the coming of the Son of Man."

"Then the sign of the Son of Man will appear in the sky, and all the nations of the earth will lament when they see the Son of Man coming on the clouds of the sky, in all his power and splendor. And he will send out his angels with a loud trumpet-call, and they will gather his chosen people from the four winds, from one end of the sky to the other." Matthew 24:37-39, 30, 31, Goodspeed.

44

God's Pledge in the Sky

Genesis 8:6-22; 9:1-17; Isaiah 54:9, 10; Revelation 4:2, 3

NOAH and his family had been shut up in the ark for over eleven months when Noah opened the window in the top of the ark and lifted out a raven, a black bird of the crow family, which has strong wings and a roving nature. The raven stretched his wings and took off in flight. But he found no place to make a home, and so he flew around and around, and always came back to rest on the ark.

Noah also sent out a dove, a gentle bird of a loving nature, to see if the waters were dried up. But the dove found no resting place, and she came back to the window of the ark. Then Noah put forth his hand and took her in. He waited a week, and sent out the dove again. This time she came back with an olive leaf in her bill; so Noah knew there was at least one place where there was no water and where an olive tree was growing.

He waited yet another week and sent out the dove again. This time she did not return, so Noah knew that the waters were gone. On his six-hundred-and-first birthday he took off all the stout cover of the window in the top of the ark and looked, and, behold, the face of the ground was dry! But still he waited for a month and twenty-seven days, until God, who had shut the door of the ark, should open it.

Then God called Noah and his family to come out, with all the creatures he had kept in the ark for a year and seventeen days. Oh, how changed was the earth! The mountains which had been so smooth and beautiful were jagged now with rocks. The waters had washed miles of sand and gravel and rock over the fair plains. The great wind which had come at the end of the Flood had broken off mountaintops and buried the dead bodies and the great forests in the earth. There were vast oceans where there had been but seas before, and water covered three fourths of the earth's surface.

There was no more the even flow of little streams under the surface, to water the ground. In some places they were there, and the ground was well moistened; but in other places there had come great deserts where before there had been fruitful plains. Forests were just getting a start. Here and there were little patches of green, where plants and trees were beginning to grow, like the olive tree from

45

which the dove had plucked a leaf. Noah and his family wondered how they could get enough to eat. They had always eaten just the food that God gave man in the beginning—fruits, grains, and nuts. But now, when there seemed so little of such food to be had, God for the first time gave them the right to eat flesh food, too.

However, they were thankful that the Lord had kept them safe and now had taken them out of the ark and set them again upon the earth. So Noah called his family together, and they built an altar of stones, and offered on it sacrifices of the clean animals they had preserved in the ark. And they thanked God for His goodness, and prayed for His favor.

Then there came up black clouds like those that had brought the Flood. And the sons and daughters of Noah cried out in fear that there would be another Deluge. But God made the sun to shine on those rain clouds, and there appeared, arching over the eastern sky, a beautiful rainbow. Never had they seen one before; for there had never been any rain. And God said to them: "I set My bow in the clouds, for a pledge to you that I will never send another flood to destroy all mankind. Hereafter it shall rain on the earth, to moisten it and make it fruitful; but when the cloud appears, there also shall be the rainbow, to remind you of My promise."

There is always a rainbow over the throne of God in heaven, as a sign that God remembers His promise; and sometimes God shows us the rainbow on earth. So, with Noah and his family, let us thank God for His goodness and His promise when the bow appears in the cloud in the day of rain.

Rainbow, rainbow! Made of sun and dew,
I think you are a window for me to peek through,
Seeing all the beauty of the city of the Lord,
    City I am traveling toward.

Rainbow, rainbow! Were you happy when
God put you in the sky for the sons of men,
To color all the storm clouds with the lights of heaven?
    What a precious promise given!

Rainbow, rainbow! All the tears of earth,
Sunning in the smile of God, turn into mirth.
Laughing with the love of God, they turn the rain to glory.
    Rainbow, rainbow! God's pictured story!

The Tower of Pride

Genesis 10:8-10; 11:1-9

NOAH was 600 years old when the Flood came, and he lived after the Flood for 350 years, so when he died he was 950 years old. His sons were Japheth, Shem, and Ham. They were all good young men when the Flood came, and the Lord saved them in the ark; but after the Flood, Ham, the youngest, began to turn toward the wickedness of the Cainites. However, in the beginning his descendants were the most powerful people in the world.

A grandson of Ham was Nimrod, who started out as a hunter of wild beasts. The animals that came out of the ark had multiplied greatly on the earth, and the wild ones, like lions and bears and wolves, began to be a danger, so men began to hunt them down and slay them. Nimrod soon became the greatest of the hunters, and so he gathered men to himself who would do anything he told them to do.

Pretty soon Nimrod decided he wanted to have all men obey him, and if they would not, he would make them. So he became the first king and tyrant since the Flood. He and the men who were with him said: "Come, let us build a city and make it the capital of the world. And let us build a tower in it which shall reach to heaven. Perhaps we can build it so high it will reach into the clouds, and we can find out what made it rain and cause the Flood. So, who knows, we might be able to prevent any more floods." You see, they did not pay attention to God's pledge, the rainbow, that He would never send another Deluge to destroy the earth.

It was in a great and fruitful plain called Shinar, along the great river Euphrates, that they decided to make their city and tower of pride. They found there clay, which they made into bricks, and burned them hard. And they found tar, which they used for mortar to bind the bricks together. So they began to build their tower and the city around it, which they called Babel, which means "the gate of God." For they said, "Through this city and this tower we shall get to heaven, and we will make a great name for ourselves, and be like God." So they built and they built and they built. They made great numbers of men to work for them, and the Tower of Babel at last grew very high. But these men were very cruel and proud and wicked.

47

God was watching this work of Nimrod and his men, and He knew the thoughts of their hearts, that they could grow to be gods, just as Satan through the serpent had told Eve. And God knew that if they were not stopped, they would bring the whole world under their hand, and make it as bad as it was before the Flood.

Now, so far, everybody in the world spoke the same language, and so everybody could understand every other body. God said: "I will stop these wicked people. I will turn their Babel—'the gate of God'—into babble, the sounds a baby makes; for though they are men, they are without understanding, like babies."

So God came down and mixed their speech all up. The tower had grown so high that they had to have men stationed at distances all the way from bottom to top, to call for what they wanted in building. Now, suddenly, their speech got all mixed up, and they could not understand one another. That made them very angry, and they fell to fighting. All was confusion. They could not go on building, and they had a terrible time getting straightened out. Here a little crowd found they could understand one another, and there was another little crowd, and so on. So they separated. And that was the beginning of the many languages into which the people of the earth have since been divided.

To make the terror greater, God struck the top of the tower with lightning and sent it tumbling down. And that was God's answer to their towering pride. They had called the name of their city and their tower Babel, "the gate of God." The city came to be called Babylon, which meant about the same thing. But because their adventure ended in confusion of tongues, so that they could not understand one another, both Babel and Babylon have come to mean "confusion." If grown men began to babble, like babies, we would think they were crazy. And that is just what all the different groups of people at Babel thought of one another.

Now those people who could understand one another formed a band which went away by itself. And every other such band went this way or that, some to distant countries. So the Lord scattered them abroad upon the face of the earth. Nimrod kept his city of Babylon, and he built other cities. But he could not be king of all the earth, as he wanted to be.

And the sons of Ham gradually fell before the sons of Shem and Japheth, so that in later times they became their servants. Shem himself lived to be 600 years old, and he was the patriarch, or great father, of all those who loved God and kept His commandments. For he and his sons and his sons' sons taught the way of the Lord.

God's Promise in the Sky

After the Flood God knew that when storms would come up, men would be afraid that another world-wide flood might be coming. To keep them from being afraid, He gave Noah the rainbow as a sign that another Flood would never come; and even now we can see God's beautiful promise in the sky.

CLYDE N. PROVONSHA, ARTIST

Ur of the Chaldees

Genesis 11:24-32; 12:1-3

THE PEOPLE of Shem spread themselves along the valley of the River Euphrates, often following the Hamites, who were the most adventurous and forward. One of the families which came from Shem was the Chaldees or Chaldeans. Down at the mouth of the Euphrates, where it emptied into the sea, they built a great city called Ur of the Chaldees. The ruins of that city are still there, but now they are 150 miles up the river from the sea, because for all these four thousand years the river has poured down its sand and silt and made land farther and farther into the sea.

But Ur of the Chaldees was a great city and seaport, where ships came in from foreign lands and went out to them again, carrying the merchandise of peoples here and there to sell. So the city became very rich. Yet, though it was built and lived in by the descendants of Shem, it was not given to the worship of the true God. Some there were who still loved and worshiped Him; but more and more the people of that city and land turned to idolatry, worshiping the gods represented by the sun, moon, and stars. And they not only bowed down and prayed to idols, but they did all sorts of wicked and vile things, which they believed their gods told them to do. Whenever the knowledge and worship of the true God is lost, people go down, down into sin.

Now among the inhabitants of Ur, or of the country just outside the city, there lived a good man named Terah, who was in the eighth generation from Shem. It was about 300 years since the Flood; but Shem was still living, and perhaps Terah and his sons saw him and listened to his teachings.

The sons of Terah were Haran, Nahor, and Abram. They were all worshipers of the true God; but of all of them Abram was the most faithful and pious. Haran, the oldest, had a son named Lot, and two daughters besides. But Haran died there in the land of Ur, leaving his children to be cared for by Terah or his other sons. Abram married Sarai, and Nahor married Milcah. The whole family were greatly troubled by the idolatry and wickedness around them, and time and again they talked together of what they should do.

Then there came to them the word of the Lord.

STORIES OF THE PATRIARCHS

Abraham to Moses

Called to Be a Pilgrim

Genesis 11:31, 32; 12:1-9; Acts 7:2-5; Hebrews 11:8-10

ABRAM prayed there in Ur of the Chaldees; he prayed that God would show him and all his father's house what they should do. For all the world about them were worshiping idols and were very wicked. Even some of Terah's family had little idols. But not Abram; he worshiped none but God.

Then God spoke to Abram, and said, "Get out of this country, away from your kin, and go to a land I will show you." So Abram talked with his father Terah and his brother Nahor and his nephew Lot, and told them what God had said to him. And they listened, because they too wanted to get away from that land and people and go where they could train their children to love and worship God.

"But where did God tell you to go?" they asked.

"To a land that He will show me."

"Don't you know more than that?" they asked. "Maybe we should go to Canaan. We hear that is a good land, and far away. Perhaps it will be easier to worship God there."

So Terah said, "Yes, we will go to Canaan." And he took Abram with Sarai his wife and Lot his grandson, the nephew of Abram, and started for the land of Canaan. He must have taken his other son, Nahor, too, and his wife Milcah, because later we find they were in the company.

So they journeyed up the valley of the river Euphrates until they came to a land called Mesopotamia, which means "the land between the rivers," because it was between the great rivers Euphrates and Tigris. It was on the way to Canaan; but when they had gone this far, Terah was tired, and he said, "Let us stop here." So they settled down in that land, in the part called Padan-aram.

Here they stayed while Terah lived. And Abram grew rich in flocks and herds and silver and gold. But most of all, he and his wife Sarai taught the people of the true God, and there came to be many who joined themselves to Abram because they loved God and wanted to be with His servant Abram.

At last Terah died, and the word of God came again to Abram, "Get out of this country, away from your kin, and go to the land I shall show you." So Abram and Sarai gathered together all the people who had joined them and become their servants, and all the cattle and camels and sheep and other animals they had, and all their wealth of tents and raiment and silver and gold, and they started west. Abram's brother Nahor did not want to leave the land where he had gained wealth, and so he and his family stayed there. We shall hear of them later, in other stories. But Lot, Abram's nephew, the son of Haran, decided to go with Abram.

So out of the land and city of Haran they went, a great company, moving with all their flocks and herds and their tents and their belongings and their riches, to go to the land of Canaan. And into the land of Canaan they came. Abram was seventy-five years old when he departed out of Haran.

In the land of Canaan they came among the descendants of Ham. In fact, Canaan was named for the oldest son of Ham. But these Hamites were not so bad as the Hamites and even most of the Shemites in the land which Abram left. There were fewer of them, and they lived more in the country and did not build great cities, where wickedness grows. Yet, though some of them still kept the knowledge of the true God, idolatry was growing among them, and long afterward, several hundred years afterward, they grew so bad that they had to be destroyed.

But now they welcomed Abram and Lot and all their people, and some of them turned to be worshipers of the true God whom Abram worshiped. Abram made his first camp near Shechem, in the center of the land, and he built there an altar, where all his family worshiped God. Soon he moved a little south, between the towns of Luz (afterward called Bethel) and Ai, and there he built another altar. Wherever he went, he built an altar of stones, on which the morning and evening sacrifices were offered, while the people prayed to God. When they left that spot, the altar remained; and wandering Canaanites who had been taught of the true God by Abram, whenever they came by that place, would remember what they had been taught. They would repair the altar where stones had fallen out, and again they would offer sacrifices and worship there.

So Abram and Sarai, with their faithful followers, filled the land with the knowledge of the truth. They worked hard, sowing and cultivating and reaping, and caring for their sheep and cattle. But more than anything else, they worked at teaching everyone the ways of God.

Lot Chooses Sodom

Genesis 13; 14; Luke 17:28-30

ONE YEAR there fell no rain in Canaan, and the country dried up, so that there was no pasture for the flocks and herds. Abram decided to take his family and possessions and go down into Egypt for a while; for in Egypt the land was watered by the River Nile, and almost never was there a famine there. But the next year Abram and Lot came back to Canaan, where now there was rain in due season, and all the fields and hills were green.

Abram and Lot both had many flocks and herds, and there was not enough pasture for them all if they stayed together. The herdsmen of Abram on the one hand and of Lot on the other quarreled about this, and fought for pasturage. So Abram said to Lot, "Let there be no strife between us, or between your herdsmen and mine, for we are brethren. Come, I will give you your choice of the country. Take what you want, and I will take what is left."

So Lot looked over all the land, and he chose the valley of the Jordan River, which was well watered and very fruitful. But it was a country next to the city of Sodom and other cities of the plain. And the people of those cities were very wicked. Abram kept the hill country, and he made his home near the city of Hebron.

At first Lot and his family only visited in Sodom, to sell their produce and do their trading. But little by little his family wanted more and more of the ease and pleasure of the city, instead of the hard work of the country. And so finally Lot's wife persuaded him to sell off his sheep and cattle, and buy a house in town, where they all went to live.

It was not very long till there came a war in that country. Four kings of the East fought with five kings of the cities of the plain, including Sodom. The Sodomites were beaten, and the kings of the East took all the spoil they could carry from Sodom, and many of its people, and started home. Lot and his family were among the captives.

When Abram, up in the hill country, heard of this, he armed all his menservants, 318 in number, and he was joined by three neighbors with their men. He followed after the kings of the East, and overtook them far to the north. In the night he fell upon them and

54

defeated and scattered them. He took back all the spoil and all the captives, and journeyed toward Sodom.

When he and all his men came near to the city of Salem (which was afterwards called Jerusalem), there came out to meet him the king of Salem, Melchizedek, with bread and wine to refresh them. Now Melchizedek was one of the few men in that country who was not an idolater; he was noted as a priest of the true God. When he met Abram, he lifted up his hands and blessed him, saying: "Blessed be Abram of the Most High God, possessor of heaven and earth. And blessed be the Most High God, who has delivered your enemies into your hand." Then Abram gave Melchizedek a tithe, or tenth, of all the goods he had taken.

Abram gave back to the king of Sodom all the people whom he had rescued, and all that was left of the goods they had recaptured. And the king of Sodom went his way with his people. Now Lot might have chosen to go with Abram; but his wife, a selfish, vain woman, did not want to. I can hear her say to Lot: "No; we'll go back to Sodom. For there we have a house and many possessions. Should we start all over again in the country, without a thing except what your uncle gives us?"

So she ruled over Lot, and he took her and their children back into the wicked city. And there Lot prospered, buying and selling and laying up treasure. But his children, as they grew up, though he taught them the ways of righteousness, grew more and more to be like the people of Sodom. When they were grown, they married Sodomites. Only the two youngest daughters were not married when it all came to an end.

———

"Blessed is the man that walketh not in the counsel of the ungodly,
  Nor standeth in the way of sinners,
  Nor sitteth in the seat of the scornful.
  But his delight is in the law of the Lord,
  And in his law doth he meditate day and night.
  And he shall be like a tree planted by the rivers of water,
  That bringeth forth his fruit in his season;
  His leaf also shall not wither;
  And whatsoever he doeth shall prosper.
  The ungodly are not so:
  But are like the chaff which the wind driveth away.
  Therefore the ungodly shall not stand in the judgment,
  Nor sinners in the congregation of the righteous." Psalm 1:1-5.

55

Father of the Faithful

Genesis 15 to 18; 21:1-5; Galatians 3:6-9

ABRAM and Sarai his wife grew to be very old without having any children. And even more than today, children were greatly desired and cherished in those old days. God told Abram that he and Sarai should yet have a son; but they said, "No, we are too old." And instead of believing just what God promised, Sarai tried to find another way. She had a servant girl, an Egyptian, named Hagar. So she said to Abram: "Now I cannot have any children. I will give you my maid Hagar for a wife, and perhaps, if she has children, I can call them mine."

Of course it was wrong for Abram or any man to have more than one wife. That always makes an unhappy home. And God had settled the matter when He created Adam and Eve; He gave Adam just one wife. That is the way it is meant to be; and in Christian countries it is not only the law of God but also the law of the land. However, back in early Bible times it was quite common for a rich man, and especially a king or a chief, to have more than one wife. So Abram and Sarai were not going against the customs of the time when they made Hagar his second wife. Hagar did bear a son to Abram, and they called him Ishmael. He grew up to be a wild sort of boy, but Abram loved him. Hagar, however, grew so proud and perky that Sarai could hardly stand her. For Hagar said, "Now Ishmael is Abram's only son, and he will inherit all that Abram has by and by." But God had other plans.

Thirteen years went by, and Abram was ninety-nine years old. Then God came again and talked to him. When Abram heard God's voice, he fell on his face and worshiped. And God said: "I will make a covenant with you. You shall be the father of many nations. And to seal that covenant I will change your name. It shall no more be Abram; it shall be Abraham." For while Abram means "high father," Abraham means "father of a multitude." And God said, "Sarai shall have a son. And to seal that covenant, her name shall no longer be Sarai, but Sarah." Now Sarah means "princess."

"On your part," God said to Abraham, "you shall keep My laws and worship no other god. For the gods of the heathen round about

56

you are many gods; but I am the only true God, who made heaven and earth. And you shall teach your children, so that they may teach their children, even to the last generation."

God knew that Abraham would be faithful. He said, "Abraham shall surely become a great and mighty nation, and all the nations of the earth shall be blessed in him. For I know him, that he will command his children and his household after him, and they shall keep the way of the Lord, to do justice and judgment, that the Lord may bring upon Abraham that which He hath spoken of him."

Shortly after this, Abraham was sitting one day in the door of his tent, under a great oak in the plain of Mamre, when he saw three strangers going by. He ran out and stopped them and said, "I pray you, come in and rest awhile. Let a little water be fetched, and wash your feet, and I will get you something to eat. And after you have rested, you may go on your journey. I'm sure that is why you have come to me."

"Yes," they said, "do just that."

Now Abraham did not know who these men were. He thought they were just strangers happening to pass by. But he entertained them anyway. And so doing, he entertained angels unawares. For two of them were angels, and one was the Lord Himself, all three of them disguised as men.

While they were eating, one of them said, "Where is Sarah your wife?"

"In the tent behind you," said Abraham.

Then said the man, "Just as I have promised you, Sarah shall have a son next year."

"Who is this?" thought Abraham swiftly. "Who is this that says, 'As I have promised you'? Surely this is the Lord Himself." And he bowed before Him.

But Sarah, listening in the tent behind, did not think who this man might be. She laughed silently, saying to herself, "After I am so old, can I be a mother?"

Then the Lord said to Abraham: "Why did Sarah laugh at My promise of a son? Is anything too hard for the Lord?"

As God said, so it came to pass. The next year, when Abraham was one hundred years old and Sarah was ninety years old, a son was born to them. And Sarah, who had laughed at the very idea because she was so old, now laughed with joy over her baby. Therefore they called his name Isaac, which means "laughter." And Isaac it was in whose line at last was to come the Saviour of the world.

When they had finished eating, the three visitors rose to go. And Abraham went with them to show them the way. Soon they stopped, and the Lord sent the two angel-men on, while He stayed to talk to Abraham. He told him He was planning to destroy Sodom, because of its wickedness.

Abraham remembered that Lot and his family were in that city. And he pleaded with the Lord not to destroy it if there could be found in it fifty righteous men.

"For fifty righteous men I will spare the city," said the Lord.

Then Abraham grew fearful that there were not so many good men in Sodom. And he pleaded for the city if there should be only forty-five.

"Yes," said the Lord.

"Forty?"

"Yes."

"Thirty?" "Yes." "Twenty?" "Yes."

"Oh, just once more let me ask, Lord. If there are only ten righteous men?"

"For ten I will not destroy it," promised the Lord. And He went on His way.

Abraham turned and went back home, with the fear in his heart that Sodom was doomed.

"Faith enabled Abraham to obey when God summoned him to leave his home for a region which he was to have for his own, and to leave home without knowing where he was going. Faith led him to make a temporary home as a stranger in the land he had been promised, and to live there in his tents, with Isaac and Jacob, who shared the promise with him. For he was looking forward to that city with the sure foundations, designed and built by God. . . . All these people lived all their lives in faith, and died without receiving what had been promised; they only saw it far ahead and welcomed the sight of it, recognizing that they themselves were only foreigners and strangers here on earth. For men who recognize that show that they are in search of a country of their own. And if it had been the country from which they had come to which their thoughts turned back, they would have found an opportunity to return to it. But, as it is, their aspirations are for a better, a heavenly country! That is why God is not ashamed to be called their God, for he has prepared a city to receive them." Hebrews 11: 8-10; 13-16, Goodspeed.

The Sinners of Sodom

Genesis 19; Jude 7; 2 Peter 2:6-8; Luke 17:28-30

LOT was a good man, but he was weak. He had been brought up as a lad and youth in the household of Abraham, and he had learned many lessons from that great man. One thing he learned and never forgot was to be hospitable; that is, to welcome people to his home and give them food and care, just as Abraham did with the three strangers who turned out to be two angels and the Lord Himself. Those two angels, when they left Abraham and the Lord, went on toward Sodom, and to Sodom they came as the night drew on.

Lot did not really want to live in Sodom. The men of Sodom were wicked and sinners exceedingly in the sight of the Lord. Their evil deeds vexed the soul of Lot. But if he ever said anything to his wife and his children about moving out of Sodom, at once they set up a cry. No; they would not go back to the country, to all the hard and dirty work of caring for the sheep and the cattle and the camels and the asses, and grubbing in the ground to raise vegetables and grain. No, indeed! Here they could walk on hard pavements, and go to shows and dances, and eat everything they liked, and drink fiery drinks, and have a gay old time. So Lot, yielding to his wife and children, stayed in Sodom.

But that night when the angels came! They did not seem to be angels; they looked like men. Lot sat at the gate of the city, among the rulers of the town; for there was where their council met. He saw the two men come in and look around as though they didn't know where to go.

So Lot went up to them, and, bowing low, he said, "My lords, come to my house and stay all night, and refresh yourselves, and tomorrow you shall go on your way."

"Oh, no," they said; "we'll just stay out in the street all night."

Lot knew they would be in danger of their lives if they did that; for the people of Sodom would abuse them and murder them. So he pressed and pleaded, and at last they gave in and went with him to his house.

Lot made a feast for them, and they had a pleasant time in the family circle. There were Lot, and his wife, and two daughters. He

59

had other daughters in the city who were married and had families; but these two youngest daughters were still single.

But just about bedtime there came a pounding on the door. Lot was afraid, for he imagined who it was. But he went to the door and opened it a crack. There was a great mob of men and boys, and they said: "Old man, bring out those strangers who came to you tonight. Give them to us!"

Lot stepped outside and shut the door behind him. "Now, my brethren," he said, "I ask you not to be so wicked. These men are my guests, and you know I cannot give them over to you to be abused."

"Ha!" they cried. "Ho! Hu! You think you are someone, don't you? You came into Sodom to stay a little while, and now you think you can be a judge over us. Now we'll deal with you worse than with your guests." And they pressed upon him, to pull him down.

Then Lot's guests, the two men he had taken in, opened the door and pulled Lot in. They shut the door, and more than that, they smote the Sodomites outside with blindness, so that they could not find the door. The mob yelled and pounded on the wall, and they cursed; but that strange blindness wearied them, and at last they went away.

"Now," said the men to Lot, "have you any other than your family here—sons, and daughters, and sons-in-law? Go out and find them. For the Lord has sent us to destroy this wicked place."

Lot went out in the darkness, in the middle of the night. He went to the houses of his children and waked them up. And he said, "Get up, and get out with me, for the Lord is going to destroy Sodom." But he seemed to them only a crazy old man. They shut the windows in his face and went back to bed.

Lot plodded home, weak and trembling. The men said, "Come, take your wife and your two daughters, and get out, or you will be consumed with Sodom."

But as Lot could not decide, and probably his wife and his daughters were crying and wringing their hands and saying they would not go, the angels took him and his wife and his two daughters by their hands and led them out of Sodom. It was almost morning. And the angels said: "Hurry! Run! Escape for your lives! Don't look back or stay in the plain. Run to the mountains, quick!"

But Lot said, "O my lord, I can't go to the mountains; some evil would happen to me. See, here is a little city, Zoar. It's very small. Spare it, and let us find refuge there."

"Go!" said the angels. "We will spare that little city for your sake. Go! For until you are gone, we can do nothing to Sodom."

Lot stumbled on with his family, all that he had left of it. His other children and grandchildren were lost in wicked Sodom. The sun came up as he entered into Zoar. But his wife stopped and looked back, so sorry and angry at having to leave all her beautiful things and pleasures in Sodom. As she looked, she saw the city fall under a rain of fire and brimstone. And even as she stood there, she felt the hot ashes and briny rain fall around her and upon her. In a minute she was dead, and the salts in the rain covered her all up and left her a pillar of salt.

Lot and his daughters fled into Zoar. All the plain behind, with Sodom and Gomorrah and other cities, was burned up and covered with ashes of a volcano, until nothing was left of them to be seen. So the Lord destroyed Sodom and Gomorrah and all the cities of the plain, except little Zoar.

Lot found the little city as wicked as the big city. And he did not dare to stay long. He took his daughters and fled to the mountains, and lived there in a cave. That was all he had left, in his old age, of all the riches and possessions for which he had given his life in Sodom.

Consider Lot's wife! Turned to a pillar of salt!
What was the matter with Lot's wife? And what was her fault?
   Discontented, nagging wife,
   She made a misery of Lot's life,
And so after a while she was turned to a pillar of salt!

Remember Lot's wife! Buried in ashes of salt!
In the wicked town, to her children's sins she called no halt.
   Careless and foolish mother,
   She thought they were just a bother,
And so in the end she was buried in ashes of salt.

Remember Lot's wife! Her tomb was a pillar of salt!
Not hers was the fate of the loved, to lie in a marble vault;
   She was caught in her pride,
   And unhappy she died,
With her monument only a powdery pillar of salt.

61

The Trial of Abraham

Genesis 22:1-19; Hebrews 11:17-19

ABRAHAM awoke in the night. Was someone calling him? Yes. "Abraham! Abraham!" And Abraham knew that it was God's voice that he heard calling.

He said, "Yes, here I am."

But when God answered, it was such a terrible message that Abraham thought he must be dreaming a bad dream. "Abraham," said the Lord, "take your son, your only son Isaac, whom you love. Take him and go to the Mount Moriah, and there offer him for a burnt offering."

Could he really be hearing God? The God who had given him and Sarah a son in their old age? The God who had said, "In Isaac shall your name be carried on," and "You shall become many nations and many people"? How could it be, if he was to slay his son and offer him, like a lamb, as a burnt offering?

Sometimes, Abraham knew, that was done by fathers in that land. They offered their oldest son as a burnt offering to their false gods. But the true God had never asked for a child or any human being to be offered to Him as a burnt offering. Could it be, Abraham thought, that he was listening to one of those false and evil gods, or devils, asking him to destroy his only hope, his only son? Isaac had grown to be about twenty years old.

Abraham struggled in his mind. And he prayed. But he had known God so long, he had heard His voice so many times, that now he could not doubt. That was his God speaking to him. And he thought, "If God tells me to, I must obey. He can raise Isaac from the dead, if He will. I must go."

So softly he aroused Isaac, and led him out of the tent. He did not waken Sarah, Isaac's mother. He could not bear to tell her what God had told him to do. Silently in the night, with Isaac and two young men, his servants, and an ass loaded with dry wood, and with fire in an iron basket, Abraham started on his three-day journey.

Finally they came in sight of Mount Moriah. Abraham said to the young men, "Stay here, and I and the lad will go yonder and worship and come again to you." He bound the wood on Isaac's back, he took the fire in the iron basket and a knife in his hand, and started with Isaac up the steep way.

Then Isaac said, "My father!"

"Yes, my son."

"Here is the fire and the wood, but where is the lamb for a burnt offering?"

Abraham could not bring himself to tell the awful truth to his son. He answered, "My son, God will provide Himself a lamb for a burnt offering."

But when they came to the top of the mountain, there was nothing to do but tell his son the truth. Isaac was astonished and dismayed, but he was an obedient son. He was indeed like a lamb. He said, "Father, if God has told you to do this, you must do it."

They built an altar of stones and laid the wood on it. Then Abraham bound Isaac as he would bind a lamb, and laid him on the wood. In an agony he reached for his knife to plunge into his son's heart.

Then he heard a voice. God called to him, and said, "Abraham!"

"Here I am."

"Lay not your hand on the lad. For now I know that you love God, seeing that you would not keep back your only son from Me."

Abraham looked around in a daze, and he saw a sheep caught by his horns in a thicket. Quickly unbinding his son, he caught the sheep and offered him on the altar instead of Isaac.

Then Abraham's eyes were opened further, and he saw what God's plan was. God would give His own, the Son of God, to be the sacrifice for men. The lamb Abraham offered and the son he was willing to offer pointed forward to the Lamb, the Son that God would provide, to die for the sins of the world. And thankfully, with a new vision, Abraham took Isaac and went home to Sarah.

———

"Faith made even Sarah herself able to have a child, although she was past the time of life for it, because she thought that he who had made the promise would keep it. . . . Faith enabled Abraham, when he was put to the test, to offer Isaac as a sacrifice. He who had accepted God's promises was ready to sacrifice his only son, of whom he had been told, 'Your posterity is to arise through Isaac!' For he believed that God was able to raise men even from the dead, and from the dead he did indeed, to speak figuratively, receive him back." Hebrews 11:11, 17-19, Goodspeed.

A Wife for Isaac

Genesis 23:1, 2; 24

SARAH was a good mother. Though she had only one son, she had many, maybe hundreds, of children and youth in the encampment of Abraham who looked to her as the grandmother of all; and she watched over them and helped them and taught them the good ways of God. Her son Isaac grew up to be his father's helper, but he was especially his mother's pride and joy. For thirty-seven years after he was born, his mother was his loved and honored companion. When she died, at 127 years of age, Isaac was indeed sad and lonely.

Three years afterward, when Isaac was forty years old, he began to think of someone else, someone who would be his wife, and in the place of his mother be his helper and comforter. But whom could he marry? He did not want a heathen wife. Neither did Abraham want his son to marry a woman of the Canaanites around them.

Then Abraham thought of the kinsmen he had left behind in Mesopotamia. So he called his oldest servant and said to him, "Go to my country and my kindred, and find there a wife for my son Isaac."

His servant obeyed his command. He took some men and ten camels, which he loaded with rich presents—dresses and robes and bracelets and rings and ornaments of silver and gold and precious jewels. Then he started for the land of Mesopotamia and the city of Nahor, Abraham's brother.

When he came to that city, at eventide, outside the wall he found a well of water, where the women of the city came with their pitchers to get water. He made his camels kneel down there. Then he stood and prayed:

"O Lord, I stand here by the well, and the maidens come out to get water in their pitchers. When I ask a girl to give me a drink, and she says, 'Yes, and I'll draw water for your camels, too,' let that be the one You have chosen for my master Isaac."

As he finished praying, he looked up and saw a beautiful young woman go down with her pitcher and fill it with water. As she came up, he said to her, "Please give me a little drink."

"Drink, my lord," said she. And when he had drunk, she said, "I'll draw water for your camels, too." And she did, pouring pitcher

God Calls Abraham

"By faith Abraham, when he was called to go out into a place which he should after receive for an inheritance, obeyed; and he went out, not knowing whither he went." Abraham's obedience makes him outstanding in faith among all Bible characters.

ROBERT TEMPLE AYRES, ARTIST

after pitcher of water into the trough for all the ten camels. And camels can drink a great deal.

Then Abraham's servant took an earring of gold and two heavy bracelets of gold, and put them on her. And he asked, "Whose daughter are you? Is there room for us to stay in your father's house?"

She said: "I am Rebekah, the daughter of Bethuel, the son of Nahor and Milcah. Certainly there is room for you and your men in my father's house, and feed for your camels."

Then she turned and ran home and told her family about the man at the well, and what he had said and done. She had a brother named Laban. As soon as he heard her tale, he ran to the well and found the man there. And he said, "Come in, blest of the Lord. Everything is ready for you, and room for your camels."

So Abraham's servant went with Laban, and they prepared supper for him and his men. But before he would eat, he told them about his master Abraham, how rich the Lord had made him, and how good he was. And he told them how Abraham had sent him to find a wife for his son Isaac. Then he told them of his prayer at the well, and how the Lord had sent Rebekah to answer it.

"Now," he said, "tell me: Will you let Rebekah go?"

They answered, "This thing is of the Lord, and we cannot say anything against it."

But in the morning they begged to have Rebekah stay with them for at least ten days. But, "No!" said Abraham's servant. "Send me on my way, for I am in a hurry to get back."

So they called Rebekah and said, "Will you go with this man now, to become the wife of Isaac?"

"Yes," she said, "I will, if you will send my dear nurse Deborah with me." It seemed a great and happy adventure to the girl Rebekah.

So away rode Abraham's servant and his men, and away with them rode Rebekah and her nurse, away to the land of Canaan.

As they came to the end of their journey, they saw a man walking in the field, meditating. Something tugged at the heart of the girl, and she said to the servant, "Who is that man walking there?"

He looked, and he said, "That is my master Isaac."

Then Rebekah alighted from her camel, and Isaac came forward to meet her. He loved her at once, and she loved him.

"Come to my mother's tent, dear one," he said. And to her tent she went with him, and that evening they were married. And Isaac—whose heart had been so sad since his mother died—Isaac was comforted, and Rebekah was glad.

The Hunter and the Shepherd

Genesis 25:19-34; 27:1-41; Hebrews 12:16, 17

ISAAC and Rebekah had two children, and only two. They were twin boys, but they were very unlike. The older was named Esau, and the younger Jacob. Esau grew up to be a wild sort of man, much like his Uncle Ishmael. He loved the free life of the hunter and was away from home a great deal, chasing the deer and other game in the desert. Jacob was quiet and thoughtful. He loved to work with cattle and sheep and goats, and he grew to be a very careful and skillful shepherd. Isaac, who was a quiet man himself, admired the bold spirit of his son Esau, and he favored him. But Rebekah, though she was adventurous herself, admired the careful and thoughtful Jacob, who was much like his father, Isaac. The two boys didn't get along very well together.

One day, when the boys had grown to be young men, Esau came home weary and weak, because his hunt had failed, and he had nothing to eat. He found Jacob cooking a kettle of pottage, which was like a stew. It smelled so good to the hungry hunter that he said to his brother, "Give me some of that pottage, for I am starved."

If Jacob had been a very kind brother, he would have said, "Surely. Take all you want, Esau." But he was crafty, and he saw a chance to get what he wanted most from his brother. Now to the oldest son belonged what was called the birthright, which meant that when his father died he would inherit not only a double amount of his goods but the right to be chief and priest of the family and clan. It was a very great privilege and right. So the birthright in this case was Esau's.

Now Jacob said to him, "Sell me first your birthright."

Esau said, "I am about to die of hunger, and if I do, what good will the birthright be to me? All right, take it!" Then Jacob fed him. So Esau thought very lightly of his birthright, and gave it away for a mess of pottage.

Now Isaac was old, and he had become blind. And one day he said to Esau, "Here I am, an old man, not knowing when I may die." As a matter of fact, Isaac lived for more than twenty years longer; but he could not know that then. So he said to Esau: "Go out hunting,

66

get a deer, and make me a tasty dish, such as I like. Bring it to me, and I will give you my last blessing." So away went Esau on the bound, to hunt.

But Rebekah had overheard what Isaac said. She knew that God had foretold that Jacob was to be the chief and priest of his people, and she knew that Esau had sold his birthright to his brother. Now if Isaac were to give the blessing to Esau, that would give him the birthright. And Rebekah decided to stop that.

So she called Jacob and told him to get a kid from the flock, kill it, and fix up a dish such as Isaac liked, and go in and pretend he was Esau. Jacob didn't want to do it. He said his father could tell him from Esau, because Esau was a very hairy man, while Jacob was smooth. But Rebekah said, "I'll fix that. Just do as I tell you."

So Jacob did. And Rebekah cooked the dish and made ready. Then she took the skin of the kid, and covered Jacob's arms and neck with it, so that it felt hairy like Esau. And she sent Jacob in.

"Father!" he said. But his voice did not sound like Esau's.

"Yes," said Isaac. "Who are you, my son?"

Then Jacob lied. He said, "I am Esau, your first-born. Here is the tasty dish you asked for. Sit up and eat."

"Come near and let me feel you," said his father.

So when he had felt the hairy arms, Isaac said, "Your voice is Jacob's voice, but your hands are the hands of Esau." And he gave him the blessing, which made him the head of the family and clan. And Jacob went out.

He had hardly gotten out of sight when Esau came in, having prepared the game he had found and had made a tasty dish. "Come, my father, eat of your son's game," he said.

"Who are you?" Isaac asked.

"I am Esau, your son."

Then Isaac trembled greatly, and he said, "Who was it, then, that brought me some game, and I ate of it, and blessed him? And he is indeed blessed."

Then Esau cried with a bitter cry: "My brother stole my birthright, and now he has gotten my blessing. Haven't you a blessing also for me, my father?"

Isaac said, "Your brother has received my blessing, and he will be the head. But I will give you a lesser blessing, my son." And he did.

With that Esau had to be content. But he felt very bitter toward Jacob, and he went around muttering what he would do when his father died. He would kill his brother, that is what he would do.

The Stairway to Heaven

Genesis 27:42-46; 28

SOME of the servants told Rebekah that Esau was threatening to kill his brother. She called Jacob to her, and she said: "Your brother is planning to murder you. Now flee away to my brother Laban at Haran, and stay there until your brother's anger cools, and then I will send for you."

So Jacob said good-by to his father and mother. All his crafty plans had come to nothing. All the wealth of his father he was leaving behind, and it seemed that his brother would get it all. But the blessing of his father he carried with him. He thought he might never see his father again, but he hoped to come back to his mother. In fact just the opposite happened; for when Jacob did come back, twenty years later, his father was still living, but his mother was dead.

Jacob went on his way with a heavy heart. His sin rose up before him, and he felt that he could not look up to God. When night came, he lay down on the ground, taking a stone for a pillow.

But as in sorrow he slept, God brought to him a beautiful and comforting dream, a vision. He saw a ladder or stairway, starting on the earth and reaching into heaven. And on that stairway he saw bright angels going up and coming down. And then he heard the voice of God, who stood over him, and said: "I am the Lord, the God of your father Abraham and of Isaac. The land on which you lie I am going to give you and your descendants. I will be with you on your journey, and guard you, and I will bring you back. I will never forsake you."

Then Jacob awoke. It was still night, and the stars were shining in the sky, the stars which he remembered his grandfather Abraham had watched as God promised him that his descendants should be as many as the stars of heaven. And now the promise was Jacob's.

Jacob said: "Surely the Lord must be in this place, and I did not know it. Oh, what an awesome place this is! It is nothing less than the house of God, and this is the gate of heaven."

So he called the place Bethel, which means "house of God." And Bethel was ever afterwards its name.

Then Jacob went on his way, a forgiven and a blessed man.

The Little Shepherdess

Genesis 29

IN THE HOME of Laban, the brother of Rebekah, over in Padan-aram, there were many problems. Laban had not prospered as well as his fathers, and he was rather hard on his children. He had several sons, whose names we do not know, and he had two daughters. The older one was named Leah, and the little one was Rachel.

Laban sometimes talked about his sister Rebekah, and told the story of how his Uncle Abraham, who had become very rich in the land of Canaan, had long ago sent his top servant, with men and camels loaded with costly presents, to seek a wife for his son Isaac. Laban said his sister Rebekah had been at the well when this servant came, and because of her courtesy and kindness she had been picked out to be Isaac's wife. He said he had run out and welcomed the man and taken him and his helpers in, and had taken good care of his camels. And all he got out of it, said Laban, was the loss of his beautiful sister, who went away the next day, and they had never seen her since. But once in a while news had come out of the West: how Abraham had died, and how Isaac and Rebekah were now the owners of all Abraham's wealth. His sister was surely lucky, he said. He wished he might have such good luck.

Of course Rachel, who was a beautiful and rather dreamy little girl, thought a good deal about her Aunt Rebekah, and she wished that she too might marry someone as rich as Isaac, and go away to live in the West. She didn't think her sister Leah, who was a rather homely girl, with weak and squinty eyes, could ever have such an adventure; but she herself, Rachel, would if she had the chance.

Her mother said that she needed Leah in the house, to help keep it. So Laban said to his younger daughter, "Rachel, you must tend my sheep." And Rachel did. Every morning, barefooted, she took the sheep out of the fold and led them to the pastures. And at noon she led the sheep to a well in the middle of a field to water them. There was a great stone over the mouth of the well, and it took all the shepherds together to roll it off, so they could get to the water.

One day Rachel was coming with her sheep to the well, and there she saw a stranger who was talking with the shepherds. Rachel did

not know who he was, but in fact he was Jacob, the son of Rebekah, and he had just come out of the West to find his mother's people. He did not come riding, as Rachel thought he might and as Abraham's servant had come, with servants and many camels and great loads of wealth. He was afoot, and he had not a bit of gold or jewels or fine raiment.

As Rachel was bringing the sheep, Jacob said to the shepherds, "Do you know Laban, the son of Nahor?"

"Yes," they said, "we know him."

"Is he well?"

"Yes, he is well. And look! There comes his daughter Rachel with the sheep."

"Why don't you water the sheep and take them back to pasture?" asked Jacob.

"We wait till all the sheep are here," they said, "for it takes all of the shepherds to roll away the stone."

Then Jacob went over to the well, and all by himself he rolled away the stone. He beckoned to Rachel to come first, and he drew the water and watered her sheep. She was so surprised! "Who can this be?" she thought. But she was more surprised when Jacob came over and kissed her.

"Who are you?" she asked.

"I am Jacob, Rebekah's son," he said, "and I have come to see your father and mother and your brothers and sisters and you."

Barefoot Rachel left her sheep right there and ran home to tell her father. Laban ran back with her, and found Jacob still at the well. Laban kissed him, and said to him, "My sister's son, you are welcome to stay with me forever."

So Jacob went home with Laban, while Rachel stayed with the sheep. But all the afternoon, while she pastured them, she kept thinking of the wonderful Jacob, who had come out of the West. And though he brought no wealth, that did not seem to matter, for he was so strong and so handsome. And Rachel thought, "Now when I am all grown up, I'll marry Jacob, and go away with him into the West, where my Aunt Rebekah is."

And that is just what she did. For Jacob loved her, and he asked Laban to let him marry her. He had no money, but he said, "I will work for you seven years, if you will give me Rachel for a wife." Laban said he would do it.

So after seven years, Rachel was all grown up, and she married Jacob. It would be fine if we could end the story there; but there was more to it. Laban did not treat Rachel right, nor did he treat Jacob right. Leah was older than Rachel, and Laban wanted to marry her off first. And besides, he wanted Jacob to work for him some more. So he talked to Leah and got her to agree to a cheat.

In those countries at that time, brides came to the wedding with a veil that covered their faces. So Laban brought Leah instead of Rachel and gave her to Jacob for his wife. In the morning Jacob found out the trick; but he was married now to Leah.

Then Laban said: "In our country we don't let the younger sister marry before the older. Come! I'll give you Rachel too, in a week, if you'll agree to work for me seven years more." And Jacob had to agree. So within a week he had two wives, which made a very unhappy home. But that was not Jacob's fault, though he must have thought that as he had cheated his brother, so his uncle now cheated him. And he made the best of it. But he always loved Rachel more.

She was a maiden fair and sweet,
    Rachel!
From lovely face to dainty feet,
    Dear Rachel!
And while she shepherded her sheep,
Her heart beat high, her thoughts ran deep.
She would a tryst with fortune keep!
    Rachel! Rachel!

Now who might woo a maid so fair?
    Rachel!
With such a sweet and artless air
    As Rachel?
He must be brave, he must be strong,
To lift the right, to smite the wrong,
And help to roll the world along
    For Rachel! Rachel!

But will you do your honest part,
    Rachel?
And give your courage with your heart,
    Sweet Rachel?
Oh, I will give my spirit gay,
And all my happy strength today,
To him who comes to take away
    Rachel! Rachel!

71

Twenty Years and Home

Genesis 30; 31

FOR TWENTY YEARS Jacob worked for Laban. Fourteen years he worked to pay for Leah and Rachel. By this time he had eleven sons, the youngest of whom was Joseph, the child of Rachel, a likely boy and much beloved.

Then Jacob said to Laban: "Now I want to go home. Send me away, with my wives and children; for I long to see my father."

But Laban said: "Stay with me; for I have learned that the Lord has blessed me for your sake. Tell me what wages I shall pay you, and I will pay them."

So Jacob said: "This is the bargain I will propose: I will tend your flocks and herds as before, and in return you shall give me all the sheep and goats and cattle that are spotted and speckled, while all that are not marked shall be yours."

"All right," said Laban.

So Jacob worked on year after year. And the spotted and speckled cattle and sheep and goats came to be more than all the unmarked ones, so that Jacob grew rich. And he had many servants to care for them all. But his increasing wealth made Laban and his sons jealous; and Laban changed the terms of their bargain ten times, hoping each time it would make a better deal for him and a worse for Jacob. It did not work out that way, however.

Finally, after six years, Jacob talked with Leah and Rachel, and they all decided to leave and go back to his father in Canaan. Laban and his sons were far away just then, shearing their sheep. And Jacob gathered all his household, his wives, his children, and his servants, and he took all his flocks and herds, his tents and his silver and gold, and stole away.

After three days Laban heard that Jacob had gone, and he took his armed friends and neighbors and started after him. Jacob could not go so fast, driving his flocks and herds; so in seven days Laban caught up with him. By this time Jacob had reached Mount Gilead, near the Jordan River, which was almost home.

The night before Laban caught up with Jacob, God appeared to him in a dream, and said, "See that you do nothing and say nothing either good or bad to Jacob." He meant not to coax him to come back nor threaten him if he would not. That stopped Laban from harming Jacob, but anyway he went on.

When he caught up, Laban said to Jacob: "What do you mean by stealing away unknown to me, and carrying off my daughters like prisoners of war? I would have made a great feast for you, and we would have had a happy parting, with song and music. You didn't even let me kiss my daughters and grandchildren good-by."

Of course Jacob knew Laban would have done no such thing. But Laban went on, saying: "It was in my power to do you harm. But last night the God of your father spoke to me and said, 'See that you say to Jacob neither good nor bad.' But now, even though you longed to get back to your father, is that any reason why you should steal my gods?"

You see Laban and his household still worshiped images. And when Jacob and his family left, Rachel stole those idols and carried them off. But Jacob did not know that. So now he said to Laban, "Search, and if you find your gods, whoever has them dies."

So Laban went through all Jacob's goods, but he did not find them. For Rachel had hidden them, and sat on them. So when Laban could find nothing of his, Jacob spoke up sharply to him. He reminded Laban of his long service, in summer and winter, in heat and cold, and how Laban had changed his wages ten times.

So Laban cooled down, and proposed to make a pledge that neither of them should ever harm the other. They set up a pillar there, and over it they said: "The Lord watch between me and thee, when we are absent one from another." And that place was called Mizpah, which means "watchtower."

Then Laban kissed his daughters and their children, and with all his men went back, while Jacob set his face toward home.

The Lord watch!
   Good-by, my daughters! Good-by, my son!
   Farewell, little children; the day is done.
   The night comes down, and far away
   The echoes are ringing: "Another day!"

   Farewell! Farewell! As brother to brother,
   While we are absent one from the other,
The Lord watch!

The Night of Wrestling

Genesis 32; 33

NOW JACOB faced toward the land of his fathers, and he marched on till he came to the River Jabbok, which flows into the Jordan. He knew that his mother was dead, but there was his old and beloved father, whom he hoped to see. And there was his brother Esau. He had not forgotten what he had done to Esau, and he was sure that neither had Esau forgotten. So he sent messengers on ahead to his brother, with a humble greeting. The messengers came back and told him, "We met Esau coming to see you, and he has four hundred armed men with him."

Jacob was greatly afraid when he heard this; for it seemed that Esau was going to kill him and all his family. So he divided his people into two companies, saying to himself that if Esau smote one company, the other might escape. Then he made up five droves, of goats, sheep, cattle, and asses, and sent them ahead as presents to Esau. Before night fell, he had all his people and all his possessions across the Jabbok; but he stayed behind to plead with God.

It was a terrible time for Jacob. All his life rose up before him— his crooked ways, his sharp dealings, his faults and his failings. Yet he knew that he had always wanted to be true to God, and he remembered that God had promised to be with him and bring him back in safety to his land. Now as he knelt, and with tears confessed his sins, it seemed to him as though he was wrestling with an enemy whom he could not overcome. He struggled and strained. The sweat rolled down his face and his body. He was in an agony.

And suddenly, in the darkness, what he had imagined, he found to be true. There was a Man wrestling with him, a terribly strong Man whom he could not throw. Jacob was very strong, but here was One stronger. An hour passed in the struggle, another hour, and another. On and on he wrestled until the dawn began to show in the east. Jacob was almost exhausted.

Then, like an electric shock, he felt the Man touch his hip, and it was thrown out of joint. In a flash Jacob knew that this was no common man, no robber trying to overcome him. It was the Lord Himself. Jacob could no longer wrestle; he could no longer stand, but he clasped his arms around the Stranger and held on as in a death grip.

And the Stranger said, "Let Me go; for the day is breaking."

"No," said Jacob, "I will not let You go unless You bless me."

"What is your name?" asked the Stranger.

"Jacob," he replied. And Jacob means "supplanter," or "cheat."

Then said the Lord, "Your name shall no longer be Jacob, but Israel." And Israel means "wrestler with God," or "prince with God." "Your name shall be Israel," said the Lord, "for you have wrestled with God and men, and you have come off the victor."

"Tell me Your name," pleaded Jacob.

"Why do you ask My name?" As much as to say, "You know who it is with whom you have wrestled. Receive My blessing!" And He was gone.

But Jacob knew that with the blessing of God he had at last conquered his old weak self. And as the morning broke, he went forward, limping, across the river and joined his company. Now he could face the future and whatever might come with confidence, for God was with him.

And so it proved. That day Esau came, but he came not with murder in his heart. He ran forward and clasped Jacob in his arms and kissed him. Then he met and greeted Jacob's family. He refused at first the presents Jacob had sent him; but as Jacob urged, he took them. He offered to stay with his men and guard Jacob's company, but Jacob gently turned down his offer.

And finally Esau went his way with his men. The brothers who had been enemies were now brothers again. And Jacob was welcomed back to his land and his home. But greatest of all his victories was the victory he gained over himself.

"Alas! for that day is great; so that none is like it:
>   It is even the time of Jacob's trouble; but he shall be saved
>   out of it.
>   Therefore fear thou not, O my servant Jacob, saith the Lord;
>   Neither be dismayed, O Israel: for, lo, I will save thee from
>   afar,
>   And thy seed from the land of their captivity;
>   And Jacob shall return, and shall be in rest, and be quiet,
>   And none shall make him afraid."

Jeremiah 30:7, 10.

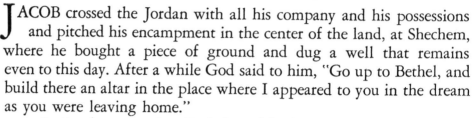

The Coat of Many Colors

Genesis 35:1-21, 27-29; 37:1-11; John 4:1-6

JACOB crossed the Jordan with all his company and his possessions and pitched his encampment in the center of the land, at Shechem, where he bought a piece of ground and dug a well that remains even to this day. After a while God said to him, "Go up to Bethel, and build there an altar in the place where I appeared to you in the dream as you were leaving home."

So Jacob removed to Bethel, and built the altar. And he called all his family and his servants to worship God. But before they left Shechem, he said to them: "Wash your clothes, and purify your hearts, to get ready to meet God. Give me the images, the little idols you have." That included the idols Rachel had stolen from her father. Then Jacob buried them all under an oak in Shechem. And at Bethel they worshiped God.

But Deborah, Rebekah's old nurse, died and was buried there. We do not know when Deborah had joined Jacob, but probably it was just after Rebekah's death, and she may have carried the sad news to Jacob in Padan-aram. Now they all mourned greatly over Deborah. Then Jacob journeyed on toward Hebron to see his father.

But heaviest of all sorrows awaited him. Rachel, his beloved wife—whose son Joseph he loved more than any other—Rachel died near Bethlehem as she gave birth to another son. As she was dying, she called the baby Ben-oni, "son of my sorrow." But his father called him Benjamin, "son of my right hand." They buried dear Rachel there, and Jacob mourned for her all the rest of his life.

When they came to Hebron, there Jacob met his beloved father, now 180 years old, and all his family bowed before the patriarch. Isaac, however, could do little more than greet and bless his long-lost son; for his days were numbered, and soon he died. Jacob and Esau together buried him in the family tomb, the cave of Machpelah, which Abraham had bought, and where Abraham, Sarah, and Rebekah were already buried, and now Isaac. In later years Leah and Jacob were also to be buried there.

But now all Jacob's hopes were centered upon Joseph, Rachel's older son, who had grown into a fine, upstanding, and handsome youth, seventeen years old. For Joseph, more than any of his older brothers, was true to God, and lived a pure and good life, while his older brothers began to depart from right doing and did many evil things.

Joseph was with them much, tending the flocks, and he reproved them for their evil deeds and words. And he told his father of those things, which made Jacob very sad. To show his special love for Joseph, Jacob made him a beautiful coat, or cloak, of many colors, such as chieftains wore. This made his brothers very jealous.

But more than that, Joseph had a dream, and he came and told it to his brothers. He said he dreamed that they were out in the field binding sheaves of wheat. And when he stood his sheaf up, all his brothers' sheaves bowed over to it. This made his brothers very angry. They said, "Do you think you are going to be king over us, and we bow down to you?"

Then Joseph had another dream, and he went and told it to his brothers when his father was with them. He said, "I have just had another dream. The sun, moon, and eleven stars bowed down to me."

This was too much even for his father, who rebuked him, saying, "Am I actually to come with your mother and your brothers, and bow down to the earth before you?"

Nevertheless, though his brothers hated him, his father thought very deeply about these dreams; for, "Perhaps," he said to himself, "they do mean something, if God sent them. Joseph is a good boy, and God may have great things in store for him."

Joseph, child of the starry-eyed,
Israel's loved one, joy, and pride;
Student of life by his father portrayed;
Sweetness of spirit by mother made;
Sower and reaper of golden wheat;
Shepherd and herdsman of unwearied feet.
Oh, what dreams did his young heart grow,
Dreams whose meaning he might not know.
Ask of his brothers, in guileless mood,
Whether their portents were evil or good.
Wrath on his head when they read them aright:
"Impudent upstart, out of our sight!
Thinkest thou chief of thy elders to be?
Out with thy dreams, and off with thee!"

77

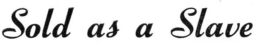

Sold as a Slave

Genesis 37:12-36

JACOB did not know how deeply Joseph's brothers hated him, or he would not have sent him on the errand he did. The brothers had been gone a long time, far to the north, feeding their flocks, and their father was anxious to know how they were getting along. So he called Joseph and said to him:

"Your brothers are feeding their flocks up in the country of Shechem. Go and find them, and come and tell me how they are."

"All right," said Joseph. And he went.

But when he came to Shechem, he could not find his brothers. He was wandering around in a field, looking for them, when a man saw him and asked, "What are you looking for?"

"I am looking for my brothers," said Joseph. "Do you know where they are feeding their flocks?"

"Why," said the man, "I heard them say, 'Let's go to Dothan.'"

So Joseph went to Dothan, about fifteen miles away, and there in the distance he saw his brothers with their flocks. He hurried forward, glad at last to find them. But they were not glad to see him. They said to one another, "Look! There comes that dreamer. Come now, let's kill him. And we'll tell our father some bad animal has eaten him. So we'll see what will become of his dreams."

And as Joseph came forward, they scowled at him and seized him and stripped off the robe of many colors and threw it on the ground. Then they were about to kill him. But Reuben, the oldest, pitied him, and he said to his brothers, "Oh, no! Let's not kill him. Throw him into this dry pit, and leave him alive; for he can't get out, and he'll die there." But Reuben meant, after the rest of them were gone, to come back and pull Joseph out and send him home.

The brothers agreed to that. They threw Joseph into the pit, and then, hardhearted, they sat down to eat. Reuben went off by himself. And while he was gone, there came by a company of Ishmaelites, with their loaded camels, going down to Egypt to trade. And Judah said to his brothers: "What good would it be to kill our brother and lie about it? Come, let's sell him to these merchants. And let us not lift our hands against him; for he is our brother."

"Yes," said the brothers, after thinking it over, "let's sell him."

So they lifted Joseph out of the pit. But when he saw the merchantmen and heard his brothers bargaining with them to buy him for a slave, he was terrified. This was worse than death. He begged his brothers not to sell him; but they had gone too far now. While the hearts of some of them pitied their brother, others argued that if they let him go home now, he would tell their father what they had done, and they would get great blame. So they all hardened their hearts, and they sold Joseph for twenty pieces of silver. And the Ishmaelites carried him away.

By and by Reuben came back and looked into the pit, but no Joseph was there. His brothers told him what they had done, and he mourned bitterly over the shameful deed. "The child is gone," he cried, "and I, where shall I go?"

But he could not bring himself to go and tell their father what they had done. He was weak and afraid. So his brothers persuaded him to join them in taking the beautiful coat, dipping it in the blood of a kid they killed, and carrying it to their father.

They asked him, "Is this your son's coat? We found it in the field."

"Oh," he cried, "it is Joseph's coat! Some evil beast has devoured him. I will go down to the grave mourning for my son."

Nothing they could do or say could comfort him. And no wonder! For they carried in their hearts the guilty secret that they had sold their brother for a slave. And they went slinking about, afraid to tell the truth, and really supposing that Joseph was dying as a hard-worked slave in Egypt.

And in Egypt he was. The Ishmaelites sold him to Potiphar, captain of the guard of Pharaoh, the king of Egypt.

Sold into slavery! Oh, what a crime!
How could you do it, brothers of mine?
Now must my father mourn me as dead.
Had you no pity for his gray head?
Yon o'er the hills lie the tents of my sire;
I go to Egypt, to sink in its mire.
God! O the God of my father, I pray,
Give me the soul of a man today!
I give Thee my life, not in part, but in whole.
O God of my fathers, possess Thou my soul!

From Prisoner to Lord

Genesis 39:1 to 41:44

POTIPHAR, who bought Joseph from the Ishmaelites, found him so faithful and able a young man that he soon made him overseer of all his house and business. Joseph seemed well favored for a slave. He was more like a son than a servant to Potiphar.

But Potiphar's wife, though she was pretty, was a very vain and deceitful woman. Joseph was handsome, and she took a fancy to him and fell in love with him. But because he would not love her in return, because she was the wife of his master, she told her husband a wicked lie about Joseph, and had him taken away and cast into prison. If Potiphar had really believed his wife, he would have put Joseph to death; but he only pretended to believe her because she was his wife, and so into prison Joseph went. Even that was a terrible fate, about what the worst of Joseph's brothers would have wanted for him.

But Joseph kept his faith in God and believed He would yet deliver him. Meanwhile he was cheerful and helpful, so that the jailer soon made him a sort of underjailer, and gave him charge over all the other prisoners.

One day Joseph saw two of the prisoners looking very sad, and he asked them what was the matter. They said each of them had dreamed a dream, and they didn't know what they meant. One of the men had been Pharaoh's chief cupbearer, whose duty was to taste the king's wine before he gave it to him, so that he should not be poisoned; and the other had been his chief cook. Pharaoh had thrown them into prison because he thought they had tried to poison him.

Joseph told them what their dreams meant. In three days the chief cupbearer would be declared innocent and would be restored by Pharaoh to his place. The chief cook would be found guilty, and would be put to death. So it came to pass. Pharaoh put the chief cook to death, but the chief cupbearer he took back into his place. As this man left the prison, Joseph asked him to plead with Pharaoh for him, because he had been unjustly thrown into prison. The chief cupbearer promised he would, but he did not. He forgot all about Joseph.

Two years went by, while Joseph stayed in prison. Then one night God sent Pharaoh two dreams. First he dreamed that he saw

80

Joseph Sold as a Slave

Joseph feared slavery more than death. He begged first one and then another of his cruel brothers not to compel him to go with the merchants. At this time some of them might have saved him, but they were afraid of the rest, and also feared that Jacob, their father, would learn of their wicked intentions.

CLYDE N. PROVONSHA, ARTIST

seven beautiful fat cows come up out of the River Nile and go to grazing on the bank. Then there came up out of the river seven other cows, ugly and thin. They went over and ate up the seven beautiful fat cows; but though the fat cows entered into the thin ones, no one could see any difference; they were just as ugly and thin as ever. Then Pharaoh awoke.

But he fell asleep again and dreamed another dream. He dreamed that he saw seven ears of grain growing on a single stalk, fine and plump. And right after them there sprouted seven other ears, thin and blasted by the east wind. Then the thin ears swallowed up the seven fine, full ears.

Pharaoh didn't know what the dreams meant, and he was so troubled over it that in the morning he called all the magicians and wise men of Egypt and asked them to interpret the dreams for him. But none of them could tell what they meant.

Then Pharaoh's chief cupbearer said to him: "I do this day confess my fault. Pharaoh was angry with me and with the chief cook, and put us in prison. There we each had a dream, but with different meanings. There was there a Hebrew youth, servant of the jailer, and he told us what the dreams meant. He told us true, for just as he said, Pharaoh took the chief cook and hanged him, but me he brought back to be his cupbearer."

Then Pharaoh sent to the prison for Joseph, and he was brought in a hurry from the dungeon. After he had shaved and bathed and put on clean clothes, he stood before Pharaoh, who told him his dreams and said there was no one who could interpret them.

Joseph answered: "God shall give Pharaoh an answer of peace. The two dreams mean the same thing. The seven fat cows and the seven plump ears of grain stand for seven years, and the seven lean and ugly cows and the seven empty, worthless ears of grain stand for seven years to follow them. There shall first be seven years of plenty in the land of Egypt; but following them there will be seven years of famine, so that the plenty will all be forgotten; for the famine will eat up all the food that was so plentiful.

"Now then," said Joseph, "let Pharaoh find a man shrewd and wise, and put him in charge of the land of Egypt. Let him appoint more men everywhere in the land of Egypt, who shall be under this headman, and all together let them gather up the plentiful food and store it in great storehouses in the cities. So when the years of famine come, there will be enough food to last through."

And Pharaoh said, "That is good counsel. I will follow it."

And he said to his courtiers, "Can we find a man with the Spirit of God in him like this man?" Of course, seeing what Pharaoh thought, they all said, "No, indeed!"

Then Pharaoh turned to Joseph again and said: "Since God has made all this known to you, there is not the equal of you in wisdom. You shall be in charge of my palace, and all my people shall obey you. Only as king shall I be higher than you. I hereby put you in charge of the whole land of Egypt."

He took from his finger the signet ring with which he signed his name, and put it on Joseph's finger. He dressed him in fine linen clothes, and put a gold chain about his neck. And he made him ride in the second of his chariots, with people shouting, "Bow down!" before him. So all the people knew that Joseph was in charge of the land of Egypt and they must do what he told them to do.

So here was Joseph—whom his brothers had sold as a slave, and whom Potiphar had thrown into prison—here was Joseph next to Pharaoh, the highest in all the land of Egypt. God certainly was with Joseph.

"He suffered no man to do them wrong:
  Yea, He reproved kings for their sakes,
  Saying, Touch not mine anointed,
  And do my prophets no harm.
  Moreover he called for a famine upon the land:
  He brake the whole staff of bread.
  He sent a man before them,
  Even Joseph, who was sold for a servant:
  Whose feet they hurt with fetters:
  He was laid in iron:
  Until the time that his word came:
  The word of the Lord tried him.
  The king sent and loosed him;
  Even the ruler of the people, and let him go free.
  He made him lord of his house,
  And ruler of all his substance:
  To bind his princes at his pleasure;
  And teach his senators wisdom."

Psalm 105:14-22.

82

Joseph's Brothers Bow

Genesis 41:45-57; 42; 43

JOSEPH was thirty years old when he stood before Pharaoh and interpreted his dreams. At that time he was put in charge of all the land of Egypt, to gather up the grain during the years of plenty. Joseph set right to work, for the seven years of plenty began at once. There was so much grain raised in the land of Egypt that Joseph had storehouses built in all the cities. And he bought from the people all their extra grain, and stored up so much that at last they lost count of it. But it was all needed for the coming years of famine.

Meanwhile Pharaoh gave to Joseph for wife, Asenath, the daughter of the high priest of Egypt. And they had two sons born to them, whom they named Manasseh and Ephraim. In after years Jacob, Joseph's father, adopted these two boys as his own, so they came to make up two of the tribes of Israel.

After the years of plenty there began the seven years of famine. That was probably caused by lack of water in the River Nile. For in Egypt it seldom rained. The ground in the Nile Valley was very fertile, but it had to be watered in the spring by the river overflowing its banks and spreading all over the land. When the river failed to do this, the ground became dry and barren, so no crops could be raised.

Of course the people became hungry, and they came to Pharaoh and said, "Give us bread."

Pharaoh said, "Go to Joseph." So to Joseph all the people went. And Joseph opened the storehouses and sold food to the famished Egyptians.

But the famine went beyond Egypt, because nowhere was there much rain. It reached away up into Canaan, where Jacob and his sons and their families lived. When hunger began to pinch, Jacob said to his sons: "Why do you stare at one another so? I have heard there is grain in the land of Egypt. Go down there and buy some, that we may all live, and not die."

So the ten older brothers of Joseph started down to Egypt. But Benjamin, the youngest, Jacob kept with him, for fear that some harm might come to him. And into Egypt went the sons of Israel, to buy grain. Little did they know who was going to sell it to them.

As soon as they came before Joseph, he knew them, but they did not know him. The last person they thought they would meet was their brother Joseph, whom they had sold as a slave. They thought this governor of Egypt was some Egyptian; for he looked and dressed and talked like one. He even had an interpreter to tell him what the brothers said and to tell them what he said, though of course he could understand them well enough.

They all bowed down before him, and begged to be sold some corn. Joseph remembered his dreams, and how they had said to him, "Do you think we are going to bow down before you, and have you rule over us?" Now here they were, bowing. He thought he would test them out. So he spoke roughly to them and said, "Where do you come from?"

"From Canaan," they answered. "We come to buy food."

"You are spies," he accused them. "You have come to find out how weak Egypt is because of the famine."

"No, our lord," they said. "We are brothers, all one man's sons. We are honest men, not spies. We were twelve; but the youngest remains with his father in Canaan, and the twelfth is dead."

"I told you," said Joseph, "that you are spies. Now I'll prove you. I will put you all in prison. But one of you I will let go home, to bring your younger brother here. That will prove that you are telling me the truth."

So he bundled them all off to prison, and kept them there for three days. And there they lay, and thought and thought on what had befallen them. But on the third day Joseph brought them before him again and said: "I am a man who fears God, and I only want to prove you. I will let you all go but one, whom I will keep in prison. Go; take grain home to your families. But when you come again, you must bring your youngest brother with you, or I'll throw you all into prison."

Then they talked among themselves in the Hebrew language, thinking no one there could understand them. They said, "Because we treated our brother as we did, selling him for a slave, all this evil is come upon us."

Then Reuben spoke up and said, "Didn't I tell you, 'Don't sin against the lad'? and you would not listen. So now we are paying for that evil deed."

They did not know that the stern-faced governor standing there before them understood what they said. But of course Joseph did. And he turned away from them, and wept. Then he came back, and taking Simeon from among them, he had him bound. Simeon had been the

84

chief one to counsel killing their brother Joseph twenty years before. And the brothers noted that.

Joseph set the other nine men free. And he told his steward to put the money they had paid back in the mouths of their sacks of grain. They loaded up their animals with the grain and started home, leaving Simeon in prison.

But at their first stopping place, as one of them opened his sack to give the animals grain, he exclaimed, "My money has been put back! It is right here inside my sack." And their hearts sank in fear, and they said, "Now what is this that God has done to us?" They thought the governor of Egypt would call them thieves.

When they reached home, they all found their money in their sacks. Jacob was dismayed at all they had to tell him. And he stoutly said that Benjamin should never go down to Egypt with them. "How have you bereaved me!" he exclaimed; "Joseph is no more, Simeon is no more, and now you would take Benjamin! All this falls on me and crushes me."

"And Judah said unto Israel his father, Send the lad with me, and we will arise and go; that we may live, and not die, both we, and thou, and also our little ones. I will be surety for him; of my hand shalt thou require him: if I bring him not unto thee, and set him before thee, then let me bear the blame forever: for except we had lingered, surely now we had returned this second time.

"And their father Israel said unto them, If it must be so now, do this: take of the best fruits in the land in your vessels, and carry down the man a present, a little balm, and a little honey, spices, and myrrh, nuts, and almonds: and take double money in your hand; and the money that was brought again in the mouths of your sacks, carry it again in your hand; peradventure it was an oversight. Take also your brother, and arise, go again unto the man: and God Almighty give you mercy before the man, that he may send away your other brother, and Benjamin. If I be bereaved of my children, I am bereaved." Genesis 43:8-14.

The Silver Cup

Genesis 43 to 45

STILL there was famine. The skies were clear. The little clouds that sometimes veiled the sun were never black and filled with rain. The fields dried up; the crops were nothing. Jacob and all his people ate as little as they could; yet the grain that his sons had brought grew less and less. Soon, unless they had more corn, they would starve. So Jacob said to his sons, "Go again. Buy us a little food."

Judah spoke up, "The man solemnly declared to us that we should not see his face, unless our brother was with us."

Back and forth they argued; but at last Jacob said: "If it must be so, take a little present for the man, take double money. And take your brother. God Almighty give you mercy before the man, that he may send back your other brother, and Benjamin."

So down to Egypt again went the brothers, ten of them; for Benjamin was one. When Joseph saw Benjamin with them, he said to his steward, "Bring the men home, and make ready a dinner; for these men shall dine with me at noon."

Joseph was so moved at seeing Benjamin that he had to weep. Hastily he went away into his private room, and there he cried and cried. By and by he washed his face and went out to them.

The dinner was served. Joseph ate by himself and the Egyptians by themselves. Simeon was brought out and restored to his brothers; and the eleven were seated in order of their ages. Several things puzzled them, but they were hungry, and they ate well.

After that, they were ready to leave; but they stayed overnight. Joseph told his steward to take his silver cup, which was a special one supposed to prevent its owner from being poisoned, and to put it in the top of the sack of Benjamin. The steward did that. No doubt he saw he was playing a game with these men, but he did not know what it meant. He just followed his master's orders.

As soon as it was light, the brothers started home. Oh, they were happy that everything had turned out so well! Simeon was with them, and they were taking Benjamin safely home.

But they had hardly gotten out of the city, when here came the steward after them. "Halt!" he cried. "What do you mean by returning

86

evil for the good my master has done you? You have stolen my master's silver cup, the one that guards him from ever being poisoned."

The brothers answered: "God forbid that we should do such a thing! Why, we brought back the money we found in our sacks. How then could we steal out of your lord's house either silver or gold? If you find the cup with any one of us, that man shall die, and we will all go back and be your lord's slaves."

"No," said the steward, "the man who stole the cup shall be a slave, but the rest of you may go free."

So they took down their sacks and opened them, beginning with the oldest and going down to the youngest. No silver cup! Every sack heaped up the proof that they had not stolen it. Of course the steward knew where it was, but he gave no hint that he was playing a game.

Wait! Here is the last, Benjamin's sack. Surely, thought the brothers, it can't be in Benjamin's sack. What? The silver cup! Oh, no! Benjamin couldn't have stolen it. But there it was! This was some mysterious thing, like finding the money in their sacks.

The steward took Benjamin, but all the brothers followed. Back to the city, back to the governor's house. And there he stood, stern and forbidding. And he said: "What is this you have done? Don't you know that such a man as I could find you out?"

Then Judah stepped forward, and he cried: "What shall we say? How can we clear ourselves? God has found out the iniquity of your servants. We will all be your slaves."

"No," said the governor. "Only the one who stole the cup shall be my servant. The rest of you go on home."

Judah came still nearer to him. He fell on his knees. And he pleaded: "Oh, let me stay in my little brother's place. You asked us, 'Have you a father? Have you a brother?' And we told you that we had a father, an old man, and a younger brother, the child of his old age, a little one. His brother is dead, and he alone is left of his mother, and his father loves him.

"You said, 'Bring him down.' And we said, 'The boy cannot leave his father, or his father would die.' But you said, 'Unless you bring him, you shall not see my face again.' Our father could hardly be brought to let him go; but we were almost starving at home, and at last he gave him into my keeping and let him come. Now if we go back and the little one is not with us, I shall bring my father's gray hairs in sorrow to the grave. I cannot! I cannot! Let me stay in his place as your slave, and send him home to my father!"

Then Joseph saw that his brothers, and especially Judah, had

wholly changed. Once Judah had been the one who proposed to sell his brother Joseph for a slave; now he was willing to be a slave himself to save his brother Benjamin. And Joseph could no longer keep back his tears. He must tell his brothers that he was their brother Joseph. He cried, "Let everyone go out!" And all the Egyptians left the room.

The brothers stood wondering. Then Joseph said, "I am Joseph! Doth my father still live?"

They could not answer him. What! This Joseph? The Joseph they had sold as a slave? They could not believe it. But it must be so. All the puzzles of their two visits were explained. Yes, this must be Joseph. He knew them all; he knew all about them. No wonder he had treated them so roughly. Now surely he would put them all to death, all except Benjamin.

Joseph said, "Come near to me! Come near, my brothers." And they came.

Then he said: "I am Joseph your brother, whom you sold into Egypt. Don't be grieved or angry with yourselves because you sold me. God sent me before you to preserve your lives. For these two years there has been the famine, and there will be five more years of famine. So now it was not you that sent me, but God. He has made me a father to Pharaoh and lord of all Egypt. Hurry now! Go up to my father and say to him, 'Your son Joseph is lord of all Egypt, and he has sent for you to come down with all your household and possessions, and live here until the famine is over.' And you see, and my brother Benjamin sees, that it is I, even Joseph your brother, who tells you this."

Then he embraced and kissed Benjamin, and then all his brothers. And they were glad. Quickly the news spread all through the house, and all through the city, and into Pharaoh's palace, that Joseph's brothers had come. And Pharaoh said to Joseph: "Send wagons for your father and the little ones, and bring them down to Egypt. And I will give them of the best of the land. And here they shall live and prosper."

So the children of Israel, the sons of Jacob, the brothers of Joseph, started home. There went with them chariots and wagons, drawn by horses with Egyptian drivers, to bring their old father and their families and all their goods down to Egypt. What a wonderful journey that was! How God had wrought for them, because they had repented and confessed their sin! And God had turned their troubles into blessings and their shame into glory. Oh, thank the Lord!

Israel in Egypt

Genesis 45:25-29; 46 to 48; 50

JACOB was Israel. The Bible seldom calls him Israel, but Jacob still. However, when he went into Egypt, it says, "Israel took his journey." And after his death, his children were called, not "the children of Jacob," but "the children of Israel." "For as a prince hast thou power with God and with men, and hast prevailed."

What a day that was when the brothers and all the great company of Egyptians, with horses and chariots and wagons, came back to Israel at Hebron in the land of Canaan! Jacob's old eyes peered down the road, and his heart kept praying, praying that his Benjamin might come safely back. This morning the road stretched dry and dusty as ever, but still Jacob watched and prayed.

Along about noon he saw in the distance a great cloud of dust. Nearer it came, and bigger it grew. What could all this be? His sons were but ten; this was a great company. Could it be bringing bad news? Jacob prayed more earnestly. No; God was good! He would not bring a last, crushing burden.

At last, at the head of the procession, he saw his sons come forth. And Benjamin with them! They came and fell at his feet, laughing and crying and weeping all at once.

"Joseph is alive!" they cried. "Joseph is governor of all Egypt! Joseph has sent for you to come down, and he will take care of us all."

"No! No!" cried the old man. "Do not deceive me! Long ago Joseph was slain by a wild beast. No! Joseph cannot be alive. What is this tale you tell, that he is governor of Egypt? Where is Pharaoh?"

"See the wagons that Pharaoh has sent to fetch you down," they answered. "Father, Joseph is truly alive. We knew he was not slain by a wild beast. Oh, Father, we are wicked. We sold him as a slave into Egypt. And all these years we have borne the guilty burden, and we have cried and we have prayed God to forgive us. But we could not tell you. O Father, forgive us! We are so wicked! Now Joseph has forgiven us. He is the governor. He is the man who tested us, who sent for his brother Benjamin. We will tell you all of it by and by. But believe that Joseph is alive; for it is true. And he is truly the head of the land of Egypt, next to Pharaoh."

At last Jacob believed. His sons told him the whole sad story, now made happy and glorious. And he forgave them, though he could hardly believe it. So he said to them: "It is enough! Joseph my son is yet alive! I will go and see him before I die."

Down into Egypt they went, all of them, all the children of Israel and servants besides, driving their flocks and herds, the women and the little ones carried in the wagons. Down they went to Goshen, the borders of Egypt. Jacob sent Judah before him, to tell Joseph. And Joseph came out in his chariot, with all his soldiers and servants attending him. He came to meet his father. And there in the land of Goshen he found him.

Joseph stepped down from his chariot, and ran forward to meet his father. He threw his arms around the dear old man's neck, and burst into tears. And Israel wept too. But their weeping was happy.

"Now," said Jacob to his son Joseph, "now let me die, since I have seen your face, because you are yet alive."

But Jacob did not die yet for seventeen years. Pharaoh invited him to court, and paid him great attention. And Israel lifted up his hands and blessed Pharaoh.

Joseph brought his sons, Manasseh and Ephraim, to his father Jacob, that he might bless them. Now Jacob's eyes were dim from age; but seeing their forms, he asked, "Who are these?"

"These are my sons, whom God has given me in this place."

"Bring them to me," said his father, "and I will bless them."

So Joseph brought them forward, Ephraim in his right hand, to be on his father's left; and Manasseh in his left hand, to be on his father's right. But Jacob crossed his hands, and laid his right on Ephraim's head and his left on Manasseh's head.

"Not so, my father," exclaimed Joseph; "for Manasseh is the firstborn. Put your right hand on his head."

"I know it; I know it," his father replied. "And truly he shall be great, but his younger brother shall be greater than he."

So all the children of Israel were settled in the land of Goshen. And when, at the age of 147 years, Jacob died, they took him, as he had made them promise, back to the land of Canaan, and buried him in the cave of Machpelah, the burial place of his fathers. But the children of Israel stayed in Egypt for generations, until the time of the great deliverance.

STORIES OF THE EXODUS

Moses and Joshua

A King and a Babe

Exodus 1; 2:1-10; Acts 7:17-21

WHEN Jacob went down into Egypt, the children of Israel were seventy in number. But they grew and they grew and they grew, until they were a great multitude. Seventeen years, and Jacob died. Seventy years, and Joseph died, and all that generation. Then there arose a new king in Egypt, who didn't know Joseph. He saw how the children of Israel had multiplied, and he said to his people: "Look! The children of Israel are more and mightier than we. Come, let us be wise, and deal with them in such a way that they cannot join with our enemies and fight against us."

So the Egyptians set taskmasters over the Israelites (who were also called Hebrews) and made them work bitterly hard, in the fields and in making brick and in building cities for Pharaoh, king of Egypt. But the more they oppressed them, the more they grew. And Pharaoh wondered how he could stop their multiplying.

So at last he made a law that all boy babies born to Israelite mothers should be thrown into the Nile River and drowned. And I suppose, though the Bible does not tell us, that a good many Hebrew boy babies were snatched from their mothers' arms and drowned in the river.

There was one family of Israelites, of the tribe of Levi, who determined to save their baby boy. The father was Amram, and the mother Jochebed. They already had two children: Miriam, about twelve years old; and Aaron, who was three. Now there was born a boy baby who had no name at first, but who came to have a name that has echoed down the halls of time as one of the greatest of men.

When he was born, his mother hid him for three months. Their home was just a little house, made of posts and rushes daubed outside and in with mud; and there was little chance of hiding a baby, especially after he grew big enough to cry loudly or babble happily. So when he was three months old, his mother saw she could no longer hide him. Then she thought and she thought and she thought; and she thought of a plan. She called Miriam to her, and she told her: "Now Pharaoh has commanded that we throw our boy babies into the river. We will obey Pharaoh, and put our precious baby boy in the river.

92

But first we will put him in a little boat, so he will not be drowned. And we will pray God to keep him and watch over him and save him."

So Miriam brought from the river some flags or rushes, and Jochebed wove them into a little boat just the baby's size. They daubed it with tar and pitch, to keep the water out; then they lined it with soft fuzz from the chaffy seeds of the rushes.

Now it was night. While Aaron lay asleep, they laid the baby in the little boat and covered him up. Then in the darkness they made their way down to the river, and placed the little boat, with its precious baby, among the reeds by the river's bank. And they prayed God to watch over him and keep him.

And God was watching. Mother in the darkness slipped quietly home. Sister stood a little way off, to watch what would become of the baby. The morning broke, and as it grew light, who should come down to the river to bathe, at that very place, but the daughter of Pharaoh, with all her maids!

They walked along on the bank of the river; and soon the daughter of Pharaoh spied the little boat out in the reeds.

"Go out," she said to one of her maids, "go out and bring that little ark to me."

So the maid waded out in the river, and brought the little boat to the shore. The daughter of Pharaoh stooped over and lifted the cover. And there was a baby boy! The baby waked up and looked, but he saw no mother's face. And the little baby cried.

"Oh!" exclaimed the daughter of Pharaoh, "this must be one of the Hebrew mothers' babies. Poor baby!" she said. "Don't cry, darling! What shall we do with him? I'll take him for my own."

Miriam, standing off a little way, saw that the princess had pity on the baby. So she came up and bowed to her, and asked, "Shall I call a nurse of the Hebrew women, to nurse the baby for you?"

"Go!" said the princess. And Miriam flew like an arrow straight to her mother. "Come!" she cried, "Mother, come! The king's daughter has found the baby and wants a nurse for him. You can be it!"

So down to the river hastened Jochebed with Miriam, and came to the princess and her maids and the baby.

"Take this child," commanded the princess, "and nurse it for me. And I will pay you wages."

So mother picked up the baby, who hushed his crying at once. And she took him home, and loved him, and cared for him, and thanked God for saving him and giving him back to her.

And the princess called the baby Moses.

In Palace and Desert

Exodus 2:9-22; Acts 7:21-29; Hebrews 11:24-26

MOTHER Jochebed kept the little Moses until he was twelve years old. No doubt his foster mother, the daughter of Pharaoh, sometimes came to see him; and it may be she never knew that Jochebed, his nurse, was his real mother. God so led her mind that she left the little fellow in the simple, humble home where he was taught in the study of nature and the history of God's people and in the ways of obedience and truth.

His mother delighted in telling him stories, and he was just as delighted to hear them. What stories did she have to tell? Because she was an Israelite mother, the daughter of Levi and Jacob and Isaac and Abraham, the stories she knew best were such as her son Moses was afterwards to write in the Book of Genesis. So she told him of the creation of the world in six days, with the seventh the Sabbath. She told him the story of the sin of Adam and Eve, and how they were cast out of the Garden. She told him of Enoch and Noah, of the Flood, and the rainbow, and the tower of Babel. And she told him of Abraham and of Isaac and of Jacob and of Joseph and all that went along with them. And so the boy Moses was taught not to bow down to idols, but to pray to the living God. For all she was worth his mother sought to fill his mind with purity and love and duty.

But at last the daughter of Pharaoh claimed him for her own son. And he was taken to the palace of the Pharaohs and the schools of the priests. The Egyptians were then the mightiest nation on earth, and their wise men had the greatest schools in the world. They put the young man Moses through all their classes and courses.

He did not forget what his own mother had taught him. He knew that God had saved him as a babe, and had kept him for the great purpose of delivering his people from their sore bondage. But the way the Egyptians had taught him was to fight, and so he thought that would be how he would deliver the Israelites.

When he was forty years old, one day he went out to see his people. He saw an Egyptian striking a Hebrew and trying to murder him. So he killed the Egyptian, and buried him in the sand. The next day he found two Hebrews fighting each other. He said to the one who was in the wrong, "Why do you strike your brother Israelite?" And the fellow said: "Who made you a judge over us? Do you mean to kill me as you killed the Egyptian yesterday?"

Moses saw that his deed was known; and very soon he heard that Pharaoh was seeking him to kill him. There was no safety for him in Egypt any more, and he fled. Away to the east he traveled, out through the desert, many, many miles. He came at last to the land of Midian. It was a wild land. The mountains rose high and rugged; the valleys were fields of sand and rock. But around the mountain of Horeb there was much water, especially in the winter. It came out in springs and ran down in streams. And along the streams there were trees and shrubs, and in the fields grass for flocks and herds.

Moses came to Midian and sat down by a well which was used by the shepherds to water their flocks. No longer the prince of Egypt, but only a desert exile, he sat there.

Now Jethro, or Reuel, the priest of Midian, had seven daughters, who tended the sheep of their father. As Moses sat there by the well, they came to water their flock. But the men shepherds came and drove them away. Then Moses stood up and helped them, and watered their flock. They were shy girls, and this Egyptian, as he looked to be, put them in awe. And so, after thanking him for his help, they turned their flocks and left him standing there.

But when they reached home, their father said, "How is it that you come home so early?"

And they said, "An Egyptian saved us out of the hand of the shepherds and also watered the flock."

"And where is he?" asked their father. "Why did you leave him? Call him, that we may take him in and give him food."

So one of the girls, Zipporah (which means "little bird"), went back and invited Moses home. And it was home to him. For with nothing else to do, he hired out to Jethro to care for his sheep. And I guess the girls were glad, though probably they still helped with the sheep. But no rough shepherds were going to knock them about after this. Especially "Little Bird" was as grateful as she was lovely.

Moses married Zipporah. They had two boys born to them, and Moses thought: "Now I have a family, and a home, and a work to do out here in the desert. I will forget all that I thought I would do about delivering the children of Israel. God must have chosen someone else to do that."

He was forty years old when he came into the desert, and he stayed there forty more years.

95

The Story of Job

Job

THIS is a story Moses heard while in the land of Midian, and which he shaped up and wrote out for us. There was a man in the land of Uz whose name was Job. He was a man perfect and upright, a man who feared God and kept out of evil. He had seven sons and three daughters, and he was very rich in the riches of that country. That is, he had seven thousand sheep, three thousand camels, five hundred yoke of oxen, and five hundred donkeys, which were used as horses. And he had a great number of servants. In fact, he was the richest man in all the East.

Now about this time Satan came before the Lord and said he had been going up and down in the earth, which he claimed for his own, to see how everything was.

"Have you seen My servant Job," the Lord asked him, "a perfect man and upright, who fears God and keeps out of evil?"

"Yes," said Satan, "but isn't he paid for it? You have set a hedge about him, so that I cannot come near to do him harm. Now just You take away all he has, and he will curse You to Your face."

"Try him," said the Lord. "I will put all he has in your power; but you shall not touch him." So Satan went out to do evil to Job.

It came to pass on a day, that everything Job had was swept away. First there came a messenger to him, all out of breath, who said, "Some wild men made a raid, and carried off your oxen and asses, and killed the servants who guarded them, and I only am escaped alone to tell you."

While he was yet speaking, there came another messenger, breathless, who said, "Lightning fell from heaven, and burned up all your sheep and the shepherds, and I only am escaped alone to tell you."

And while he was speaking, there came still another messenger, who said: "The Chaldeans made up three bands, and fell upon the camels and have carried them away; and they slew the servants with the edge of the sword. And I only am escaped alone to tell you."

And while he was yet speaking, there came another servant with the worst news: "All your sons and daughters were feasting in their oldest brother's house, when there came a great wind that blew down

96

Young Moses Sees His People's Distress

While Moses spent forty years at court, he often thought of the enslaved condition of his people. He frequently visited them and assured them that God would eventually deliver them. As he saw them oppressed and unfairly dealt with, he longed to strike a blow to free them from oppression and slavery.

ROBERT TEMPLE AYRES, ARTIST

the house and killed them all and the servants too; and I only am escaped alive to tell you."

Terrible! Terrible! All that he had and all that he loved (except his wife) were gone. But Job did not murmur. He rose and tore his robe to show his grief, and he shaved his head, and fell down on the ground and worshiped God. He said: "Naked was I born, and naked shall I die. The Lord gave, and the Lord has taken away. Blessed be the name of the Lord!"

So then when Satan came before the Lord again, God said to him, "Have you seen My servant Job, who still worships God, though I have let you afflict him sorely?"

"Oh, yes," said Satan, "skin for skin! Everything that a man has will he give for his life. But You have only let me take away his possessions; You would not let me touch his person. Now just You touch him with sickness, and he will curse You to Your face."

"Try him," said the Lord. "Only you shall not make him die." So Satan went out to do his worst. And he sent sore boils upon Job, from head to foot, very itchy and painful, and he was sick all over. Job went and sat on the ash heap, and took a broken piece of pottery to scrape himself with.

Then there came to visit him three of his friends: Eliphaz, and Bildad, and Zophar. They hardly knew him, he was so changed. They felt so sorry they could not say a word, but sat down and kept still for a whole week. Then they began to talk to Job.

Almost all the rest of the Book of Job is taken up with their reasonings and Job's replies. They said he had been bad somewhere, somehow, or God would not let him be afflicted so. But Job said he had not done anything bad, and he could not understand why he was punished in this way.

After a while a young man, Elihu, joined in the talk, but he did not help Job any. Yet what these men said and what Job said make a most interesting and helpful part of the Bible. For they were among the wisest men of the East, and they knew a great deal about the things of creation and the history of man, and they poured forth their wisdom as it is told in the Book of Job.

In the end a great thunderstorm came up, and it was no common thunderstorm. The sky grew black, the lightnings flashed, the whirlwind blew, and there was a great tempest. Then out of the whirlwind came the voice of God, speaking to Job:

"Gird up your loins like a man, and hear Me," said the Lord. "Where were you when I created the world, and when all the angels

97

sang and shouted for joy? Were you there?" Then the story goes on, how the Lord told of the many things in creation, in the waters, on the earth, in the air. "How much do you know of all this, Job? Are you able to judge, not knowing the deep wisdom of God?"

At last Job answered: "I know that Thou canst do everything, and that nothing can be hid from Thee. Therefore I abhor myself, and repent in dust and ashes."

Then the Lord let Job know that he had been afflicted by Satan to test him, whether he loved the Lord because of the things God gave him, or because he purely loved Him. And the Lord said Job had passed the test well. But He told Job's three friends they had not spoken much truth, but if Job would pray for them, they would be forgiven. Job did. And they were.

Then the Lord healed Job, and gave him back twice the amount of riches he had in the beginning. He had also seven sons and three daughters, who were the fairest in all the land. So again Job had a happy home.

Thus Satan was defeated, and God was proved just, and Job, the righteous man, lived to a good old age.

The Burning Bush

Exodus 3; 4; Acts 7:29-36

FORTY years is a long time in the life of a man, and forty years was a long time in the life of Moses. It was half the length of his life up to then; for he was forty years old when he fled from Egypt, and he was eighty years old when he was called back.

Many things can happen in forty years. Things happened in Egypt. The Pharaoh whose daughter found and adopted Moses died, and probably his daughter died also. It may be that Moses' own mother, Jochebed, was still living. His father, Amram, surely was; for he did not die till he was 137 years old. Good men and women then lived, very often, to be over one hundred years old, and sometimes nearly two hundred. Miriam, Moses' sister, must have been over ninety years old, and Aaron, his brother, was eighty-three, when Moses was eighty; yet they all were as strong as most people nowadays at half that age.

The Israelites were in hard bondage, under great affliction; for the new Pharaoh who came to the throne was hard and cruel, and he made the children of Israel suffer with hard work and no pay. They cried to God, and God heard their cry. It was time for them to be delivered. Moses, the one whom God meant to be their deliverer, was long since gone out into the wilderness; but now God sent Aaron to find him. So Aaron started out into the desert.

Meanwhile, in all this time, Moses had been going to school. What! Going to school, away out in the desert, away from all the great buildings and all the great learning of Egypt? And for forty years? Yes; for God's school is different from man's. His schoolroom is the earth; His schoolbooks are all the things He has made and the stories of His dealings with men. And these were the books that Moses read. He learned to be quiet and gentle and patient and to endure hardship in caring for the helpless sheep. And thus also he learned to be gentle and patient with men and women and children.

And Moses remembered the stories his mother had told him, of God's great work of creating this world and making man, of the Garden, and the sin, and the plan of salvation pictured forth in the sacrifice of the lamb. And then the long continued story of God's

99

dealings with men both bad and good, but especially with such good men as Adam and Enoch and Noah, with Abraham, Isaac, and Jacob and Joseph. And in the quiet of his country life Moses wrote out those stories and made the Book of Genesis.

Now one day, as he led his flock in the valley below Horeb (which was also called Sinai), Moses, whose eye was always quick to catch the unusual, saw a strange sight. Out there on the desert one of the thorn bushes, dry and brittle, was afire. But, strange to say, it did not burn up. It kept blazing and blazing away, as though some secret fuel were feeding it. And Moses said, "I will now turn aside and see this great sight, why the bush is not burned up."

Little did he know that late, bright winter morning what was going to come from his curiosity about a burning bush. If he had just passed it by, and had said, "Oh, something set it afire, and I guess it will soon be gone; I don't care," then Moses would never have been anything more than a shepherd of the desert, and the Israelites would have gone on being slaves in Egypt. But Moses was not a careless man. He knew and loved the things of nature, and what was strange drew his attention, to find out its secret. And what a secret was here!

As he drew near to the burning bush, suddenly he heard a Voice speaking from it: "Moses! Moses!"

He stopped. "Here I am," he answered.

And the Voice said: "Do not come near. Take off your sandals from your feet; for the place where you are standing is holy ground. I am the God of your fathers, Abraham, Isaac, and Jacob."

Then Moses hid his face; for he dared not look upon God, who was in the fire of the burning bush. He put off his sandals; for so men worshiped in those days, as men today take off their hats in a holy place.

And the Lord went on and said: "I have seen the troubles of My people Israel in bondage in Egypt. And I have heard their cry. I have come down to deliver them from the Egyptians, and to bring them into a good land, a land flowing with milk and honey. So come now, and I will send you to Pharaoh, that you may bring My people Israel out of Egypt."

But Moses had lost all thought of being the deliverer of Israel. He said, "Who am I, a shepherd, to go to Pharaoh and tell him to let Israel go?"

Once, when he was a young man, Moses had thought he was quite able to bring the Israelites out from under bondage. But now, having learned his lessons in the desert, he felt too small and humble to do so great a work. But the Lord knew it was just that humbleness that fitted him to be a tool in God's hand to do this important work.

Moses asked, "When I go to the children of Israel and they ask, 'Who sent you?' what shall I say?"

Then God gave to Moses His secret name. He said, "Tell them, 'I AM has sent me.'" That name, I AM, means that God is self-existent, that no one created Him, and that He lives always, yesterday, today, and forever. That name became the one by which He was afterwards called, in the Hebrew tongue, Jehovah. But because that name was so sacred, the people of Israel would not speak it, and they wrote in its place, THE LORD, which is what we generally read in our Bibles.

Moses kept objecting, and God kept insisting. Moses said, "Suppose the people of Israel will not believe me when I tell them Jehovah, the Lord, has sent me."

God said, "What is that in your hand?"

"A staff," said Moses.

"Throw it on the ground." Moses threw it. And it became a serpent, a deadly snake, wriggling over the ground.

"Put out your hand and take it by the tail." Moses took it by the tail, and lo! it was again the staff in his hand.

"Put your hand in your bosom. Now take it out."

And Moses saw his hand all leprous, white as snow. And leprosy was the deadliest disease.

"Put it back in your bosom. Now take it out."

And lo! his hand was healed and healthy, like all his body.

"By these signs and others I shall give you," said the Lord, "I will make you known as My messenger."

"But, oh!" said Moses, "O Lord, I cannot speak well. I have not spoken Egyptian for forty years. I am slow of speech, and my tongue stammers."

"Who made man's mouth?" said the Lord. "Did not I? I will help you to speak, and I will tell you what to say."

"O Lord, I beg You to send someone else, whomever You will."

Then the Lord's anger blazed against Moses; for now his humility had become cowardice and stubbornness. God said, "Your brother Aaron I know is a ready speaker. He is coming to meet you, and he will go with you to Pharaoh. He shall be your spokesman, and I will go with you both. Take this staff in your hand, and go!"

Then Moses gave up. He led his flock back, and stood before Jethro. "Let me go," he asked, "and visit my people in Egypt, and see how they do."

And Jethro said, "Go in peace."

The Deliverer Comes

Exodus 5 to 10; Psalm 105:26-35; Hebrews 11:27-29

MOSES and Aaron came back to Egypt. And first they called the elders of the Israelites together and told them what God had sent them to do. The people believed, and when they heard that the Lord had pity on them and was about to deliver them, they worshiped. But they did not know through what trials they must pass and what terrible things the Lord must do to the Egyptians before they would let His people go. God had mercy on the Israelites and helped them along little by little.

Moses and Aaron then went before Pharaoh and boldly said: "Jehovah, the Lord God of Israel, says, 'Let My people go, that they may worship Me in the wilderness.'"

Pharaoh answered: "Who is Jehovah, that I should obey Him, and let Israel go? I do not know Jehovah, and I will not let Israel go." And he gave orders to the taskmasters to make the Israelites work harder. He said, "The people are idle, and that is why they say, 'Give us three days' vacation, that we may go into the wilderness and worship the Lord.'"

Many of the Israelites were used in building cities for Pharaoh, and others were used in making the brick with which they built. In making the brick they used chopped straw, to help hold the brick together; and this had been furnished to them for their brickmaking. But now Pharaoh said, "Give them no more straw. Let them go out and get it in the fields, yet they shall deliver just as many brick as before."

They could not do it, and when they failed, they were beaten. Then the Israelites complained to Moses and Aaron and said, "You have not delivered us. You have made our lot harder. You have put a sword in Pharaoh's hand to slay us."

Moses cried to the Lord and prayed: "Why have You sent me? Since we came with Your message to Pharaoh, he has only made the lot of the people harder; and You have not delivered the people at all." Moses, too, had lessons yet to learn in trusting the Lord no matter what happened.

Then God gave Moses power to bring ten plagues upon Pharaoh

and the Egyptians, each worse than the one before it. And He said, "In the end Pharaoh will let My people go."

With the first plague, Pharaoh hardened his heart, saying he would not let the people go; but with the second he weakened and promised. Yet when the plague was removed, he again said, "No." Every time a new plague was brought, Pharaoh yielded a little more; but when the plague was taken away, he went back on his word and would not let the people go. Until the very last one.

The first plague was turning the river to blood. At the command of God Moses stretched out his rod over the river, and suddenly it was like the blood of a dead man. The River Nile was worshiped by the Egyptians; they called it "Father Nile," because by its overflowing in the spring it moistened and enriched the ground and gave them good crops. Now it was stinking blood, and they hated it. To get any water to drink, they had to dig holes; for that water, right from the earth, was not harmed.

The second plague was frogs, which came out of the river in great hordes, and covered the ground, and filled their houses, and got into their bread dough and into their beds. But, at Pharaoh's plea, the Lord killed all the frogs, and the people had to shovel them up into heaps, and they poisoned the air.

The third plague was lice. The Egyptians, and especially the priests, made a great deal of being clean and free from vermin; but now the lice covered the priests as well as the people. And the priests said to Pharaoh, "This is the finger of God." But he hardened his heart and would not listen.

The fourth plague was swarms of gnats and flies, which not only filled their houses but got into their eyes and noses and ears, till they screamed. But in all the last seven plagues the Lord made a difference between the Egyptians and the Israelites, for in the land of Goshen none of them fell. And the Israelites gathered themselves together in the land of Goshen.

The fifth plague was a disease which killed off most of the Egyptians' cattle and other stock. The sixth plague was boils, torturing sores that covered the Egyptians from head to foot. The seventh plague was a dreadful storm of hail, with lightnings and thunders such as Egypt had never known. It broke down all the trees and destroyed the crops in the field which had come up. The eighth plague was swarms of locusts, which ate up every green thing that was left, so that Egypt, the fruitful land, was left bare. The ninth plague was darkness, thick darkness that could be felt. But in the land of Goshen

all the people had light. And many Egyptians fled into the land of Goshen, so that there was a mixed multitude there.

At each plague, Pharaoh had called on Moses and Aaron to have it removed, and he promised a little more and a little more of how he would let the people go. But when the plague was gone, he went back on his word. This last time, when the plague of dreadful darkness was removed, he said to Moses: "I will let the people go and their little ones with them. But you cannot take your flocks and herds with you."

Moses said, "We must go with our flocks and herds and everything we own."

Then Pharaoh's anger flared, and he shouted: "Moses and Aaron, get out of my sight! Get out! And take care of yourselves, for you shall see my face no more!"

And Moses answered, "You have spoken well. I will see your face again no more."

There was yet to come the last, most dreadful plague.

The Passover

Exodus 11 to 13; Psalm 105:36-39

NOW," said the Lord to Moses, "I will bring yet one more plague upon Pharaoh and upon Egypt. And after that, he will let you go. Yes, he will thrust you out, glad to be rid of you."

"About midnight," said the Lord, "I will go out into the midst of Egypt; and all the first-born, the oldest child in every family of the Egyptians, shall die, from the first-born of Pharaoh who sits on the throne to the first-born of the servant woman who grinds the grain in the kitchen. Yes, even the first-born of the beasts that are left in the land shall die.

"And there shall be a great cry throughout the land of Egypt, such as never was and never shall be again. And then Pharaoh and all the Egyptians shall push you out. But I will save the children of the Israelites, both their first-born and all the rest.

"Only, if they believe Me, they must do this: Every family must take a lamb on the tenth day of this month, the first month, and must keep it up till the fourteenth day. In the evening of that day they shall kill the lamb and take of its blood, which they shall sprinkle on the two side posts and the upper doorpost of the house. Then they shall roast the lamb whole, without breaking a bone; and all the family, every father and mother and every child, shall eat it, with unleavened bread and bitter herbs, before the midnight hour. And you shall be all dressed for your journey, with your loins girded and your shoes on your feet and your staff in your hand. And be ready to go.

"Then at midnight I will send My destroying angel forth and smite the first-born of Egypt. But when My angel comes through your land, he will look to see if the blood is on the doorposts. And when he sees it, he will pass over that house and not bring death into it.

"This is the Lord's Passover. And throughout all your generations hereafter you shall keep this Passover every year, on the fourteenth day of the first month, to remember this day and this night, when the Lord delivered you from bondage, when He smote the first-born of Egypt but passed over you."

Through most of their long time of slavery, the Israelites had not been able to make the morning and evening sacrifice and to pray

openly to the Lord; for this was against the religion of the Egyptians, and they stopped the Israelites from worshiping God as much as they could. So now, as they were being delivered, the Lord gave them the Passover as a grand beginning again of His worship.

Just as it had been from the beginning, when Adam and Eve and Abel worshiped, the lamb stood for the Redeemer, the Son of God, who was to come and die for sinners who wanted to be saved from their sins and eternal death. The blood of the lamb which was sprinkled on their doorposts represented the life of the Saviour ("For," the Lord told the Israelites, "the blood is the life") which He would give for poor sinners, and so the angel of eternal death would "pass over" them.

So the Israelites did as the Lord commanded. Each family took a lamb and kept it penned up for four days. Then on the evening of the fourteenth day of the month they killed the lamb, they sprinkled the blood, and they prepared and ate the Passover supper. They stood all ready for the journey, with their clothes girded up for traveling, their shoes on their feet, their staffs in their hands, their little ones with them, and their flocks and herds all ready to be driven before them as they should go out from the land of Egypt.

At midnight every Israelite family had finished the Passover supper. They had marked the doorposts with the blood of the lamb. Now, as the Lord had told them to do, they burned all parts of the lamb which could not be eaten. And in awe and great expectation they awaited the coming of the angel of death, who was to pass over them.

Then death struck. And over the land of Egypt there arose a terrible cry, the voice of a people whose first-born children were slain. The Israelites heard it, and they thanked God that when He had seen the blood on the door, He had passed over them, and their children were safe.

Then Pharaoh called in haste for Moses and Aaron. "Go out!" he cried. "Get up and go out from among my people, both you and all the children of Israel. Take your flocks and your herds, and be gone! And bless me also!"

The Egyptians pressed upon the children of Israel to go. They gave them gold and silver and precious stones and clothing and everything they asked for. And they said, "Go! Go! Let us be rid of you forever!"

And out of Egypt, marching in order, driving their flocks and herds and carrying the wealth of Egypt, out of the house of bondage marched the children of Israel.

Through the Red Sea

Exodus 13:17-22; 14; 15; Psalm 106:7-12;
1 Corinthians 10:1-13; Revelation 15:2, 3

THE ISRAELITES came out of Egypt marching in order, six hundred thousand men, besides women and children, no doubt over a million. And there went with them, too, a great many Egyptians or half Egyptians, called a "mixed multitude." And there were great flocks and herds which they owned, led or driven by chosen men and youth. And they bore great stores of riches which they had taken from the Egyptians.

From the midnight hour when they started, there appeared before their marching host the presence of God in a pillar of fire. When day came, it was a pillar of cloud, but at night it was a pillar of fire. From this day till they reached the Promised Land, forty years afterward, the pillar of fire and cloud never left them. It led them on the way, it gave them light by night, it protected them from their enemies, and it showed that God was with them. For the Lord was in that pillar of cloud and fire, and often He spoke from it to Moses.

They marched from Egypt, east to Etham, on the edge of the desert. Now the shortest way from there to Canaan was along by the Mediterranean and through the country of the Philistines. But the Lord did not take them that way, for two reasons. First, they would meet the Philistines, a warlike people, and the Israelites were unused to war. Second, they had so long been in slavery that most of them were poor and ignorant of the ways and worship of God; and the Lord wanted to give them a course of teaching, a year or two; but He did not at first mean it to be forty years, as it proved to be.

So at Etham He said to Moses, "Turn and march south, and encamp by the Red Sea." So they did, and they came to a plain shut in by mountains on their right and left, with the sea in front. And here the Lord gave them their first lesson.

For when Pharaoh heard that they had turned south, against the sea, he said: "They are entangled in the wilderness. Why did we let them go? I will take my army and go after them and bring them back."

So he gathered a great army, with foot soldiers, and horsemen, and six hundred chariots, and marched after them. The Egyptians came

upon the Israelites shut in by mountains and the sea. The Israelites were terribly frightened, and they accused Moses of bringing them into this place where Pharaoh would kill many of them and take the rest back to Egypt.

But Moses said to them, "Stand still, and see the salvation of the Lord. For the Egyptians you see today you shall see no more forever."

And the Lord said to Moses, "Tell the people of Israel to go forward. And you lift up your rod and stretch it over the sea. I will divide the sea, and the people of Israel shall march through on dry ground."

Then the pillar of cloud and fire lifted up from before the camp of Israel and went behind, between them and the Egyptians. To the Egyptians it was a black and threatening cloud; but to the Israelites, as night came on, it was a bright and shining light, piercing the darkness over the sea.

Moses stretched out his rod over the sea. And the Lord sent a strong east wind, which cut a path through the sea as the Israelites marched forward. They found dry ground, with the waters walled up on their right hand and on their left. Through the night they marched —men, women, and children, flocks and herds, marching to the other shore.

Right after them, on the other side of the cloud, marched and rode and drove the Egyptians, saying, "Where these slaves can go, we can go." But as the morning drew near, they found themselves in trouble. Their chariot wheels were clogged, the dry ground became mud, and they could scarcely move. Then they cried: "Turn! Turn! Flee from the Israelites! For the Lord is fighting for them against the Egyptians."

But now in the morning the Israelites were all over on the other shore. Then, as the Lord commanded, Moses stretched out his rod over the sea. And it caved in, swallowing the Egyptians and drowning them—footmen, horsemen, and charioteers and their horses. And the sea washed up their dead bodies at the feet of Israel.

Then how the hosts of Israel rejoiced and shouted and sang for joy. They sang with Moses a triumphal song: "I will sing unto the Lord; for He hath triumphed gloriously!" And Miriam led the women, with timbrels and dancing, answering to Moses and the men:

> "Sound the loud timbrel o'er Egypt's dark sea!
> Jehovah has triumphed! His people are free!"

Angel Food and Water of Life

Exodus 12:22-27; 16:1 to 17:8;
Psalm 78:12-25; 1 Corinthians 10:1-4

GOD'S people were free! No longer slaves, but free men! Egypt with its bondage was left behind on the other side of the sea which had swallowed Pharaoh's army. Israel had taken themselves out of Egypt in body, but oh, how much they needed to have their minds free from the darkness of Egypt! God had delivered them, and He went before them in the pillar of cloud and fire. But would they trust Him? Would they obey Him?

The pillar of cloud and fire turned south, and led the Israelites into the desert of Shur. Three days they marched, but they found no water, and all the water they had carried was gone. Then they came to a well, but when they began to drink its water, they cried, "Marah! Marah!" that is, "Bitter! Bitter!" And they could not drink it. They murmured against Moses. But God told him to cut down a certain tree and throw it into the water. When he did, the water was cured of its bitterness, and the Israelites drank their fill.

Then they came to Elim, where there were twelve wells of water and seventy palm trees, and they encamped there awhile. Then they turned southeast toward the mountains of Horeb, or Sinai. By now all the food they had brought from Egypt was eaten up, and they had nothing left. What could they do? How could a million people be fed in a desert where almost nothing grew? The people cried to Moses and Aaron: "Oh, that we had stayed in Egypt, when we sat by the flesh-pots and ate bread to the full. You have brought us out into this desert to kill us all."

Then the Lord said to Moses: "I will rain bread from heaven for you. And the people shall go out and gather it every morning, for six days of the week. But on the Sabbath day there will be none to gather; so let them gather on the sixth day twice as much, and keep some for the Sabbath."

Because the people were not yet used to a fleshless diet, that evening the Lord sent quails which settled about the camp, and the Israelites caught them and ate them. But in the morning the dew fell heavily, and as it dried up the people saw covering the ground a

small, white thing like snow or ice pellets. And they said, "Manna? Manna?" that is, "What is it? What is it?"

And Moses said to them, "This is the bread which the Lord has given you to eat. Every one of you gather it, just enough for each person. You shall each have an omer [which is about three quarts]."

So the name of it was called "What is it?" or "manna." It was a perfect food, and it tasted like wafers made with honey. For forty years afterwards, until the children of Israel came into the Promised Land, the manna never failed to fall and give them food every day except on Sabbath. When the sun came up, all that was left upon the ground melted. And if anybody tried to keep some overnight, it got wormy and became rotten. But on the sixth day they gathered twice as much and kept a part overnight for the Sabbath food. And then it kept perfectly. So the Lord began to teach them to keep the Sabbath, which they had largely forgotten in their bondage in Egypt.

They journeyed on into the land of Rephidim, where again there was no water. And the people cried to Moses, "Give us water to drink! Have you brought us out of Egypt to kill us and our children with thirst?"

Moses cried to the Lord, "What shall I do to this people? They are almost ready to stone me."

And the Lord said: "Take some of the elders of Israel with you, and bring the people up to the rock wall on the side of the camp. Then take your rod and strike the rock, and there shall come water out of it for all the people to drink."

So Moses did. And lo! a great stream of water, a river, burst forth from the rock, enough for all the people and all their flocks and herds to drink. And though when they left that encampment, the waters there dried up, wherever they came, Moses had only to speak to the rock, and the water gushed forth.

"He clave the rocks in the wilderness,
    And gave them drink as out of the great depths.
    He brought streams also out of the rock,
    And caused waters to run down like rivers.

"And had rained down manna upon them to eat,
    And had given them of the corn of heaven.
    Man did eat angels' food:
    He sent them meat to the full."

Psalm 78:15, 16, 24, 25.

The Hands That Prevailed

Exodus 17:8-16; Deuteronomy 25:17-19;
1 Samuel 15; Psalm 105:37

WHEN the Israelites came out of Egypt, they were not all healthy. There were some sick and feeble among them. The Egyptians had worked them hard and abused them. Also, the Israelites had formed some bad habits of eating and living, and that had helped to break down their health. Disease comes from breaking the laws of nature, which are God's laws. And God told the Israelites, "If you will listen to Me, and do right, and keep My laws, I will put none of the diseases of the Egyptians on you." Through their journeying, God taught them how to live, so that they grew strong. Those who would not obey His laws died; but those who obeyed lived so that it could be said of them at last that "there was not one feeble person among their tribes."

But when they had been on their journey only two months and came into the land of Rephidim, Moses tells us that there were some weak and faint persons straggling behind, and there were fainthearted and rebellious ones, especially among the mixed multitude. Because of their rebellion and murmuring, the Lord could not protect them as much as He would. So a new danger befell them.

There dwelt in that land a people called the Amalekites, who were mean and cruel. And they said: "Now here is our chance to kill some of these Israelites, and take what they have." So they fell on the hindmost stragglers and killed them.

Then Moses called a strong young man of the tribe of Ephraim, Joshua by name; and he said to him: "Choose out strong men, the most fit for war, and go out and fight the Amalekites. And I will stand on the top of yonder hill, with the rod of God in my hand, and I will pray for you."

So Joshua chose the strongest and best of the men and armed them with the weapons they had picked up from the dead Egyptian soldiers on the shore of the Red Sea. With these he went out and fought against the Amalekites.

Moses took with him his brother Aaron and his brother-in-law Hur, the husband of Miriam, and the three of them climbed to the top of the hill. They could see the battlefield where Joshua was fighting.

111

Moses lifted up his arms, with the rod of God in his right hand, and prayed for victory of the Israelites. Aaron and Hur soon saw that while Moses' hands were raised, Joshua and the Israelites prevailed, but when he grew weary and let his hands drop, the Amalekites prevailed.

So Aaron on one side and Hur on the other held up his hands as he prayed. And Joshua and his men drove the Amalekites from the field and taught them a lesson they would not forget. Because of their meanness and treachery, the Lord doomed the Amalekites to utter destruction; several hundred years later that was accomplished, and Amalek as a nation was wiped out.

Moses now built an altar on the spot where he had pleaded with God and where Aaron and Hur had held up his hands. He called the place and the altar Jehovah-nissi, which means "the Lord my Banner"; because, like a banner of victory, his wavering hands had been strengthened and the enemies of God's people had been defeated.

Moses now took Joshua, the brave young captain, as his own companion and servant and began to train him as a leader. Neither of them knew it as yet, but forty years later Joshua was to be the one to take Moses' place as the leader of God's people.

Lift up your hands, O man of God,
    And pray for victory.
The Amalekites despise your rod
    With which you cleft the sea.
Look! There upon the plain they fight!
Lift up your rod, and plead the right!

Lo, Moses prays, and on the plain
    Brave Joshua smites the foe.
The Amalekites in crowds are slain,
    And Israel triumphs so.
Pray on, pray on, O man of God!
Hold high the consecrated rod!

But weary grow the pleading hands,
    And stronger war's alarms.
Quick! Hur and Aaron, where he stands,
    Support his wavering arms.
Lo, fervently again he pleads,
And victory comes where Joshua leads.

Giving the Law at Sinai

God showed Himself to His people, not only as a lawgiver and a judge, but as a merciful guardian. The God who brought them out of Egypt, who guided and protected them on the journey and opened the Red Sea before them, destroying Pharaoh and his army, thus proving Himself supreme—this was the God who now spoke to them His law.

CLYDE N. PROVONSHA, ARTIST

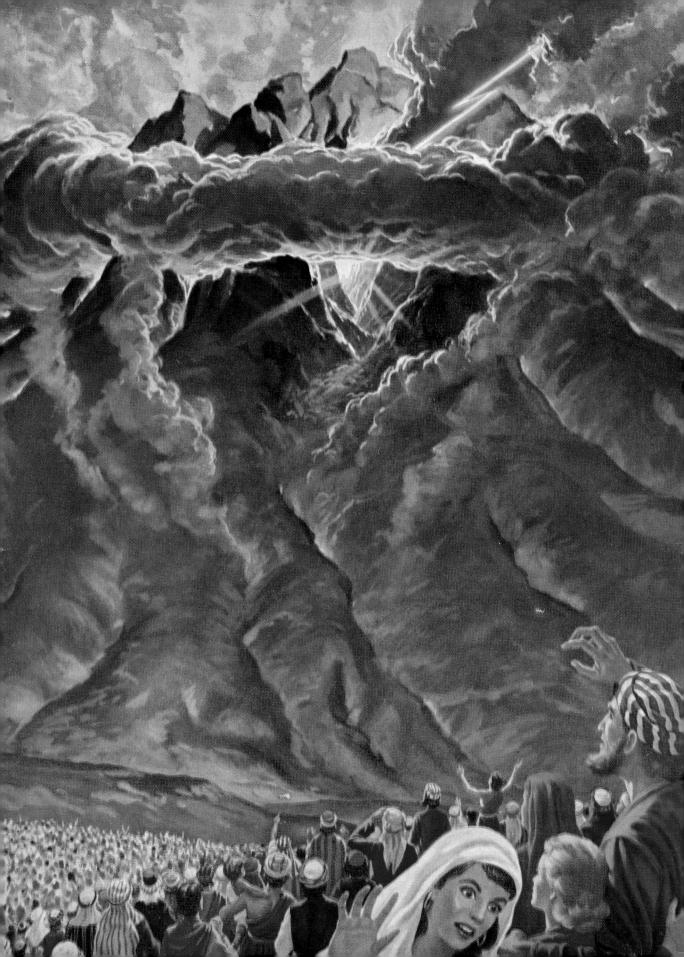

At the Mount of God

Exodus 18 to 20

IN THE third month after they left Egypt, the hosts of Israel came to Mount Sinai. How Moses' heart must have thrilled as they came to that sacred ground! For here was the land where he had led his flock that bright morning a few months before. Here he had seen the burning bush and had heard the voice of God out of it calling him to go back to Egypt and deliver His people Israel. Now the months seemed years or ages away. Such great things had been done in Egypt as had never been done before. Israel, which was then a nation of slaves, was now out of the house of bondage and journeying to the Promised Land flowing with milk and honey.

But here at the Mount of God they were to encamp for a year and go to school to God. They were to see the glory of God, clothed in black clouds that flashed lightnings and crashed thunders. They should hear God's voice speaking His law. They should build a wilderness sanctuary, a movable house of God, rich and beautiful, housing the ark of God where His Presence dwelt. Here they should learn terrible but glorious lessons of the great God who had delivered them.

The pillar of cloud and fire led the Israelites through the mountains to the plain at the foot of Mount Sinai and then rested upon the mountaintop. As they began to pitch camp, there came from the other direction a man, a woman, and two boys. Who are they? Behold! Out from the host of Israel steps their leader, Moses, to meet the little band. He bows before the man; it is his father-in-law, Jethro. He clasps in his arms the woman, his wife, Zipporah. He gathers to his bosom the boys, his own dear sons. The little family that was broken up when Moses was called to his great mission in Egypt is now united and happy.

The camp of Israel was laid out in perfect order through the valley. The mountain above them was clothed with cloud and fire. And God called to Moses out of the cloud and said: "Thus shall you say to the house of Jacob, to the children of Israel: You have seen what I did to the Egyptians, and how I brought you out from bondage. Now if you will obey My voice, and keep My laws, I will make you a kingdom of priests and a holy nation."

113

Thus Moses told the children of Israel. And all the host of them answered, "All that the Lord has spoken we will do."

Then the Lord said to Moses: "Sanctify the people today and tomorrow, and be ready on the third day. For then the Lord will come down in the sight of all the people upon Mount Sinai. Set bounds around the mountain, which the people may not pass over; for the mount on which the Lord descends shall be holy ground."

So the people cleansed themselves and prayed for pure minds and got themselves all ready for the great third day. And when the morning of that day dawned, there were thunders and lightnings and a thick cloud upon the mountain. And the voice of the trump of God sounded loud and louder, so that the people in the camp trembled. And Moses brought them out of the camp to meet with God, and they stood outside the bounds.

Mount Sinai was all asmoke, because the Lord descended upon it in fire, and the whole mountain shook. And God called Moses up into the mount. "Come up again," God said, "and bring Aaron with you." So Moses and Aaron went up.

Then, after the roar of thunder and of the trumpet of God, there came a calm, while God spoke all the words of His Ten Commandment law:

"Thou shalt have no other gods before me.

"Thou shalt not make unto thee any graven image, or any likeness of any thing that is in heaven above, or that is in the earth beneath, or that is in the water under the earth: thou shalt not bow down thyself to them, nor serve them. . . .

"Thou shalt not take the name of the Lord thy God in vain; for the Lord will not hold him guiltless that taketh his name in vain.

"Remember the sabbath day, to keep it holy. Six days shalt thou labour, and do all thy work: but the seventh day is the sabbath of the Lord thy God: in it thou shalt not do any work. . . .

"Honour thy father and thy mother: that thy days may be long upon the land which the Lord thy God giveth thee.

"Thou shalt not kill.

"Thou shalt not commit adultery.

"Thou shalt not steal.

"Thou shalt not bear false witness against thy neighbour.

"Thou shalt not covet thy neighbour's house, thou shalt not covet thy neighbour's wife, nor his manservant, nor his maidservant, nor his ox, nor his ass, nor any thing that is thy neighbour's."

Exodus 20:3-17.

114

The Golden Calf

Exodus 24; 31:18; 32 to 34; Deuteronomy 9:9-21

AFTER God with His own voice had proclaimed His law from Mount Sinai, He said to Moses: "Come up to Me in the mount and bring with you Aaron and his two oldest sons and seventy of the elders of Israel. They shall worship afar off; but you, Moses, come near to Me in the cloud."

So Moses went up, and with him Aaron and the others. And they saw the likeness of God, "as it were the body of heaven in his clearness." And then with Moses they went down.

Again the Lord called Moses up into the mount, saying, "I will give you tablets of stone, on which I will write My law." Then Moses said to the elders of Israel: "Stay here till I come to you again. Aaron and Hur shall be in charge." Then he took the young man Joshua with him, and they went up into the mount.

For six days they waited on the mountain before the cloud. And the glory of the Lord appeared to the Israelites below as a consuming fire. On the seventh day God called Moses, and he entered the cloud, while Joshua remained outside. God laid out before Moses the pattern of a sanctuary the Israelites were to make for Him, and the manner of the priests who were to minister in it. There in the cloud on the mountain God gave to Moses the tablets of stone on which the law was written by the finger of God. And Moses was in the cloud with the Lord for forty days and forty nights.

But down in the camp of Israel the people grew weary, because their minds were empty. They might have spent their time in studying the law of God and learning more of His ways. Some of them did. But the mixed multitude of Egyptians and half Egyptians were not spiritually minded. They thought of the riotous times they had back in Egypt, feasting and dancing, and of the gods and idols which they believed taught them to be so loose and riotous. They talked with others in the camp who were weak and wavering; and gradually, day by day, they got almost all the Israelites to go with them. Aaron saw this spirit growing, but he did not put a stop to it; he hoped every day that Moses would come back. Aaron could not put his foot down, as Moses would, and put a stop to evil.

115

Then suddenly it came to a head. The people came before Aaron and said: "We don't know what has become of this man Moses, who led us here. He may be dead. Now make us gods which shall go before us."

"What gods? There is one God, Jehovah, who brought you out from the land of Egypt."

"We never saw that God. We want gods we can see. Make us a god Apis, the bull god which we saw in Egypt." For the Egyptians worshiped many animals, and one of them was the bull. And in their worship they did many wicked things too shameful to tell about. Now the Israelites, led by the mixed multitude, turned back to this heathen worship.

All this was terrible treason, a turning away from God, who had spoken the law in their hearing. Some faithful men tried to stop the folly. They called to the people to remember God, who was even now in their sight in the cloud of smoke and fire on the mountain, where Moses had gone to talk with Him. But the riot grew, and some of the wicked ones lifted their hands to slay the good.

What about Hur in this time? The Bible does not tell us; but an old story says that he stood up against the idolatry, and the rebels killed him. The story says that when Aaron saw his dead body, then he was afraid for his own life, and he gave up to the people. We do not know, because the Bible does not tell this; but it says no more about Hur after this time, and it may be he died a noble martyr.

Aaron trembled. He feared the people would take his life. He thought he would turn them aside by demanding a sacrifice. "Break off the golden earrings that are in your ears," he cried, "and in the ears of your wives and of your sons and daughters, and bring them to me." He thought they would not want to part with them.

But they began to tear off the golden earrings and cast them before Aaron, till there was a huge pile. Now Aaron had lost control, and he went along with the crowd. He took the gold and melted it in a furnace. Then he cast the flowing gold into a mold he had made in the form of a bull calf. And when it was cooled and solid, he took it out and shaped it with a tool until it was the perfect image of the evil Egyptian god Apis. And the people shouted, "This is your god, O Israel, which brought you out of the land of Egypt!"

When Aaron saw the frenzy of the people, he feebly tried to call their minds back to the true God by saying, "Tomorrow, before this image, there shall be a feast to Jehovah." Oh, shameful, wicked thing, to call this golden calf by the sacred name of Jehovah, the God who could not be seen save as the flaming fire from the midst of which He had spoken the words: "Thou shalt have no other gods before Me. Thou shalt not make unto thee any graven image, nor bow down to it nor serve it."

But on the next day the feast was held. The people worshiped the golden calf. They ate and drank till they were drunken. They danced and played before the image and sang, "These are thy gods, O Israel, that brought thee up from the land of Egypt."

Up on the mountain God said to Moses: "Go down at once! For your people have gone quickly out of the way. They have made a molten calf, worshiping before it and dancing and saying, 'This is your god, O Israel, that brought you out of the land of Egypt.' I have watched this people," said the Lord, "and they are a stiff-necked people. I will destroy them and make a great nation out of your children."

Then Moses pleaded with the Lord to forgive. But he quickly did as God told him to do. He went out and took Joshua, and together they went down the mountain. As they came near to the camp and heard the sounds of tumult, Joshua said, "There is the sound of war in the camp."

But Moses answered, "It is not the sound of the cry of might, nor the sound of the cry of defeat. It is the sound of singing that I hear."

Then they came to the camp. And Moses saw the golden calf, mounted high, and the people dancing and leaping and singing and shouting before it. His anger blazed; and as they turned to look at him, he flung down the tablets of stone on which God had written His law, and they broke in pieces. The people had broken them in their lives, and the broken law on the stones was the symbol of their sin.

Moses strode through the crowd. He knocked down the golden calf. He broke it to pieces, melted it, ground it to powder, and scattered the dust on the water, which he made them drink, bitter as it was.

Then he turned upon Aaron. "What did this people do to you," he demanded, "that you have made them sin this great sin?"

Aaron shrank before him. "Let not my lord's anger blaze," he begged. "You know how bad these people are. They said to me, 'Make a god to go ahead of us, for we don't know what has become of this man Moses.' So I told them to tear off their gold and bring it to me. Then I threw it into the fire, and lo! there came out this calf!" He tried to make Moses think the calf was a miracle, as though God had formed it in the fire.

The people were still unruly. Moses took his stand at the gate of the camp and cried, "Whoever is on the Lord's side, come to me!" And there came almost the whole tribe of Levi, who had not worshiped the golden calf. Many others, from all the tribes, repenting of their sin, came also.

"Thus commands Jehovah, the God of Israel," Moses cried to the Levites: "Gird on your swords, and go out and slay everyone who does not repent of this folly." So the men of Levi did as he told them, and there fell that day about three thousand of the wicked leaders in the riot.

Moses returned to the Lord and pleaded: "Alas, these people have committed a great sin. But, O Lord, if Thou wilt forgive their sin—and if not, blot me, I pray thee, out of Thy book which Thou hast written."

God said, "Whoever sins against Me, him only will I blot out of My book. But lead the people where I told you. My angel shall go ahead of you. But on the day that I punish, I will indeed punish."

Still Moses pleaded, and God forgave. He told Moses to pitch the tent of meeting outside the camp and call all the people there. He told them to strip their ornaments off and plead for forgiveness. This they did; but many besides the three thousand were slain by the Lord, because they repented not.

Then God told Moses to hew out two tablets of stone like the first and come up into the mount again. There he stayed for another forty days and nights, receiving the words of God. And God again wrote on the new tablets His Ten Commandment law.

This time Israel waited patiently. Aaron, deeply repenting his sin, joined with the good leaders of Israel in teaching the way of the Lord. And when Moses came down, he was greeted by a more sober and earnest people, who listened eagerly to what work God had for them to do.

———

"Who is on the Lord's side? Come to me!"
 Moses stood a-beckoning in the gate.
Little Phinehas answered him: "We are! We!
 All the men of Levi! God is great!"
Eaglet of the priesthood, zealous for the Lord,
 Aaron's little grandson led the way,
Lifted high the banner, waved the sacred sword,
 Made atonement for that sinful day.

118

"Let Them Make Me a Sanctuary"

Exodus 35 to 40; Numbers 4; 9:15-23; 10:1-28;
Hebrews 9:1-5; Psalms 90; 91; 103

WHILE Moses was in the fiery cloud of God on Mount Sinai, God showed him a blueprint of a sanctuary which the people of Israel were to make for Him. Sanctuary means "holy place." It was called a holy place because God's presence was there. It came to mean, too, a refuge place, a place of safety; for where God is, there His people are safe.

And God told Moses to take Aaron and his sons and set them apart to be His priests, Aaron the high priest and his sons priests under him. The priests were to be the go-betweens of God and the people: to offer the sacrifices for the people, to pray for them, and to give God's messages to them. In the beginning of the world the father of a family was the priest, and in a sense that is true even today; for God made parents to be the go-betweens of their children and God. The father might be called the high priest, and the mother a priest.

But the Israelites, like the rest of mankind, had gone so far away from God that the fathers and mothers were not often good priests. So now, when God was making the laws and the forms of government for His people, he took one tribe, the tribe of Levi, to be His go-betweens. All the men of the tribe of Levi were to be ministers, or servants, of the Lord, caring for the sanctuary and its service and teaching the people.

But one family in the tribe, Aaron's family, were to be especially the priests. The tribe of Levi was taken for this service because it had been the most faithful to God through the trials of the wilderness. And though Aaron had failed when the people rebelled and compelled him to make the golden calf, yet he had been so faithful in most things and had repented so deeply of this sin, that God took him and kept him for His priest.

Since the Israelites were on the march much of the time and were living in tents, this sanctuary had to be made so that it could be moved from place to place. So God showed Moses the pattern of a building, part house and part tent, which could be taken apart and carried with them when they moved, and set up again when they

camped. Caring for this sanctuary was part of the work of the Levites.

It was a very beautiful and costly building. The main part was the tabernacle. It was made of boards covered with gold, set upright in sockets of silver, and of curtains of the finest linen beautifully embroidered. The boards made three sides of the tabernacle, but the front was closed only with curtains. The top or roof had three covers. The lowest or inner one was of woven goat's-hair. The next or middle one was of ram's-skins dyed red. The third and outer one was of sealskins. All these coverings hung down on the outside of the golden boards.

The tabernacle was ten cubits wide, ten cubits high, and thirty cubits long. In our measurements this meant perhaps eighteen feet wide, eighteen feet high, and fifty-four feet long. There were two rooms. The first one was twice as long as it was wide; it was called the holy place. The second one was square; it was called the most holy place, because the Presence of God was there whenever the tabernacle was set up.

Outside the tabernacle and surrounding it was a great space closed in by curtains; it was called the court. The greater part of it was in front of the tabernacle. The curtains that closed the front of the court were usually drawn aside, so that the people could look in.

The furnishings of the tabernacle were these: In the court were the altar of burnt offering and the laver or great basin of water for the priests to wash with. In the holy place there were a seven-branched lamp, a table of showbread, and a little altar of incense. In the most holy place there was the sacred ark of God, made of acacia wood covered with gold. The cover of the ark was called the mercy seat. Bowing over the mercy seat were two golden figures of angels, called the cherubim. And inside the ark were the two tablets of stone on which God had written His holy law.

This was the sanctuary Israel was to make for God, and which they did make there at Mount Sinai. Over it towered God's pillar of fire and cloud; and in it, on the mercy seat, dwelt the bright light that no man could look upon; for God was there.

The tabernacle was pitched in the very middle of the camp of Israel. Nearest to it camped the tribe of Levi, the tribe that God had taken as His special ministers. Right in front of the tabernacle were the tents of Moses and Aaron. On the other three sides were the three clans of Levi. Each of them had a special work to do in caring for the tabernacle, both when it was carried on their journeys and when it was set up.

Then, outside the Levites, the twelve tribes of Israel pitched in regular order, three tribes on each of the four sides. On the east, behind Moses and the priests, was the camp of Judah, with Issachar and Zebulun. On the south side was the camp of Reuben, with Simeon and Gad. On the west side was the camp of Ephraim, with Manasseh and Benjamin. And on the north side was the camp of Dan, and with them the tribes of Asher and Naphtali.

When the pillar of cloud and fire lifted, it was the signal to break camp and march. Then the sons of Aaron blew on two silver trumpets; and all the tribes of Israel packed up and stood ready to go. The camp of Judah marched first. Then the tabernacle was taken down and carried forward by two of the clans of Levi. Then marched the camp of Reuben. After them came another clan of Levi, bearing the ark and the furnishings of the tabernacle. Next marched the camp of Ephraim; and last came the camp of Dan, making the rearguard.

So in order marched forth from Sinai the host of Israel, and in such order they marched through all their wilderness wanderings.

If you had been a little lass,
    Or else a little lad,
Back there in Israel's Sinai camp,
    Now wouldn't you be glad?
Each lovely morning you'd go out,
    And pan or bucket take,
And scoop up manna from the ground
    As white as frosty cake.
Then you would run to mother quick
    And help her boil or bake it;
More kinds of ways than you could think
    There were for you to take it.
And you would wander by the brook
    That flowed from out the rock,
And pick the lovely violets
    And sleepy four-o'clock.
And just suppose one happy day
    Bezaleel should spy you
And call, "Come here, my little one,
    For messenger I'll try you."
So you would run his errands then,
    And all his orders carry
To workmen here and there, and help
    To build the sanctuary.

121

The Daily Worship

Exodus 35:4-35; 36:1-7; 40; Leviticus 1; 8; 9; Isaiah 53;
Hebrews 2:9-18; 3; 9:6, 9-25

THE TABERNACLE was the most beautiful and costly tent-house that ever was made. And how do you think Moses got all the gold and silver and brass and wood and fine cloth and skins and embroidery that went into its making? Did he put a tax on the people and make them give up their wealth for the tabernacle? No! God did not want a sanctuary that people were compelled to make. He told Moses to take a freewill offering from the people. And everyone that was of a willing heart brought the material in abundance, until there was so much that Moses had to stop them. The people were so glad and happy after the Lord had forgiven them for their idolatry that they just poured out the wealth they had taken out of the land of Egypt and everything the desert could furnish. So there was enough and more than enough to build the tabernacle.

Then God took two men who were very skillful, and He put His Spirit upon them to make them more skillful. And they led all the best workmen and skillful needlewomen in the camp in plating the golden boards and the brazen altar, and in shaping the silver sockets and the altars and the laver and the other furnishings, and in weaving and embroidering the curtains. Greatest of all their work was the sacred ark, covered all with gold, and the figures of the angels bowing over it.

The first of these men was Bezaleel, who was the grandson of Hur. He was of the tribe of Judah. His helper was Aholiab, of the tribe of Dan. Though they had learned in Egypt to be skillful workmen in metal, the wisdom that God gave them for this work made them the best artists and artisans in all the world. So with all the wisehearted they prepared the tabernacle. It took about a year.

On the first day of the second month of the second year, Moses reared up the tabernacle in the midst of the camp of Israel. Then the Lord came down in blinding light, in the pillar of cloud and fire, and rested on the tabernacle. His glory filled it so that even Moses could not enter. After a while God veiled His glory a little, so that Moses and Aaron and the priests his sons could come near and do their duties there. But never were any but the priests to go into the holy place

122

of the tabernacle. This they had to do each day. And never were any of the common priests to go into the most holy place. Only the high priest could enter there, and he but once a year, veiling his face from the glory with a cloud of fragrant smoke from the incense on the burning coals of his censer.

Every day of the year the priest offered sacrifices of animals upon the brazen altar of burnt offering in the court of the sanctuary. He brought a little of the blood of the slain sacrifice and sprinkled it in the sanctuary. He filled the cups of the seven-branched lamp with oil, and put fresh unleavened bread upon the table of showbread, and burned incense upon the little golden altar before the veil of the most holy place. But never was he to part the curtain and go in.

There were very particular laws about all this work of the priests. And every one held some meaning, which the priests and the people were to study. The sacrifice of the lamb or other animal represented the death of the coming Christ, who was to die for the sins of the world. The lamp in the holy place represented the ever-living Spirit of God which was to enlighten His people. The showbread upon the table represented the word of God which they were daily to take and live thereby. The incense burned upon the altar represented the prayers of God's people. And before a priest went into the holy place, he washed his hands and his feet with water from the laver outside the tabernacle, to represent the cleansing of anyone who would approach unto God.

The high priest represented the Son of God, who is the mediator or go-between of man and God. The Son of God, the Christ, is both the sacrifice and the priest. And all His life and work and sacrifice were shadowed forth in the service of the sanctuary. Let us thank and praise and worship our Lord, the Lamb of God, our High Priest, who died to save us, and who pleads for us continually before the throne of God.

Of course the sanctuary and its service, though so beautiful and impressive, were only the symbols of things they represented. They could not even approach in form or glory the real things. The tabernacle represented heaven, and the court outside represented the earth where the sacrifices took place; but no more was the tabernacle like heaven than the court outside was like the earth. They were only figures of real things. But since they were figures and pictures, they were to be studied for the meanings they held. So the Israelites were to study, and we too may study and learn what is the actual work of our sacrificial Lamb and of our High Priest, the Son of God.

123

The Day of Atonement

Leviticus 16; 23:26-32; Daniel 8:13, 14; 9:20-27;
Hebrews 9:6-28; 10

ALL the year long, day by day in the sanctuary of God in Israel, the priest was to offer the sacrifice of the lamb or other animal in the court before the tabernacle, as the Lamb of God, the Christ, was to be offered in the earth for the sins of men. Every day the priest was to bring a little of the blood of the sacrifice and sprinkle it in the holy place, before the veil of the most holy, as a sign of the sins of men brought into the sanctuary of God in heaven, but sins forgiven through the sacrifice of His beloved Son.

Then on the tenth day of the seventh month came the Day of Atonement, when the yearly round of service was to be finished. Every year this whole service was thus repeated. The year was long, as the history of earth and sin is long. The Day of Atonement was, in comparison, short, as the final work of Christ, our great High Priest, is in comparison short.

While the priest could not every day enter the most holy place, yet as he sprinkled the blood before the veil outside, in the holy place, it signified the bringing of the sins of the people into the presence of God in the most holy. And so it was said that the sins of men, sins which God abhors, polluted the inner sanctuary. Just so do the sins of men in all ages of this world pollute the universe and the heaven of God.

But on the Day of Atonement the sanctuary was to be cleansed of these sins, as in the end of the world the universe and heaven itself are to be cleansed forever of sin and all its evil results, so that nevermore will there be sin or sorrow or sickness or death.

On this Day of Atonement no one was to do any unnecessary work. Everyone was to fast; no one was to eat anything at all. By this they were to show their sorrow for their sins and that they wanted God to blot out their sins forever.

First in the service on that day came the sacrifice on the altar of burnt offering. This sacrifice was of a bullock, which the high priest offered for himself as well as for all the people. Since he was but a man, though he represented the Son of God, he was sinful, and with

124

experiences of doubt and faultfinding, and of punishment an[d re]pentance, until at last they came to the borders of the Promised [Land] and camped in a place called Kadesh-barnea.

"Now," said Moses to them, "the Lord has set the land b[efore] you. Go up and take it. Don't be afraid or discouraged."

But they said to him, "First let us send men to spy out the [land] and bring us word again how to go and what we shall find."

So Moses took twelve men, one from every tribe, and sent [them] on to spy out the land. They were gone for forty days. When [they] came back, they reported: "It is surely a land flowing with milk [and] honey; and here are some of the fruits of it." And they showed ba[skets] of figs and pomegranates and a great bunch of grapes so large it [was] hung from a pole carried between two men.

But ten of the spies seemed very glum. They said: "The pe[ople] there are very strong. And they live in cities walled up to hea[ven.] And there are giants there, too. We can never conquer them. [Now] that the Lord has brought us to this land, to fall by the sword, [and] leave our wives and little ones to be a prey. Wouldn't it be better i[f we] chose a captain to take us back to the land of Egypt?"

But two of the spies, Joshua of the tribe of Ephraim and C[aleb] of the tribe of Judah, stilled the people and told them: "It is a g[ood] land. And Jehovah our God will conquer it for us. Come, let us g[o up.] The Lord will give us the land."

But all the people cried, "Stone them! Stone those two me[n to] death! They want us to die by the sword!"

Then the glory of the Lord appeared in the cloud over [the] tabernacle. He called Moses and Aaron to Him, and He said: "T[his] people are so rebellious that I cannot take them into the lan[d of] Canaan. I will make them wander in the wilderness till all this gen[era]tion of older people are dead. As their spies were gone for forty [days,] so I will make them wander for forty years, a year for a day. O[nly] Joshua and Caleb of this generation shall go into the Land of Prom[ise."]

Now the people were sorry. They came up the next morn[ing] and said, "We will now obey the Lord and go to war against [the] heathen." But Moses said, "No! It is too late. The Lord has pa[ssed] sentence, and you must bear it." Nevertheless they did go up to ba[ttle,] but the Canaanites and Amalekites beat them, and slew many, [and] chased them back to the camp.

So the Israelites failed to enter when they might have, wi[thin] two years after they left Egypt. And for forty years they cam[ped] and traveled to and fro in the wilderness.

his people he must have forgiveness; and the sacrifice represented that forgiveness.

The high priest then carried some of the blood into the tabernacle. He went through the holy place, carrying a censer. He put some live coals in it from the altar of incense, and placed some incense upon it. Incense was made of sweet gums, which when burned gave off a dense, sweet-smelling smoke. Veiling his face with the smoke of the incense, he parted the veil and entered the most holy place. There he sprinkled the blood upon the mercy seat of the ark, which represented the throne of God. Then he came out.

He came again to the great altar of burnt offering in the court. There were brought to him two goats. Lots were cast to tell which goat should be the Lord's and which goat should be the scapegoat. The Lord's goat was offered as a sacrifice on the altar. Like the sacrificial lamb or bullock, it represented the sacrifice of the Son of God for the sins of men.

Again the high priest took of the blood and carried it into the sanctuary; and as he had done before, he entered with it into the most holy place and sprinkled it upon the mercy seat. He then came out bearing in symbol all the sins of the whole year which had been brought into the most holy place by the daily sprinkling of the blood. Daily the sins had been forgiven; now on the Day of Atonement they were to be blotted out. This was called the cleansing of the sanctuary.

Outside, the live goat was now brought to him. At the door of the tabernacle the high priest placed his hands upon the head of the scapegoat and confessed over him all the sins of the people of Israel, which he had brought out of the sanctuary. The scapegoat was then sent away in the care of a strong man and turned loose in the wilderness. This represented the final banishment of sin and the cleansing of the whole universe from all its evil. So ended the ceremony.

Our Father who art in heaven,
    Hallowed be Thy name.
Be my sins forgiven;
    Take away my shame.
Let Thy sanctuary
    No more be defiled.
Ever with me tarry,
    And bless this little child.
    Amen!

"To Spy Out the Lan[d]"

Numbers 9 to 14; Deuteronomy 1[...]

FOR ALMOST a year the Israelites [...] great things took place in that time. [...] of God in the third month after coming [...] Sinai on the twentieth day of the secon[...]

There at Sinai they had seen and [...] law from the mountaintop. There within [...] from Him and had worshiped the gold[...] God's judgments and had repented of [...] brought their gifts in plenty to make the [...] and there they had worked and gladly [...] they had set up the tabernacle and ha[...] blinding flash of His glory. There they ha[...] and sacrifices that were to go on for fifte[...] had kept their first Passover since comin[...] last God said to them: "You have staye[...] tain. Take up your journey to the land [...] to give you."

So they broke camp at Sinai, and j[...] terrible wilderness toward the land of C[...] Lord went with them. In the pillar of cl[...] with the pillar of fire He gave them lig[...] of the children grew tired and sore, an[...]

> "We are weary, oh, so[...]
> Is it far, is it far
> To Canaan's la[...]

It was to be farther than any of th[...] their wanderings, their clothes never gr[...] wore out. The Lord gave them manna [...] vided pasture for their flocks. When ther[...] God gave them water from the rock. [...]

But there were many among them, [...] multitude, who murmured and complain[...]

126

Through Forty Years

Numbers 16; 20; 21; Deuteronomy 2; 3:1-8

FORTY years! Oh, how long a time of disappointment and weary waiting! But the Israelites had not yet learned their lesson. At one time Korah, a man of Levi, and Dathan and Abiram, men of Reuben, rose up in rebellion against Moses and Aaron. Korah wanted to be high priest in Aaron's place, and the others wanted to take Moses' place. But the Lord made it clear that He had appointed Moses and Aaron to be head and priest of the people. And when the rebels would not listen and obey, the Lord made the earth to open where they stood, and they were swallowed up in it.

At another time the people were discouraged by the hard road, and they complained against Moses, saying he had not brought them into the Land of Promise. As though Moses were responsible for their sin at Kadesh and had sentenced them to the forty years of wandering! Then the Lord let poisonous serpents come into the camp, and many who were bitten died. The people repented, and the Lord in mercy told Moses to make a brazen serpent and lift it on a pole. All who would look at the brazen serpent were healed.

So it went on. There were murmuring and rebellion and punishment; and sometimes many, sometimes one by one, the older people, those above twenty years of age, who grumbled and rebelled, were taken away in death. You can imagine the way they looked upon Joshua and Caleb, still strong, still faithful, still with the promise of God that they should go alive into the Promised Land.

And all the young people and the children looked to them and to Moses and Aaron and Miriam, and followed their teaching, and grew, most of them, to be strong and true men and women of faith. But when at last, after thirty-eight years, the Israelite host came back to Kadesh, there Miriam died, and was buried. And there Moses and Aaron failed. For the people found no water. And though they knew that God would give them water, as He always had, if they would be patient for a little while, they came and complained to Moses and said again that he had brought them out of Egypt to slay them in the wilderness. Then God told Moses to go and speak to the rock, and water would come forth.

128

Going Through Jordan

When the feet of the priests who carried the ark touched the water of the Jordan, the water from above stopped flowing. Then, when the water below had flowed on, the people walked through the river bed. This great miracle reminded the people that the same God who divided the Red Sea forty years before was with them still as their Guide.

CLYDE N. PROVONSHA, ARTIST

Moses and Aaron went to the rock, and the people followed them. But now for the first time Moses was out of patience. His long years of bearing the burden overcame him, and he spoke out roughly to the people. "Hear now, ye rebels!" he said. "Must we fetch water out of this rock for you?" And instead of speaking to the rock, he struck it twice with his rod. The water gushed out, and the people drank. But the Lord said to Moses and Aaron: "You have dishonored Me before the people. Therefore you shall not take them into the land which I have given them." So it came about in the end that of all the people over twenty years of age who came out of Egypt, only Joshua and Caleb went into the Promised Land.

The land of Edom was in their way to Canaan, and Moses sent messengers to their king, asking to go through peaceably on the highway. But the king of Edom came out with his army and forbade their passing. The Lord told Moses that they should not fight the Edomites, who were the descendants of Esau; for He had given their land to them. So Israel turned back south again, to go around the land of Edom.

On the way they came to the high Mount Hor. There God told Aaron to go up the mountain, with his son Eleazar and Moses, and die on the top of the mountain. They obeyed; and on Mount Hor Moses took off from Aaron the high priest's garments and put them on Eleazar, who thus became the high priest. Then Aaron died and was buried there by Moses and Eleazar. Now there were left of the old leaders only Moses and Joshua and Caleb.

The people journeyed a long way to go around the mountains of Edom and the land of Moab, to come at last to the east side of the Jordan River. On the way they had to fight three kings and their people, who came out to stop them. These kings were Arad the Canaanite, Sihon the Amorite, and Og the giant, king of Bashan. But the Lord gave Israel the victory in every case, and they took all these lands, from the border of Moab up to Mount Hermon in the north.

So they came at last to the plains of Moab, next to the Jordan River. And the forty years were finished.

A Prophet Who Failed

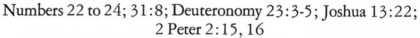

Numbers 22 to 24; 31:8; Deuteronomy 23:3-5; Joshua 13:22;
2 Peter 2:15, 16

THE ISRAELITES were encamped in the plains of Moab, and the Moabite king, Balak, was greatly afraid of them, though they had no thought of harming him or his people. He heard of a prophet in far Mesopotamia named Balaam, who was said to possess great power, so that whom he blessed would be blessed and whom he cursed would be cursed. Perhaps this prophet was a descendant of Nahor and the family of Rebekah and Rachel; for he lived in their country and worshiped God as they did. But all we really know is that he was a believer in the true God and was a prophet.

So Balak sent some princes of Moab and of Midian, a tribe of whom dwelt with the Moabites. They came to Balaam and they said: "Balak, the king of Moab, asks you to come and curse the Israelites, who have come out of Egypt; for he is afraid of them. He will give you great riches and honor if you will do this."

Balaam said to them, "Stay overnight, and I will ask the Lord about this."

That night God said to Balaam, "You shall not curse the Israelites; for I have blessed them." So in the morning Balaam sent the princes away. But Balak sent back more and greater princes and promised Balaam more money and greater honor if he would come and curse Israel.

Now Balaam, though a prophet, was a greedy man, and he very much wanted the money that Balak promised. So he asked the Lord again that night if he might not go. Seeing that Balaam had set his mind on it, God said, "If the men call for you in the morning, go with them; but you shall speak only the words I give you."

In the morning Balaam set out, with two servants, to go with the Moabite princes. Probably they had gone ahead, not expecting he would come; for what happened to him seems to have been while he was alone. God was displeased with Balaam, and He sent an angel to teach him a lesson. The little donkey, or ass, that Balaam rode saw what Balaam could not see, an angel standing in the way with a drawn sword, ready to slay his master. So the ass left the road, and ran

130

into a field. Balaam was very impatient to get along, and he beat the little beast back into the road.

Twice after that the ass stopped, and finally lay down, because she saw the angel in the way. Then Balaam was angry indeed, and he beat the little beast unmercifully. God made the dumb animal to speak then. She said to Balaam, "What have I done to you, that you beat me these three times?"

He said, "Because you have made a fool of me. I wish I had a sword, and I would kill you."

Then the Lord opened Balaam's eyes, and he saw the angel with drawn sword in his hand, waiting as though to kill him. Balaam was scared, and he fell on his face before the angel.

"O Lord," cried Balaam, "if my way is displeasing to you, I will go back." But he did not want to go back, and the Lord let him go on.

The next day Balak took Balaam up on high places, where he could see the camp of Israel. Three times Balaam tried to curse Israel, but every time only blessings came from his mouth.

In a rage Balak cried: "Get out! Go back to your own country! I thought I would give you great riches and honor, but your God has kept you from them."

So Balaam turned and went back home. He did not feel very good. All that money and all that honor he thought he would get, he had lost. He kept thinking and thinking about it, until by the time he reached home he had made up his mind he would get them somehow. So he turned and went back to Balak with a very wicked scheme.

"Get the most beautiful women of Moab to tempt the men of Israel into the worship of your gods," he said. "That's my curse."

And Balak and the princes and the women planned it all out. And they did get some of the Israelites to sin and go against God's commandments.

Then the anger of the Lord blazed out and consumed the wicked ones among them. And in this last trial all those who were left who had come out of Egypt when they were over twenty years of age perished.

There was war then between Israel and Moab; and among the slain was Balaam the prophet, who thus lost his money and his honor and his life, because he had forsaken God and brought a curse upon His people. Nevertheless God used it to weed out the remnant of the rebels in Israel, and they died along with the greedy prophet who failed.

131

On Nebo's Lonely Mountain

Numbers 27:12-23; Deuteronomy 1 to 3; 31;
32:42-52; 34; Jude 9; Matthew 17:1-3; 1 Thessalonians 4:13-18

THE LIFE of Moses, the man of God, was now drawing near to its close. He was 120 years old, yet he was as strong as ever. His eye was not dim nor his strength lessened. He prayed to God: "Let me go over Jordan and see that good land which Thou shalt give to Thy people."

But the Lord answered him: "Say no more to Me of this matter. Ascend this Mount Nebo and view the land which I am giving your people. And when you have seen it, you too shall be gathered to your fathers, as your brother Aaron was. You rebelled against My word at Kadesh, when the people complained because there was no water. And then I told you both that you should not go into the Land of Promise."

So Moses submitted himself to God. And he prayed, "Let the Lord name someone to take my place over the children of Israel."

And God said, "Take Joshua the son of Nun, and set him before Eleazar the high priest, and before the people give him a charge to be the leader of My people."

So Moses took Joshua and did with him as the Lord commanded. And all the people knew that God had appointed Joshua to take the place of Moses. And they promised that they would follow and obey him.

Moses then recounted, in a long speech and a song, all that the Lord had done for His people Israel, and how He had brought them into the border of the land He had promised. Now they were soon to go over Jordan and possess it. God would go before them and drive out the wicked inhabitants. And God would bless them if they would keep His commandments and walk in His ways.

Then Moses turned and ascended the mountain. When Aaron was to die, he climbed the mountain not alone, but with his brother and his son to support him and to comfort him in his last hours. But Moses! All Israel's hearts went with him, but never a single body. Up Nebo's lonely mountain, step by step, he climbed alone, save that, unseen, God went with him.

Nebo was the headland of the Mount Pisgah chain of mountains.

132

It was a very high mountain, and from it one could see north and south and west, far over the country. From this height of Pisgah, Mount Nebo, the Lord showed Moses more than the natural eye could see: all of Gilead at his feet, on the east side of Jordan; all the north country, as far as the headwaters of Jordan River; all the country on the west of Jordan, north and south, bounded by the Great Sea, which we now call the Mediterranean; all the country in the south, where Abraham, Isaac, and Jacob had lived; and all the valley of Jordan, with Jericho just across the river.

And God said to Moses: "This is the land about which I swore to Abraham, Isaac, and Jacob, saying, 'I will give this land to your descendants.' Now I have let you look upon it, but you shall not go over there."

So Moses, the servant of the Lord, died there on Nebo's height. And the Lord buried him in a valley in the land of Moab. But no man knew the place of his burial, and no man knows to this day.

But that was not the end. In the long history of the human race, two men had been taken to heaven without seeing death; they represented those whom God will take alive to heaven when He comes in the end of the world. Now Moses, raised from the dead, was to represent those whom God will bring from the grave.

Very soon after Moses' burial, God came down to his grave to call him forth to life. Satan stood there to contend against the resurrection. But all the power of Satan, who had brought death, could not keep the servant of God in his grave. With a triumphant shout he rose at the call of his Lord. And ever since he has been in heaven with Elijah and with Enoch and with God.

Up from the plains of Moab, up to the mountain's height,
With stately tread, to the march of the dead,
    He passed from his people's sight.
No man was there to comfort, no comrade at his side;
Alone with God in the way he trod,
    He laid him down and died.

Down from the heights of heaven, cascading in wave on wave,
The legions streamed and the chariot gleamed
    To lift him from the grave.
"Come forth, O faithful servant! There is an end to strife!"
In glory bright, with rapturous flight,
    He rose to immortal life.

The Walls of Jericho

Joshua 1 to 6; Hebrews 11:30, 31

ACROSS the river rose the walls of the city of Jericho, such a city, with such great walls, as had terrified the ten spies forty years before. How could they take it? Some time before they crossed the Jordan, Joshua sent two men ahead to spy out the land. These men entered Jericho and went to an inn, or hotel, kept by a young woman named Rahab.

The king of Jericho was told that two strange men had come in and were suspected to be spies. So he sent to Rahab and said, "Bring out those men to me." But Rahab's heart turned toward Israel, and she believed that God was going to give the city and all the land to the Israelites. So she hid the men, and she said to the king's messengers, "Yes; the men did come, but they are gone."

Then, when it was dark, she took the men out, and they promised that when the Israelites should take the city, they would spare her and all her family. So, since her house was built against the city wall, she let them down outside by a scarlet rope, and they escaped. They said to her, "Bind this scarlet cord on your window, so our people may know where your house is." All this they told to Joshua.

So Joshua commanded the children of Israel, and they came to Jordan and rested there for three days. It was in the time of the spring floods, and Jordan had overflowed all its banks, until it was a mile wide. How could they cross? No boats, no bridges. A million people, with their flocks and herds.

As God commanded Joshua, so they did. The priests took up the sacred ark and marched in advance of all the people. As they came to the brink of the river and the priests' feet touched the water, lo, all the water above stopped and piled up, flooding the valley, while the water below flowed on, leaving an ever-widening path across the river. The priests with the ark marched to the middle of the river bed and stayed there, while all the host of Israel passed over. Then the priests with the ark came out; and Jordan with a roar sent its waters down to the sea.

Now when the host of Israel was across the river, the city of Jericho was shut up tight; for they had seen the miracle of the crossing,

134

when Jordan stayed his rolling flood, and they were terribly afraid. But high on the wall at the window of Rahab's house gleamed the red cord that told of her faith.

Then God commanded Joshua: "Take all the men of war and form them in line. Have the priests carry the ark at their head. Have seven priests, each one with a trumpet, go before them. All this host shall march around Jericho, silently, the ark at their head. Then they shall return to their camp.

"On the second day they shall do the same, and on the third day, and every day for six days. But on the seventh day they shall march around the city seven times. And when they have finished the seventh march and are ringed around the city, they shall all face inward, and the priests shall blow a long blast on the trumpets, and all the host shall shout with a great shout. And the walls of Jericho shall fall down flat. Then go in and possess the city."

So Joshua and the Israelites did exactly as God had commanded. They marched around the city the first day, no one saying a word, and no sound coming forth but the sound of their marching feet. The men of the city crowded upon the top of the walls, ready to fight. But nothing happened. The Israelites marched around once, and went back to their camp. "Ho!" said the people of Jericho. "They are afraid! They don't dare to fight against the city."

But when the Israelite men of war, with the priests and the ark at their head, did so the second time, and the third time, and the fourth, and the fifth, and the sixth, silently, fearsomely, a mysterious dread crept into the hearts of the men of Jericho. Their shouts ceased. They looked with awe upon this silent army, marching, marching, around their city every day.

Then on the seventh day, early began the march. Once, twice, thrice, seven times the host marched around. Then they halted and faced inward, while the people upon the walls held their breaths. And then! The long blasts of the trumpets! And then! The mighty shout of the host of Israel! And the walls of Jericho trembled, and shuddered, and shook, and fell, and all the people with them! Only that part of the wall where the scarlet cord gleamed at the window, that stood upright; for Rahab and her family were within. And the two men she had saved went to her house and brought out all her people in safety.

So the city of Jericho was taken. And all the people of all the land of Canaan heard of it, and an overwhelming fear struck into their hearts.

Sin and Sorrow

Joshua 7; 8

NOW when the Israelites had taken Jericho without a fight, they thought, "Oh, this is easy. We shall not have much trouble in conquering all the people of the land." So they began to be careless. And when carelessness comes in, sin lurks at the door. And sin brings defeat and death.

There was a little city up in the hills called Ai. It was the nearest to Jericho, and Joshua sent men to look it over. They came back and said, "Ai is just a small city. It will not take all the host of Israel to conquer it. Just send about three thousand men. They will be enough to take Ai." So Joshua sent three thousand men of war. They marched up boldly to the gates of Ai. But the men of Ai came out fiercely and attacked them and killed some of them and drove them away.

When they came back to the camp and told the woeful story, all the hearts of Israel fell. And Joshua was terribly discouraged. He went and lay before the tabernacle of the Lord and cried, "O God, what shall we do? For the Canaanites will hear of this, and they will come and surround us and cut us off."

But God said: "Joshua, get up! There is sin in the camp of Israel, and that is why they could not stand before their enemies. I commanded that all the spoil from the city of Jericho should be given as an offering, and no man should take any of it for himself. But My commandment has been broken. Find the guilty man, and purge the evil from the camp."

So when they had cast lots, they found the sinner, Achan, of the tribe of Judah. And he confessed that he had seen among the spoils a fine Babylonish garment and two hundred shekels of silver and a wedge of gold. He took them and buried them in the earth in his tent.

They found them even as he said, and they took Achan and put him to death, because he had disobeyed the commandment of the Lord and had brought defeat to Israel and death to many of its men and disgrace to all the cause. And all the children of Israel took it to heart that they could not deceive the Lord nor trespass upon His law, else Israel would suffer and the cause be lost.

Then they went up with all the host and took Ai.

136

Conquest of Canaan

Joshua 9 to 11

ONE nation in Canaan was the Gibeonites. They came to the camp of Israel in old clothes and with moldy provisions and said that they came from a far country. They said that because they had heard of the great deeds of Jehovah in bringing Israel out of Egypt they wanted to make a league with them and be friends.

Without ever asking the Lord, Joshua and the princes of Israel believed what the Gibeonites told them, with the proof of their old clothes and provisions, and they made a league with them not to hurt them in any way. But within three days they found out that these people with whom they had made the league were their neighbors, inhabitants of the land.

Joshua told the Gibeonites, those proud and wicked people, that they might live, but they would be made the servants of Israel, the hewers of wood and drawers of water for all the congregation. The Gibeonites said, "Whatever you say. Only let us live."

Now when the king of Jerusalem found out that Gibeon had made a league with Israel, he sent to all the kings and cities round about, and made a league with them to fight against the Gibeonites. All the host of the Canaanites, with their horses and chariots, were arrayed against them. They sent word to Joshua to come in haste. And Joshua brought all the warriors of Israel to the aid of Gibeon. He marched by night and fell upon the Canaanites in the morning. There was a great battle all day. But the Lord sent a hailstorm, with great hailstones raining down upon the Canaanites, and more of them died from the hailstones than from the sword.

As night was coming on and the battle was not finished, Joshua stood, and in the might of God he called to the sun: "Sun, stand still upon Gibeon, and Moon, stand still above the valley of Ajalon." So the miracle happened. The day was lengthened until the host of the Canaanites was swept away. Never was there before a day like that, nor ever after was there one.

From this time on Joshua fought against the kings of Canaan and destroyed them. All the kings of the South, all the kings of the North, all the kings in between, did Joshua defeat for Israel.

STORIES OF THE JUDGES

Joshua to Samuel

The Last Works of Joshua

Joshua 13; 14; 18; 20; 23; 24

AFTER he had led the Israelites into Canaan, Joshua lived for about twenty-five years. He and Caleb were the only ones of those who came out of Egypt as grown men who lived to enter the Land of Promise. Caleb stayed with Joshua through the years spent in subduing the land and fought with him shoulder to shoulder.

Then, about five years after they had crossed the Jordan, Caleb came to Joshua and said: "You remember that forty-five years ago you and I were two of the twelve men sent in to spy out this land. And we were the only ones who said it could be taken, in the strength of the Lord. Then Moses promised I should have the city of Hebron, which I spied out. So please carry out Moses' promise."

And Joshua said: "Right, Caleb! You shall have Hebron, and the Lord will go with you and destroy the giants and all those who hold with them. All this south land shall belong to your tribe of Judah, and you their chief shall possess the land you spied out."

So Caleb went with his tribesmen of Judah and took Hebron and drove the giants out. His nephew Othniel, a vigorous young man, helped him greatly, taking one of the strongest cities. He married Caleb's daughter, Achsah; and in after years he delivered the Israelites when they were in trouble and became the first of their judges.

Joshua made his home in the land of his own tribe, Ephraim, which was about in the middle of Canaan. There, too, near Shechem, in the piece of land which Jacob had bought of the prince of Shechem, they buried the body of Joseph, which they had brought with them out of the land of Egypt, as he had made his brethren promise.

Joshua called the heads of the tribes to him at Shechem, and there he divided the land among them, and wrote the record in a book. Two of the tribes, Reuben and Gad, and half of the tribe of Manasseh, had been given their land by Moses on the east side of Jordan. All the other nine and one-half tribes were now given their territory. These tribes were Judah and Simeon in the south, Benjamin and Dan next to them, Ephraim in the middle, and the half tribe of Manasseh above them. Then in the north part came the lands of Issachar, Zebulun, Asher, and Naphtali.

But the tribe of Levi was not given any territory, because they were to be scattered in Israel to teach the people the law of God and His ways. Instead of a territory, they were given certain cities scattered all through the tribes, forty-eight cities in all, and the land about them for cultivation. Besides this, they were to be supported by all the Israelites, who paid a tithe of all their income, and thank offerings and freewill offerings besides, all of which went to the priests and Levites.

Then, as Moses had commanded, Joshua set aside six cities as cities of refuge. These were needed because of a law which seems strange to us. It was not a law made by God or by Moses; but it was made long before in that eastern land, and the Israelites just adopted it. With us, if a man has been killed, the man who killed him is tried in a court. If he meant to kill him, he is a murderer, and he may be put to death; but if he did not mean to kill him, he is set free or punished less. But back in Joshua's time, when a man was killed, his nearest of kin was supposed to slay the killer, without his being tried and found guilty. To save the innocent, God made these cities of refuge, to which the slayer might flee and be safe till he was tried. Three of these six cities were on the east side of the Jordan River, and three of them were on the west side, in the south and in the middle and in the north.

Now, as Joshua came to the end of his life, he called the people with their elders to come to him at Shechem, and he said to them: "Now the Lord has given you this land, though there remain in it many of the former inhabitants. You are not to mingle with them, letting your sons marry their daughters and taking their daughters for your sons' wives. You are not to let them entice you into the worship of their gods; and if they try to do it, you are to destroy them or drive them out."

"We will do that," the people said.

"Choose you this day," Joshua went on, "whom you will serve: whether the gods of Egypt and the gods of this land, or whether your own God, Jehovah. But as for me and my house, we will serve the Lord Jehovah."

And all the people answered, "Jehovah is our God. Him will we serve, and none other."

So Joshua sent them to their homes. And he died, in a good old age, being 110 years old. They buried him there in his home estate in Ephraim. And as long as that generation lived, they kept their word, and worshiped only the God of Israel.

Rise of the Judges

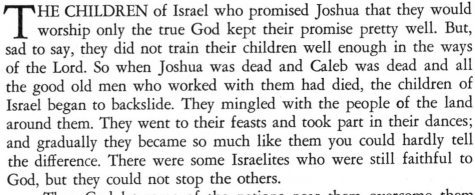

Judges 2 to 5

THE CHILDREN of Israel who promised Joshua that they would worship only the true God kept their promise pretty well. But, sad to say, they did not train their children well enough in the ways of the Lord. So when Joshua was dead and Caleb was dead and all the good old men who worked with them had died, the children of Israel began to backslide. They mingled with the people of the land around them. They went to their feasts and took part in their dances; and gradually they became so much like them you could hardly tell the difference. There were some Israelites who were still faithful to God, but they could not stop the others.

Then God let some of the nations near them overcome them and rob them and afflict them in many ways. After a while they came under the rule of Jabin, king of the Canaanites, whose city was Hazor, north of their land. He had 900 iron chariots and many horsemen. The captain of his host was Sisera. For twenty years the Israelites suffered under him.

Then the Lord raised up a judge, a woman, named Deborah, who lived in the land of Joshua, Mount Ephraim. She taught the people the way of the Lord. And when they cried for deliverance, she sent to Barak, a captain of Israel in the northern tribe of Napthali. She said to him: "Jehovah, God of Israel, commands that you gather ten thousand men of war from Naphtali and Zebulun and march to Mount Tabor, the high mountain in your country. And I will give Sisera and all his army into your hands."

But Barak was afraid, and he said to Deborah: "If you will go with me, I will go. But if you will not, then I will not go."

Said Deborah: "Surely I will go with you. But the honor will not be yours; for God will give Sisera into the hand of a woman."

Well, Barak mustered up his courage when Deborah came. He gathered 10,000 men out of Naphtali and Zebulun and Asher and Ephraim and Benjamin and marched to Mount Tabor, the top of which is flat.

As soon as Sisera heard of this uprising, he came to fight Barak and the Israelites. He brought his army, with their nine hundred chariots, into the plain below the mountain, where they could drive swiftly. They looked terrible to the Israelite army watching high up on the mountain.

But Deborah prayed, and Barak prayed. And suddenly black clouds gathered in the sky, the lightning flashed, the thunder rolled, and rain swept the valley. The River Kishon, which flowed through the valley, swiftly rose and flooded the land. The ground became miry, so that the chariots were stuck.

Then Deborah said to Barak, "Up! Up! Down on them! Charge down the mountain! And the Lord will fight for you." Down from the mountaintop swept the army of Israel and fell upon the host of Sisera and scattered them.

Sisera leaped from his useless chariot and fled on foot. His great army was lost. He was alone and afraid. Soon he came to a tent, where lived Heber, a Kenite. Now the Kenites were descended from Jethro, the father-in-law of Moses. Most of them lived in the south, in Judah or just below. But Heber had moved up north, on the border of Naphtali. And Sisera thought, "I can hide here in Heber's tent and rest awhile."

Jael, the wife of Heber, came out and welcomed him, saying, "Come in, my lord, and rest." She covered him up. Then he asked for a drink, and she gave him milk. He told her to stand in the door, and if anyone should inquire whether a man was there, she should tell him, No. Then Sisera went to sleep.

Heber and Jael were not Israelites, and they had the nature of the wild people of the desert. Jael thought, "Here is my chance to rid the land of this cruel oppressor." And while Sisera slept, she took a tent peg and a hammer and came up softly and drove it into his temple. So he died.

Then she went and stood in the door of the tent. And here came Barak, hot on the trail of his enemy, Sisera.

"Come in," said Jael, "and I will show you the man you are looking for."

Barak went in carefully, with his sword ready; for he expected to meet a live warrior who would fight. But there lay Sisera dead. And Barak remembered that Deborah had said to him, because he was afraid, "The honor shall not be yours; for God will deliver Sisera into the hand of a woman."

Then Deborah and Barak sang a song of triumph. And because Deborah judged the people and led them in the way of the Lord, the land had rest for forty years.

143

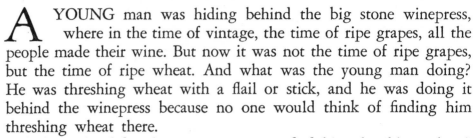

A Man of Valor

Judges 6

A YOUNG man was hiding behind the big stone winepress, where in the time of vintage, the time of ripe grapes, all the people made their wine. But now it was not the time of ripe grapes, but the time of ripe wheat. And what was the young man doing? He was threshing wheat with a flail or stick, and he was doing it behind the winepress because no one would think of finding him threshing wheat there.

But why didn't he want anyone to find him threshing wheat? Oh, this was in a time when the Israelites were in great trouble. The Midianites came up in great numbers at harvesttime and took away all the food of the Israelites and robbed and broke things up and abused the people. They were so mean that many of the Israelites fled away and lived in caves and dens. For seven years now this had happened. And the young man Gideon, having reaped a little wheat, was threshing behind the winepress to hide it from the Midianites. This was in the tribe of Manasseh and the clan of Abiezer. And Gideon was the son of Joash, a chieftain of the Abiezrites.

Suddenly Gideon looked up, and there, sitting under a great oak by the winepress, was a man watching him. Before Gideon could speak, the man said, "The Lord is with you, mighty man of valor!" Such a greeting showed that he was no enemy, but, Gideon thought, perhaps a messenger of Jehovah. And Gideon was right, more right than he thought he was.

Gideon said: "O sir, if Jehovah is with us, why has all this happened to us? And where are all His wonderful deeds that our fathers tell of, when He brought us out of Egypt? But now Jehovah has forsaken us and delivered us into the hand of Midian."

Then the man turned to him and said: "Go in this your might and save Israel from the power of Midian. Am I not sending you?"

It came like a thunderclap to Gideon. What! He deliver Israel? He a mighty man of valor? Now he knew for sure that this was an angel of God. But he felt very humble, like Moses at the burning bush; and he said: "O my lord, how can I save Israel? My clan is the weakest in Manasseh, and I am the lowliest in my father's family."

144

The Attack of the Three Hundred

At Gideon's signal the three hundred broke their pitchers and blew their trumpets. The Midianites were awakened and saw that they were surrounded. In every direction they saw flaming torches and heard the blaring of trumpets. Panic seized them, and they ran for their lives, fighting each other to get away. Thus only three hundred routed an army.

CLYDE N. PROVONSHA, ARTIST

And the angel said, "I will be with you, and you shall destroy the Midianites altogether."

Then Gideon said: "If I have found favor with you, show me a sign that it is really the Lord who speaks to me. Wait here, I pray you, till I come back with an offering."

And the angel said, "I will wait."

So Gideon went in and prepared some food, meat and bread and broth, and brought it out to the angel under the oak. And the angel said, "Take the meat and the cakes and put them on the rock here. And pour out the broth on them."

Gideon did. Then the angel reached out his staff and touched the offering. And fire burst forth from the rock and burned it up. Then the angel vanished.

When Gideon saw that, he was afraid; for it was thought that no man could see the face of even an angel and live. But the Lord said to him, "Don't be afraid. You are safe. You will not die."

Then Gideon felt courage pouring into him. And that night, at the command of the Lord, he went with ten of his servants to the hill-top where his father had set up an image of Baal, the false god, and where the people worshiped. He tore down the image, threw down his altar, chopped up wood, built an altar of stones to Jehovah, and offered a sacrifice on it.

In the morning the men of the town came to worship Baal. And they found the idol and his altar torn down, and a new altar of Jehovah, whereon a sacrifice had been offered. They asked, "Who has done this?" They soon found out it was Gideon. And they said to Joash, "Bring out your son, that we may put him to death, because he has destroyed the image of Baal and thrown down his altar."

But Joash was ashamed that he had made this image and encouraged the people to worship the false god. And he said: "Will you take Baal's part? Whoever will, let him die. If Baal is a god, let him take his own part; for his altar has been torn down." That ended that. For the people said, "Surely if Baal were a god, he could defend himself."

Then Gideon blew a trumpet and sent messengers all through the town and country of Abiezer and the tribes of Manasseh and those in the north. And there came men from all of them, till 32,000 were gathered to him. That did not seem very many to Gideon, when he looked on the great host of the Midianites spread through the valley, like grasshoppers for multitude. But he was a man of valor, and he did not lose heart.

Noble Three Hundred

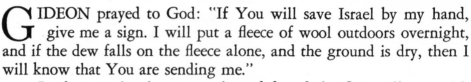

Judges 7

GIDEON prayed to God: "If You will save Israel by my hand, give me a sign. I will put a fleece of wool outdoors overnight, and if the dew falls on the fleece alone, and the ground is dry, then I will know that You are sending me."

In the morning he rose early and found the fleece all wet with dew, so that he wrung out of it a bowlful of water. But he wanted to be more sure. He thought, "Wool naturally draws water. Maybe I should have asked for just the opposite thing." So he prayed to God: "Don't be angry with me, but let me try just once more. Tonight let the fleece be dry and all the ground wet."

And God did so that night; for in the morning the ground was wet with dew, but the fleece was dry. Then Gideon roused his little army, and marched them to the edge of the mountain overlooking the multitude of Midianites in the valley.

But God said to him: "The people with you are too many for Me to give you the victory, lest they say, 'Our own might has saved us.' Say to them, 'Everyone that is afraid and timid, go home.' "

Gideon did as the Lord told him to do. And with a sinking heart he saw twenty-two thousand, more than two thirds of his army, slink away. There were left only ten thousand men. Could he gain a victory over the great host of the Midianites with just ten thousand men?

Then the Lord said: "The people are still too many. Bring them down to the water." This was the brook that flowed from the spring Harod—which means "the waters of trembling." "Let them pass through," said the Lord, "all ready for battle, and let them drink. But watch, and set on one side those who kneel down and take time to drink deep. And set on another side those who hasten through, catching up water in their hands to drink."

Gideon wondered, but he did as the Lord commanded. And there were just three hundred out of the ten thousand who caught up water in their hands to drink. These were the ones so eager to battle for the Lord that they would not kneel down to drink.

"Keep the three hundred," said the Lord, "and send the others home."

Gideon's heart sank, but he did what the Lord commanded. Just three hundred men; but every man of them was a hero.

Gideon had made provision for his army of 32,000 soldiers. Maybe he had thought of making a night attack on the Midianites when he had so many men; and so he had a good many lamps and pitchers, or pottery covers, for them, to hide their light until they should be wanted. And he had plenty of trumpets. "Now," maybe he thought, "those are all wasted." But not so.

While his men were sleeping that evening, Gideon heard the Lord tell him to go down to the camp of Midian. With Phurah his servant he did so, and creeping next to a Midianite tent, they heard a man wake up his tent mate and tell him a dream he had dreamed. He said, "I dreamed that a loaf of barley bread came tumbling into the camp of Midian. And it came to a tent and knocked it over, so that it lay flat. Now what do you suppose that means?"

And his tent mate answered, "That means nothing else but the sword of Gideon, a man of Israel. For God has delivered Midian and all the host into his hand."

Gideon was listening outside; and when he heard that, he thanked the Lord, and he and his servant stole away to their own camp.

"Get up! Get up!" he called to his men. "The Lord is delivering the Midianites into our hands."

They sprang to their feet. Gideon gave them every one a lamp and a pitcher and a trumpet. "Now," he said, "come with me and do just what I do." Down the hill he led them to the camp of the Midianites. He spread them around the camp, scattered out. Then he broke his pitcher, so the light flamed out, and he blew a mighty blast on his trumpet. All the 300 men broke their pitchers and flared their lamps and blew their trumpets. And they shouted, "The sword of the Lord, and of Gideon!"

The Midianites woke up in panic. All around them, spaced far apart, they saw the flaming lamps, they heard the blaring trumpets, there echoed the shout, "The sword of the Lord, and of Gideon!" They thought there must be thousands and tens of thousands attacking them; and scared almost to death, they ran and stumbled and fought one another to get away. The 300 brave men closed in on them, still blazing and blaring and shouting. And all that mighty host of Midianites melted away.

A great victory was won that night by the act of God and the courage of Gideon and the faith and valor of his noble soldiers. Never again did the Midianites trouble Israel.

A Victory and a Vow

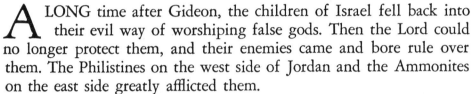

Judges 10; 11

A LONG time after Gideon, the children of Israel fell back into their evil way of worshiping false gods. Then the Lord could no longer protect them, and their enemies came and bore rule over them. The Philistines on the west side of Jordan and the Ammonites on the east side greatly afflicted them.

Now the Israelites were so miserable they cried to the Lord to save them. But He sent a prophet to say to them: "I have delivered you many times from your enemies, but always you have turned away from Me after you were delivered. Now go and call on the gods you have chosen; let them deliver you."

"Oh, we are sorry," said the Israelites. "We know we have sinned. Those false gods cannot deliver us, for they are no gods at all. Only, we pray, deliver us this time." And they really put away their idols and tried to keep God's commandments.

In the land of Gilead, on the east side of Jordan, there was a man of Israel whose name was Jephthah. He was a bold, brave sort of man, but his brothers hated him and drove him away. He went and lived in a land called Tob, on the border of Israel. Bold and reckless men gathered around him, and he became noted as a desert chief who fought and plundered and made a great name for himself.

Now when the Israelites gathered for battle against their oppressors the Ammonites, they had no leader. So they sent to Jephthah and asked him to come back and be their captain. Back came Jephthah with his band of fighters, and the Israelites put him at their head.

Jephthah sent word to the king of Ammon, "Why are you come out to fight against me in my land?"

The Ammonite king was surprised to find Jephthah at the head of the Israelites. But he answered, "Because Israel took away my land when they came up out of Egypt."

"No," said Jephthah, "Israel did not take away your land. We took away the land of Sihon, king of the Amorites, because he came out to fight against us, and God delivered him into our hand. So now the Lord God of Israel gave the land of the Amorites to us; and should you have it?"

But the king of Ammon would not listen, but came with his army to fight Israel. Then Jephthah went out and fought the Ammonites and defeated them. He took their cities and subdued them until they were no longer able to oppress Israel.

But just before he went into battle, he vowed a vow to the Lord that if God would give him the victory, he would offer up as a burnt offering the first thing that should come out of his house to meet him on his return. It was a very foolish vow; for God would not give the victory to Jephthah for any sacrifice, but because it was His will to deliver His people. It was the sort of vow the heathen make, because they think their gods can be bought by gifts. And Jephthah could not know what would meet him at his door.

He came back after his victory, and lo! who should come out of his house but his daughter, his only child, a beautiful young woman. She came with her companions, gay and happy, singing the praises of the hero her father, who had delivered Israel.

But suddenly her song ceased. She looked upon her father, stricken now with horror, as he realized what his vow had done for him. Here was his beloved daughter, his only child, come out of his house the first to meet him, and he had vowed to offer her to God as a burnt offering!

The law of God forbade all human sacrifices, though the heathen sometimes offered their children in death to their gods. But God's law provided that only animals were to be sacrificed, and they by the priests. But Jephthah had long been separated from his people, and he was used to heathen ways and sacrifices.

No doubt he had no thought of offering his child when he made his vow. But now that he had made it, and now that his daughter had become the victim, he thought he could not go back on his promise. He could have, and he should have; for God abhorred such sacrifices. But Jephthah was influenced by heathen customs.

When he told his daughter what he had done, the sweet girl told him to do what he had vowed, only she asked for two months, in which with her girl companions she might go out on the mountains and bewail her fate.

And after that—sad, sad story of that evil time—the Bible says that her father "did with her according to his vow."

149

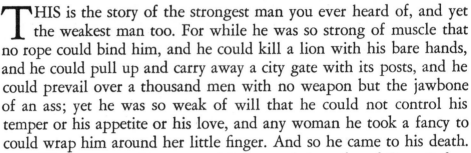

The Weak Strong Man

Judges 13 to 16; Numbers 6:1-21

THIS is the story of the strongest man you ever heard of, and yet the weakest man too. For while he was so strong of muscle that no rope could bind him, and he could kill a lion with his bare hands, and he could pull up and carry away a city gate with its posts, and he could prevail over a thousand men with no weapon but the jawbone of an ass; yet he was so weak of will that he could not control his temper or his appetite or his love, and any woman he took a fancy to could wrap him around her little finger. And so he came to his death.

His name was Samson, and he was of the tribe of Dan. Before he was born, his father and his mother were told by an angel that he was to be a Nazarite for all his life. A Nazarite was a man who took a vow not to drink wine or eat grapes either fresh or dried, or ever to cut his hair or shave. He could take this vow for a short time or a long time, as he chose; and when the time was up, he could be free of his vow and be like other men. It was supposed that by doing all this a man would be more holy and give himself more fully to the service of God. But as it proved with Samson, unless the heart was right, he was no better for his vow.

Samson did not become a Nazarite by his own will. It was put upon him by his parents, and he did not seem to like it very well; for he broke all its laws except the keeping of his long, thick hair. But the benefit he got from it was having greater strength than any other man. And when at last he was tricked into having his hair cut off, all his great strength left him, and that was the end.

Samson's enemies, and the enemies of his people, were the Philistines, who lived in the cities of the plains just below the Danites. When Samson had become a young man, he went a-roving into the land of the Philistines, showing off his strength. And the young women of the Philistines thought he was great and handsome and all that. And their praises went to his head. One of the young women pleased Samson so much he determined to marry her. On his way down to see her one day a hungry lion sprang out upon him; but he took that lion in his hands and tore him apart and threw him to one side. Later, when he was going down with his parents to his wedding, he went aside to see the carcass of the lion, and he found it all dried up and a swarm of bees in it. Samson took some of the honey and ate it and gave some to his father and his mother, but he told them nothing about the lion.

During the wedding feast with thirty young men his guests, they fell to telling riddles. Samson said: "I'll tell you a riddle. If you guess it, I'll give you each a suit of clothes. If you can't guess it, you must each one give me the same." This is the riddle:

> "Out of the eater came something to eat;
> Out of the strong came something sweet."

Of course they knew nothing about his killing the lion nor about his finding honey in it; so they could not guess. But they went to his young wife and told her to find out the answer, or they would burn her up in her father's house. They were savage young fellows.

So she coaxed and she coaxed Samson, and she wept on his shoulder, and she said: "You simply hate me! You don't love me at all! You have told my friends a riddle, and you haven't told me the answer to it."

"Why should I?" he said. "I haven't told anyone."

"But I'm your wife." And she coaxed and she cried. And at last he grew so tired of it, he told her. Then she ran and told her friends. They said to Samson:

> "What is sweeter than honey?
> And what is stronger than a lion?"

Samson was very angry; and to pay the penalty he went out and killed thirty Philistines and took their clothes and gave them to the young men. Then he stalked off home to Dan and left his wife.

That was the beginning of his singlehanded warfare against the Philistines. He burned their cornfields, he killed their men, he broke the ropes with which they bound him. He walked among them as he pleased, and they could do nothing with him. He liked to be with the Philistines more than with the Israelites. Though he despised their men, he loved their women because they praised and coddled him.

Finally he took a fancy to a woman named Delilah, and he stayed with her a great deal of the time. The Philistines went to her and said, "Now coax Samson and find out the secret of his great strength, and every one of us will give you a lot of money."

So Delilah begged Samson to tell her why he was so strong. At first he joked with her and told her lies. When she had the Philistines try them out, they all proved wrong, for they found that Samson was as strong as ever. But Delilah kept at him, till at last he weakened and told her the truth. She believed him, and the Philistines believed her. So she put Samson to sleep and had a man come in and cut his hair. The last of his vow was broken, and his great strength left him. The Philistines rushed in and bound him and put him in prison. They put out his eyes and set him to turning the mills that ground the corn.

Now indeed Samson was sorry for his sins. He repented deeply, and the Lord forgave him. He took the vow of the Nazarite anew for himself; and as his hair grew his strength grew too. One day, a great feast day, when thousands of the Philistines crowded the temple of their god Dagon, they took poor blind Samson out to plague him before them all. They did not know that he had gotten back his strength.

Then Samson asked the boy who led him to take him to the two main pillars that held up the temple. And he put his hands on the two pillars, and he prayed: "O God, remember me, and strengthen me just this once." Then, crying, "Let me die with the Philistines!" he bowed himself with all his might and pulled the pillars down. And the whole temple fell to pieces, with thousands of Philistines under it! And Samson too.

Poor Samson! Strong as a steer and weak as a worm. He could defeat the Philistines, but he could not conquer himself. But by his deeds he did keep the Philistines from troubling the Israelites so much.

———

Poor little Samson! Just a willful boy.
    Wouldn't mind his mother or his dad;
Ate what he wanted, delighted to destroy,
    Found a naughty pleasure in just being bad.

Poor big Samson! Strong as any ox.
    Couldn't keep his temper or his spite;
Played with the Philistines, gave them some hard knocks,
    Took a heavy beating when he tried to do right.

Poor blind Samson! Set to grinding corn.
    Tormented by his captors, not a single friend;
Wished a useless wish he never had been born,
    Died with the Philistines. And that was the end.

152

The Girl Who Chose God

Ruth

IT CAME to pass in the days of the judges that there was a famine in the land of Israel. In the little town of Bethlehem, in Judah, there lived a man by the name of Elimelech, and his wife Naomi, with their two little boys Mahlon and Chilion. Since the famine was so bad, Elimelech took his family and moved to the land of Moab. There they had enough to eat; but it was not long till Elimelech died, and Naomi was left with her two sons.

In about ten years the boys had grown up, and they both married girls of Moab. Chilion married Orpah, and Mahlon married Ruth. But soon both Chilion and Mahlon died, and Naomi was left with none of her family but her two daughters-in-law. She heard that now there was plenty of food in the land of Judah, and she said to her daughters-in-law, "I'm going back home." So she started, and Orpah and Ruth started with her.

But they had not gone far till Naomi thought of their future, and she said to them: "Now it is good-by. Return to your people, and marry again. May the Lord bless you."

The girls both wept. Orpah turned back, but Ruth clung to Naomi. And she said: "Urge me not to leave you. For wherever you go, I will go; and wherever you stay, I will stay. Your people shall be my people, and your God my God. Wherever you die, I will die, and there will I be buried. The Lord be my witness that even death shall not part you and me."

So Naomi let Ruth go with her. They came to the little town of Bethlehem, where Naomi had lived. And all the townspeople were stirred by her coming. They said, "Can this be Naomi?"

"No!" she said, "don't call me Naomi [for that means "pleasant"]; call me Mara [which means "bitter"]; for the Lord has dealt very bitterly with me." You see she had lost her husband and her sons; and she didn't even have a house or lands; because what Elimelech owned had either been sold or taken up by someone in their long absence. However, they found a place to stay; but they were very poor.

It was in the beginning of the barley harvest, which comes before the wheat harvest. Now it was in the law of Moses that the poor

of the land might go out, when the grain was being reaped, and gather up for themselves the scattered stalks of grain that the reapers dropped. This was called gleaning. So Ruth said to Naomi, "Let me go and glean wherever I can find a field."

And Naomi said, "Go, my daughter."

So Ruth went out and found a field where the reapers were reaping; and she went in with the other gleaners. It happened to be a field belonging to Boaz, a kinsman of Elimelech. But Ruth did not know that. Boaz was a wealthy man, owning houses and rich fields, and he had many servants. His father was Salmon, and his mother was Rahab, the woman of Jericho who saved the Israelite spies and whom they saved when Jericho was destroyed. Boaz was now in middle age, old enough to be Ruth's father, but he was not married.

Pretty soon this morning Boaz came from his house and greeted the men and women in his field. He noticed the new arrival, Ruth. And he asked his foreman, "Who is this girl?"

"Oh," said the foreman, "that is the Moabite girl who came back with Naomi. She asked me to let her glean here, and I did, and she has kept at it all morning."

So Boaz went over to Ruth and spoke kindly to her and told her to stay right there with his maidens and glean. Ruth was very grateful; and she worked harder than ever, gleaning, for she wanted to make the best showing she could to Naomi. At noon Boaz asked her to come and eat with his reapers. And after they had eaten, he told the reapers to drop some handfuls just on purpose for her. So she gleaned all afternoon, and when evening came she beat out the grain and found she had almost a bushel of barley. She carried this home, and when her mother-in-law saw it, she exclaimed, "Why, Ruth, wherever have you gleaned today, to get so much?"

"Why," she said, "the man's name in whose field I gleaned is Boaz. Do you know him?"

"I should say so!" said Naomi. "Boaz is a near kinsman of Elimelech, my husband. Now Ruth, you do as he told you and stay right with his reapers and gleaners. Thank the Lord for this! Something is going to come of it."

So Ruth stayed in Boaz's field all through the barley harvest and the wheat harvest that followed. Naomi was watching and thinking and praying. And now at last she said to her daughter-in-law: "Ruth, this Boaz is of near kin to us, and he has shown you great kindness. He is not married, and I think he wants you for his wife. But of course he's older, and I suppose he thinks you'd rather have a young man for your husband. So he has not said anything. Today he winnows barley at the threshing floor. Now you bathe and perfume yourself, and put on your best clothes, and go down there. And when he has finished his work and has eaten and lain down and gone to sleep, you go softly and lie down near him. He will know by that that you are asking for his help, and he will let you know what to do."

And Ruth answered softly, "I will do just what you say, Mother Naomi."

And she did. Boaz was astonished that she would prefer him to any of the young men; for she was very beautiful, and any one of them would have been glad to have her for a wife. However, it was a law in Israel that if a man died and his family lost their possessions, the nearest of kin might redeem them and give them back. He might also marry the man's widow. And right then Boaz saw that it was not only his pleasure but his duty to buy back the lands of Elimelech and Naomi, and, oh, joy! here was the widow of Mahlon, the son of Naomi, this beautiful Ruth, waiting to marry him. He had loved her, but he never thought she could love him.

However, there was a hitch in the plan. He told Ruth: "It is true that I am near of kin to you, but there is one other man who is nearer than I. I will go in the morning and find out if he will redeem; and if he will not, then I will do it. And, my dear, I will gladly claim you for my wife."

And Boaz lost no time. The next morning, in the presence of the elders of the city, he asked this other man if he would redeem Naomi's possessions.

"Yes," said the man, "I'll do that."

Boaz's heart sank. But he said, "At the same time you must marry Ruth, the widow of Naomi's son."

"I can't do that," said the man. "I'm already married, and I don't want another wife. Next to me, you are nearest of kin. You redeem the land and marry Ruth."

Boaz's heart leaped. "I will," he said. And he took the elders to witness. Thus Ruth and Boaz were married. And they had a son born to them whom they named Obed. How they loved him! And Naomi loved the baby too, and so she found that her name, "Pleasant," not "Bitter," was right.

They couldn't know it then; but Obed, when he was grown, became the father of Jesse; and Jesse became the father of David, the great king of Israel. So Ruth, the Moabite girl who chose the God of Israel, was chosen by Him to be the mother of kings.

155

A Little Boy Who Listened

1 Samuel 1 to 3

THERE was a little boy in the house of God at Shiloh, where the tabernacle was pitched, and the ark of God in it—a little boy who, though a child, acted the part of a priest; for the high priest, Eli, loved the little lad who had been put in his care, and he gave him some of the duties of a priest to do.

The boy's name was Samuel, which means "asked of God." And that was the name his mother, Hannah, gave him. Why? Because, since she had never had any children, she prayed to God to give her this boy. And she promised that if God answered her prayer, she would give the boy to the Lord for all the days of his life.

God did answer her prayer, and the baby was born; and his mother said, "Because I asked God for him, he shall be called Samuel." She kept him till he was weaned, and when he was about three years old she brought him up to the tabernacle and gave him to the high priest Eli for the service of the Lord.

Now Eli, the high priest, was a good man himself, but he was too easy with his sons, Hophni and Phinehas; and though they were priests, they grew up to be wicked and unjust men, breaking God's laws and doing all sorts of evil things to the people they were set to help. Eli rebuked them, but he just didn't have the courage to put them out of the priest's office. So they went on.

The Lord sent a prophet to tell Eli that because he did not stop his sons' evil ways, God would punish them and him and all his family. Still Eli did nothing. He was very old, and he put all his affection upon the boy Samuel, who loved the Lord and was perfect in all his ways.

One night, when both Eli and Samuel had lain down to sleep, the Lord called to the boy, "Samuel."

Samuel thought it was Eli calling him. So he ran in to Eli, and said, "Here I am; for you called me."

"Oh, no, little Samuel," Eli said, "I didn't call you. Go lie down again."

So Samuel walked back to his bed and lay down. But before he had gone to sleep or shut his eyes or closed his ears, again the Lord called, "Samuel."

Again Samuel jumped up and ran in to Eli: "Here I am; for you called me."

"No, my son; I didn't call you," said Eli; "lie down again."

So back went Samuel and lay down on his bed. But the third time the Lord came and called, "Samuel!"

And Samuel quickly rose and ran in to Eli, and he said, "Here I am; for you did call me."

Then Eli knew that it was the Lord who was calling Samuel. And he said, "Go lie down again; and if He calls you again, say, 'Speak, Lord, for Thy servant heareth.'"

"Oh," thought Samuel, "it is the great God who has come down to speak to me, a boy." And he lay down, but he didn't go to sleep. He kept his eyes open and his ears open, and he listened.

And sure enough, just as before, the Lord came and softly called, "Samuel, Samuel."

And Samuel said, in the tiniest voice, "Speak; for I hear You."

Then God told Samuel what He had told the prophet He had sent to Eli. He said that because of the wickedness of Eli's sons, and because Eli did not stop them or punish them and take them away from being priests, God would bring all the evil He had promised upon Eli and his sons in one day.

Samuel could not sleep after that. He stayed awake all night. In the morning he arose and went about his duties. And he said nothing to Eli; for he was sad and afraid. But Eli called him to him, and said, "Samuel, tell me what the Lord said to you last night. Hide not a thing from me."

Then Samuel told him every word that the Lord had said.

And poor old Eli, who could not discipline his sons, bowed his head and said: "It is the Lord. Let Him do what seems good to Him."

Softly sighs the evening breeze, hush-a-by,
Whispering sweetest thoughts of peace where you lie,
    Samuel.

Duties done and vesper said; day is o'er.
Let the sad world vex your head nevermore,
    Samuel.

List! Upon the spirit clear a voice is falling!
Prophet, tender, do you hear? God is calling:
    "Samuel! Samuel!"

"The Glory Is Departed"

1 Samuel 4

NOW the Israelites went out to battle against the Philistines, and they were beaten. The Philistines killed about four thousand of them. When the Israelites came back into camp, they cried, "Why has the Lord let us be defeated? Come, let us bring the ark of God out of Shiloh into our midst, so that it may save us from our enemies."

They were like the heathen about them, who thought that if they had the image of their god in their hands, they could make him do whatever they wished. The Israelites did not have an image of God, but they had the ark, on which, in the most holy place of the tabernacle, God shone with a bright light. When the ark was taken out, God withdrew His light; but the people believed that God was in the box. But God had really departed from their midst. It was very wicked for them to take the ark out of its sacred house and carry it into battle; but the Israelites had become very heathenish, and their priests, the sons of Eli, were the most wicked of all.

Hophni and Phinehas listened to the people, and they took the ark out of the tabernacle and had it carried into the camp of Israel. And when it came, all the Israelites shouted with a great shout, so that the earth rang again.

When the Philistines heard that mighty shout, they were scared. And they asked, "What does that great shout of the Israelites mean?"

Some of their scouts who had spied on the camp told them, "The ark of Jehovah has come into the camp of Israel."

Then the Philistines were afraid. They said: "God is come into the camp! Woe to us! These are the mighty gods that smote the Egyptians with the plagues. Who can deliver us? Be strong, O ye Philistines, and fight, that ye be not slaves to the Hebrews, as they have been to you."

So they encouraged one another, and when the battle was joined they fought harder. The Israelites had taken the ark right into the midst of their army, but it did them no good. When God is not in the hearts of men, He is not in the midst of men. So the Israelites were beaten again, worse than before; for 30,000 of them fell.

The battle was hardest around the ark, and thousands of the

Israelites fell there. The two wicked priests, Hophni and Phinehas, were slain before it. And the Philistines captured the ark and carried it with them.

Oh, how terrible! The ark of God was taken, and the Israelites felt that their God was taken too. That, of course, was foolish; for God is in heaven and in all the earth and in all the universe. But the poor heathenish Israelites thought He was shut up in the ark, and now the Philistines had captured Him!

There ran a man out of the battle to Shiloh. Now Eli had spoken against the ark being taken out of the sanctuary, but what he said had no weight with his sons or with the elders of Israel. He was an old man now, just two years short of being a hundred years old, and blind and feeble. He went out of the city and sat by the gate, his heart trembling for the ark of God.

When the man came into the city and told his news, all the people cried with a great cry. Eli heard them and had the man brought to him. "What has happened?" he asked.

The man said: "Israel is smitten. There has been a great slaughter. Your two sons, Hophni and Phinehas, are slain! And the ark of God is taken!"

When Eli heard that last terrible word, "The ark of God is taken," he fainted, and fell off his seat backward. And being very old and very heavy, he broke his neck and died. The word ran quickly through the city, "The high priest is dead!" It came to his daughter-in-law, the wife of Phinehas. In that hour her baby was born. But when she heard that her husband and her father-in-law were dead, and that the ark of God was taken, she cried: "Ichabod! Ichabod! The glory is departed from Israel, for the ark of God is taken." Then she died grieving for the ark and her husband and her father-in-law.

And they named the baby Ichabod, which means "Where is the glory?"

Ichabod!
Because thy father scorned the good,
And shamed his post and fatherhood;
Because the ark of God was lost,
The glory gone at fearful cost;
Because thy mother felt the shame;
Poor baby! thou must bear the name,
    Ichabod!

The God of Might

1 Samuel 5; 6

"AH, HA! AH, HA!" shouted and sang the Philistines. "We have taken the God of Israel! He is not a god like our Dagon, in the likeness of a man and a fish. He is just a box, though a most beautiful and costly box, all of gold, and curiously wrought. On the top are angels made of solid gold, and they are bowing toward the center and the top of the box. It is said that their God sits there in light, but we see no light there. Perhaps He is inside." But they did not dare to open it to see.

They took the ark and put it in the house of Dagon, in their city of Ashdod. They set it right before the image of their god, which was made like a fish but with the head and the hands of a man. "Now," they said, "we have two gods, Dagon and Jehovah, for that is the name of the God of Israel." So they closed the doors and went home.

But when they came in the morning and opened the doors, lo, there was Dagon fallen over on his face before the ark of God! They were shocked, but they set Dagon up in his place. On the next morning, however, when they opened the doors, there was Dagon not only fallen down, but with his head and his hands broken off, and only the fishy part of him was left.

Then things began to happen. A great sickness seized upon the men of Ashdod, and many died. And out in the fields, where their grain was growing, a plague of mice came and ate it up.

Then the men of Ashdod said: "This is the work of the God of Israel. This ark shall not stay with us." And they sent it to another of their cities, Gath. But the plagues followed to Gath. So they sent the ark to another city, Ekron. But the men of Ekron cried: "They have sent the ark of the God of Israel to us, to slay us and our people."

Then all the lords of the Philistines gathered together. They called for the priests and diviners and asked them, "What shall we do with the ark of Jehovah? Tell us!" And the priests and the diviners answered: "Send the ark back to the land of Israel, with a trespass offering of gold. Why harden your hearts, as Pharaoh and the Egyptians did? Their land was smitten to the very death, until they let Israel go. Send back the ark!"

160

"Now do this," said the priests and diviners: "Make a new cart, and put the ark on it. Fasten to the cart two milch cows, take their calves away from them, and turn them loose. If they start off on the road to Bethshemesh in Israel, we'll know that Jehovah has done this great evil to us. But if the cows refuse to go and stay by their calves, we will know that it was not the God of Israel, but a mere chance."

So the Philistines did. They made the cart, and they put the ark on it. They put the jewels of gold, the trespass offering, in a little box by its side. They took two cows, and took their calves away from them, hitched them to the cart, and turned them loose. And the cows, leaving their calves, went away from them on the road to Bethshemesh.

The lords of the Philistines followed the cart with the ark on it until it came to where some Israelites were reaping wheat in the field of a man named Joshua of Bethshemesh. The men of Bethshemesh looked, and, behold, here came their precious ark on a cart drawn by two cows. They shouted for joy. They crowded around the cart, and the Levites among them took the ark and set it on a great stone which was there in the field. And the men of Bethshemesh built an altar of stone before the ark; they killed the cows and offered them for a sacrifice upon it. When the lords of the Philistines had seen this, they went back and told their people. And the plagues stopped.

Now the Lord had given through Moses careful directions how the ark was to be treated. It was never to be touched by any but the priests or the Levites, who carried it, covered with a cloth, when they journeyed. But the Philistines, of course, did not know this; and the Lord was kind to them and did not punish them for handling the ark.

The men of Bethshemesh at first rightly dealt with the ark, offering sacrifices before it. Later their curiosity got the better of them. They crowded around it, and at last some of them put their hands upon it and lifted off the cover. And then they all came around and looked into it. There were the tables of stone on which God had written His law, and there were a pot of manna and Aaron's rod that budded, which Moses at the command of God had put into the ark. Then God struck the people with a great slaughter. And they were afraid. They sent to the men of Kirjath-jearim, nearby, and said, "The Philistines have sent back the ark of God. Come down and get it."

The men of Kirjath-jearim came. They handled the ark reverently. And they put it into the house of a man whose name was Abinadab, and made his son Eleazar the caretaker. God blessed the home of Abinadab. And the ark stayed there for twenty years. But Shiloh, where the tabernacle was, never had the ark again.

The Stone of Help

1 Samuel 7

SAMUEL the boy had become a young man. There was now no high priest; for Eli was dead, and his grandson, Ichabod, was but a babe. Samuel, though he was of the tribe of Levi, was not of the family of Aaron, who were the priests. But God spoke to Samuel constantly, and all Israel came to know that Samuel was a prophet of the Lord.

The people began to repent of their sins and to turn to the Lord. Then Samuel arose and called them to him and said: "If you will return to the Lord with all your hearts, and put away the strange gods that are among you, then the Lord will deliver you out of the hand of the Philistines." And the people began to obey Samuel. They put away their false gods and sought the Lord.

Samuel gathered all Israel together at Mizpah and prayed for them. The people drew water and poured it out before the Lord and fasted and prayed, saying, "We have sinned! We have sinned!" And Samuel judged the people there at Mizpah.

When the Philistines heard of the gathering of Israel at Mizpah, they came up with their army to attack them. Then the Israelites said to Samuel, "Cry to the Lord for us, to save us from the Philistines." And Samuel prayed, and the Lord heard and answered.

Samuel stood at the altar, offering the sacrifice, and the people bowed in prayer. Then the Philistines drew near to fight against the Israelites; but the Lord brought up a terrific thunderstorm. The lightnings struck, the thunder crashed, the storm broke in fury upon the Philistines and drove them away in terror. And the Israelites chased them back to their own country. Not again in the time of Samuel did the Philistines have the mastery over Israel.

So Samuel set up there a great stone to remember the victory. And he called it Ebenezer, the "stone of help." For, said he, "Up to this time the Lord has helped us."

The Israelites took back the cities and towns which the Philistines had taken from them, and they had peace with the Philistines on the one side and with the Amorites on the other side. Everywhere it became known that in Samuel Israel had a great judge and leader.

"Make Us a King"

1 Samuel 8 to 10

A S SAMUEL grew older, he grew ever wiser and ever more the spokesman for God. He was the last and the greatest of the judges of Israel, and he was the first of their prophets. Before his time, in Israel the prophets were called seers. Seer means "one who sees"; prophet means "one who speaks," that is, who speaks forth the word of God. Although God had set the fathers and mothers to be the teachers of their children, and the priests and Levites to be the teachers of all, this plan had not been carried out very faithfully in Israel; and that is why it was so easy for the Israelites to backslide and go to worshiping false gods and doing evil things.

Now Samuel, who was a Levite and whom God made His priest and prophet, set up a school at his home in Ramah. It was called the school of the prophets. This kind of school lasted long in Israel. In after years we find Elijah and Elisha at the head of such schools. The students were called the sons of the prophets, and the teachers were called their fathers.

For all the days of the years of his life Samuel taught Israel. And the Israelites steadily grew in the knowledge and love of God. While there were among them still many who were evil and of wicked mind, they were not, as a people, so bad as they had been. And this was due to the goodness and the teaching of that son of Hannah who as a little boy listened to the voice of God, and as a man spoke the will of God.

As Samuel grew old, he set his sons, Joel and Abiah, as judges under him. But the young men, while they were not so bad as the sons of Eli, were not altogether righteous, either. They took bribes from men whose cases they judged, and they gave judgment according to the one who paid them best. This had a very bad effect upon the people, and they came to Samuel and said: "Now you are old, and your sons do not walk in your steps. Make us a king, such as all the nations around us have, and he will be our head, and go out to war against our enemies."

Samuel was greatly disappointed. He was sorry about his sons; and I think he corrected them; for they seem to have straightened up. Anyway, Joel's son Heman was one of the chief choirmasters that

163

David appointed; so he must have had a good upbringing from his father. But Samuel was even more deeply grieved that the Israelites asked for a king. For God had told them through Moses that He alone was to be their King and their God, and He would rule them through His priests and prophets. If the priests and the judges and the prophets had all been as true as Samuel, there would never have been a king in Israel.

But the Lord told Samuel to do as the people asked; for, said He, "They have not rejected you; they have rejected Me. Nevertheless, show them what a bad step they are taking." So Samuel did. He foretold to them how their kings would tax them and oppress them and often lead them astray. But still the people said, "We want a king!"

Now there was a young man of Gibeah, in the tribe of Benjamin, named Saul, the son of Kish. He was very tall and well formed, and looked like a king; but he had never thought of being one. With a servant he was out one day looking for some strayed animals. They came to a hill on which was built a city where Samuel was visiting. And the servant said, "Let's go up here and ask the seer where our animals are."

So they went up. And as they came to the city, Samuel met them. Now the Lord had told Samuel the day before, "Tomorrow I will send you a man out of Benjamin whom you shall anoint captain of My people, to save them out of the hand of their enemies." And now He said to Samuel, "This is the man."

But Saul did not know Samuel, never having seen him. So he went up to him and said, "Sir, will you tell me where the seer's house is?"

And Samuel said, "I am the seer. Go with me to the sacrifice and eat with us. Tomorrow I will let you go."

So Saul ate with Samuel that day and with his thirty guests. And afterwards Samuel took Saul up on the flat roof of the house and talked long with him. He found the young man gracious and humble, and he was sure that God had chosen him.

So on the morrow, as he went down the hill with him on the way, Samuel stopped Saul and said, "Stand still while I tell you the word of God." Then he took a little bottle of oil and poured it on Saul's head; for so were priests and afterwards kings consecrated to their offices in those days. And Samuel said: "The Lord has anointed you to be captain over His people."

Then he told Saul several things that would happen to him before he reached home, and all those things happened just as he said.

And he also instructed him in the things he was to do as king. So Saul went on home and quietly went to work on his father's lands, saying nothing to anyone about having been chosen by Samuel.

But in a few days Samuel called Israel together at Mizpah to choose a king. He told the people again that God was their King; but since they had called for a human king, God would give them one.

Usually when a choice was to be made, it was done by the casting of lots. Lots were pebbles or pieces of wood marked so as to tell them apart. When the Israelites cast lots to decide a thing, the priest or whoever was in charge first prayed the Lord to have the lot turn up which He wanted to have. So by the casting of lots, they believed they read the will of God. They said, "The lot is cast into the lap, but the decision rests wholly with the Lord."

Exactly how they did it we do not know, but we suppose the different colored pebbles or the pieces of wood would each stand for one of the parties concerned. For instance, when one of the twelve tribes of Israel was to be chosen, there were twelve lots, each marked with the name of a tribe. These were shaken together in the lap; then the priest or someone reached in and took out a lot, and whatever name or mark was on it, that was the tribe chosen.

Now Samuel had the representatives of the tribes come before him, and he probably used the lot to decide which one to choose. So the tribe of Benjamin was taken. Then he had the several clans of Benjamin come before him, and of them all the clan of Matri was taken. Then he had the families of the clan of Matri come before him, man by man, and Saul the son of Kish was taken. So it was decided to be the will of God that Saul should be their king.

But Saul was nowhere to be found; for he had hidden himself among the baggage. He did not feel worthy to be king. They searched and found him and brought him out; and Samuel stood him up among them, he a head taller than any. And Samuel said, "See him whom the Lord has chosen! Is there anyone his equal?"

And all the people shouted, "Long live the king!"

The King Saves the City

1 Samuel 11

BEYOND the Jordan River, eastward, lay the city of Jabesh-gilead. And beyond Jabesh-gilead lived the Ammonites. The Ammonites had a king named Nahash, who brought an army and laid siege to Jabesh-gilead. And when he was about to take the city, the men of Jabesh said to him, "Make a treaty with us, and we will be your servants."

And the savage Nahash answered: "I will make a treaty with you on this condition, that I put out the right eye of every one of you."

This was a hard condition, and the men of Jabesh said to Nahash: "Give us a week, to send for help to all Israel; and if at the end of the week no help comes, we will come out to you."

So the men of Jabesh-gilead sent out messengers across the river, to the tribes of Israel: "Send us help!" Messengers came to Gibeah of Benjamin, the city of Saul. And when the men of Gibeah heard the news, all the people made a great cry. It was evening when Saul came in from the field; and when he heard the city crying, he asked, "What is the matter? Why are all you people weeping?" So they told him.

And when he heard the news, Saul was greatly stirred, and the Spirit of God came upon him. He took a yoke of oxen and chopped them in pieces. Then he sent men with the pieces, quickly, through all the land of Israel, and told the men to say: "Whoever does not come out after Saul and Samuel, so shall it be done to his oxen." The fear of the Lord fell upon Israel, and they came out as one man. When Saul numbered the host, there were 330,000 men. But it had taken nearly a week to get together.

He told the messengers from Jabesh-gilead, "Go back and tell your people, 'Tomorrow, by noon, you shall have help.' " Then he set his army on the march, and they crossed the Jordan. In the night Saul divided his army into three parts, and they surrounded the Ammonites on three sides.

Now the men of Jabesh-gilead had said to Nahash, "Tomorrow we will come out to you." Nahash thought that surely no help would come to the city from the Israelites, so he was careless, just waiting for the morning to put out the right eyes of the men of Jabesh.

166

But before morning Saul struck. So swift and sure was his attack that the Ammonites were slain before they knew what was happening to them, and what were left of them were so scattered that no two remained together. The men of Jabesh did indeed come out to Nahash, but not in the way he expected.

When Saul had been made king, there were some men who grumbled, saying, "How can this man save us?" Perhaps they were from some of the larger tribes, while Saul was of the smallest tribe, Benjamin, and they were jealous. But now all the people believed in Saul, and they cried, "Who said, 'Shall Saul reign over us?' Bring out those men, and we will put them to death."

But Saul said, "No man shall be put to death today; for the Lord has wrought salvation in Israel."

Then Samuel said, "Come, let us go over to Gilgal, and renew the kingdom there." And all the people went to Gilgal and made Saul king over again. And they offered sacrifices to the Lord in Gilgal. And Saul and all the men of Israel rejoiced greatly.

"The Lord hear thee in the day of trouble;
  The name of the God of Jacob defend thee;
  Send thee help from the sanctuary,
  And strengthen thee out of Zion;
  Remember all thy offerings,
  And accept thy burnt sacrifice;
  Grant thee thy heart's desire,
  And fulfill all thy plans.
  We will shout with joy over thy victory,
  And in the name of our God we will set up our banners.

"Now know I that the Lord saved His anointed;
  That He will save him from His holy heaven
  With the saving strength of His right hand.
  Some trust in chariots, and some in horses;
  But we will remember the name of the Lord our God.
  They are brought down and fallen;
  But we shall arise, and stand upright.
  O Lord, give the king victory,
  And hear us when we call."

Psalm 20, King James Version and J. M. Powis Smith.

Two Chase Ten Thousand

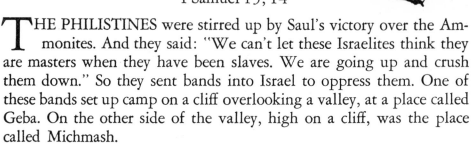

1 Samuel 13; 14

THE PHILISTINES were stirred up by Saul's victory over the Ammonites. And they said: "We can't let these Israelites think they are masters when they have been slaves. We are going up and crush them down." So they sent bands into Israel to oppress them. One of these bands set up camp on a cliff overlooking a valley, at a place called Geba. On the other side of the valley, high on a cliff, was the place called Michmash.

After his victory over the Ammonites, Saul sent all the people home except three thousand. Two thousand of these he kept with him at Michmash, and one thousand he put in charge of his son Jonathan, a brave young man and one who trusted in the Lord. Jonathan and his thousand men were at Gibeah, Saul's home town, which was south of Geba. Jonathan believed in action, so he suddenly took his men and captured the garrison of the Philistines at Geba.

The news of this angered the Philistines, and they gathered a great army, 3,000 chariots, 6,000 horsemen, and so many foot soldiers they were said to be like sands of the seashore. They came up and took Michmash and made it their headquarters, while they sent out bands this way, that way, everywhere to spoil the country.

Saul called for all the Israelites to come to him at Gilgal. And they came, but the terror of the Philistines was so great that they kept leaving. Some hid themselves in caves and holes and dens; some went over Jordan to safer land. So Saul's army melted away.

Samuel was to meet Saul in Gilgal in seven days. When the seventh day came, and no Samuel, Saul grew impatient. He said: "Bring me animals for burnt offerings." And when they brought them, Saul took on himself the office of priest and offered the sacrifice. This was very wrong; for he was not a priest or even a Levite. But he was really saying by this act that he was both king and priest.

He had no sooner finished offering the sacrifice than Samuel came. And he said, "What have you done?"

Saul said that he had to do it, because the people were leaving in crowds and Samuel had not come. But Samuel said: "You have done foolishly. God called you to be king, not priest. Now He will choose

168

another man for king who will do His will." And Samuel left. The Israelites then deserted so fast that Saul had only six hundred men left. He joined Jonathan at Geba, but even the six hundred followed trembling.

There was great fear in Israel. But one true heart beat strong. Jonathan was a young man of faith. He said to himself, "It is the time for bold action. It is the time for God to work." So early on a morning he said to the young man who bore his armor, "Let us go over and smite the Philistines on the heights of Michmash, the other side of the valley. It may be that the Lord will work for us; for He can work through few as well as through many."

Then his armor-bearer said, "Do all that is in your heart. I am with you!" So they stole away from the camp and went down into the valley. The Philistine guards saw them, and they called, "Come up to us, and we will show you something." Jonathan and his armor-bearer went forward under the cliff, where the Philistines could not see them; and they climbed up the heights on hands and feet. They burst over the top on the startled Philistines, who fell back in dismay. Jonathan and his armor-bearer plowed right in, smiting the Philistines right and left.

Then a panic took hold of the Philistine host, and they ran, fighting one another to get away. The Lord sent a quaking in the ground, so that the Philistines were greatly frightened. They ran faster and faster, leaving their chariots; and Jonathan and his armor-bearer were right after them.

Back in Geba the guards saw the tumult in the Philistine camp, and they told Saul. He found that Jonathan and his armor-bearer were gone, and he knew at once that his daring son was at the bottom of this. First he called the priest who was with the army, and told him to ask counsel of God what he should do. But as he talked with the priest, the tumult in the Philistine army over across the valley kept increasing, and Saul grew impatient. He said to the priest, "Withdraw your hand!"

Then Saul ordered his little army of six hundred to follow him down into the valley and across and up the other side, and they joined the battle. Then the Israelites who had hidden in caves and dens came out and helped in the pursuit. So the Philistines were overthrown with a great slaughter on that day.

Brave Jonathan and his faithful armor-bearer proved what Moses had sung: that one should chase a thousand, and two put ten thousand to flight.

169

The King Disobeys

1 Samuel 15

KING Saul fought against the enemies of Israel on every side—on the north, on the south, on the east, on the west; and he was successful in his wars. Yet the Philistines, who were on the seacoast, west and south, troubled Israel all during the life of Saul, and he had almost continual war with them.

Now the Amalekites, who dwelt in the south and in the desert, even unto Egypt, were the first enemies of Israel. They attacked the Israelites in the desert when they first came out of Egypt and killed some of the weak and fainting ones who straggled behind. Joshua fought against them there and drove them off. And the Lord said that He would destroy the Amalekites for their cowardly and wicked acts.

So now Samuel called Saul and told him to go and destroy the Amalekites, not only the people, but even their flocks and herds, everything that they had. Saul gathered a great army and went forth against the Amalekites. He did destroy a good many of them, all that he found, except— And it was in making that exception that he disobeyed the Lord.

He thought it would be quite an honor if he took the Amalekite king, Agag, alive, and brought him back to the land of Israel, to show him off as his prisoner. So he spared Agag and took him along. And then, all those flocks and herds! He couldn't see why all of them should be destroyed. He had his men kill off the worst of them, but he kept the best and took them along. "I'll sacrifice the finest of them in a great offering to God," he said, "and so He'll be pleased, and excuse my keeping the rest."

So Saul came back to the land of Israel with his army and his captive king and the great lot of cattle and sheep. And at last he came to Gilgal.

Then the Lord came to Samuel and said: "I am sorry that I chose Saul for king. He has gone back from following Me and has not done what I commanded." Samuel was grieved; and he prayed to God all night. But the Lord told him to go and tell Saul his fate.

Therefore in the morning Samuel rose up and went to Gilgal. Saul came out to meet him and exclaimed: "Blessed be thou of the

Lord! I have been faithful and have done all the Lord told me to do."

And Samuel said, "What means, then, this bleating of sheep and lowing of cattle that I hear?"

"Oh," said Saul, "the people brought them from the Amalekites. They kept the best to sacrifice to the Lord. But the rest we have utterly destroyed."

"Stop!" said Samuel, "and I will tell you what the Lord said to me tonight."

"Say on," said Saul.

And Samuel said: "When you were little in your own sight, you were made the head of the tribes of Israel. And the Lord sent you on an errand, saying, 'Go, smite the Amalekites until they are utterly consumed.' Why then did you not obey the Lord?"

"I have obeyed the Lord," said Saul, "and have done what He told me to do. I have destroyed the Amalekites and have brought Agag, their king. But the people took some of the animals, which of course they should have destroyed, and they are going to sacrifice them to the Lord."

Then said Samuel: "Has the Lord as great delight in burnt offerings as in obeying the word of the Lord? To obey is better than sacrifice, and to hearken than the fat of rams. Because you have rejected the word of the Lord, He has rejected you from being king!"

Then Saul was afraid, and he confessed: "I have sinned because I feared the people and listened to their voice. Pardon me, I pray, and come with me to worship the Lord before the people."

But Samuel answered, "I will not go with you to worship the Lord. For you have rejected the word of the Lord, and the Lord has rejected you from being king of Israel."

He turned away to leave. But Saul was now in terror, and he grasped the mantle of Samuel to hold him. The mantle tore in his grasp; and Samuel said to him: "Today the Lord has torn the kingdom of Israel from you and has given it to your neighbor, who is better than you. Moreover the Glory of Israel will not lie or change His mind; for He is not like a man, to change His mind."

Then Saul really humbled himself. "I have sinned," he said. "Yet now honor me before my people and go with me to worship the Lord your God."

Samuel at last consented to go with Saul while he worshiped. Then he put Agag to death. Samuel went back to his home at Ramah, and he never saw Saul again to the day of his death. But he mourned over Saul, because he loved him.

God Chooses Another King

1 Samuel 16:1-13

THE LORD said to Samuel: "How long will you mourn over Saul, since I have rejected him as king? Fill a horn of oil and go to Jesse of Bethlehem; for I have found a king among his sons."

So Samuel went to Bethlehem and found Jesse, who was the grandson of Boaz and Ruth. And Samuel said to Jesse, "Bring your sons in." And Jesse first called the oldest, Eliab. He was a tall, good-looking young man; and Samuel thought, "Surely this is the Lord's choice."

But God said to him: "Look not to his face nor his stature; for I have refused him. The Lord sees not as man sees; for man looks on the outward appearance, but the Lord looks on the heart."

So Jesse brought the next, Abinadab, and then Shammah. But the Lord said, "Not he," and, "Not he." Then Jesse brought four more, seven sons in all. But Samuel said to Jesse, "The Lord has not chosen these. Are these all your sons?"

"Well," said Jesse, "there is the youngest, David, but just now he is shepherding the sheep."

"Send for him," said Samuel. "We will not sit down to the feast till he comes."

So Jesse sent a messenger to the field where David was shepherding his sheep. And he said to David, "Your father wants you, quick! The prophet Samuel is there, and he said to send for you. Go! I'll take care of the sheep."

So away went David, running, and soon he came into the midst of the family, where with Samuel they were waiting. He was a beautiful lad, perhaps fifteen years old, with his dark curls and his red cheeks and his sparkling eyes. And he was all a-panting from his run. He wondered what Samuel could want of him.

Then God said to Samuel, "Arise, anoint him: for this is he."

And Samuel took the horn of oil and anointed David in the midst of his brethren. But they did not know what he anointed him for. From this day on, however, the Spirit of the Lord was upon David.

And Samuel walked back to his home in Ramah.

The Shepherd Boy and the Giant

1 Samuel 17; Psalm 23

DAVID was keeping the sheep. He did not know why Samuel had anointed him; for Samuel had not said that he was to be king. But David kept thinking and thinking. He had a harp with him, and he kept playing and playing, and singing and singing. It soothed his sheep to hear his voice, and he loved to play and sing. He made up a song about a shepherd and his sheep. So he sang:

> "The Lord is my Shepherd;
> I shall not want."

And all was peaceful out there on the Bethlehem hills.

But suddenly there was trouble. Into the flock there sprang from the thicket a great yellow lion, gaunt and hungry. He seized a lamb from its mother and ran away with it. David dropped his harp and ran after him. He had a sling, and as he ran he fitted a stone in his sling and slung it and hit the lion, which turned and reared up to claw him. But David ran in, seized the lion by his beard, yanked him over, and killed him. Then he took the lamb back to its mother.

But scarcely had he gotten back when, boom! out of the woods came a great black bear, and he seized another lamb and ran away with it. Right after him ran the shepherd boy. Another rock, another hit, and then David killed the bear and set the lamb free.

That was enough for one day, David thought. And as soon as he got the sheep quieted down, he took his harp again and played and sang:

> "The Lord is my Shepherd;
> I shall not want.
> He maketh me to lie down in green pastures,
> He leadeth me beside the still waters."

Then here came a messenger from his father. "What now?" said David. "Has Samuel come again?"

"No," said the messenger, "but your father wants you to go

173

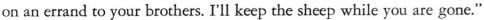

on an errand to your brothers. I'll keep the sheep while you are gone."

Now Saul and the Israelites were at war again with the Philistines. And the three oldest of David's brothers—Eliab, Abinadab, and Shammah—were in the army of Saul. Jesse said to his youngest son: "David, here are some provisions for your brothers in the army—ten loaves of bread and a bushel of parched corn. I want you to take them to your brothers, and also a present of these ten cheeses to their captain. See how your brothers are doing, and bring me word."

So David next morning rose early and loaded the provisions on a beast and journeyed to the army to find his brothers.

He came to the camp just as the army was going to the battle line, raising the shout of battle. He left his supplies in care of the keeper of the baggage, ran to the battle line, and greeted his brothers.

While he was talking with them, suddenly he heard a hoarse voice bellowing out: "I am a Philistine. You are servants to Saul. Send me a man to fight with me. If he kills me, all the Philistines will be your servants. If I kill him, you shall be our servants. I defy the armies of Israel this day. Send me a man to fight with me!"

"Who is that?" David asked the men around him.

"That," they answered, "is Goliath, the champion of the Philistines. He is a giant, ten feet tall, with a helmet of brass and a coat of mail and leg armor, and a spear like a weaver's beam. And an armor-bearer goes before him with his shield. He has been coming out every morning and bellowing that taunt. No man, not even Saul or Jonathan, dares to meet him."

And David said: "What shall be done for the man who goes out and slays the giant?"

"Why," said the men, "King Saul will give him great riches and will give him his daughter for a wife, and he will make his father's family great in Israel."

"I'll go and fight him," said David.

Now Eliab, David's oldest brother, heard what David said. He was pretty jealous of his young brother since Samuel had anointed him, though he did not know what for. And now he spoke up:

"You! David! Keeper of the sheep! Why are you here? With whom did you leave those few sheep in the wilderness? I know your pride and your naughty heart. You have come here to see the battle."

"What have I done that you scold me?" asked David.

But the men around David said: "Come with us to King Saul." So they took David before the king. And David said to Saul: "Let not my lord's courage fail. I will go and fight this Philistine."

Saul looked on him, standing there in his eager, youthful beauty, and he said, "You can't fight him. You are only a youth, and he is a man of war."

Then David told Saul about the lion and the bear. And he said: "God who delivered me out of the mouths of the lion and the bear will deliver me from this Philistine, because he has defied the God of Israel."

And Saul said, "Go! And the Lord be with you."

Then he put his own armor on David. But it was all too big and heavy, and David was not used to wearing armor. He struggled to go, but then he said, "I can't go in these, for I have not tried them."

So he put off the armor. And he took his shepherd's staff in his hand, and his sling, and went out to meet the giant. On the way he picked up five smooth stones from the brook and put them in his shepherd's bag.

Goliath saw someone coming down the hill to meet him, and he got all ready for a fight. But when they drew nearer to each other, the giant saw the man was but a youth, and he with nothing but a stick and a sling. And he bellowed: "Am I a dog, that you come to me with sticks? Come on! I'll give your flesh to the birds of the air and the beasts of the field." Then David fearlessly called back to the Philistine:

"You come to me with a sword and a spear;
　But I come to you in the name of the Lord of hosts,
　The God of the armies of Israel,
　　Whom you have defied.
　This day the Lord will deliver you into my hand,
　That I may slay you, and deliver Israel from your taunts."

The giant strode forward to meet David, and David ran forward to meet him. Goliath in a rage pushed back his helmet on his head. David paused and put a stone in his sling. He whirled his sling around his head, and then, straight as an arrow, he slung it at the giant.

The stone struck Goliath in his forehead and sank in, and the giant fell to the ground. David ran forward, and with the giant's own sword he killed Goliath.

Then the Israelites rose up as one man and shouted and ran down the hill toward the enemy. And when the Philistines saw that their champion was dead, they ran away. And on that day a glorious victory was won for Israel, because a shepherd boy, in the strength of God, killed the giant.

Brothers in Heart

1 Samuel 17:55-58; 18 to 20

WHEN David came up from slaying the giant, he stood before King Saul. And Saul asked him, "Whose son are you, my lad?" David said, "The son of thy servant Jesse the Bethlehemite."

Jonathan stood by while his father talked with David. And he was so taken with the young man that he loved him as his own soul. Right then a friendship was formed between David and Jonathan which held strong through many troubles, a friendship that has never been matched by any other. To show how much he thought of him, Jonathan took his own royal robes and put them on David and gave him his own sword and bow.

Saul looked admiringly upon the young man and said: "You are my own now. You cannot go back to your father and keep sheep. You are a man of war, and I shall keep you and make you a captain." So David stayed with Saul and went on war raids and beat the Philistines. And everybody thought David was the finest young captain they ever knew.

After a while, the war being over, Saul marched his army back in triumph to the cities of Israel. And the young women of those cities came out with song and dance, singing to the conquering heroes:

"Saul has slain his thousands,
But David his ten thousands."

Suddenly Saul was struck with jealousy. He said: "They have sung of David's slaying his ten thousands, and of me only thousands. And what more can he have but the kingdom?" He remembered that Samuel had said the Lord would choose another man who would do His will; and Saul thought, "Now perhaps David is that man!" An evil spirit settled upon him, and he determined he would kill David.

At first he just sent him against the Philistines, hoping they would slay him in battle. But David always came off victorious. And when Saul let the evil spirit overcome him, David would play on his harp before him and sing, and that seemed to cure Saul. But one day as David played, Saul rose from his seat and cast his spear at him, trying

David Defeats the Giant

Goliath looked upon David with scorn and rage. He cursed the shepherd boy, but David was not afraid. Instead he ran toward Goliath, at the same time hurling a stone from his sling at the giant's forehead. The armies saw Goliath stagger and fall to the ground. Then the Philistines fled in terror.

ROBERT TEMPLE AYRES, ARTIST

to pin him to the wall. David slipped to one side, however. Next day Saul did the same, but again David escaped.

But David was loved by Saul's own family; not only by Jonathan, but by his sister, Michal. And Saul said: "I will give Michal to him for wife, and she will be on my side." But when it came to a test, and Saul sent to get David in his house, Michal let David down from the outside window, just as his great-great-grandmother Rahab had let the spies down; and David escaped.

Jonathan pleaded with his father not to try to kill David, because he had done nothing wrong. And sometimes Saul listened to Jonathan; but then the evil spirit in him would drive him again, and he would be just the jealous, murderous king. At last, one day when Jonathan was pleading for David, Saul threw his spear at his own son, trying to kill him. Then Jonathan rose from the table in fierce anger and went out to meet David.

They had agreed that David would hide in the field by a heap of stones, and Jonathan would come out with a boy. He would shoot an arrow and send the boy to find it. Then if he should call to him, "The arrow is this side of you," David would know that Saul felt good toward him. But if he should call, "The arrow is beyond you," David would know that Saul indeed meant to kill him.

So Jonathan went out near to David's hiding place. He shot the arrow, and as the boy ran to find it, he called to him, "Is not the arrow beyond you? Be quick! Don't stand still!" Then he sent the boy home, and the lad knew nothing of what it all meant.

Then David came out of hiding and came to Jonathan. They kissed each other and wept much and said a farewell. Jonathan said to David: "Go in peace. We have sworn a friendship in the name of the Lord, and He will unite us, and our children after us." Then David fled away, and Jonathan went back to the city.

"Lo, how good and lovely it is
    When brethren dwell together as one.
Like the goodly oil upon the head,
Which flows down upon the beard, Aaron's beard,
That flows down upon the edge of his robes,
So is the dew of Hermon that flows down upon
        the mountains of Zion;
For there has the Lord commanded the blessing:
Life for evermore."
                                    Psalm 133, J. M. Powis Smith.

177

Saul Hunts David

1 Samuel 21 to 23

DAVID fled, but he did not know where to go. Everybody but Jonathan seemed to be against him. Yet all Israel, except some of the servants of Saul, loved David. But they did not dare take his part against the king.

As David came to the city of Nob, where the tabernacle was now pitched, he found there the high priest, Ahimelech, the grandson of Eli. Ahimelech gave David some food, and also the sword of Goliath, which David had taken from the giant and laid up in the tabernacle. But Ahimelech did not know that David was fleeing from Saul. Afterward, however, this did not help him; for Doeg, a servant of Saul, saw David, and told the king, who charged Ahimelech with helping David, and killed not only him but also all his family except one son, Abiathar, who escaped and joined David.

But now, because he thought no place in Israel was safe, David fled to Achish, king of the Philistine city of Gath. Very soon, however, the lords of the Philistines planned to kill David, because he had been their enemy. Then David escaped and fled into the wilderness of southern Judah. Poor David! Cast down from his high place in the kingdom and made a fugitive, with no place to go. So he sought the wildest country he had seen in his shepherd days. In the hills were many caves; and David went to one of the largest of them, the cave of Adullam. And when his father's family in Bethlehem heard where he was, they all left and came to him. Among them were three of his nephews—Joab, Abishai, and Asahel, sons of his sister Zeruiah.

His old father and mother came too, leaving all they owned, because the whole family were sure Saul would kill them, since they were related to David. Now David took his father and mother to the land of Moab, from which his great-grandmother, Ruth, had come. The king of Moab received them kindly, and they stayed there all the time David was in the wilderness.

There came also to David in the great cave of Adullam many men from among the Israelites who were in trouble, and he became their captain. Soon there were four hundred of them, and they grew to be six hundred. Many of them were wild and rough, but David was very firm, and he controlled them. Also he brought them to be worshipers of the Lord, men who obeyed His word.

Now when Saul heard that David was hiding in the wilderness, he took some men and went to hunt for him. Time and again, when word was brought to Saul where David was, he set out to get him, but David always slipped away.

By this time David had changed his headquarters to the wilderness of En-gedi, which was near the Dead Sea. There were many great caves in these mountains. David and his men were hidden deep in a cave when Saul with three thousand men came searching for him. Saul left his men outside, while he went into the cave and slept.

Then David's men said to him, "The Lord has told you that He would give your enemy into your hand. Now strike him dead!"

But David would not. However, he cut off a part of Saul's robe as he lay sleeping. When Saul woke up in the morning and went out of the cave, David followed after him, and holding up the cloth he had cut off, he cried, "My lord, the king!"

When Saul looked behind him, David bowed low, and said: "Why do you listen to those who say, 'David will hurt you'? The Lord gave you into my hand this night, but I did not touch you. See, here is the proof, in the piece of your garment I cut off."

Then Saul wept. And he said: "David, you are more righteous than I am. Now I know that some day you shall be king in my place. Swear to me by the Lord that you will not harm any of my children, or their children."

So David swore. And Saul took his men and went home.

"Why do you boast of evil, O mighty man?
  The kindness of God is all day long.
  Your tongue contrives guile,
  Like a sharp razor it works deceit.
  You love the bad better than the good,
  You would rather lie than tell the truth.

  .   .   .   .

"But I am like a green olive tree in God's house;
  I trust in the kindness of God forever and ever.
  I will praise thee forever because thou hast done it;
  And in the presence of thy saints I will proclaim that thy
        name is good."

                              Psalm 53, J. M. Powis Smith.

179

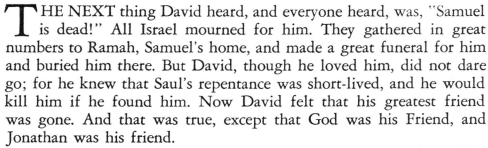

David Spares the King

1 Samuel 23:16-18; 26

THE NEXT thing David heard, and everyone heard, was, "Samuel is dead!" All Israel mourned for him. They gathered in great numbers to Ramah, Samuel's home, and made a great funeral for him and buried him there. But David, though he loved him, did not dare go; for he knew that Saul's repentance was short-lived, and he would kill him if he found him. Now David felt that his greatest friend was gone. And that was true, except that God was his Friend, and Jonathan was his friend.

Once more Jonathan had met and visited with David. He had come out into the wilderness, not like his father Saul, to hunt and kill; but, like the noble brother and friend that he was, to comfort and strengthen David. Jonathan said to David: "Don't be afraid; for the hand of Saul my father shall not find you. You shall be king, and I shall be next to you, the king's friend. And that my father Saul knows."

So again they made their pledge to each other. David stayed with his men in the wilderness, and Jonathan went home. It was the last time they ever met.

Now Saul received word from the Ziphites that David was in their neighborhood, and he took three thousand men and went out to hunt for him. He pitched his camp by a hill and lay down to sleep. Right by him was his captain, Abner. They were all very weary, and they fell into a sound sleep.

There David found them. And David said to two of his men, "Who will go down with me to Saul in the camp?" And one of them, his nephew Abishai, said, "I will go with you."

So they two stole quietly down to Saul's camp, and there was not a guard awake. They went in and stood by the sleeping Saul. Abishai whispered to David: "God has delivered your enemy into your hand. You needn't touch him; just let me do it. I will strike him with a spear just once, and I'll not have to strike him the second time."

"No," said David; "you shall not kill him. He is the Lord's anointed, and the Lord will see to him. But take his spear and his canteen of water, and let us go."

It was coming morning as David and Abishai stole away. When they had reached the top of a hill opposite, they stopped, and David began calling: "Abner! O Abner! Can't you hear, Abner?"

Abner the captain roused up, and shouted, "Who is it that's calling the king?"

And David said, "Abner, aren't you a valiant man? Why have you not kept your lord the king? One of the people wanted to kill him, but I would not let him. You are fit to die, because you did not protect your king. Now see where the king's spear is, and the canteen of water that was at his head."

Now Saul was thoroughly awake. And he shouted, "Is this your voice, David, my son?"

"Yes," answered David. "Why do you pursue me, since I have not lifted my hand against you, even this second time?"

And Saul, once more shamed and sorry, said, "I have sinned. Return, my son David; for I will no more do you harm, because my life was precious in your sight today. I have played the fool and sinned greatly."

"Let a young man come over and get your spear," said David. "May the Lord give every man what he deserves."

Then said Saul (and they were the last words he ever spoke to David): "Blessed may you be, my son David. You shall do great things, and shall prevail."

Then David went on his way, and Saul returned to his place.

(When the Lord delivered David from all his enemies and from the hand of Saul)

"In my distress I called upon the Lord,
And unto my God I cried for help;
He heard my voice from his palace,
And my cry unto him reached his ears. . . .
And the Lord thundered from the heavens,
The Most High uttered his voice.
He let fly his arrows and scattered them;
Lightnings he hurled and routed them. . . .
And the foundations of the world were bared. . . .
He delivered me from my strong enemy,
From my foes; for they were too strong for me."

From Psalm 18, J. M. Powis Smith.

David in Ziklag

1 Samuel 27; 28:1, 2; 29; 30

AT LAST David said to himself: "If I stay out here in the wilderness, I shall surely perish at the hand of Saul. What shall I do? Perhaps Achish, the king of Gath, will take me in. Then Saul cannot get me there."

So David arose and took his men and all their families and all that they had and went into the land of the Philistines. David had lost his wife Michal, the daughter of King Saul; for when David fled, Saul took her and gave her to another man for his wife. But out in the wilderness, David married two other wives, whose names were Ahinoam and Abigail. For in those days kings and chieftains very often married many wives, though it made trouble in the home. But anyway, David had now married the two, and he took them along, of course, when he moved to Gath.

Achish received him very well; and when David asked for a town somewhere in the country, where he might keep his people, Achish gave him the little city of Ziklag, which was really in the land of Judah. There David and his men set up their homes and stayed for a year and four months. When Saul heard that David had gone to the Philistines, he did not hunt for him any more.

But after a year or so, the Philistines decided they would conquer King Saul and the Israelites once and for all. And Achish called David and said, "Now you shall go with me to battle, you and your men."

Poor David! He did not want to fight against his people or against Saul; but he had gotten himself into this fix, and he did not know how to get out. So he took his men, leaving all their families in Ziklag, and went along with the Philistines. They marched far north into the valley of Jezreel, about one hundred miles away, and got ready for battle. Saul gathered his army right over against them, on Mount Gilboa. And there was David with the Philistines, about to fight with them against his own people, the Israelites.

But God watched over him and delivered him. He set the lords of the Philistines to complaining about David. They came to Achish and said: "What are these Hebrews doing here in our army? Don't you know David will turn in the battle and fight with his own people

182

against us? Send him back home at once." And Achish had to give in. So he told David, "I know you are all right; but the lords do not want you. So now go, return home."

David was glad. And in the morning early he rose with his men and marched back south to his city of Ziklag. It took them over two days to make the journey; and when they got there, what did they find? Nothing but smoking ruins. For the Amalekites had come in while David and his men were gone, and they had captured all the people, wives and children, burned the city, and gone away with the captives.

David's men were so grieved they talked of stoning him. But he asked of God, through the high priest Abiathar, what he should do. And God told him to pursue after the Amalekites, and he should get back everyone and everything.

So David, with his six hundred men, started out after the Amalekites. So swift was his march that two hundred of his men could not keep up. They had to be left behind, at the brook Besor, while with the other four hundred David went on.

Soon they came to a man in the desert who was faint and almost dead. They took him and gave him food and drinking water, and he came to. They found he was an Egyptian, a servant to an Amalekite, who had left him because he was sick. He guided David and his men to the camp of the Amalekites, where he found them spread out carelessly, feasting and dancing and rejoicing over their raid on David's city and others, and over all the captives and spoil they had taken. David came on them at evening, and he smote them all that night and all the next day, till none of them escaped except four hundred young men who fled on camels.

David and his men got back all their people, wives and children, and all the spoil, besides much more which the Amalekites had taken from other places. Then they turned homeward. Soon they came to the two hundred who had been so faint they could not go on. And some evil-minded men in David's company said, "We will not give them anything but their families, because they did not fight." But David said: "Not so, my men! You shall not do this to your brethren who fainted. Who will listen to you in this matter? This is my law: Those who go on to the battle and those who stay by and guard our baggage, they shall share and share alike." And he made it a law forever in Israel.

So they all got back home and started to build up their city again. But David was waiting for word from the battle in the north.

The Woe of Gilboa

1 Samuel 31; 2 Samuel 1; 1 Chronicles 10

THREE days after David and his men had returned to Ziklag, a man came running into the camp from the north. His clothes were torn and there was earth on his head, sure signs that he brought bad news. He fell at David's feet.

David said to him, "Where do you come from?"

"Out of the camp of Israel," panted the man.

"How went the battle?" asked David. "Tell me quick!"

"Oh," he cried, "the people are fled from the battle. Many are slain. And Saul and Jonathan his son are dead."

"How do you know they are dead?" demanded David.

And the man said: "I was there, in the battle, on Mount Gilboa. And I saw Saul leaning on his spear, wounded and dying. And the Philistine horsemen and chariots were after him hard. When he looked back, he saw me and called me. 'Here I am,' I said. And he said, 'Stand over me and slay me.' So I did as he said, because I knew he could not live. And I took the crown from his head and a bracelet from his arm and have brought them to you. Here they are."

He really thought David would be glad at the news he brought. But instead David mourned and wept. And all his men did likewise. Not a morsel of food would they touch; and they kept up their mourning till evening. Especially did David mourn for Jonathan, who was like a brother to him.

As evening drew on, David called the messenger before him and asked him, "Who are you? Where did you come from?"

The young man said, "I am a stranger, the son of an Amalekite." If anything more was needed to condemn him, that was it. David said to him sternly, "Why were you not afraid to slay the Lord's anointed?" And he called one of his young men, who put the evil fellow to death.

As the truth became known afterwards, this Amalekite had not done what he said he had at all. For Saul, wounded indeed, and pursued by the Philistines, had told his armor-bearer to put him to death. But the armor-bearer would not slay the king. Then Saul fell on his sword and took his own life. Somewhere in the battle his three sons, Jonathan and two others, also died.

This Amalekite was doubtless just a camp follower, more likely in the army of the Philistines than in the army of the Israelites. And after the battle had swept over the field, he came sneaking behind, to rob the dead. And there he saw King Saul, already dead, with his crown and his armor and sword; for the Philistines had not yet turned back, as they did later, to find his body.

So the Amalekite thought this was a good chance to get in favor with David, and he took Saul's crown and a bracelet and escaped from the army and ran south. He thought that David would reward him for what he brought. But by his lie he brought death upon himself.

Now Ziklag was a sorrowful place. But David saw that God had removed Saul from his way, and he was thankful that he had waited for God to act. Poet and singer that he was, he sat down in his sorrow and composed a song which was a lament for both Saul and Jonathan, a very beautiful song. He sang it and taught his people to sing it.

"Your beauty, O Israel,
  Is slain upon thy high places.
  How are the mighty fallen!

"Tell it not in Gath,
  Publish it not in the streets of Askelon,
  Lest the daughters of the Philistines rejoice,
  Lest the daughters of the uncircumcised triumph.

"Ye mountains of Gilboa, let neither dew fall,
  Nor rain be upon you, O fields of death!
  For there was the shield of the mighty thrown aside,
  The shield of Saul, not anointed with oil. . . .

"Saul and Jonathan, beloved and lovely!
  In life and in death they were not divided;
  Swifter than eagles were they,
  And stronger were they than lions. . . .

"O Jonathan! By your death am I mortally wounded,
  I am distressed for you, my brother Jonathan!
  You were exceedingly dear to me,
  Your love was more marvelous to me than the love of women.

"How are the mighty fallen,
  And the weapons of war perished!"

185

STORIES OF THE KINGS

David to Josiah

David Is King

2 Samuel 2 to 4; 5:1-5; 1 Chronicles 11:1-3

AT LAST the long, hard road had come out upon a fair view. David was king! At least he was king of Judah, and soon he would be king of all Israel.

When the people of Israel heard that Saul and Jonathan were dead, they fled from their cities, and the Philistines came and dwelt in them. So all the country north of Judah and west of the Jordan was in the hands of the Philistines. Abner, the captain of Saul's army, escaped from the battle, and he took the last and weakest of Saul's sons, whose name was Ishbosheth, and crossed the Jordan. There he set up the feeble Ishbosheth as king; but Abner was really the strong man and the power that made what was left of the kingdom of Israel.

But Judah, in the south, was steady and strong, though they trembled at the dangers surrounding them. Now David asked the Lord if he should go up to any of the cities of Judah, and the Lord said, "Yes." "What city?" he asked. "Hebron."

So to Hebron David went, with all his men and their families. And there the men of Judah came and anointed him king over them.

Now David's nephews, Joab and Abishai, were two of the most valiant men in David's army. And their younger brother, Asahel, who was swift of foot, hoped to become as noted as they. There began a war between Judah and the kingdom of Israel, with Joab on David's side and Abner on the other.

The two armies met at the pool of Gibeon, which was in Benjamin. Abner proposed a grim game. It would seem that he meant it to decide whether David should have all twelve tribes, or whether the son of Saul should have them. For he said to Joab, "Let twelve of your men come out and fight twelve of my men."

"All right," said Joab, and set forth his twelve men. These two parties fought, and they all fell down dead. That settled nothing. So Joab set all his men to fighting, and Abner did too. The battle went against Abner, and he and all his men fled.

Now Asahel started out to get Abner, and as he was a very swift runner, he soon caught up with him.

"Is that you, Asahel?" asked tired Abner, looking behind him. "It is," said Asahel.

"Turn aside," said Abner, panting with the run. "Turn aside and take one of my young men instead of me."

But Asahel would not, though Abner warned him the second time: "I don't want to kill you. How then could I hold up my face to your brother Joab?"

But Asahel kept on, and he was almost ready to strike Abner down, when that stout warrior thrust his spear backward, and the sharp point pierced Asahel's breast, and he fell down and died.

As the sun went down and the day ended, the men of Benjamin rallied around Abner on a hill. As Joab and his men came up, Abner called to him, "Shall the sword devour forever? Don't you know it will be bitterness in the end?"

Then Joab blew a trumpet and called his men back. They took up Asahel and carried him to burial at Bethlehem. But Joab and Abishai were bitter against Abner and looked for a chance to kill him.

In this war Ishbosheth and Abner's side grew weaker, while David and Joab's grew stronger. At last Abner decided he would turn all the Israelites over to make David king. And he went down to Hebron to talk with him. David made an agreement with Abner and sent him away in peace.

Now Joab and Abishai were away with their men when Abner came, and he had gone before they came back. Then Joab sent messengers after Abner and brought him back. When he came, Joab did one of his wicked deeds; for he took Abner aside in a very friendly way, and then he stabbed him to death.

When David learned of this, he said: "I and my kingdom are not guilty of this crime. It rests upon Joab, and God will punish him for it. But I am today weak, though anointed king, and these men the sons of Zeruiah my sister are too hard for me." He made a great funeral for Abner; and he compelled Joab and all his men to make a deep show of grief at the grave.

All Israel heard of this, and they said David had acted right; they knew that it was not his fault that Abner was killed. And since there was no one now to lead Israel, they all turned to David. They came to him at Hebron, and made him king over all Israel.

David was thirty years old when Saul died and he came to the throne. He reigned for seven years and six months in Hebron, and after that for thirty-three years over all Israel. So his reign lasted for over forty years. He did great things for God.

The City of David

2 Samuel 5:6-10; 1 Chronicles 11:4-9

THERE was in the midst of the land a city that was to become famous to the end of time. It was a very old city; for in Abraham's time it was there, and it was called Salem, which means "peace." By Joshua's time it had come to be called Jerusalem, which means "the place of peace." It was built on several hills, which made it a very strong city. The Israelites took the lower city several times; but they could not drive out the Jebusites, who held the high-walled hill of Zion, and so they dwelt among them.

But when David became king, he determined to have Jerusalem for his capital city. So he set out from Hebron with his army and besieged the upper stronghold of Zion. The Jebusites were very sure that no one could take their strong city. They laughed at David, and they put some lame and blind people on the wall, and said, "Even the blind and lame could stop you from coming in here."

But David said to his men: "Go up over the wall. Whoever first gets to the top, I will make him captain over the host."

Of course Joab, David's nephew, had been captain ever since the wilderness days, but David did not want him to be captain because he was so ruthless. He thought that by promising this, he could get someone very brave to take the place of Joab. But Joab was not going to let that happen. He put himself at the head of his men and was the first to mount to the top of the wall and smite the enemy. So he kept his place as captain.

Thus David took the stronghold of Zion, and he called it the City of David. He built great and strong walls to tie the hills together, and so united the upper and the lower cities into one. And he made Jerusalem a very strong city, and his capital.

Many great men have lived in Jerusalem since then, and many great deeds have been done there. The Lord himself put his Presence there in the sanctuary that came to be built. And greatest of all, a thousand years later, the Son of God walked and taught there and died there for the sins of the world. So now for many ages Jerusalem has been called the holy city.

Ark Brought to Jerusalem

2 Samuel 6; 7;
1 Chronicles 13; 15; 17; 28; 29:1, 2

THE HOLY ark of God, which Moses made at the command of the Lord in the camp at Sinai, was housed in the most holy place of the tabernacle. This beautiful tent-house, with the ark in it, was kept in Shiloh until the ark was captured by the Philistines in battle. When they sent it back to Israel, it was taken, not to Shiloh and the tabernacle, but to the city of Kirjath-jearim and into the house of Abinadab. There it stayed for many years. And the Lord blessed the home of Abinadab for keeping the ark safely and reverently.

After David had taken Jerusalem and made it his capital, he thought it would be well for the ark to be brought there. So he prepared to do it. He made another tent for it in Jerusalem, and then he went with part of his army and many musicians to the house of Abinadab to get it.

Now the Lord had told the Israelites how the ark should be carried. Only the priests were to touch it, as they covered it up with three covers. It had two staves or poles, run through rings on each side, and carrying these poles on their shoulders, the priests were to take the ark whenever it was to be moved. Sometimes the Levites were allowed to carry it, but never to touch it. The Philistines sent it back on a new cart; but the Lord forgave them because they did not know better. Strange as it may seem, David did not know how God had said it should be carried. He should have known, and the priests should have known; but, you see, there had been much breaking up of the priests' family in David's time; and as there were very few copies of the law, all they knew was what they had been told and remembered. So it really was not strange that David thought the ark could be carried in the same way the Philistines sent it, in a new cart.

He had such a new cart made. They hitched a yoke of oxen to it, and put the ark on it. Then they started with it toward Jerusalem, singing and playing instruments of music, and dancing before it in joy. Two of Abinadab's sons, Uzzah and Ahiah, who were not priests, went along to drive the oxen. Ahiah went ahead, and Uzzah walked alongside. By and by they came to a rough place in the road, and the oxen stumbled and shook the ark. Uzzah, fearing it would be jostled

191

off the cart, put his hand on the ark to steady it. And suddenly he was struck dead! Thus God showed that the ark, wherein He put His Presence, could not be treated like a common box.

But David was terrified, and all the people were struck dumb. The music stopped; they hung their heads. They were all afraid. After a few stunned moments, David had the ark taken off the cart and put in the house of Obed-edom, which stood by the road. And there it stayed for three months. But the Lord blessed the house of Obed-edom, as he had blessed the house of Abinadab.

So after three months David decided to bring it on to Jerusalem. Now he had studied and inquired about how the Lord had told Moses the ark should be cared for. And he assembled the priests and the Levites and gave the ark into their charge. And they took the ark out of the house of Obed-edom and carried it to Jerusalem, to the tent that David had made for it. And all the people rejoiced and had a wonderful holiday.

But as David sat in his house, talking with Nathan the prophet, he said to Nathan: "Now I dwell in a beautiful house, but the ark of God is housed in a tent. I think I should make a wonderful and beautiful temple for God to dwell in."

And Nathan said: "That's a splendid idea, David. Go ahead and do it."

But that night God spoke to Nathan, and told him that was not right, and he should carry a different message to David. So, as God told him, Nathan went the next morning and said to David: "The Lord says you shall not build a house for Him to dwell in; for you have been a man of war, and you have shed much blood. His house shall be a house of peace, and He will have a man of peace to build it. He will give you a son who shall be a man of peace, and he shall build the house for Him."

So David was content. He did not know who that son would be. The sons he had then were a disappointment. One was self-indulgent, one was stupid, one was proud and vain, one was more anxious to be king than to be good. But David believed the Lord and was content to wait for His leading. And after that he set himself to gathering material for his son to build the temple. Great stores he gathered of gold and silver and brass and iron and cedar and all the wealth that was to go into the making of the temple.

The Son of Jonathan

2 Samuel 4:4; 9

IT CAME to pass that when David was well established as king of
Israel and the Lord had given him rest from his enemies, he remembered the old days when Jonathan was his dear friend, and how
he had sworn to him that he would not forget his children but would
do them good.

So David called an old servant of Saul's, whose name was Ziba,
and he asked him: "Is there anyone left of the house of Saul? If so, I
want to help him."

And Ziba said: "There is a son of Jonathan, named Mephibosheth. He is lame in his feet, so that he cannot walk. For when he was
five years old, and the tidings came to Gibeah of the death of Jonathan
his father, his nurse picked him up to flee, but she dropped him, and the
bones of his feet were broken."

"Where is he?" David asked.

"Over across the Jordan at Lo-debar, in the house of Machir."

"Send at once and get him," ordered David.

For most of his childhood and all of his youth Mephibosheth
had been crippled. Perhaps, too, he did not know of the great friendship of his father with David or of David's promise, and he may have
thought that David was his enemy because he was of the house of
Saul. So he had been content to keep quiet and say nothing.

But now, oh joy! David, the friend of Jonathan, had sent for
him and had promised to help him. So Mephibosheth hastened and
got ready and rode to Jerusalem. When he came into the king's presence, he fell before him on his face. That was the way that humble
men did to kings and great men whom they would honor.

And then David said softly, "Mephibosheth."

"I am your servant," answered Mephibosheth.

"Rise up, my son," said David. "Don't be afraid. Listen! I will
show you kindness for the sake of Jonathan your father. All the lands
of Saul your grandfather I will restore to you, and I will have Ziba
take care of everything and be your servant. You shall live with me,
and I will care for you all the days of your life."

And Mephibosheth was very glad.

David's Great Sin

2 Samuel 11; 12; Psalm 51

THE BIBLE tells of good men and of bad men. But no man is altogether good. There is only one perfect, and that is God. When good men did bad things, the Bible tells of it without covering it up. But when they repented and asked the Lord to forgive them, the merciful God did forgive them, and they became good again.

David was a good man, and the Lord said that he was a man after God's own heart. Yet he did some bad things in his life. There was this difference, though, between David and Saul: David did not argue that he had done right when he knew that he had done wrong. He repented at once and asked forgiveness; and that was one reason why he was a man after God's own heart. The Lord forgave him. But still he had to suffer, and other people had to suffer, from the evil which he had done.

The greatest sin that David committed was to steal another man's wife and then to have that man put to death so that he could keep her. That was about the greatest sin a man could sin. And God did not excuse David, but punished him. Yet, because David repented at once, He did not reject him, but forgave him.

The Israelites were at war with the Ammonites. Joab, David's commander of the army, was fighting against the city of Rabbah, the capital of the Ammonites. One of the captains he had was Uriah the Hittite, who had joined the Israelites, and who was very faithful to David and loved him.

Now Uriah had a beautiful wife, whose name was Bath-sheba. Their home was in Jerusalem. And one day at sunset, as David was walking on the flat top of his palace, he looked over into Uriah's yard and saw Bath-sheba. She was so beautiful that David wanted her for himself. He did not stop to think how wicked it was to break God's law. He just wanted Bath-sheba; and since he was king, he thought he could do just anything he wanted to. So he sent for Bath-sheba, and he took her for himself.

Then he thought of Uriah, out there in the army fighting against the Ammonites. So he sent Bath-sheba home. And he sent word to Joab to have Uriah go into the worst part of the battle and be killed.

194

Joab did that very thing; for he was a very unprincipled man, and he would carry out David's orders no matter what they were, if it suited him to do so. And perhaps Joab thought it would cover up some of his own bad deeds if he did this wicked thing for David. So Uriah was killed. Then David sent for Bath-sheba again, and she became his wife. David thought that no one but he and Joab knew how bad he had been. But God knew. And God sent the prophet Nathan to David to tell him this parable:

"There were two men in a certain city," Nathan said to David, "one of them rich, and the other poor. The rich man had many flocks and herds, but the poor man had only a single ewe lamb, which he loved very much. Now there came a traveler to the rich man, and to feast him he refused to take any of his own flock or herd, but he took the poor man's lamb and killed it and prepared a feast for the traveler who had come to him."

David's anger flared at once, and he said to Nathan: "The man who did that is worthy of death. He must give back seven lambs to the poor man, and then he shall die!"

Nathan pointed his finger at David, and he said: "You are the man! Thus says the Lord God, 'I anointed you king over Israel, and delivered you out of the hand of Saul. I gave you houses and wealth and wives and servants. And if that had been too little, I would have given you anything you asked for. Why, then, have you despised God and His law and have slain Uriah the Hittite and have taken his wife for your own? Now therefore I will raise up evil against you from your own family. You did this secretly, but I will do what I do to you before all Israel.'"

David was stricken to the heart. He saw himself as God saw him, not as a great king, but as a great sinner. And he said at once to Nathan, "I have sinned against the Lord."

Then Nathan said—and the pity of God was in his voice: "The Lord also has forgiven your sin: you shall not die. But because you have made a mockery of God, you shall be punished. The child that is born to you and Bath-sheba shall die." And the child died.

David was most deeply repentant. If you would know how he mourned for his sin, read the fifty-first Psalm, which he wrote as soon as Nathan had left him. It was his prayer to God for forgiveness and mercy. And it is a prayer that all of us may pray. For though we have not sinned David's sin, we have every one of us committed some sins, and we have need to pray to God, "Create in me a clean heart, O God, and renew a right spirit within me."

195

The Beautiful Bad Prince

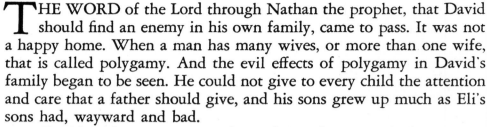

2 Samuel 13 to 19

THE WORD of the Lord through Nathan the prophet, that David should find an enemy in his own family, came to pass. It was not a happy home. When a man has many wives, or more than one wife, that is called polygamy. And the evil effects of polygamy in David's family began to be seen. He could not give to every child the attention and care that a father should give, and his sons grew up much as Eli's sons had, wayward and bad.

David had one son more beautiful and more gifted than any other. His name was Absalom, which means "father of peace"; but his name did not become him. Inwardly he was not peaceful, though outwardly he was fair. From the sole of his foot to the crown of his head there was no blemish in him. His face was handsome, and his eyes were bright. His hair was very thick and wavy, and fell to his shoulders. He cut it only once a year, and by then it weighed several pounds.

Absalom had a full sister, the daughter of his mother; her name was Tamar. That means "palm tree"; and like a palm, she was tall and graceful and very beautiful. There was also an older half brother, named Amnon, the oldest of David's children. Absalom did not like Amnon very well; and when Amnon did wrong to his sister Tamar, Absalom came to hate him with a deadly hatred. He hated him so much that one day, when he had Amnon in his power, he had his servants kill him. Then Absalom had to flee, and he ran away to his mother's father, who was king of Geshur. There he stayed for three years.

When he came back, his father forgave him, and Absalom soon rode high in favor. He had chariots and horses, and fifty men to run before him and cry, "Make way for Absalom!" He would stand beside the gate of the king's palace and greet every man who came to the king for judgment. He would take him by the hand and kiss him, and he would say: "Your cause is good and right, but there is no one appointed by the king to hear you. Oh, that I were made judge in the land, and I would do justice to everyone." That made them feel good. They thought Absalom was the best man ever, and so he stole the hearts of the men of Israel. But in fact he was evil in heart; for he planned all this so that he could become king in place of his father, who loved him so.

Finally Absalom made a plot against his father. He went to Hebron and proclaimed himself king. He had sent this word all through Israel: "When you hear the trumpet blown, shout, 'Absalom is king!'" And so the word went swiftly, and the trumpets were blown, and the people made Absalom king.

When word was brought to David that his son had conspired against him and had set himself up as king, David said to his old and tried servants and warriors: "Let us flee, or Absalom will come on us suddenly, and kill everybody in the city."

So they said, "We'll do whatever you say."

Then David arose, and went out of the city. And there went with him all his tried servants, the best warriors in Israel, Joab and Abishai and Ittai the Gittite, and their men with them. And the priests, Zadok and Abiathar, came bearing the ark of God. But David sent them back with the ark; for he would not take it into exile with him.

Away across the Jordan David and his followers passed that night and came to the city of Mahanaim. This they made their headquarters, and prepared for battle.

But Absalom came to Jerusalem in great state, with the people shouting, "Long live the king!" And the trumpets blew, and the drums beat, and there was a great to-do over the young king, the beautiful and bad son of David. But in many hearts in Jerusalem and through all the land there were trouble and doubt and prayer.

Then Absalom gathered a great army and passed over Jordan to fight his father David and his soldiers. He was not ashamed or sorry. He meant to kill his own father, so that the kingdom might come to him. Yet David loved him; and when his men passed out of the city gate to go to the battle, and the captains, Joab and Abishai and Ittai, went by, David said to them all: "Deal gently with the young man Absalom, for my sake." But that was one command Joab did not intend to obey.

The battle was begun in a forest called the Wood of Ephraim. It was a thick and heavy forest, with great trees; and the many men of Absalom were lost in it, while David's fewer but mightier men made the most of it. Then Absalom's army was beaten, and fled. And Absalom himself turned to flee with them. He was riding a mule, and as he drove the mule heedlessly, it ran under a great oak tree, and Absalom on its back had his head caught in its branches, and his great mass of hair got all tangled up in it. The mule ran out from under him, and left him there hanging in air.

When Joab heard of this, he ran and thrust three darts into the heart of Absalom; so he died. They cast his body into a pit in the forest, and raised a great heap of stones over it. And all the army of Absalom were scattered, and ran away to their own homes.

Then Joab sent runners to tell David, who sat in the gate of the city, waiting for news. When they came and told him the battle was won, all he said was, "Is the young man Absalom safe?"

The last runner said, "May all the enemies of my lord the king be as that young man is." Then David knew that Absalom was dead. He turned and went up the stairs to the room above, crying: "O Absalom, my son, my son Absalom! Would God I had died for thee, O Absalom, my son, my son!"

As the army came back in triumph, they heard King David mourning for his son. And they slunk in as men ashamed. Then Joab went up and stood before David, and he said: "I see now that you love those who hate you, and hate those who love you. If we all had died, and Absalom had lived, you would have been well pleased. Now stop this nonsense, and go down and speak cheeringly to your men, or you will not have one man staying with you this night."

Then David saw how wrong he had been. He dried his tears, and went down and greeted his brave soldiers who had won the battle and the kingdom for him. And soon they were all back in Jerusalem, and David sat again upon his throne, and all the men of Israel welcomed him. They saw how foolish they had been, and how bad was the beautiful young prince who had broken his father's heart.

"Who can ascend into the hill of the Lord?
And who can stand in his holy place?
He who has clean hands and a pure heart,
Who has had no desire for falsehood,
And has not sworn to a lie.
He will receive a blessing from the Lord,
And justification from the God of his deliverance.
This is the generation of those who search for him,
Who seek the face of the God of Jacob.
Lift up your heads, O gates!
And lift yourselves up, O ancient doors,
That the king of glory may come in!"
Psalm 24:3-7, J. M. Powis Smith.

The King of Wisdom

1 Kings 1 to 4; 10; 2 Chronicles 1; 9

THE LIFE of David drew to a close. Who should be king after him? Usually the oldest son of a king became king in his place; but God might change that. Amnon, David's oldest son, was dead. Probably his second son, Chileab, had died too; for we hear no more of him than that he was born. Absalom was the third son, and in his rebellion he was slain. The fourth son, the oldest then living, was Adonijah, and he thought he would be king.

But God had told David that his son Solomon should be king after him. David had taken great care in training Solomon, as he had not done with his other sons. And Solomon, whose name means "peaceable," was a young man who loved the Lord and tried to learn and to do all things right. Now Adonijah declared himself king, and some of the chief men, like Joab and Abiathar the priest, followed him. Nathan the prophet and Bath-sheba the mother of Solomon went in before King David. They told him what Adonijah was doing and reminded him that he had promised Solomon should be king, as the Lord had directed.

Then David called Zadok the priest, and Nathan the prophet, and Benaiah the captain of his guard, and told them to make Solomon king. This they did, with great rejoicing and loud celebration. And Solomon came and sat on the throne of David his father, and David was content.

Adonijah and Joab and Abiathar and all the people who were sitting at the feast where they had made Adonijah king, when they heard the noise of this celebration, were afraid, and they scattered. Solomon later gave them each one justice, according to what they deserved, and as David told him to do. And David especially charged Solomon to build the temple of God, for which David had gathered great stores of material. Then David died.

Shortly after the death of David, the young King Solomon went to Gibeon to worship, for there was the tabernacle. It was the one which Moses made, and which had been moved from Shiloh to Gibeon. And there was the brazen altar of sacrifice. Solomon offered great sacrifices there and asked for God's direction.

So in the night God came to Solomon in a dream and said, "Ask what I shall give you."

And Solomon answered: "O Lord, my God, you have made me king over all this great people, in the place of David my father. But I am as a little child; I do not know how to go out or to come in. Give me, therefore, an understanding heart, that I may be able to judge all things aright."

God was pleased with Solomon for asking this favor, and He said: "Because you have asked for wisdom, and not for long life, nor riches, nor the life of your enemies, see, I have granted your request; I have given you a wise and understanding heart. And I have also given you what you have not asked for, both riches and honor; and if you will walk in My ways, to keep My laws, I will give you long life."

Therefore Solomon became the wisest man in all the earth. And he became the richest. And he built great buildings, the greatest of which was the temple of God. Royalty honored him and sent him presents and made treaties of friendship with him. One was the queen of Sheba, a very wise woman herself, who came from her far country with a great train of servants and with presents of spices and gold and precious stones. She said she had heard of Solomon's wisdom in her far country, and she had come to prove him with hard questions.

And when she had talked with Solomon, and he had answered all her questions, and she had seen all his great works, she said: "The half was not told me. Happy are your family. Happy are your servants. Happy are your people who have so wise a king set over them. Blessed be the Lord, who has delighted in you, and set you over the throne of His people Israel." Then she went home.

And Solomon set himself to the great work that David had appointed him to do.

"I am but a little child," said he,
    Young King Solomon.
That was what God wanted him to be,
    Young King Solomon.

"For like a little child, you can be taught,"
    Said God Almighty.
And wisest grew King Solomon, in the thought
    Of God Almighty.

Solomon Builds the Temple

1 Kings 5; 6; 8; 2 Chronicles 2 to 7

SOLOMON was the youngest son of David; but he was the wisest and the best. That was because of two reasons. First, his father was very careful to teach him, and to live with him, and to love him. And second, Solomon himself gave his young heart to God and made up his mind to do all that God wanted him to do. So when he became king, Solomon was known all over the world as the wisest and the greatest king that had ever lived.

David had wanted to build a temple for the worship of God, and to put the holy ark in the central place in it; because, so far, since he had brought the ark to Jerusalem, it had had only a tent or tabernacle over it. God told David he could not build that temple because he had been a man of war; but He told him that his son Solomon, a man of peace, should build it. So David made great preparations, gathering material in abundance, and he commanded his son Solomon to be sure to build that temple.

And Solomon did. Very soon after he became king, even before he had built a palace for himself, he set to work upon the great temple. And he was seven years building it. It was the richest and most beautiful house that had ever been built.

There was a king of the city and land of Tyre, up on the seacoast north of Israel, in whose country were the great mountains of Lebanon, on which grew mighty trees of cedar and fir. This king's name was Hiram; he and David had been great friends. Now Solomon sent and proposed to King Hiram that he furnish the timber of the cedars and firs of Lebanon for the building of the temple. And Solomon said he would pay for all the work. Hiram was very glad to do this; for he had learned of the true God through David, and he wanted a part in building the temple.

Hiram sent to Solomon a master workman, whose name was also Hiram. This Hiram was the son of a Tyrian father and an Israelite mother of the tribe of Dan. You remember that when Moses built the beautiful tabernacle at Sinai, the two master workmen were Bezaleel of the tribe of Judah and Aholiab of the tribe of Dan. And perhaps, though the Bible does not tell us so, this Hiram of the tribe of Dan,

201

who was to be the master workman on the temple of Solomon, was a descendant of that Aholiab who was one of the master workmen on the tabernacle of Moses. For the temple was now to take the place of the tabernacle.

Solomon built the temple on a hill called Mount Moriah, which David had bought of a man named Araunah, and which was right next to Mount Zion, where the king's palaces were. After the temple was built, it was included in the city of Jerusalem, and in the Bible it is often called, like all Jerusalem, Mount Zion. But the actual place of the temple was on Mount Moriah, the very same mountain where the Lord, to test Abraham, told him to go and offer his son Isaac; and then the Lord delivered him, for as Abraham said, "The Lord will provide Himself a lamb." Right there the temple was built; and there in the court were offered as burnt offerings the lambs and other animals which represented the Lamb of God. That Lamb was Jesus, the Christ, the Son of God; and many hundreds of years later it was on this very spot that Jesus taught, and in this very Jerusalem that He was condemned to die, and on a hill outside that He was crucified as the Lamb of God to take away the sins of the world.

Solomon's temple, like the tabernacle, was a central building with two rooms: the holy place, with the altar of incense, the golden lamps, and the table of showbread; and the most holy place, in which the ark of God was placed. Outside this building was the first court, or the court of the priests, just as there had been in the tabernacle, except that while the tabernacle court had been enclosed in curtains, the temple court walls were built of stone. And outside this first court there was another, called the great court. The great court was lowest on the hill; the priests' court was on a level with the temple; but the temple was so much higher that it stood out above all, so it could be seen from every part of the city of Jerusalem.

The temple was built of great rocks, every stone of which was shaped and fitted before being brought there, so that it was put together without sound of hammer or ax or any other tool. The inside of the temple was covered with cedar wood, carved into forms of angels and flowers and fruits; and all of it was then covered with pure gold. The whole temple and the courts were made of the most beautiful and costly materials, so that it was the most wonderful temple in all the world.

When everything had been completed, there came the dedication of the temple. King Solomon and the people of Israel went to the tent or tabernacle where the ark stood. The priests covered the ark and all the holy vessels; then the Levites brought them out and started for the temple. With sacrifices and music the procession moved, rejoicing, up to Mount Moriah. When they reached the temple, the priests put the ark in the most holy place. Then the bands played, and the trumpets blew, and the people shouted and sang:

> "Praise the Lord! Praise the Lord!
> For His goodness faileth never.
> Praise the Lord! Praise the Lord!
> For His kindness endureth forever."

Then Solomon stood before all the people and prayed, thanking the Lord for His acceptance of His temple, and asking that His mercy might endure forever upon His people. And then, as it had been in the wilderness when the tabernacle was set up, the temple was filled with a cloud of glory; for the Lord came down and put His Presence upon the mercy seat of the ark. And the glory was so great that the priests could not stay in the temple, and they went outside and worshiped with all the people.

So was dedicated the great and beautiful temple of God in Jerusalem.

And Solomon prayed:

"O Lord, the God of Israel, there is no God like thee in the heavens above nor upon the earth beneath, who keepest loving faith with thy servants who walk before thee with all their heart, who hast kept with thy servant David, my father, that which thou didst promise him; for thou didst speak with thy lips, and with thy hand thou hast fulfilled it, as it is this day. Now therefore, O Lord, the God of Israel, keep with thy servant David, my father, that which thou didst promise him, saying, 'You shall never lack a man in my sight to sit on the throne of Israel, if only your sons take heed to their way, to walk before me as you have walked before me.' Now therefore, O God of Israel, let thy word be confirmed . . . which thou hast spoken to thy servant David. . . .

"Listen thou to the supplication of thy servant and of thy people Israel, when they shall pray toward this place; yea, hear thou in the heavens, thy dwelling place, and when thou hearest forgive."

1 Kings 8:23-30, J. M. Powis Smith.

The Kingdom Is Divided

1 Kings 11 to 13; 2 Chronicles 10 to 12

IT WOULD be good, wouldn't it, if we could know that Solomon was faithful to God all his life? But sad to say, that was not so. He knew more about more things than any other man; and at first he was humble, and so he was wise. But as time went on, and people everywhere praised him and gave him gifts and made him rich, Solomon grew careless, and then he became sinful.

More than that, he married many wives, and most of them were not Israelite women, but women from heathen lands. And they brought their idols with them and worshiped their own gods. They got Solomon to worship with them, and he forgot the Lord. So the Lord sent a prophet to tell him that when his son should come to reign, God would divide the kingdom into two parts, and give ten tribes to another. Whether at that time or later, Solomon did repent, and came back to the Lord; but he had done great mischief and folly, and the penalty had to be paid.

There was a young man, Jeroboam, whom Solomon, seeing that he was very quick and able, put over all the workmen from his tribe of Ephraim. And one day, as Jeroboam went out of the city into the field, he met the prophet Ahijah, who said to him by the word of the Lord that when Solomon's son should come to the throne, God would give him but one tribe, and He would give Jeroboam the rest of the kingdom. Solomon heard of this, and he sought for Jeroboam to kill him; but Jeroboam fled into Egypt and stayed there until Solomon was dead.

Solomon's oldest son was Rehoboam. Though Solomon was so wise, he was not wise enough to bring up his son in the right way. He had so many wives and so many children, no wonder he could not keep track of them all, and he did not train a single one. This Rehoboam was a wild young man, and he ran with a lot of young fellows who were as reckless as he. His mother was an Ammonitess, and he had more of her nature than he had of Solomon's.

After a reign of forty years, Solomon died. Then the Israelites came together at Shechem, ready to elect Rehoboam king. They sent to Egypt for Jeroboam, and he came. Now the people of Israel had borne very heavy burdens under Solomon, taxes and forced labor and all. So, with Jeroboam at their head, they came to Rehoboam and said: "Your father made our yoke heavy. Now if you will make that yoke lighter, we will serve you."

"Give me three days to think it over," answered Rehoboam, "and then I will answer you."

So they gave him three days, and he went first and talked with the old men who had been counselors to his father. And they said to him, "Do as the people ask you to do." But that did not please Rehoboam, and he turned and talked to the young men who had grown up with him. They said: "Go and tell this people, 'Instead of making your yoke lighter, I will add to it. My father whipped you with whips, but I will whip you with scorpions.'" And that is just what Rehoboam went and said.

That set the people off. They cried, "What part have we in David? To your tents, O Israel! Now look to your own house, David!" And with Jeroboam at their head, they rushed away and set up the kingdom of Israel, with Jeroboam as king. Only the tribe of Judah stayed with Rehoboam and made the kingdom of Judah. From that name came the name of Jews, which this people were afterwards called. After this there were the two kingdoms, Israel and Judah.

Rehoboam was going to fight them and make them come back, and he gathered an army to do it. But a prophet from the Lord told him to stop, because this was the Lord's punishment for what his father Solomon had done. Rehoboam obeyed, but he did not feel very good. He kept up the temple worship, but he very soon strayed after the heathen gods, his mother's and others, and he went on to do wickedness as Solomon had done in his later life.

Jeroboam, though, was not any better; he was worse. He had learned in Egypt to worship the same god Apis that the Israelites at Sinai had worshiped. Its image was a bull. And Jeroboam set up in Bethel a golden calf, and another in northern Dan; and he made priests of the lowest of the people. So most of the people of the kingdom of Israel came and worshiped this false god. Jeroboam said he did this because if he let his people go up to the temple of God in Jerusalem, they would soon leave him and go back to the kingdom of David's line. But his real reason was that he had an idolatrous heart. It made a great trouble in Israel through many generations. Later, when Rehoboam's grandson, Asa, became king of Judah, many of the truehearted in Israel moved there and stayed where they could worship God. So Jeroboam lost out after all, because he turned his back on God.

Wicked King and Wickeder Queen

1 Kings 16; 21

FOR 250 years after the kingdom was divided, the two kingdoms of Israel and Judah lived next to each other. But things went worse in Israel than in Judah. There were some good kings in Judah, but there were none in Israel. In Judah all the kings came of the line of David; but in Israel the families of the kings kept changing. Jeroboam had only one son to follow him as king. Then there came an overturning, and another overturning; and after about twenty-five years there came to the throne of Israel a king named Ahab. He was weak and wicked; but he might not have been so bad if he had not married a princess of Zidon named Jezebel, who was wickeder than he.

Jezebel brought in the worship of the heathen god Baal. There were very wicked things done in this worship, and Ahab and Jezebel were at the bottom of it all. Jezebel persecuted all the people who wanted to worship the true God; and she and Ahab murdered and stole whenever anyone got in their way. Many things happened in the twenty-two years that Ahab reigned. Some of them will be told in the next stories. But in the last part of his reign, one of the wickedest things he and his wife did was to murder a good man named Naboth, who had a vineyard and land next to the king's ground. Ahab wanted it to extend his gardens, but Naboth would not sell it. This made Ahab so angry that, like a naughty child, he went and lay down on his bed, turned his face to the wall, and would not eat a thing—he just lay there and pouted.

Jezebel came in and said, "What's the matter with you? Are you sick?"

"Naboth won't sell me his vineyard," whined Ahab.

"Well!" said Jezebel. "Well, I say! Are you king of Israel, or not? Get up and eat something. I'll get Naboth's vineyard for you."

So she wrote letters to the chief men of the city, and signed them with the king's name and sealed them with his seal. The letters said: "Get two men, wicked men, to testify before the people that Naboth cursed the king and God."

The rulers did as Jezebel told them to do, because they were afraid of her, and they were not good men either. They got two fellows to testify that Naboth had blasphemed God and the king. Then they all took him outside the city and stoned him to death.

Then Jezebel went in where Ahab was still moping and said to him, "Get up! for Naboth is dead!"

Ahab sprang off the bed, delighted. He didn't ask how Naboth had come to die; he just left that to his wicked queen Jezebel. Down he hurried to the vineyard of Naboth and took possession of it.

But while he stood there, gloating over his easy victory, getting Naboth's vineyard for nothing, there came to him Elijah the prophet, who said: "Have you killed, and also taken possession? Thus says the Lord: In the place where dogs licked up the blood of Naboth, right there shall they lick up your blood, even yours. And the dogs shall eat Jezebel. And I will leave you not a son nor a daughter, for they shall all be slain."

And so it came to pass.

"Obadiah, who was in charge of the household, . . . deeply revered the Lord. For when Jezebel ordered the prophets of the Lord exterminated, Obadiah had taken a hundred prophets and hidden them by fifties in a cave and supplied them with bread and water."

1 Kings 18:3, 4, Waterman.

Ho, comrades, I will sing a song of cheer to you
Because the way is weary and the road is long.
And for that a lilt of joy will help to bear you through;
Listen now, I pray you, listen to my song.

Oh, the fathers long and long ago, they trod this weary road;
They dragged the tired, dusty feet; they bore the heavy load.
They went through waters and through fires; they faced bloodthirsty foes,
In dungeons foul, in deserts drear, in trial, in bonds, in woes.
But when they fainted, faltered, fell, they paused to praise and pray;
And the God who answered to their need is just the same today.

Ho, comrades! Let us sing a song of cheer today;
For though the way is weary and the road is long,
Ten thousand thousand saints have sanctified the way,
And all the harps of heaven echo to our song!

Elijah the Tishbite

1 Kings 17; Luke 4:25, 26

THE KINGS of Israel were all bad kings, and they drove the people away from God. Yet there were many people in Israel who loved the Lord and held to Him. Up to the time of Ahab, though most of them had worshiped the golden calves which Jeroboam had set up, all of them, even the kings, professed to worship also Jehovah, the Lord, the God of Israel. But Ahab and Jezebel brought in the worship of Baal the sun god and of Ashtoreth the moon goddess, a worship that was vile and wicked and cruel. Really the worship of false gods was the worship of devils, for there were no such gods as they named; but behind the worship of these false gods was the devil who invented them. And this wicked king and wickeder queen led the people of Israel more and more to forget God and to do the evil deeds that the devils taught them to do. Of all the kings of Israel, there was none like Ahab, who sold himself to work wickedness in the sight of God, stirred up by his wife Jezebel.

Then God struck. Over across the Jordan River, in the land of Gilead, there had grown to manhood, near the town of Tishbi, a youth named Elijah. He loved the Lord, and in the quiet of his mountain home he learned the greatness and the power and the love of the God of Israel. He mourned over the evil of the worship of Baal and Ashtoreth, and he prayed God to show His might by some great sign, to bring Israel back to Him. And God answered through him.

Elijah the Tishbite arose one day in the Spirit of the living God and journeyed across the Jordan to Samaria and to the palace of the king. He wore no costly robes; he carried no royal badge. He was clothed in a garment of camel's hair with a leathern belt, and the dust of the road was upon his sandaled feet. Into the royal palace, past the staring guards, he strode into the presence of the king. None stopped him, none questioned him; for upon his brow there rested the light of heaven, and men were afraid.

Elijah stood before Ahab, and, lifting his hand toward heaven, he declared: "As the Lord God of Israel lives, before whom I stand, there shall be neither dew nor rain these years, except by my word."

Thunderstruck, the king could say no word. His courtiers and his

208

guards were silent. Elijah turned and took his way out of the palace and was lost to view. Behind him rose a babble of voices: "What means this mad fellow?" "How dared he come before the king? His words are nothing. Do not be afraid. Baal, the sun god, will give us warmth. Ashtoreth, the moon goddess, will give us dew and rain. Go to the high places, go to the temples. Offer sacrifices. Burn incense. Pray to Baal. Are there not 450 of the prophets of Baal, and 400 of the prophets of Ashtoreth? What is one prophet of Jehovah against them all?"

But the sun poured down and the rain was withheld. Day after day, month after month, a year, passed by. No rain, not even dew. The grass dried up, the leaves fell from the trees, the earth was parched. Where is the fellow that said the curse? Find him! Kill him!

But Elijah had been hidden by the Lord Himself. "Go to the gorge of the brook Cherith," said the Lord to him; "for I have commanded the ravens to feed you there." And to the wild ravine of the stream that flowed into Jordan Elijah went and dwelt in a cave. He drank of the brook, and the ravens brought him bread and flesh in the morning and in the evening. No man knew his hiding place.

Ahab sent his messengers everywhere, searching for Elijah, with orders to kill him on sight; but they did not find him. Ahab sent men to every country around, asking for word about Elijah the Tishbite, that strange prophet in the camel's-hair robe with a leathern girdle about his loins; but all the kings and rulers of the countries swore he was not with them.

Still the drouth continued, the blazing sun by day, the dewless moon by night. Baal and Ashtoreth gave no sign of help, though their prophets and their worshipers prayed and sacrificed and pleaded. The brooks dried up; scarcely was there a well or a spring anywhere with water. The flocks and herds perished. Men thirsted. Where was Elijah?

After the first year, the brook Cherith dried up. Where now could Elijah find refuge and food? God said to him: "Leave here. Go to Zarephath, in the land of Zidon. I have commanded a widow woman there to support you." And Elijah arose and went, according to the word of the Lord. None knew him as he passed; none told the king.

There was famine in Zarephath too, for the drouth had reached there as well. But when Elijah came to the gate, he saw a woman outside gathering sticks. He called to her, "Please bring me a little water to drink." She started to get it, and he called, "Bring me a bit of bread, too, please."

209

Then she said, "As Jehovah your God lives, I have not a cake of bread in the house, but only a handful of meal in the barrel and a little oil in a bottle. And now I am gathering two sticks for a fire to bake it. And after that my little son and I must die."

But Elijah said: "Fear not. Go and do as you have said. But first make me from it a little cake and bring it to me, and afterward make one for yourself and your son. For thus says the Lord, The barrel of meal shall not fail, nor the bottle of oil be spent, until the day that the Lord sends rain on the ground."

She believed him. And she went and did as he told her. And lo, the meal did not fail nor was the oil spent, as day after day she baked the bread, and they ate together, the widow and her son and Elijah.

But one day the boy fell sick. Sicker and sicker he grew, until there was no breath left in him.

"Alas, O man of God!" cried the mother, "my little boy is dead!"

"Give me your son," said Elijah. He took him and laid him on his own bed and cried to the Lord to raise the boy from the dead. God heard him and answered. And he took the child alive back to his mother.

"Now indeed I know," she exclaimed, "that you are a man of God, and the word of God is in your mouth."

And Elijah stayed there with her and her son until God gave him another mission.

"An upright man can do a great deal by prayer when he tries. Elijah was a man like us, and he prayed earnestly that it might not rain, and for three years and six months there was no rain in the land. Then he prayed again, and the heavens yielded rain and the earth produced crops."

James 5:16-19, Goodspeed.

The words of the widow's son:

Mother, Mother, why must I die?
   I have been a good boy.
We have been friends, the prophet and I.
   Was he sent here to destroy?

Mother, Mother, I am alive!
   I heard Elijah pray;
And my spirit, fleeing, turned to revive.
   Oh, I am alive today!

Jehovah Is God

1 Kings 18; James 5:17, 18

IT CAME to pass after many days, even the third year, that the Lord said to Elijah, "Go show yourself to Ahab, and I will send rain on the earth."

So Elijah arose and left the kind widow and her son and returned to the land of Israel.

There was in the king's house a man named Obadiah, who was the governor of the palace, but a man who loved the Lord. He would not bow to Baal or worship him. Jezebel must have hated him, but he was so careful and so capable that Ahab would not part with him; for he trusted him greatly. Now about this time when the drouth was so great, Ahab said to Obadiah: "Let us go through the land, to see if there are any springs and brooks and grass for the animals. You go that way and I'll go this." So Obadiah set out.

Suddenly there stood before him the man whom the whole kingdom was seeking, Elijah. And Elijah said, "Go tell your king that Elijah is here."

"O my lord Elijah!" cried the poor man. "There is no nation or kingdom where the king has not sent to seek you. And he has taken an oath of everyone that you were not there. Now if I go and tell him, 'Elijah is here,' why, the Spirit of God will catch you away. And when Ahab can't find you, he will put me to death. Haven't you heard how, when Jezebel slew the prophets of the Lord, I took a hundred of them and hid them in a cave and fed them? I have been true to your God, the God of Israel. Do not send me to death with this word to Ahab."

Then said Elijah, "I promise you I will be here. I will show myself to Ahab this day."

Then Obadiah went and told the king. Ahab hastened to meet Elijah. He thought, "If he is really there, I'll put him to death." But when he came into Elijah's presence, all his courage melted away. He just said, "Are you he who is troubling Israel?"

"I have not troubled Israel," answered Elijah, "but you and your father's house have done the troubling, because you have forsaken Jehovah and followed Baal. Now send and gather to me to Mount

Carmel all Israel and the 450 prophets of Baal and the 400 prophets of Ashtoreth, who all eat at Jezebel's table."

Ahab had to obey. He sent out word all over Israel, and he took all the prophets of Baal and Ashtoreth with him and led them out to Mount Carmel. Now the mountains of Carmel were very fruitful. There were many springs there, and brooks flowing down its sides; and at least one of them, in spite of the drouth, was still flowing.

As the people gathered there in the morning, and the priests of Baal, led by Ahab, came in the front, Elijah came forth and faced them. He called to the people: "How long will you go limping between two minds? If Jehovah is God, follow Him; but if Baal is God, then follow him." But the people answered never a word.

Then said Elijah: "I, even I only, remain a prophet of the Lord, but Baal's prophets are four hundred and fifty men. Let them therefore give two bullocks, one for themselves and one for me. Let them sacrifice theirs, and lay it on wood on the altar, but put no fire under it. And I will dress the other and do the same. Then call on the name of your god, and I will call on the name of the Lord. And the God who answers by fire, let Him be God!"

And all the people shouted, "It is well spoken."

Said Elijah to the priests of Baal, "You go first." So they prepared their altar with the wood on it, they slew the bullock and laid it on the wood. Then they called on Baal to send fire to burn it up. All the while they were trying by tricks to put some fire under the wood themselves. But Elijah watched them so closely they could not manage it. They grew more wild and loud every hour, leaping and dancing about the altar, and praying to Baal.

Noon came, and no fire from Baal. Then Elijah mocked them, saying: "Cry aloud! Cry louder! For Baal is a god! Either he is talking, or he is chasing someone, or he is on a journey, or maybe he is asleep and needs to be waked up!"

That made them more frantic than ever. They leaped and danced and cut themselves with knives till the blood gushed out. But still no fire. And Elijah watched them every moment, lest they slyly put some fire under the wood. The time of the evening sacrifice drew near, but from their god there was neither voice nor hearing nor any attention. The devil would have been glad to answer his worshipers and priests and send fire to burn up their sacrifices. But the hand of God was upon him and kept him back from doing anything.

Then Elijah called to the people, "Come near to me!" And they drew near. Silently Elijah took twelve great rocks, according to the

212

number of the tribes of Israel, and he built with them an altar to Jehovah, the Lord, the God of Israel. Then he dug a trench about it. He laid the wood on the altar, and the slain bullock on the wood. And he said to the people, "Bring from the fountain yonder four barrels of water and pour it on the sacrifice and the altar." They did so. And he said, "Do it the second time." And they did. And he said, "Do it the third time." And they did, till the water ran all around and filled the trench.

Then Elijah came up to the altar, and he prayed: "O Jehovah, God of Abraham, Isaac, and Jacob, let it be known today that Thou art God in Israel, and that I have done all these things at Thy word."

There was a bright flash, a blazing fire that fell from the sky upon the altar and burned the sacrifice and the wood and even the stones and the dust and licked up the water in the trench. And when all the people saw it, they fell on their faces and cried, "The Lord, He is the God! The Lord, He is the God!"

"Take the prophets of Baal," commanded Elijah. "Let not one of them escape!" So they took them and carried them down to the valley below and slew them there. So they who had brought death to so many of the people of God were put to death.

Then Elijah said to Ahab, "Get up! Eat and drink; for there is the sound of abundance of rain." There was not a cloud in the sky, but Elijah knew. He went up to the top of the mountain with his servant and knelt down and prayed. And he said to his servant, "Go up to the headland and look toward the sea." His servant went and looked and came back and said, "There is nothing."

"Go again," said Elijah. And he kept on praying. Seven times he told his servant to go and look. On the seventh time the servant came back and said, "There comes up a little cloud out of the sea, the size of a man's hand."

"Go to Ahab," said Elijah, "and say: 'Get your chariot ready, and drive for home, lest the rain stop you.'"

And the heavens grew black with thunderclouds and rain and wind, and there came a great burst of rain. Ahab drove with all his might toward Jezreel. And Elijah, girding up his robe with his leathern girdle, ran before him, faster than the horses could go, until they came to Jezreel.

So Jehovah, the Lord, the God of Israel, showed His might and His power over the things of nature, over the sun and the moon and the rain and the growing things of earth. And He showed that Elijah was His prophet.

"Seven Thousand in Israel"

1 Kings 19

AHAB came to his palace and told Jezebel what had happened: how Elijah had called down fire from heaven and proved that Jehovah is God, and how all the prophets of Baal had been slain. He was greatly shaken himself, and perhaps he thought that those things which had occurred would convince Jezebel too. What a triumph that would be, to convert the queen who upheld Baal and Ashtoreth, and make her a servant of Jehovah!

But Jezebel had no such idea. She was filled with fury. She sent a messenger to Elijah with a dreadful threat. Tired and worn, the prophet had lain down to sleep. The messenger came and awoke him and said, "The queen, Jezebel, says to you: 'You have slain my prophets. The gods do so to me and more also, if I do not make your life as one of theirs by this time tomorrow!'"

Suddenly Elijah's faith failed. He knew what the terrible wrath of Jezebel could do. He was worn and weary and faint, and his spirit was low. Instead of meeting the threat as he had bravely met all other dangers before, he took his servant and fled for his life, south, through Israel, through Judah. He came to Beersheba at the edge of the desert, and there he left his servant and fled on into the wilderness. All his toil and sacrifice and all God's great works had come to naught! Israel had not been converted; he only was left. So he thought. He lay down under a juniper tree and asked that he might die. "It is enough," he said; "now, O Lord, take away my life; for I am not better than my fathers." Then he fell asleep.

He was awakened by a touch upon his face. He started up, fearing an enemy. But it was an angel who had touched him and awakened him. And the angel said, "Arise, and eat." He looked, and there on a bed of live coals was a baked loaf of bread, and nearby a bottle of water. So he arose and ate and drank, and lay down again to sleep.

After a while the angel came again and awakened him, saying, "Arise, and eat; for the journey is too great for you." So he did. And then, in the strength of that food, he went for forty days into the wilderness, to Horeb, the mount of God. And there he went and lived in a cave.

The Lord came to him and said, "What are you doing here, Elijah?"

He answered: "I have been zealous for the Lord of hosts. But the children of Israel have forsaken Thee, thrown down Thine altars, and slain Thy prophets. And I, even I only, am left, and they seek my life to take it."

"Come out," said the Lord, "and stand upon the mountain before Me."

As Elijah came out of the cave, the Lord passed by. A wild wind came that broke in pieces the rocks of the mountain; but the Lord was not in the wind. Then there was a great earthquake; but the Lord was not in the earthquake. And after the earthquake there was a fire; but the Lord was not in the fire. And after the fire there was a still, small voice.

And when Elijah heard it, he wrapped his face in his mantle. And the Lord said to him in that still, small voice: "Go back to Israel. Anoint Hazael to be king of Syria. Anoint Jehu to be king of Israel. Anoint Elisha the son of Shaphat to be prophet in your place." Then the Lord continued: "You think you are the only one left? No! I have yet seven thousand people left in Israel who have never bowed the knee to Baal."

So Elijah turned back and went through the wilderness to the land of Israel. There he found Elisha, the son of a wealthy farmer. He had twelve yoke of oxen plowing, eleven of them with servants before him, and he with the twelfth, so he could look after them all. The Lord knew Elisha. He knew him as one of the seven thousand in Israel who, He said, had never bowed the knee to Baal or with his lips kissed him. He knew that he was fit to be Elijah's successor, and so He took him from the plow to be His prophet.

Elijah went by and silently threw his mantle over the shoulders of Elisha. Not a word did he speak, but passed on his way. But Elisha knew by that act that he was called to take up the work of Elijah. He left his oxen and his plow and ran after Elijah. And when he had caught up with him, he said, "Let me, I pray you, kiss my father and my mother good-by, and then I will follow you."

To test him, Elijah appeared cold. "Go back," he said; "for what have I done to you?"

But Elisha knew that he had had his call, and nothing would turn him aside. He went back, but not to stay. He offered a burnt sacrifice to the Lord, bade his father and his mother good-by, and then he followed Elijah and became his servant.

The Good King Jehoshaphat

1 Kings 15; 22; 2 Chronicles 13 to 20

DOWN in Judah things went better. The temple of God in Jerusalem was always there, to remind the people that their God was the true God. They worshiped there, and their kings worshiped there. Still they were not perfect in following the Lord and doing His will; some of them also worshiped in what were called "high places," the tops of hills where images of false gods were set up. But they were so much better than the kings and most of the people of Israel that the Lord prospered them.

When Rehoboam died, his son Abijah reigned for three years. He was much like his father, now in and now out of the worship of God. But his son Asa was a different sort, more like David, and the Lord greatly blessed him. He took away the images of the false gods and the high places and commanded the people of Judah to seek the God of their fathers. He gathered the tribe of Benjamin into the kingdom of Judah, and also much of the land of Ephraim beyond, and he taught them all the way of the Lord.

When the truehearted in the kingdom of Israel saw the good spirit and the good works of Asa, king of Judah, and how the people of Judah followed him in obeying the God of Israel, they came in great numbers out of the kingdom of Israel into the land of Judah. They gathered together in Jerusalem and pledged themselves to obey the Lord and with all their power to bring others to Him.

Of course this did not please the king of Israel, who at that time was Baasha. He made war against Asa, but he could not conquer him. And so the kingdom of Judah grew stronger and the kingdom of Israel weaker. Asa reigned for forty-one years, longer than any king before him, and he was deeply mourned when he died.

But he had left a good son in his place as king. That was Jehoshaphat. He was determined to root out all the evil from his kingdom, and he turned his people wholly to the worship of God. He sent some of his princes, with Levites and priests, to teach the law of God in the cities of Judah and in the lands that his father had taken from Israel. He was victorious against his enemies who came against him, and he was very strong.

In one thing, though, he made a very great mistake. He thought that he might win the king of Israel and his people to the true God if he showed them he was their friend. But the king of Israel at that time was the wicked Ahab, who was led by his wickeder queen Jezebel. It was not the Lord's will for Jehoshaphat to make friends with a man who was so wrong-headed and weak that he let his queen lead him into all sorts of wickedness. And the results showed why.

Jehoshaphat went to Ahab in his capital of Samaria and his summer palace in Jezreel. Ahab made a great feast and celebration for Jehoshaphat's coming; and even Jezebel welcomed him. She must have hated the godly king; but then, he was a king, and Jezebel could pretend to like anyone who was a king.

Then Jehoshaphat made the mistake of his life. He arranged with Ahab and Jezebel to give their daughter, Athaliah, for a wife to his son Jehoram, who would be king after him. That was a way kings had then, and have still, to try to keep peace and strengthen their kingdoms by intermarrying their sons and daughters. But this was a good kingdom uniting with a bad kingdom. Jehoshaphat thought a good deal of his son Jehoram, and he had begun to teach him how to rule by making him his helper in the ruling of the kingdom. Perhaps he thought that Jehoram could convert Athaliah to the true worship, when he should have made her his wife; but it turned out the other way, that Athaliah moved Jehoram just as her mother Jezebel had moved Ahab.

Pretty soon Ahab proposed to Jehoshaphat to join forces with him, to go and fight against the Syrians, and take back the city of Ramoth-gilead, which the Syrians had taken from him.

"Will you go with me?" he asked.

And Jehoshaphat answered: "I am as you are, and my people are as your people. We will go with you to the war. But first, will you not ask counsel of the Lord?"

"Oh, yes," said Ahab. "I have four hundred prophets here. I'll call them in, and ask of the Lord."

But the prophets were not the Lord God's prophets at all, but prophets of Baal, the god of the Zidonians, Jezebel's god. "Baal" in their language means "lord"; so Ahab could pretend he was asking of the Lord, the God of Israel.

"Certainly!" said the prophets to Ahab and Jehoshaphat. "Go on to war. God will give you victory over the enemy."

Jehoshaphat, though, was not satisfied. Those prophets didn't look to him like the prophets of the Lord. "Isn't there yet another prophet, that we may inquire of the Lord through him?" he asked.

"Well," said Ahab, "there is one other prophet, Micaiah. But I hate him, because he always prophesies evil about me."

"Don't say that," said Jehoshaphat. "Call him."

So when Micaiah came, Ahab said to him: "I've told you many times to tell me nothing but the truth in the name of the Lord." He didn't want the truth, but he did want to show Jehoshaphat that Micaiah would say something bad about him.

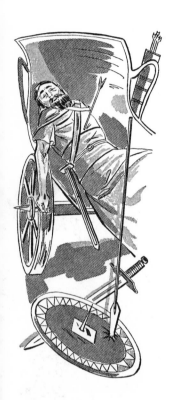

And Micaiah said: "Go up! But the Lord will deliver you into the hand of the Syrians. I saw all Israel scattered upon the mountains, as sheep that have no shepherd."

"Didn't I tell you?" said Ahab to Jehoshaphat. Then he told his guards to take Micaiah and shut him up in prison until he should come back.

But Micaiah said, "If you come back at all, the Lord has not spoken by me."

So the two kings went with their men to battle against the Syrians at Ramoth-gilead. And Ahab said to Jehoshaphat: "I'll disguise myself before I go into battle. But you put on your royal robes." That didn't sound very good to Jehoshaphat; he knew what Ahab was up to. But he was a brave man, and he did not try to sneak like Ahab. So he put on his royal robes and went forth bravely into the battle against the Syrians.

Now the Syrian king had told his men to seek out the king of Israel and fight against him, and him only. When they saw Jehoshaphat in his royal robes, they said, "There's the king of Israel!" And they pressed around him to slay him. But Jehoshaphat gave a shout, and with his men pressed through. The enemy saw it was not Ahab, and they left him. But one of them shot an arrow at another man in a chariot, and smote him between the joints of his armor, so that he was wounded to death. And that man was Ahab!

Ahab made his chariot man take him out of the battle. He lived the rest of the day, until the battle was over, but then he died. They took him back to Samaria and buried him. They washed the blood out of his chariot, and the dogs licked it up, as Elijah had foretold.

Jehoshaphat went back home in safety. But a prophet met him and said, "Should you help the ungodly, and love them that hate the Lord? There is wrath upon you from the Lord for this."

The king was sorry. But he had done mischief, not only in helping Ahab, but still more in taking Ahab's daughter for his son's wife. So after his death there came trouble upon Judah.

Elijah Goes to Heaven

2 Kings 2

DO YOU think that because Elisha was elected to become prophet in Elijah's place, he now put on airs and said: "Look at me! I was just a farmer plowing in the field; but now I am a prophet, to take Elijah's place"? No! Do you know what he did? He waited on Elijah, and took care of all his needs. Now in those days and in that country, when men washed their hands, they did not wash them in a basin; they had a servant pour water over them, so that they always washed in clean water. And that is one of the things Elisha did for Elijah. So when it was said, "Here is Elisha, who pours water on the hands of Elijah," it was just saying, "Here is Elisha, who is a servant to Elijah, and who does all the duties of a servant."

But while Elisha was Elijah's servant, and cooked his food, and washed his dishes, and built the fires, and swept the floors, and mended his clothes, and poured water on his hands, all the while Elisha was listening to his master's teaching, and he was learning more and more of the word of the Lord, and he was diligently studying to do his master's will and the will of God.

The schools of the prophets which Samuel had started were revived by Elijah, and there came to be many prophets and sons of the prophets, or students, in the land. Elijah and Elisha now went together the rounds of these schools and taught and labored with the students; and Elijah saw that his work had not been in vain. These young men were some of the seven thousand God said He had left in Israel. And there came to be more, as the people listened, and many repented and left the worship of Baal to return to Jehovah. Even King Jehoram, the son of Ahab, though he was bad enough, worshiping the golden calves that Jeroboam had set up, yet did not so evil as his father and mother had done. He often prayed to God and listened to His prophets.

The time drew near when God would take Elijah alive to heaven. This was told to Elisha and to the students in the schools of the prophets. It was a solemn time, and they were very serious and earnest; for such a thing had not been known since Enoch was translated, two thousand years before.

Elijah and Elisha made their last visits to the schools; and the last three they visited were at Gilgal, Bethel, and Jericho. As they started to leave Gilgal, Elijah, to test Elisha, said to him, "Stay here; for the Lord has sent me to Bethel."

But Elisha, knowing that his master was about to be taken away, would not leave him. "No," he said, "as the Lord lives, and as you yourself are alive, I will not leave you." So they went on to Bethel.

The sons of the prophets at Bethel came to Elisha and said, "Do you know that the Lord will take away your master today?"

"Yes," said Elisha, "I know it. Say no more."

As they were leaving Bethel, Elijah said, "Elisha, stay here; for the Lord has sent me to Jericho."

"No," said Elisha, "I will not leave you." So they two went on.

When they came to Jericho, the students in the school of the prophets there came to Elisha and said, "Do you know that the Lord will take away your master today?"

"Yes," he answered, "I know it. Say no more."

As they were leaving Jericho, Elijah said, "Stay here; for the Lord has sent me to Jordan."

"No, never!" said Elisha. "I will not leave you." So they two went on to the River Jordan.

But fifty of the sons of the prophets followed afar off, and they gathered on a high hill and watched Elijah and Elisha as they came to Jordan. And what did they see? Elijah took his mantle, folded it, and struck the water. And lo, the waters parted as they had for Joshua, and the two went over on dry land. Still the fifty watched, straining their eyes to see the two beyond Jordan.

And Elijah, knowing that the end of their life together was at hand, and admiring his servant for refusing to leave him, said to Elisha, "Ask what I shall give you before I am taken from you."

Wealth, or an easy time, or authority, Elisha did not ask for. Like Solomon in his youth, he felt his need of the wisdom of God, and for this he asked. It was a law in Israel that the oldest son, at his father's death, should receive a double portion of his wealth, as well as the headship of his people. Elijah's wealth was in his spirit, the Spirit of God in him that enabled him to do his wondrous work. So Elisha, as the oldest spiritual son of Elijah, answered, "Give me, I pray, a double portion of your spirit."

"If you see me taken from you, it shall be so," answered Elijah. And they two went on, talking together, as Elijah gave his last instruction to his servant.

Suddenly a great light shone around the two. A chariot of fire flashed down from heaven and parted them. A whirlwind of glory covered Elijah, and he was carried away in the chariot of fire.

"My father, my father!" cried Elisha, "the chariot of Israel, and the horsemen thereof!" In the blaze of the glory he hardly knew what he was saying.

Elijah, remembering his promise, looked back upon his faithful servant, and he let fall his mantle, the mantle he had first thrown around the shoulders of the plowman Elisha, the mantle with which he had parted the waters of Jordan. Then he was gone in the chariot of glory, gone to heaven. And Elisha saw him no more.

He picked up Elijah's mantle and turned back to his duties. He came to the Jordan River, and folding the mantle, he struck the water with it, crying, "Where is the God of Elijah?" The God of Elijah was there! For the waters parted as before, and Elisha walked across on dry ground into the arms of his students. And beholding him with the light of the Spirit upon his brow, they took him to their hearts, saying, "The spirit of Elijah rests on Elisha."

The high trails are the hard trails;
    They double the aching back,
They plant the stone, and they twist the groan
    From the song's track.
And the panting breath in the crisis fails,
And the ice betrays, and the sleet assails,
    And the lightning's thunders crack,
        Crack, crack!

But the hard roads are the high roads;
    And I give you challenge there
To the far view, and the vision new
    And bright and fair,
To the castles of glory, the saints' abodes,
And the harping of harps and the singing of odes,
    And the voice of thanks-giving prayer,
        Immortal prayer.

A Boy Who Lived Again

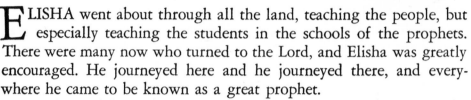

2 Kings 4:8-37

ELISHA went about through all the land, teaching the people, but especially teaching the students in the schools of the prophets. There were many now who turned to the Lord, and Elisha was greatly encouraged. He journeyed here and he journeyed there, and everywhere he came to be known as a great prophet.

Elijah had fought against the evil worship of Baal, brought in by Jezebel, when it threatened to overwhelm all the worship of Jehovah; and the road that Elijah trod was a hard road. But now the worship of Baal was lessening, though many followed after the gods that Jeroboam had set up. So the way of Elisha was easier, but not easy. And he was highly honored in Israel, both by the king and by the people.

One of the places where he used to stop as he went on his journeys was in the city of Shunem and at the house of a good and great woman there. After several visits, the woman said to her husband: "I see this is a holy man who stops and eats with us sometimes. Let us build a room for him on the side of the house, and put in it a bed and a table and a stool and a lamp, and let it be for the man of God only, when he comes."

Her husband said, "All right; let's do." And they built the room and furnished it. And when Elisha came, she took him up and showed him the room, with all its nice furniture. And he was glad. So he asked her what she wanted, but she said, "Nothing." However, when she was gone, he asked his servant, Gehazi, what he might do for the good woman. And Gehazi said, "I'll tell you, master. She has no child of her own, and she does so much wish for a son."

Then Elisha called her back and said, "Listen! Next year about this time you shall have a baby boy born to you."

She was so thrilled she could hardly believe it. And she said, "O my lord, don't tell me any lies."

"No, indeed!" said Elisha. "Truly, you shall have a son."

And so it came to pass. For the next year there was born to her a baby boy. How she loved him! He grew to be quite a lad. When he was perhaps five years old, one day he followed his father out to the wheat field. The sun was hot, and it beat down on the little boy's head

222

and made it ache. He went to his father and said, "My head! My head!"

His father said to a big boy, "Take the little chap up and carry him to his mother." So the big boy carried the little boy to his mother. She took him in her arms and sat down with him and rocked him. But he grew sicker and sicker, until at noon he died.

She took him up in her arms and laid him on the prophet's bed and shut the door. Then she called to her husband and said, "Have the ass saddled for me. I want to go to the prophet."

"Why do you want to go to the prophet?" he asked. "This isn't new moon or Sabbath."

She didn't tell him the little boy was dead. She just said, "It's for the best." So he had the ass saddled.

And she said to her servant, "Go behind and drive fast and faster." And she rode to Mount Carmel, where the prophet Elisha was. He saw her coming, and he said to his servant, "Here comes this Shunammite woman. What can be the matter?"

When she came up to him, she fell down at his feet, and she cried, "Did I ask for a son? Did I not say, 'Tell me no lies'?"

Then he knew her little boy was dead. And he said to Gehazi, "Take my staff, and go ahead and lay it on the face of the child." So his servant took his master's staff and went ahead. But the mother said to Elisha, "I'll not go unless you go with me." He arose then and went with her. On the way they met Gehazi, and he said, "I laid the staff on the face of the lad, but he is not awaked." So they went on till they came to the house.

Elisha went up to the room alone, and opened the door. There lay the little dead boy. Elisha looked at him; then he walked up and down in the room and prayed to God. Then he went and laid himself on the little boy. He put his mouth on his mouth, and his eyes on his eyes, and his hands on his hands; and the little boy's flesh grew warm. Again Elisha walked up and down and prayed to God. And again he went and laid himself on the little boy, eyes to his eyes, mouth to his mouth, hands to his hands. And the child sneezed seven times, and he opened his eyes, and he was alive!

Elisha summoned his servant, and said, "Call this Shunammite." And when she came, he said to her, "Take up your son."

She looked over to the bed where she had laid her little dead son. But now his eyes were open! He smiled at her and stretched out his hands to her. She fell at the prophet's feet and thanked him. Then she took up her little boy and carried him out, more thankful for him now than when first as a little babe he had been laid in her arms.

The Girl Who Saved Her Master

2 Kings 5

THERE was a little girl in Israel in the days of Elisha who was snatched away from her happy home by a band of Syrians and carried to Damascus. We do not know her name, but because she was captured by the Syrians, she is called the Captive Maid.

The great man among the Syrians, next to the king, was Naaman, who was captain of the army. The Captive Maid was given as a servant to the wife of Naaman, and waited on her. I suppose she was up early every morning, and perhaps she took the lady's breakfast in to her on a tray, and carried the dishes out and washed them. Then, when the lady arose from her bed, the little girl helped her dress, and brushed her hair, and handed her her paints and her bracelets and her rings and the jewels that she wore; for the lady of course was a beautiful lady, but she was a heathen. And the little girl ran errands for her and did everything she could think of to make the lady happy.

For the little Captive Maid was very unselfish. She might have mourned and cried because she had been snatched away from her mother and her father and made to be a servant in a strange land. But instead of that, she kept a bright and smiling face, and thought of other people's troubles, and tried to help them. And most of all she loved her mistress and gave her every care and attention.

One day the lady's friends were calling on her. And they admired her jewels and her fine clothes and the rich curtains and carpets and furniture and the servants and all. And they said to Naaman's wife: "You must be very happy with all these beautiful things, and all these servants to wait on you, and so great a man as Naaman for your husband."

But the poor lady burst into tears. She said, "They are nothing to me, because my husband Naaman is a leper."

Now leprosy was a dreadful disease, which ate away fingers and toes and face, until the poor victim at last died of it. And there was no cure for it. At first it came just as a little white spot that could hardly be seen, but it grew and grew and grew until it was all over. I suppose that Naaman had only just begun to feel the leprosy, so it would hardly be noticed; but he knew and his wife knew that it would grow

224

Elijah Taken to Heaven

Elisha asked Elijah for a double portion of his spirit, and Elijah said that if Elisha saw him taken to heaven, he would receive it. "And it came to pass . . . that, behold, there appeared a chariot of fire, . . . and parted them both asunder, and Elijah went up by a whirlwind into heaven. And Elisha saw it."

CLYDE N. PROVONSHA, ARTIST

worse till it killed him. So she cried, "My poor husband is a leper!"

The little girl stood there by her mistress' couch, and she felt, oh, so sorry for her! She thought and she thought, and then she thought of Elisha, back home, who had done so many miracles, even raising a little boy from the dead. And suddenly she spoke right out: "I wish that my master were with the prophet that is in Israel, and he would cure him of the leprosy."

"Why, little girl," all the ladies exclaimed, "no one can cure the leprosy!"

But she said, "The prophet that is in Israel can. He can do anything. Why, he even raised a little boy from the dead."

"Is that so!" they cried. "Let's tell the king."

So they told the king what the little girl had said. And the king called Naaman and said: "The little girl at your house says you can be cured of the leprosy down in Israel. Come, I'll send you with a letter to the king of Israel, and with presents of gold and silver and fine clothes. And you go down and get cured of the leprosy."

So Naaman got ready his chariots and his horsemen, and took a great store of gold and silver and fine clothes for a present, and his king's letter which said to the king of Israel, "I am sending Naaman to be cured of the leprosy." And away rode Naaman to the land of Israel.

The little girl watched him go, with all his horses and chariots and soldiers. She might have wished he would take her along and give her back to her father and mother; but really all she thought of was the healing of her master. And she prayed God to see that he was cured; for of course she knew it was God who would work through the prophet to cure him.

Away rode Naaman with all his horsemen and servants. And he came to the king of Israel and gave him the letter. And when the king of Israel had read the letter, he said to his servants: "See how this man seeks a quarrel with me, asking me to cure a man of the leprosy. Am I God, to kill and to make alive?"

But when Elisha heard of it, he said, "Let him come now to me, and he shall know there is a prophet in Israel."

So Naaman rode down to Elisha's house, with all his servants and horses and chariots, and he stopped at Elisha's door, and sent in word to him to come and cure him of the leprosy. But Elisha just sent a messenger down to say, "Go and wash in Jordan seven times, and you shall be cured."

That made Naaman very angry. He said: "I thought he would

come out and stand and call on the name of the Lord his God, and strike his hand over the place and cure the leprosy. I have better rivers than Jordan back in Damascus. I can go and wash in them, if that will cure me." And he turned his chariot and rode away in a rage.

But his servants, who knew the Captive Maid and had come to believe in her God, came to Naaman and said: "If the prophet had asked you to do some great thing, wouldn't you have done it? How much better to do the little thing he tells you, 'Wash, and be clean'!"

Naaman listened to them, and he was ashamed of himself. So he drove down to the Jordan River. He got out of his chariot and walked down to the water's edge. He waded out a little way and stooped down under the water. Once! But he was not cured. Twice! And the leprosy was still there. The third time! And the fourth time, and the fifth, and the sixth. But still there was the spot of leprosy.

Once more! Seven times! And, lo, when he rose from the water, the leprosy was gone!

Then he rejoiced, and all his servants rejoiced. He rode back to the house of Elisha. This time he did not call for the prophet to come out. The once proud Naaman, now humble, went in and stood before Elisha and thanked him over and over. "Take a present, I pray you," he said, "of gold and silver and fine clothes."

"No," said Elisha; "this is the gift of Jehovah, the God of Israel. I will take no present for it."

"Then," said Naaman, "let me take a load of Israel's soil back to Damascus, that I may build on it an altar to Jehovah. And after this I will worship none but the God of Israel, for He is the only one who could cure the leprosy."

"Go in peace," said Elisha.

And when Naaman came back to his home, all cured of the leprosy, wasn't his wife glad! And wasn't the king glad! And weren't all the people glad! But most of all, wasn't the little girl glad!

She was a little captive maid,
    Whose name we do not know;
She might have mooned and moaned and told
    A wretched tale of woe.

But, no! She let her happy face
    Bring sunshine to the ill.
She loved not self, but other folk;
    And so we love her still.

What the Lepers Found in Camp

2 Kings 6:24-33; 7

BENHADAD, the king of Syria, was not a very grateful soul, nor did he long remember the kindness that had been shown to him in the cure of his captain, Naaman. It came to pass after a while that Benhadad gathered his army and went up and besieged Jehoram, the king of Israel, in his city of Samaria. And soon there was a great famine in the city, because all the food had been eaten up. They ate almost all the animals, though the king saved a few horses for his chariots. And then a dreadful thing came to light.

The king was passing along one day, when a woman cried to him and said: "This other woman here had a child, and I had a child. And because we had nothing to eat, this woman said, 'Boil your son, and we'll eat him. And afterwards we'll boil my son, and eat him.' So we boiled my son and ate him; but now she has hid her son."

Then the king rent his clothes, and he said, "Is it come to this, that my people will be cannibals? It's all the fault of Elisha; for he could have done something to save us if he would. I'll take his head off." And he sent a man to get him. But the king did not wait for that; he went right on the man's heels, to get Elisha himself.

Now Elisha was sitting in his house, with the elders of the people about him. And when the king came, Elisha said: "Hear the word of the Lord. Tomorrow about this time a measure of fine meal shall be sold for a shekel, and two measures of barley for a shekel, in the gate of the city." This meant there would be food—at low prices.

Then the third officer of the king, who was close to him, said, "Ha! Even if the Lord should open the windows of heaven, that couldn't be!"

And Elisha said: "You shall see it, but you shall not eat of it."

Now outside the wall of the city, by the gate, were four lepers. They were not let into the city, and they were afraid to go to the Syrians outside. But finally they were so hungry they said to one another: "We shall die if we stay here. We might as well go to the Syrians. They can't any more than kill us."

So at twilight they took their way to the camp of the Syrians. But when they came to the camp, they heard no sound in it. Strange! they

227

thought. Can the Syrians all be asleep? They came to the first tent, and went into it. No one was there. They went to the next tent. No one was there. No one was anywhere.

What had happened? Why, the Lord had made the Syrians to hear the sound of chariots and horsemen and a great army. And they said, "Listen! The king of Israel has hired the Hittites and the Egyptians to come against us!" And they arose and fled for their lives, leaving everything as it was in their camp.

So the lepers came and sat down in a tent, and ate and drank. Then they arose and carried away gold and silver and fine clothes, and went and hid them. They came back to another tent, and carried away what was there. Then they said, "We are not doing right. This is a day of good news, and we keep still. Let's go to the city and tell them."

So they came to the city gate and told the watchman. And he sent word to the king. Then the king arose in the night, and he said to his servants, "I will tell you what the Syrians have done to us. They know that we are hungry, so they have gone out of their camp and hid in the field. And they say, 'These Israelites will come out to rob our camp, and then we'll catch them. And the gate of the city will be open, and we'll go in and capture it.' "

"Well, anyway," said one of his servants, "let us find out for sure. Send out five horsemen to see."

They didn't have five horses left; but the king sent out two horsemen, saying, "Go and see." They rode all the way to the Jordan, and found nothing but the goods which the Syrians had thrown away in their flight. So the horsemen came back and told the news. Then the gate was opened, and the people poured out and gathered in the food and all the wealth of the Syrians.

In the morning there was a great jam of people at the gate. Now the king had set his third officer at the gate to control the crowd. What must he have thought when the news was brought to the king! And then he was sent down to the gate, and so he heard them calling, just as Elisha had foretold: "A measure of fine flour for a shekel! Two measures of barley for a shekel!" He tried to control the hungry people pressing through the gate, but he could not. They just ran over him, and he fell and was trodden underfoot, and died. So he who had said, "If the Lord should open the windows of heaven, this thing could not be," saw it, but he did not eat thereof.

Jehu Executes Judgment

2 Kings 9

THE LORD had said to Elijah that the family of Ahab should be utterly destroyed; and He told him to anoint Jehu king over Israel. Elijah was taken to heaven before the time for this came; and it was left to Elisha to do it.

Jehu was captain of the army of Israel, and right then he was at Ramoth-gilead, which he had taken from the Syrians. Elisha called one of the sons of the prophets and said, "Take this flask of oil, and go to Ramoth-gilead, and anoint Jehu king of Israel."

So the young man took the flask of oil and went to Ramoth-gilead. There he found all the captains in a meeting, with Jehu over them all. He called him into an upper chamber, and pouring the oil on his head, he said: "The Lord anoints you to be king of Israel. You shall destroy the family of Ahab, until not one remains." Then he opened the door and fled.

Jehu came out and stood at the top of the stairs. The captains asked him, "What did that mad fellow want? What did he do to you?"

Jehu said, "He anointed me king of Israel."

Then all the captains cheered and threw their outer garments under Jehu's feet. They blew with trumpets, and they shouted, "Jehu is king!"

Jehu ordered his chariot to be made ready. And then he took a few of the captains with their chariots, and he rode for Jezreel, where he knew King Jehoram and his mother Jezebel were.

In Jezreel the watchman on the wall saw a great cloud of dust coming. And he reported to the king. The king sent out a horseman to inquire who it was and what it meant. But Jehu just made him join his crowd. Then the watchman said, "The messenger came to them, but he is not coming back."

"Send another horseman," commanded Jehoram. The horseman went, but the watchman reported, "He reached them, but he is not coming back. And the driving of the chariots is like the driving of Jehu the son of Nimshi, for he drives furiously."

Now Jehoram's nephew, Ahaziah, king of Judah, had come to visit him, as he was getting well of wounds he had received in battle.

229

So the two of them rode out in their chariots to meet Jehu. As they drew near, Jehoram called out, "Is it peace, Jehu?"

And Jehu answered: "What peace, so long as the evils of your mother Jezebel are so many?"

Then Jehoram turned his chariot about, exclaiming, "Treachery, Ahaziah!" And they both fled. But Jehu fitted an arrow to his bow, and shot Jehoram, so that he fell down and died. Then he pursued after Ahaziah, and slew him too.

As Jehu rode into Jezreel, Jezebel, who had been told what he had done, looked out of a window and mocked him. He looked up and cried, "Who is on my side, who?" Two or three servants looked out.

"Throw her down!" he cried. And they threw Jezebel out of the window, and there she died under the horses' hoofs. Left there, she was soon found by the dogs, who ate her up. So died Jezebel, and her son, and her grandson, and in the end, all the house of Ahab. For though Jehu was himself a wicked man and made a wicked king, the Lord used him to execute judgment for the horrible sins of Ahab and Jezebel.

"I have taken refuge in the Lord;
  How then can you say to me:
  Flee like a bird to your mountain?
  For, lo, the wicked bend the bow,
  They fit their arrow to the string,
  To shoot in the dark at the upright in heart.
  When the foundations are torn down,
  What has the righteous done?

"The Lord is in his holy temple,
  The Lord, whose throne is in the heavens;
  His eyes behold, his eyelids test the sons of men.
  The Lord tests the righteous and the wicked,
  And he hates the lover of violence.
  On the wicked he will rain coals of fire;
  Brimstone and scorching wind will be the portion
      of their cup.

"For the Lord is righteous; he loves righteousness;
  The upright will behold his face."
                 Psalm 11, J. M. Powis Smith.

The Boy King

2 Kings 11; 12:1-16; 2 Chronicles 21:1 to 24:16

AT THIS time, down in the kingdom of Judah, things were not going well. For the queen they had was the daughter of Jezebel; and where the children of Jezebel were, there was always evil. This is how it came about.

Jehoshaphat, the king of Judah, had thought he could help the kingdom of Israel by marrying his son into the family of Ahab and Jezebel. So he made a marriage between their daughter Athaliah and his son Jehoram. This son had the same name as Athaliah's brother Jehoram, who afterwards became king of Israel and was slain by Jehu; but we must not mix up the two men. Both of the Jehorams are sometimes called Joram, much as we might call an Alexander just Alex; but you may know it is the same person, nevertheless.

Perhaps Jehoshaphat thought that Athaliah, married to his son, would settle down into a nice, purring kitten, but it did not turn out so. For Athaliah was a tiger, just like her mother Jezebel, and she made her husband Jehoram into another son of Ahab. No sooner was Jehoshaphat dead than Jehoram rose up and slaughtered all his brothers and reigned as king. But he and Athaliah made the worship of Baal common in Judah as it was in Israel.

Jehoram reigned for eight years, and then he died. His son Ahaziah became king, and he was just as bad, for his mother Athaliah was his counselor to do evil. When he had been king for only one year, he went up to visit his uncle, Jehoram, king of Israel. It was then that Jehu, coming to Jezreel, slew both Jehoram and Ahaziah, and they died.

When Athaliah, back in Jerusalem, found that her son Ahaziah was dead, she arose, that wicked woman, and slew all her own grandchildren, except one that she missed. He was only a baby, and his name was Joash. His Aunt Jehosheba, the sister of Ahaziah, had married a good man, Jehoiada, the high priest in the temple of God. She snatched the baby up before Athaliah's soldiers could kill him, and she hid him and his nurse in the temple, where she and Jehoiada cared for him. Six years they kept him in secret, while his wicked grandmother Athaliah reigned over Judah and made a most terrible time of blood

231

and crime and worship of Baal. She thought she had killed the last of the descendants of David and had made naught the promise of the Lord. But it was not so.

Jehoiada and Jehosheba taught the little lad Joash as he grew, and instructed him in the law and way of God. So when he was seven years old, Jehoiada gathered all the Levites in the kingdom to Jerusalem. He gave them weapons of war and set them as guards in the temple. He showed them the little prince and told them what he was going to do. And they were glad.

So on the set day Jehoiada brought out Joash and put the guards all around him. Then he put a copy of the law of God in his hand, and set the crown upon his head, and anointed him king of Judah. And all the people shouted, "God save the king!" By this time all Jerusalem was stirred. The people came running to the temple, saying to one another, "Little Joash is made king!"

Athaliah heard all the noise and tumult, and she came out to the temple to see what it meant. There she saw the little king standing by the pillar, with the crown on his head and the law in his hand, and all the people shouting, "Long live the king!"

Athaliah saw that she was undone. And she cried, "Treason! Treason!" But Jehoiada said to the guards, "Take her out! Do not slay her in the temple!" So they took her out, and before they came to the palace, they put her to death.

Now the boy king Joash reigned, and all the people rejoiced. He overthrew the worship of Baal. He repaired the temple, where the wicked Athaliah had wrought havoc. And as long as Jehoiada lived— and it was long—Joash the king obeyed the word of the Lord, and things went well in Judah.

But sad to say, after Jehoiada died, King Joash listened to princes who were bad counselors. They said to him, "Come now, you are no longer a boy, and you have no master to control you. Come, let us have some fun and do as the other gods tell us to do."

So Joash consented, and they left the God of their fathers.

Then God sent prophets to warn the king and the people. One of these prophets was Zechariah, the son of Jehoiada, who told them, "You cannot prosper, because you have forsaken the Lord." But the king commanded them to stone Zechariah to death, and they did. So Joash repaid with evil the good that Jehoiada had done him.

But soon he paid for it with his life. For some of his servants made a plot against him and killed him. Therefore he came to a sad end.

232

The Prophet
Who Ran Away

2 Kings 14:25; Jonah

THERE was a prophet in the kingdom of Israel in the days of the sons of Jehu, whose name was Jonah. Jonah did good work for God in Israel; but one day God bade him go out of his land, to a far country, a great city called Nineveh, and carry a warning for Him to a wicked people.

But Jonah did not want to go to Nineveh. He knew that his God was a merciful God; and he thought if he cried woe against the king and the people of Nineveh and if they repented, then God would not punish them as he prophesied. So Jonah rose up to flee away from God. He went down to the seaport of Joppa and found a ship going to Tarshish, which is Spain. He took passage and paid the fare, and the ship sailed away with him. Soon Jonah felt sleepy, and he went down into the ship and fell asleep.

But while he slept, a great storm came up. The wind blew hard, and the waves ran high, and the little ship labored and twisted and creaked, and seemed about to go to pieces. All the seamen were heathen, some worshiping this god and some that. Every one of them prayed to his god to save them.

The master of the ship, going down into it, found Jonah fast asleep. He woke him up and said, "What do you mean, you sleeper? Get up and cry to your God to save us." Jonah came up on deck in the midst of the storm, and he knew that God had caught him. The men cast lots to see who had brought this storm on them, and the lot fell on Jonah. Then the men clamored around him:

"Who are you? What is your country? What is your occupation? What evil thing have you done, to bring this destruction upon us? Come, tell us!"

And Jonah told them. "I am an Hebrew," he said, "and I fear Jehovah, the God of heaven. He told me to go to Nineveh and cry against it. But I went not. Instead, I took passage in this ship to go to Tarshish."

"What shall we do to you," the seamen said, "so that your God will stop this storm?"

Jonah said, "Take me up and cast me into the sea. And then the

233

storm will stop." But the men did not want to do this. They rowed hard to come to shore, but the storm grew ever fiercer. So then they took up Jonah and threw him into the sea. Immediately the storm stopped. And the men feared Jehovah exceedingly, and worshiped Him.

But what had become of Jonah? Was he drowned? No. The Lord had prepared a great fish, which opened its mouth and swallowed Jonah. And the Lord kept him alive in the belly of the fish for three days and three nights.

There Jonah prayed. He was sorry for his disobedience, and he believed that God would yet save him. And then, he promised, he would do whatever the Lord told him to do.

Then the Lord commanded the great fish, and he vomited up Jonah on the land. And God said to Jonah the second time, "Go to Nineveh, that great city, and tell them what I bade you tell."

So Jonah arose and went to Nineveh. It was a big city, so great it would take three days to walk through it. There were in it more than 120,000 infants, and probably a million grown people. Jonah started going through the city, crying out, as the Lord bade him: "Yet forty days, and Nineveh shall be overthrown! Forty days, and Nineveh shall be destroyed!"

The people of Nineveh looked, and wondered, at this strange figure, clad in the garb of a prophet of Israel—camel's-hair robe and leathern girdle, and sandals—and with a long gray beard. They did not lay hands on him. They were afraid. They ran to their king, and they said, "There is a prophet of Israel going through the city, crying, 'Yet forty days, and Nineveh shall be destroyed.' "

The king, too, feared. He knew that he and his people were wicked, and he knew that God could punish. So he rose from his throne, laid aside his royal robe, and put on sackcloth, the garments of mourning. And he made a proclamation to his people: "Let the city fast. Let neither man nor beast, herd nor flock, taste anything. Let them not eat, nor drink water. But let everyone put on sackcloth, and cry mightily to God. Let them turn everyone from his evil way and from the violence that is in his hand. Who can tell if God will not repent, and turn away from His fierce anger, that we perish not?"

The people obeyed their king; for they too knew their deeds were evil, and they repented. Then God, the merciful God, seeing how they turned from their evil and were sorry for their sins, said He would not do to them the evil He had threatened. And He did it not. So Nineveh was saved.

But Jonah was very angry. The mercy of the Lord had seemed to show Jonah to be a false prophet. He said to the Lord, "Is not this the thing I thought while I was in my own country? Therefore I fled to go to Tarshish. I knew you were a merciful God, slow to anger and of great kindness. Now, O Lord, take away my life; for it is better for me to die than to live."

The Lord said to Jonah, "Are you doing right to be angry?"

"Yes," said Jonah, "I am." He went out of the city and made a booth by the wall, and there he stayed, waiting, and thinking that perhaps God would yet destroy Nineveh.

God made a gourd vine to grow up over Jonah's booth of branches, and it shaded him from the hot sun. Jonah was glad for the gourd. But in the night a worm gnawed its roots, and it withered away. Then again Jonah was angry, and prayed to die.

And God said to him, "Are you doing right to be angry?"

"Yes," said Jonah, "I am so angry I wish to die."

Then said God, "You had pity on the gourd, which you did not make grow. Should I not have pity on Nineveh, that great city, in which are more than 120,000 infants?"

Jonah was silent. He saw that God was right.

Jonah means "dove." We might guess that his mother named him that because he was a cooing baby, and she loved to cuddle and pet him. Cooing is natural to healthy babies, and cuddling and petting are natural to fond mothers and fathers. But too much of it, especially when the baby has grown up to be a boy or a girl, is likely to make a spoiled child. We may suppose that Jonah as a child was somewhat spoiled because when he became a man, he was afraid to tackle a hard job, and so tried to run away from the Lord. And then he pouted and sulked when the Lord forgave the men of Nineveh, and afterward when the gourd vine that shaded him wilted.

"Then some of the scribes and Pharisees addressed him, saying, 'Master, we would like to have you show us some sign.'

"But he answered, 'Only a wicked and faithless age insists upon a sign, and no sign will be given it but the sign of the prophet Jonah. For just as Jonah was in the maw of the whale for three days and nights, the Son of Man will be three days and nights in the heart of the earth. Men of Nineveh will rise with this age at the judgment and condemn it, for when Jonah preached they repented, and there is more than Jonah here!' "

Matthew 12:38-41, Goodspeed.

235

Israel Goes Into Captivity

2 Kings 15:29; 17; 18:9-12

THE LAST years of the kingdom of Israel were sad years. From the time that the kingdom of Solomon was divided, and ten tribes went and made the kingdom of Israel, to the time when they were all taken captive, was a little over 250 years. And during all that time they had not one good king. Every one of their kings followed the way of Jeroboam or the way of Ahab; and most of the people of Israel did the way their kings did.

Nevertheless God loved them, and He sent many prophets to them to turn them from their evil ways. Hosea, Amos, and Jonah were some of those prophets, and then there were the great prophets Elijah and Elisha. But only a few of the people would heed them. Some of those who did moved to the kingdom of Judah, where the worship of the true God was better held. Some of them were put to death by wicked kings and people. Yet a few were left who kept the way of the Lord; but they were not enough to save Israel.

After Jehu there were more than a hundred years of murders and bloodshed and worship of false gods in Israel. King after king was killed by someone who wanted to be king in his place. There were nine of these kings, some of whom reigned only a few months, and one but four weeks. They were all evil men, and they led their people in doing evil.

So all these years were sad years of blood and crime and evil-doing. The kings and the people worshiped the golden calves of Jeroboam, doing the vile and wicked things it called for; and some even worshiped Baal, though that heathen god had been cast down by Jehu. They broke all the commandments of God. They made for themselves molten images and carved images, and worshiped the sun and the moon and the stars. They sacrificed their children in fire in the worship of Molech. They communed with evil spirits, who were devils, and they sold themselves to do wickedness in the sight of God.

Therefore God was very grieved with them, and removed them out of His sight. There was none left but the kingdom of Judah. God let the kings of Assyria come and destroy Israel. The capital of Assyria was Nineveh, the city to which Jonah had gone at the command of

236

God to warn it. The king and people of Nineveh repented at that time, and the Lord did not destroy them. But they soon forgot and went back to their gods and their evil ways. They were very fierce and cruel, and it was a terrible judgment that the Lord let them come.

First a king of Assyria came and carried away the people in all the northern part of the country and all the east that was across Jordan. So there was left to Israel only Samaria and the country around it. The king of Assyria took the captive Israelites to his own land and scattered them among the people there, and most of them lost all sight of God and became like the heathen around them.

Then, about twenty years later, another king of Assyria came up against Samaria, where Hoshea was king. As it proved, he was to be the last king of Israel. The Assyrian army besieged Samaria for three years and finally took it. There was nothing now left of the kingdom of Israel, which had lasted about 250 years. All the remaining Israelites were carried away and scattered in cities far off, which the Assyrians had conquered. Except those who joined the Jews, they were lost out of the Israel of God.

To fill the cities and the country of Israel, the king of Assyria brought people from other cities which he had conquered, and settled them there. They were all heathen, and they had many gods, some one and some another. But there were not enough of these people to fill all the cities and the land; and lions and other wild beasts began to multiply and attack them. So they sent to the king of Assyria and said to him, "Because we do not know the God of this land, He has sent lions among us, and they slay us, and we are miserable."

So the king of Assyria took one of the Israelite priests, and sent him back to that land, saying, "Go and teach the people I have put there about your God." The priest probably was one of the priests of the golden calves of Jeroboam; for he came and lived in Bethel, the place of those idols, and the true priests of God were all in Jerusalem in the land of Judah. Anyway, he was not able to teach the people very much about God. They learned a little, but still they all worshiped their false gods. And so they mixed up their religion. In after years their descendants were known as Samaritans. They were not Jews, though they did believe in the God who made heaven and earth. But they made a great deal of trouble for the Jews, as you will learn in later stories.

Still the kingdom of Judah lived on for over a hundred years. And you shall hear of two good and great kings who kept the knowledge and worship of the true God alive in Judah.

237

Good Son of a Bad Father

2 Kings 16; 18; 19; 2 Chronicles 28 to 31

THE KINGDOM of Judah had about as many good kings as bad kings through its history. One of the worst of their kings was Ahaz. His name, you see, is very much like that of Ahab, and he was to Judah what Ahab was to Israel. He did not do what was right in the sight of the Lord, as David and Asa and Jehoshaphat had done, but he walked in the ways of the kings of Israel. He made his son to pass through the fire to Molech, and worshiped Baal and the gods of the nations round about. He took away the treasures of the temple and shut up its doors, so that men might not worship there, while he made altars and shrines to the false gods in Jerusalem and all through the land. Sixteen years he reigned and did evil. Then he died, and Hezekiah his son reigned in his stead.

Hezekiah was twenty-five years old when he became king. He was altogether different from his father; for he loved the Lord and kept His commandments and taught the people to worship the only true God. How is it that he was so good when his father was so bad? Well, he had a grandfather, the good King Jotham, who lived until Hezekiah was nine years old; and he taught him. And his mother was Abi, the daughter of Zachariah. This Zachariah was probably the Zachariah who was the son of Jehoiada, and high priest after him. So the good word of the Lord came to Hezekiah through his faithful mother. And the good teaching of his mother and his grandfather overcame the evil influence of his father. Then, too, there was in the land one of the great prophets, Isaiah, who worked mightily to save the worship of God. And Hezekiah listened to him and obeyed the word of the Lord. That is how a good son came from a bad father.

In the very first month of his reign Hezekiah opened the doors of the temple, which Ahaz had shut up. He gathered the priests and the Levites, and he preached to them in the east street by the temple. He said: "Our fathers have sinned and done evil; therefore the wrath of the Lord has been upon us. Many have been killed, and many have gone into captivity. Now it is in my heart to make a covenant with Jehovah the God of Israel, to turn away His wrath from us. Therefore now, my sons, do not be careless and slow; for the Lord has chosen you to serve Him and to minister before Him in His holy temple."

Then the Levites arose under the eye of the king, and they cleansed the house of God. Seven days they were in cleansing it, and on the eighth day they came to Hezekiah and said, "We have finished, and the house of God is clean." So Hezekiah rose early in the morning and gathered the elders together, and with many people he went up to the temple and offered sacrifices. So the worship of Jehovah God was revived in Judah.

And Hezekiah called all the people of the kingdom of Judah, and he sent letters to the people of the kingdom of Israel, calling them to the keeping of the Passover in Jerusalem. For the kingdom of Israel was not yet destroyed; it lasted until Hezekiah had reigned over Judah for six years. And many of the people of Israel came and joined with the people of Judah in worshiping the Lord.

But those were very troublous times; and Hezekiah, the good king, with all his people, was made to feel the trouble. The Assyrians who had captured Samaria, in the sixth year of Hezekiah, looked with greedy eyes upon the riches of Judah and Jerusalem. Hezekiah had reigned about fourteen years when Sennacherib, the new king of Assyria, came up with a great army and overran Judah. He was going against the king of Egypt, but he took all the cities on his way. He came to Lachish, in the lowland near the sea, and besieged it.

And from Lachish he sent officers to Jerusalem. When they came, the city gates were shut against them, but Hezekiah sent out officers to talk with them. The Assyrians stood and talked so loud that the people on the walls could hear them.

"Speak to us in the Syrian language, for we understand it," pleaded Hezekiah's officers, "and do not speak in the Jews' language so the people can understand."

"Huh!" said the Assyrians, "do you think our master has sent us to speak just to you? He has sent us to speak to all the Jews." Then he shouted louder than ever to the people on the wall: "Don't let Hezekiah deceive you. He is trusting to the king of Egypt, but Egypt is a broken reed. If he says that Jehovah, the God of Israel, will deliver you, why, he has taken away all the high places of Jehovah and told you to worship alone in Jerusalem. Do you think we have come up without Jehovah? Why, He told us to come and take this city."

But the people on the city walls answered him not a word; for so Hezekiah had commanded them. Then his officers came back and told Hezekiah all the words of the Assyrians. Hezekiah sent word to Isaiah the prophet; and Isaiah, praying to the Lord, had a comforting message for him. He told him: "The Lord says, 'Do not be afraid of the words of the king of Assyria, wherewith he has blasphemed Me. I will send a blast upon him, and he will fall by a sword in his own land.' "

Then the king of Assyria sent a letter to Hezekiah, threatening him again. Hezekiah took the letter up to the temple and spread it out before the Lord. He prayed, and the Lord heard him. He sent Isaiah to him, saying, "Thus saith the Lord to the king of Assyria, 'Because your pride reaches up to heaven, and you have spoken words against Me, I will put a hook in your nose, like as an ox, and a bridle on your head, like as a horse, and I will turn you back by the way you came.' And, Hezekiah, the Lord to whom you have prayed will deliver you."

That night the angel of the Lord went out into the camp of the Assyrians and struck to death 180,000 of the Assyrians. So Sennacherib broke up his camp and took the remnant of his army and retreated fast to his land. Scarcely had he reached there when he went into the house of his god to worship; but two of his own sons found him there and slew him. So Hezekiah and Judah were delivered.

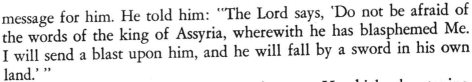

"The Assyrian came down like the wolf on the fold,
And his cohorts were gleaming in purple and gold;
And the sheen of their spears was like stars on the sea,
When the blue wave rolls nightly on deep Galilee.

"Like the leaves of the forest when Summer is green,
That host with their banners at sunset were seen;
Like the leaves of the forest when Autumn hath blown,
That host on the morrow lay withered and strown.

"For the Angel of Death spread his wings on the blast,
And breathed in the face of the foe as he passed;
And the eyes of the sleepers waxed deadly and chill,
And their hearts but once heaved, and forever grew still!

.   .   .   .

"And the widows of Ashur are loud in their wail,
And the idols are broke in the temple of Baal;
And the might of the Gentile, unsmote by the sword,
Hath melted like snow in the glance of the Lord!"

Byron.

240

Jonah Cast Into the Sea

"Then they said unto him, What shall we do unto thee, that the sea may be calm unto us? . . . And he said unto them, Take me up, and cast me forth into the sea. . . . So they took up Jonah, and cast him forth into the sea. . . . Now the Lord had prepared a great fish to swallow up Jonah."

ROBERT TEMPLE AYRES, ARTIST

The Last Good King of Judah

2 Kings 21 to 23; 2 Chronicles 33 to 35; Jeremiah 1:1, 2

BUT, OH, sad to say, the people of Judah went over again the same track they had traveled so many times before! Upon Hezekiah's death his son Manasseh came to be king. He was only twelve years old, but he must have been a very wayward boy; for he forsook the way of his father Hezekiah and the teaching of the prophet Isaiah and of the prophet Micah. He reigned long, even fifty-five years; and as he grew older, he grew worse and worse.

Then God sent prophets, who declared that the Lord would give them up to their enemies and send them into captivity, as he had the people of Israel. But they only mocked.

Soon there came bands of Assyrians, and they captured Manasseh, bound him with fetters, and carried him away to Babylon. There he was put in prison. And now he came to his senses. He had nothing to do but think upon the evil way he had gone and the messages the prophets had brought to him. He repented of his sins and prayed God to forgive him. And the merciful, loving God did forgive him, and brought him again to his kingdom and Jerusalem.

After this Manasseh tried to undo the evil he had done, but not many of the people followed him. His son, Amon, despised the reform his father tried to begin. At once he started in to make the tide of evil run strong. But he had not long to reign. After two years some of his servants made a plot against him and slew him. Then the people of the land made Josiah, his little son, king in his place.

It was now eighty-six years since Hezekiah came to the throne, and fifty-seven since he died. Judah was in as bad a state as when Hezekiah became king. But lo, another king of righteousness was now to reign, the best king that Judah ever had.

Josiah was younger than Hezekiah when he was crowned. He was but eight years old. But his heart was turned strongly toward the God of Israel. Perhaps, as in the case of Hezekiah, his mother taught him of the Lord. Her name was Jedidah, which means "beloved," or "darling"; and so we like to think that she was a sweet and noble young mother, who felt that the Lord had given her little son into her hands to make him a man of God. And until he was six years old,

there was his old grandfather, Manasseh, who had been so bad but who had repented; and perhaps he tried to teach the little boy of the true God. And though there was at first no great prophet like Isaiah, there were others, like the prophetess Huldah, who taught the way of the Lord. May we not suppose that Jedidah, Josiah's young mother, had been instructed by Huldah, and they were friends, and Huldah helped her teach the little boy? Surely God was speaking to the heart of little Josiah; for he made up his mind even so early that he would follow the Lord. He loved the Lord, and he hated idolatry with all his soul, and he turned not to the right hand or to the left from the ways of God all the days of his life.

For eight years after he became king he studied and learned and sought to do right. Then, when he was sixteen years old, he took his public stand for God. And four years later, when he was twenty, he began to clear the kingdom of the false gods and their altars and their shrines. Old Manasseh had tried, after he repented and came back, but he did not succeed very well. So there was much to do.

Josiah went out with his soldiers and his workmen and stood over them while they smashed the idols and cut down the heathen images and broke to pieces the shrines in the high places. And he purged Jerusalem and the land of Judah of heathen worship as it had never been purged before, even by the best of the kings. There was not an idol left in Judah.

Then he went farther, up into the land that had been Israel's. There were foreigners living there now, heathen who worshiped the gods of their fathers, though they had learned a little of the true God. Josiah went through all their land, through Ephraim and Manasseh and up into Naphtali. And everywhere he smashed the altars and the temples of the heathen gods.

He came back to Bethel, where 350 years before Jeroboam had set up the worship of the golden calves. Through all these years the house of idols he built there had stood, and the worship he had started had kept on. Back there in the first days of Jeroboam, the Lord had sent a prophet from the land of Judah, who stood and told Jeroboam that there would be a child born to the house of David, a child named Josiah, who should destroy the altar and the worship. And now, three centuries and a half afterward, that Josiah had come as prophesied. He tore down the house of idols, and broke down the altar, and took dead men's bones and burned them on it. And as he did at Bethel, so he did at Samaria and the land about. So the Samaritans learned a little more of the true God.

242

Now the Lord sent a great prophet, Jeremiah, to help Josiah. He was just a young man when, in the thirteenth year of Josiah's reign, he stood up and helped the king rid the land of heathen worship; but he was to grow strong and great, and he was true to God to the end of his life.

In the eighteenth year of Josiah's reign, there was found in the temple the book of the law written by Moses. It had been lost when Manasseh stopped the worship of God; and as books were very scarce then, having all to be written by hand, there had not been a full copy, and much of it had been forgotten.

Now the book was taken before the king, and there were read to him the woes which Moses had foretold would come upon this people if they departed from the Lord. "They shall be burnt with hunger and devoured with burning heat and with bitter destruction. The sword without and terror within shall destroy them."

King Josiah was dismayed; for he knew how terribly his fathers and his people had sinned. He rent his clothes, and he sent to Huldah the prophetess, saying, "Inquire of the Lord for me and for them that are left in Israel and Judah, concerning the words in this book; for it tells of great wrath to be poured out upon a people who have been so wicked as we."

Then Huldah sent back word: "Thus says the Lord God of Israel, 'I will bring upon this place and this people the curses that are written in the book, because they have forsaken Me. But say to the king, "Because your heart was tender, and you have humbled yourself before God, this evil will not be brought during your life, and you shall not see it." ' "

Josiah assembled all the elders and the people of Jerusalem, and the priests and Levites, and he read the book of the law to them. Then he pledged himself and he pledged them to love the Lord and keep His commandments. And like Hezekiah before him, he called all the people to observe the Passover. All the people in Judah and thousands from the land of Israel came to this Passover, the greatest that had been held since the days of Samuel. And the land had peace while Josiah reigned for thirteen more years.

But when he was only thirty-nine years old, Josiah was slain in a battle with Pharaoh-necho, king of Egypt. Oh, how the people mourned for him, the truest and the best king that Judah ever had! Then came swiftly the woes that Judah had earned and that had been foretold would come upon them. And of this you will be told in the Stories of the Prophets.

STORIES OF THE PROPHETS

Isaiah to Daniel

The Prophet of Hope

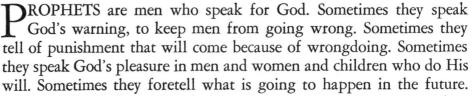

Isaiah 1; 3; 5

PROPHETS are men who speak for God. Sometimes they speak God's warning, to keep men from going wrong. Sometimes they tell of punishment that will come because of wrongdoing. Sometimes they speak God's pleasure in men and women and children who do His will. Sometimes they foretell what is going to happen in the future.

God has had prophets from earliest times. Enoch was a prophet; Abraham is called a prophet; Moses was a great prophet; there were prophets during the time of the judges; and Samuel was one of the chief prophets. Prophets during the time of the judges, and for some time after, were often called seers, because they saw the visions of God.

Samuel founded the schools of the prophets, to teach young men the word of God and all the things they needed in their lives and work. In David's court there were the prophets Gad and Nathan, who were probably trained by Samuel. And during the times of the kings of Israel and Judah there were many prophets, including Elijah and Elisha.

But it was in the last years of the kingdom of Judah that the great prophets came; and all the books of the Bible after the songs and sayings of David and Solomon are books of the prophets. Some of the books are long, and some of them are short. They are called the major prophets and the minor prophets. The major prophets are the first four in order: Isaiah, Jeremiah (with Lamentations), Ezekiel, and Daniel. The minor prophets follow, twelve in number. A few of the prophets spoke to the kingdom of Israel, but most of them to the people of Judah. Most of the prophets tell us just when they spoke, so we know their time.

Isaiah lived in the times of Uzziah, Jotham, Ahaz, Hezekiah, and Manasseh, kings of Judah. He belonged to the royal family, and that made him a prince of men. But far better than that, he belonged to the Lord's family, and that made him a prince with God. And a prince of the prophets he has always been, not only in his lifetime but in all the nearly three thousand years since. He was a good counselor, to keep the kings in the right way, and he often carried to them messages from the Lord. But also he spoke to the people; and that was still more im-

246

portant, for as the people are, so are their priests, and so are their princes.

Isaiah had many times to rebuke God's people for their sins, because the worship of false gods was very common, and the careless and evil lives that went with that worship were ruining the people. But Isaiah also was a prophet of cheer and hope. He believed that God would save His people; and so he welcomed the messages of God that told of that salvation, and he faithfully gave the messages to his people. Sometimes so happy was he that he sang, and his words written in his book make some of the most beautiful parts of the Bible.

Isaiah counseled Ahaz; and he greatly helped Hezekiah, as you heard in the story "A Good Son of a Bad Father." And when Hezekiah died, and his son Manasseh did such evil, we may be sure that Isaiah still faithfully bore the messages of God to him. He died during the reign of Manasseh, we do not know for sure just how. The Bible does not tell us, but a tradition of the elders says that Manasseh put Isaiah to death, as he certainly did put to death many of the people of God. But Isaiah, prince of the prophets, still lives for us in what he has written.

ISAIAH'S FIRST PROPHECY

"Hear, O heavens, and give ear, O earth: for the Lord hath spoken, I have nourished and brought up children, and they have rebelled against me. The ox knoweth his owner, and the ass his master's crib: but Israel doth not know, my people doth not consider. Ah sinful nation, a people laden with iniquity, a seed of evildoers, children that are corrupters: they have forsaken the Lord, they have provoked the Holy One of Israel unto anger, they are gone away backward. . . .

"Wash you, make you clean; put away the evil of your doings from before mine eyes; cease to do evil; learn to do well; seek judgment, relieve the oppressed, judge the fatherless, plead for the widow.

"Come now, and let us reason together, saith the Lord: though your sins be as scarlet, they shall be as white as snow; though they be red like crimson, they shall be as wool. If ye be willing and obedient, ye shall eat the good of the land."

Isaiah 1:2-4, 16-19.

A Vision of God

Isaiah 6

WHILE Isaiah was yet young, in the last year of King Uzziah, one day he went up into the temple to worship. Isaiah was a prince, but he was not a priest, and only the priests were allowed to go into the temple itself; but the people, as well as the kings and the princes, were allowed in the court. The priests ministered every day in the holy place; but only once a year did the high priest go into the most holy place, where God's Presence dwelt on the ark; and then the high priest veiled his face from the glory with the smoke of incense.

But since the worship of the temple was so often hindered and stopped, and even the priests were sometimes bad, we do not suppose that the round of the temple services was carefully kept, especially in the last years. And we are not sure that the high priest every year observed the Day of Atonement, when he went into the most holy place. If he was a bad high priest, I should not think he would dare go in where the glory of God shone on the ark.

Isaiah and all the people had had a lesson of what would happen, even to a king who presumed to go into the sacred rooms where only the priests had the right to go. For King Uzziah, though he had been a good king, at last grew so proud that he thought he was above everyone, and that he might do anything the priests did. So one day he pushed right into the first room, or the holy place, of the temple. The priests stood in his way and told him he was trespassing upon God's holy ground. And in that instant God struck King Uzziah with the leprosy. So he hastened out, but he was a leper to the day of his death, and lived in a separate house, away from all his people.

So Isaiah did not think of going into the temple itself, but in the court he prayed so earnestly, and gave himself so completely to God, that the Lord showed Himself to him in a vision. Now in a vision a prophet loses sight of every natural thing around him, and he sees only what God shows him. And this is the vision that was given to the young prophet Isaiah:

He saw the Lord sitting upon a throne, high and lifted up, and His glory filled the temple. Above the throne stood two great angels of the highest order, called the seraphim. Each of them had six wings.

248

With two he covered his face, with two he covered his feet, and with the other two he flew. And the two seraphim cried each to the other:

"Holy, holy, holy, is the Lord of hosts;
The whole earth is full of His glory!"

So mighty and so moving were the tones of the seraphim that the doorposts quivered like the strings of a harp, and the house was filled with the sweet smoke of incense.

The young prophet quaked with fear. He exclaimed: "Woe! Woe is me! I am stricken! For I am a man of unclean lips, and I live among a people of unclean lips. For my eyes have seen the King, the Lord of hosts!"

Then one of the seraphim flew to him, bearing in a pair of golden tongs a live coal from off the altar of incense. He laid it upon the lips of the young man, and he said: "Lo, this has touched your lips; and your iniquity is taken away and your sin cleansed."

Then the voice of the Lord said, "Whom shall I send?"

The young prophet answered, "Here am I. Send me!"

"Go," said the Lord to him, "go and bear My word to this people. They will hear, but not understand. They will look, but not see. If only they would, they could understand and be converted."

"O Lord," cried the prophet, "how long shall this be?"

"It will be," came the answer, "until I have wasted the cities and made the land desolate and scattered men far away. Then there will be some who understand, and a remnant shall return. Like an oak tree that casts its leaves in the fall but awakes in the spring and brings forth more leaves and fruit, they shall come back."

Then Isaiah awoke from his vision. And he understood that though Judah should resist his word, yet in the end, after God's judgments had fallen, a remnant should return and bring forth the fruits of righteousness. So he kept heart as a prophet of hope should.

———

Alleluia! Alleluia!
Praise Him, ye seraphim above;
Praise Him, ye angels of His love;
Ye winged spirits of His grace,
That day by day behold His face,
Sing, sing the rapture that ye know,
And lend your joy to earth below;
For earth is full of the glory of God.
Alleluia! Alleluia! Alleluia! Amen!

Dangers Without and Within

Isaiah 7; 8; 36 to 39; 2 Kings 15:32-38; 16; 20

ISAIAH went out of the temple after his vision of God upon His throne. And he was filled with the glory he had seen and heard. "Go," the Lord said to him, "go and tell this people My message. But they will not listen and they will not understand, until I have punished them for their iniquity and scattered them to far countries. Yet in the end there shall be a remnant that revives, like a tree in the spring that brings forth its new leaves."

Isaiah set to work with courage to teach the people. King Uzziah died that year, and his son Jotham became king. Since Uzziah was a leper in the last years of his life, Jotham had really reigned for him for some time; but after his father's death he reigned alone for sixteen years. He was a good king and did his best to lead his people in the ways of God. So Isaiah had good help.

But Ahaz, Jotham's son, was a wild young man, and he became a wicked king. Isaiah labored with him, even after Ahaz openly joined himself to idols. The Lord sent trouble upon him, but he would not heed. Two kings, the king of Israel and the king of Syria, fought against him, and Ahaz was in great trouble. Then the Lord said to Isaiah, "Go and find Ahaz, and say to him: 'Be calm, and do not fear because these two kings have joined against you and threaten to destroy Judah. They shall not do what they plan; for their plans shall be broken.' " But Ahaz shut his mind against the Lord and would not listen.

Then Isaiah said to him, "Ask a sign of the Lord that what I tell you is true."

But Ahaz sullenly said, "I will not ask any sign of the Lord."

So Isaiah said: "The king of Israel and the king of Syria will be taken out of the way, but in their place there shall be a greater scourge, even the king of Assyria."

So it came to pass. For the king of Assyria, pretending to help Ahaz, stripped him and Judah of nearly everything they had. But all this did not drive Ahaz and his people to the Lord. They worshiped the gods of the nations which oppressed them; for their ears were heavy, and their eyes were dull.

250

Yet there were some people in Judah who listened to Isaiah and who sought the Lord. Among them was the little son of Ahaz, Hezekiah, who drank in what Isaiah had to teach him. And he grew up to be a good man. When at twenty-five years of age he became king, he overthrew the worship of false gods and turned the people to God.

But he too was troubled by the Assyrians, who invaded the land and threatened to take Jerusalem, as you have heard in the story about Hezekiah. It was then that Isaiah was a tower of strength to Hezekiah; and, as he prophesied, the Lord destroyed a great part of the Assyrian army and sent its king hurrying back to his own land, where he soon was slain by his own sons.

At this time Hezekiah fell sick, and the Lord sent Isaiah to him to say: "Set your house in order, for you are going to die." Then Hezekiah turned his face to the wall and wept. And he prayed to the Lord to let him live. So God sent Isaiah back, before he had gone out of the palace, with this message to the king: "I have heard your prayer, and I will heal you. In three days you will be able to go up to the temple to worship. And I will add fifteen years to your life."

And so it was. And in those fifteen years there was good and there was evil. It was good because Hezekiah and Isaiah had fifteen more years in which to try to bring the people of Judah to the side of the Lord; but it was bad because in those years there was born the son of Hezekiah, Manasseh, who when he was twelve years of age became king, and a bad king, the worst king that Judah ever had. Yet the seeds of truth that Isaiah sowed bore fruit in many lives in Judah; and Isaiah kept his faith and hope to the last.

And Hezekiah prayed:
"O Lord, by these things men live,
And through all of them is the life of my spirit
          sustained;
Therefore do thou restore me, and bring me to life
          again!
For thou hast cast all my sins behind thy back.
The grave cannot thank thee, death cannot
          praise thee;
Those who go down to the Pit cannot hope for thy
          love.
The living, the living man thanks thee, as I do
          this day."
Isaiah 38:16-19, King James Version and Goodspeed.

The Coming Redeemer

Isaiah 2; 9:6, 7; 11; 12; 42; 52; 53; 55; 60; 61; 65; 66

"WHAT will be the end of all this battle for the Lord?" asked the young prophet Isaiah. "Must we go up and down, up and down, forever? Must there be a good king, then a bad king, then a good king, then a bad king, and so on, never ending? Will the people worship Jehovah for a while, then Baal, and then turn around and go over the same ground again? Will there never come an end? Will God not conquer evil at last?" Isaiah thought it over and over. He asked God to tell him. And God did.

There had been many prophets before Isaiah, good men, men who like him had fought evil and loved good, men who had stood for God though all the world about them was evil. And there had been promises of victory. Even Adam and Eve had had the promise of a coming Son who would bruise the serpent's head. Enoch had seen the Lord coming with ten thousands of His saints. Abraham had been told that all the earth would be blessed in his children. Moses had foretold the coming of a great Prophet who would be the Lord's mouthpiece. Job had spoken of a Redeemer who would stand upon the earth in the last days. David had sung of God as his Redeemer. But no one had made the matter as clear as Isaiah wanted it. So he prayed to know more. And the Lord answered him.

The Redeemer, God told him, would be born as a child of the line of David. The Spirit of the Lord would rest upon Him, and He would judge righteously, doing justice to the poor and slaying the wicked. Yet He would be despised and rejected of men. He would carry the sorrows of men and bear their sins. He would be the Lamb of God, dying for the sins of the world. He would be the great High Priest, pleading for the forgiveness of God for His people. And in the end He would see victory in the salvation of the righteous. And Isaiah remembered how David had said that though God's Holy One would die, the Lord would not leave Him in His grave. But He would rise and be king over all the world. And not only from His people Israel but also from the nations around, the Gentiles, would come multitudes to join His kingdom of righteousness. And they who would not have Him rule over them would perish. And all the world would be righteous and pure. "They shall not hurt nor destroy in all My holy mountain; for the earth shall be full of the knowledge of the Lord, as the waters cover the sea."

Isaiah was the first great prophet to tell so much about the coming Redeemer and His kingdom. What he told opened to men the splendors of the kingdom of God. He also told that to have this come to pass, there must be a change of heart, a turning to the Lord, by His people. If they did not do this, they could never see the kingdom come and be a part of it.

After Isaiah came other great prophets who told more and more of the coming Redeemer. About one hundred years later, Jeremiah took up the tale and told of the coming King and what His people must do to be ready for Him. And then Ezekiel added more to the story, telling of the kingdom of the Redeemer, who would be both Priest and King.

As it was the custom in Israel, when making either a priest or a king, to pour a little oil on his head (that is, anoint him), the coming Redeemer came to be called the Anointed. In the Hebrew language the word for Anointed is Messiah, and in Greek it is Christ. Those three words, in three languages, all mean the same: the Anointed, the Messiah, the Christ.

Last of the four major prophets, Daniel spoke of the Redeemer as the Messiah. And he not only told of His work and reign, but of the exact time when He should come. Some of the minor prophets added bits of information about the Messiah and His coming. And all together, these prophecies are known as the Messianic prophecies, or the prophecies about the Messiah, who in our time is called the Christ.

The morning's banners faintly flash
　　Upon the eastern sky,
And still the foeman's cohorts dash
　　Against the bulwarks high.
But cheerily rings the trump the hour,
　　And bravely runs the word;
For from his high-thrust warden tower
　　The watchman's voice is heard:
　　　"A-ll's w-e-ll! A-a-ll's well!"
　　The watchman saith,
"The King, with all His armies, comes!"
　　And loud the people answereth:
"The King! The King! He comes! He comes!"

253

The Prophet
of Heartbreak

Jeremiah 1 to 6

AMONG the priests in the town of Anathoth, about three miles from Jerusalem, there was growing up in the last years of Manasseh, king of Judah, a little boy named Jeremiah. He was about the same age as Josiah, the little grandson of Manasseh, who at the same time was growing up in the palace of the king in Jerusalem. These two boys probably did not know each other, for people in those times did not travel or visit so much as now; but the Lord was shaping the minds and the lives of both of them to work together when they should become men, to try to save the people of Judah.

Jeremiah was the son of a priest, Hilkiah, who faithfully taught him the laws of God and trained him to do the work of a priest when he should be grown.

So he was in much the same place as Samuel of old. But while the work of a priest was a part of God's work, Jeremiah never came to act as a priest in the temple; for the Lord chose him for a greater work, even to be His prophet. Jeremiah was a thoughtful lad, somewhat timid, but very determined to keep the law of God, which he studied day and night. Later in life he said to the Lord: "Thy words were found, and I did eat them; and Thy word was unto me the joy and rejoicing of mine heart."

He was perhaps eighteen or twenty years old when the Lord spoke to him, saying: "Jeremiah, you shall be My prophet. Even before you were born, I chose you and ordained you to be My spokesman to the nations."

But Jeremiah shrank back. "Ah, Lord God," he said, "listen, I pray. I cannot speak; I am only a child."

Just so had Solomon spoken when he came to be king. But it is the men who do not think that they are great and wise, who think of themselves as being only children, whom the Lord can use as His spokesmen. And the Lord said to young Jeremiah: "Do not say, I am a child. You shall go to everyone to whom I send you; and whatever I command you, you shall speak. I have set you this day over the nations, to tear down what I would have torn down, and to build and plant what I would have to grow. I have made you to be like a walled city,

like an iron post, like a wall of brass, to stand against the kings of
Judah, against the princes, against the priests. They will fight against
you, but they shall not overcome you; for I am with you to deliver
you."

So Jeremiah entered upon his work in the thirteenth year of
Josiah's reign. That was one king of Judah against whom he did not
have to fight; for just the year before, Josiah, then twenty years old,
had started to clear his kingdom of the wicked idol worship with which
his father and his grandfather had sowed it. Jeremiah rejoiced to see
this work begun, but he knew that it must go into the hearts of the
people, and not merely be the king's work. So, filled with the Spirit
of God, he spoke out what the Lord told him, calling upon the people
to forsake their false gods and their evil ways and turn to the Lord.

Josiah was greatly encouraged by the voice and the words of this
young prophet. Like Jeremiah, he hated idolatry with all his heart.
And for nearly twenty years the two worked together to put down the
false religion, not only in Judah but in the land that had been Israel's.
All over the land the king threw down the idols and lifted up the
name and worship of the Lord. And the prophet preached and prophesied to turn the people to God. Many listened and bowed their heads
and hearts before Jehovah.

But still there lingered in the lives of most of the people the love
of evil. The king might smash their idols and tear down their shrines,
and they might all make a showing of worshiping the Lord. But when
Josiah was killed, in the thirty-first year of his reign, and his sons came
to the throne, then down went the people into the slime of idolatry.
All that Jeremiah could do and say could not keep them true to God;
and his heart ached and broke over their iniquity. Yet his life and
work were not lost; for out of the wreck of Judah came some of the
brightest and best of the children of God, as you will hear in stories
that follow.

Jeremiah said:

"As the thief is ashamed when he is found, so is the house of
Israel ashamed; they, their kings, their princes, and their priests, and
their prophets; saying to a stock, Thou art my father; and to a stone,
Thou hast brought me forth: for they have turned their back unto
me, and not their face: but in the time of their trouble they will say,
Arise, and save us. But where are thy gods that thou hast made thee?
Let them arise, if they can save thee in the time of thy trouble: for ac-
cording to the number of thy cities are thy gods, O Judah!"

Jeremiah 2:26-28.

255

The Heart of the Redeemer

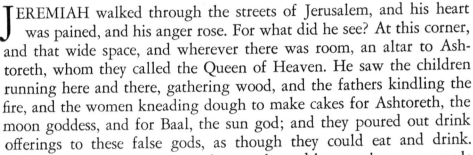

Jeremiah 7; 15; 17; 23; 24

JEREMIAH walked through the streets of Jerusalem, and his heart was pained, and his anger rose. For what did he see? At this corner, and that wide space, and wherever there was room, an altar to Ashtoreth, whom they called the Queen of Heaven. He saw the children running here and there, gathering wood, and the fathers kindling the fire, and the women kneading dough to make cakes for Ashtoreth, the moon goddess, and for Baal, the sun god; and they poured out drink offerings to these false gods, as though they could eat and drink.

And then he went up to the temple, and he saw the same people come and make offerings to Jehovah, in His house, the house of God. Yet in their lives they were stealing and murdering and committing adultery, and swearing falsely, and burning incense to Baal, and walking after other gods. And then they came and stood in the house that was called by Jehovah's name, and said: "It is all right for us to do these things, because now we bring an offering, and Jehovah will receive us." So mixed was their worship that though they, and their princes and their kings, knew the name of Jehovah, and were even called by His name, and asked for His protection, yet they also worshiped the false gods, and lived and acted as the priests of those gods taught them. Even the priests of God's temple entered into this wickedness; and that is why the people who worshiped the false gods in the streets and on the high places could come and pretend to worship God in the temple.

Then Jeremiah stood in the gate of the Lord's house and cried: "Thus says Jehovah, the God of Israel, 'Mend your ways and your doings, and I will make you to dwell safely in this place. But you do not mend them. You lie and steal and commit murder and every evil thing, and then stand here and say, "We are innocent." Has this house, which is called by My name, become a den of thieves in your eyes? Go now to Shiloh, where the tabernacle was, and see what I have done to it. For the sons of Eli polluted the holy place, and I slew them, and destroyed it. That is what I will do to Jerusalem unless you change your hearts.' Oh," cried Jeremiah, "the heart of man is deceitful above all things, and desperately wicked; who can know it?"

Yet God would not leave His people. As Isaiah had declared the word of God, "I am Jehovah your God, your Saviour, your Redeemer, the Holy One of Israel," so Jeremiah declared: "Your Redeemer is strong; Jehovah of hosts is His name. He says to you, 'If you will thoroughly mend your ways, if you will show right judgment between a man and his neighbor, if you will not oppress the stranger and the widow and the orphan, if you will no longer shed innocent blood, if you will not walk after other gods to your hurt, then I will make you to dwell safely in this land which I have given to your fathers forever and ever. If you will diligently listen to Me, and will keep the Sabbath, the heart of My law, then there shall be peace in your land, and through the gates of this city shall go to and fro the kings and princes who sit upon the throne of David. And this city shall remain forever.' "

Moreover Jeremiah prophesied: "The days come, says the Lord, that I will raise up a Redeemer, a righteous Branch, a King who shall reign with judgment and justice. And in His days Judah shall be saved, and Israel shall dwell safely. And this is the name by which He shall be called, The Lord our Righteousness. And I will give you a heart to know Me; you shall be My people, and I will be your God."

But when the priests and the false prophets and the people who followed them heard the words of Jeremiah, they rose up against him and said, "You are fit to die, because you have prophesied against this place, and have said the Lord would do to it as He did to Shiloh."

But among the princes of Judah were some who still feared the Lord. They came up to the temple and delivered Jeremiah out of the hands of the priests and the false prophets. And Ahikam, one of the chief princes, took Jeremiah under his protection; so that for a while Jeremiah was safe from the wrath of the evildoers. Yet, because they turned against the word of the Lord, and rejected the heart that He offered to them, the loving heart of their Redeemer, the doom of Jerusalem was settled, and nothing could change it.

"There's a wideness in God's mercy,
    Like the wideness of the sea;
There's a kindness in His justice,
    Which is more than liberty.
For the love of God is broader
    Than the measure of man's mind,
And the heart of the Eternal
    Is most wonderfully kind."
                    Faber.

257

Rebels and Woes

2 Kings 35:1-7; 2 Chronicles 36:11-21; Jeremiah 25 to 28; 32 to 39;
Ezekiel 1:1, 2; Daniel 1:1, 2

GREAT was the mourning for King Josiah, slain in battle by Pharaoh-necho, king of Egypt. Jerusalem and all Judah mourned for him. Jeremiah lamented for him. All the musicians played sad music, and all the singers sang dirges. And well might they mourn; for Josiah had been the best king that Judah ever had. He loved the Lord, and glorified His name, and taught the people to worship Him. Now Josiah was dead, and all the land mourned.

The people looked over the sons of Josiah to choose from them a king. And they chose Jehoahaz (who was also called Shallum), and made him king. But Pharaoh-necho came to Jerusalem when Jehoahaz had reigned for only three months, and he said: "Here! These Jews have made you king, but you shall not be king. I will make your brother Eliakim king, but I will change his name to Jehoiakim, and he shall be subject to me." So Pharaoh-necho did, and Jehoiakim reigned for eleven years.

Jehoiakim would not listen to Jeremiah. He was not long the servant of Pharaoh-necho; for Nebuchadnezzar, the king of Babylon, defeated Pharaoh and drove him out. Then Nebuchadnezzar came to Jerusalem, and Jehoiakim became his servant. For three years he kept his oath to serve Nebuchadnezzar; but then he rebelled, and the king of Babylon besieged Jerusalem and took it. He put Jehoiakim in chains, intending to take him captive to Babylon. But he changed his mind, and when Jehoiakim promised to be good, he left him on the throne. However, Nebuchadnezzar carried away some of the people and especially some of the princes. Among these were four young men of whom we shall hear further: Daniel, Hananiah, Mishael, and Azariah.

Now Jeremiah counseled the king to remember his father Josiah, and to turn from his evil way and do justice. He counseled him also to keep his promise to be the servant of Nebuchadnezzar. Then, in the fourth year, the Lord told Jeremiah to write out the doom that He had made for Judah if it continued rebellious.

Books in those days were not like ours. Instead of having the leaves fastened at the back, to be turned page by page as we do, they were written on one long sheet and rolled on rollers at either end, as each page was read. Jeremiah had his helper, Baruch, write the book, and read it to the people at the temple. When the king heard of this, he commanded the book to be brought and read to him. But before the reader had gone very far, Jehoiakim reached out, took the book, slashed it with his penknife, and threw it on the coals of the fire before him. That is how he despised the word of God.

Nebuchadnezzar came again and besieged Jerusalem. Jehoiakim was slain, and in his place Nebuchadnezzar put his eighteen-year-old son, Jehoiachin. But Jehoiachin did no better than his father; and in three months Nebuchadnezzar sent a captain with soldiers and took him in chains to Babylon. At the same time the captain stripped the temple of its wealth, and carried it away. He also took many of the people. Among them was a young priest, Ezekiel, who later became a great prophet.

Then Nebuchadnezzar set up the youngest son of Josiah, Mattaniah, now twenty-one years old, and changed his name to Zedekiah. He was the last king of Judah. Weak and changeable, he sometimes listened to Jeremiah, but more often disobeyed and did him damage. By this time the state of the people had become very bad, and Jeremiah was made to suffer. He was thrown into prison and into the dungeon, deep, deep down. They lowered him into the dungeon with ropes. The bottom was deep in mire, and Jeremiah sank in it.

Now one of the servants of the king was an Ethiopian named Ebed-melech. When he heard what they had done to Jeremiah, he went to the king Zedekiah, and said: "These men have done evil in putting Jeremiah into the dungeon. He will die there of hunger; for they are not feeding him."

"Well," said the king, "take thirty men with you as a guard, and go lift Jeremiah out of the dungeon before he dies."

So Ebed-melech got some old rags and some ropes, and went to the dungeon and looked down at Jeremiah. "Put these rags under your armpits," he said, "and then these ropes, and we'll draw you up." So they drew Jeremiah out of the mire, and he stayed in the prison court.

Then Zedekiah sent secretly for Jeremiah, and asked him what to do. For the army of Nebuchadnezzar was all around the city, and about to take it. Jeremiah advised him to give himself up to Nebuchadnezzar, and he promised by the word of the Lord that if Zedekiah would do this, he should not be hurt. But the king listened to his own men and refused the counsel of Jeremiah.

The Prophet of Submission

Ezekiel 1 to 3; 9; 10

WHEN Nebuchadnezzar's captain took captive the young king Jehoiachin and ten thousand of his people, and took them all to Babylon, one of the captives was a young priest named Ezekiel. Like Daniel and his friends, Ezekiel had listened to Jeremiah, and believed all that he prophesied. Their parents, too, were believers in the word of the Lord; and though all Judah went astray, these faithful followers of God kept their faith and their actions pure.

The priests of the Lord in Israel entered upon their duties when they reached thirty years of age. Ezekiel was twenty-five years old when he was taken captive; and for five years he lived quietly among some of his people whom Nebuchadnezzar settled on the River Chebar in Chaldea. Then in his thirtieth year the Lord called him to be His prophet.

Like Isaiah before him, Ezekiel saw a vision of God upon His throne. If you read the two visions, in Isaiah 6 and Ezekiel 1, you will note some differences in what they saw of the glory of the Lord and of His throne. But that is no wonder, because the throne of God is so marvelous that probably no two persons will ever see it exactly the same. There was a third prophet, John, many hundreds of years later, who also saw God upon His throne. If you like, you may read his account in Revelation 4, and you will find some other differences.

The most marvelous thing about the throne of God is that it is a living throne. Mortal kings have made thrones out of wood and silver and gold and ivory and precious stones, so that they sparkled and gleamed in beauty; but the prophets tell that God's throne is a living creature or made of several living creatures, like nothing else on earth or in heaven. The prophets did their best to describe to us this glorious throne, and we may do our best to get some idea of it, but nothing can make us know its wondrous beauty until, please God, we see Him face to face upon His throne.

Ezekiel stood by the river, and saw in the visions of God a great whirlwind come out of the north. And the whirlwind was a fire rolling and folding within itself, and in the midst of it a brightness that shone with an intense light. And as he looked, he saw that brightness become four living creatures, or cherubim (cherubs), whose form was that of a man. Each of them, however, had four faces and four wings. Their legs were straight, and their feet like hoofs, and they sparkled like polished brass. Under their wings appeared their arms, and hands like the hands of a man. Their four faces were so different from anything the prophet had ever seen that all he could compare them to were these four faces: a man, a lion, an ox, and an eagle; but we may well believe that they were more beautiful than he or we could imagine. An eagle's face is keen, with a piercing eye. An ox's face is strong and patient. A lion's face is majestic. And a man's face is everything that the others are not.

Ezekiel also watched their wings. Doubtless those wings were not like anything ever seen elsewhere. When we speak of wings, we think of the wings of a bird, and they are beautiful. But then there are wings of airplanes, too, in many different forms. And there are wings on some seeds, like the seeds of the maple and the elm trees. And there are even wings on some houses. And all of them are different. So the wings of the angels and other heavenly creatures may be like nothing we have ever seen.

The wings of these creatures which made up the throne of God were used to cover them and to fly with. The cherubim could go straight up, and forward, and backward, and sidewise. Perhaps you have watched a hummingbird hovering before a flower dart up and forward and backward, and its wings go so fast you cannot see them except as a blur. I think that if Ezekiel had ever seen a hummingbird, he might have compared the cherubim to it. And the Spirit that filled them all made them act together, whatever the Spirit wished them to do and wherever He wished them to go.

These cherubim were part of the throne of God. But there were other parts too. By every one of them was a wheel, a wonderful wheel that gleamed like the yellow or gold of the precious stone called topaz. These wheels, too, were something alive, and they had eyes in all their spokes and their rims, eyes that sparkled like jewels. Wherever the cherubim went, the wheels went with them, and the prophet could only say that they looked like wheels within wheels. Perhaps you have seen neon lights that whirl and whirl around and within themselves, and they may give you some idea of the splendor of the throne.

Now above the heads of the cherubim and living wheels there was a firmament or platform, glittering like blue ice. And on it was the appearance of a throne. And upon the throne was the form as of a man, shining with a luster beyond anything upon earth. And there

261

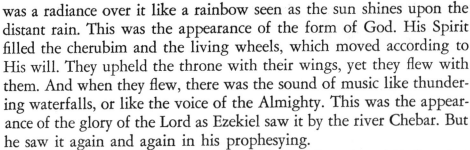

was a radiance over it like a rainbow seen as the sun shines upon the distant rain. This was the appearance of the form of God. His Spirit filled the cherubim and the living wheels, which moved according to His will. They upheld the throne with their wings, yet they flew with them. And when they flew, there was the sound of music like thundering waterfalls, or like the voice of the Almighty. This was the appearance of the glory of the Lord as Ezekiel saw it by the river Chebar. But he saw it again and again in his prophesying.

Then there came a voice from the throne, the voice of God, saying to Ezekiel: "Son of man, I am sending you to the children of Israel, who have rebelled against Me, and you shall tell them what I say. They will rebel against My words, but you are not to be dismayed. Whether they will heed or not, they shall hear, and they shall know that My prophet is among them."

Then the Spirit of the Lord lifted him up and carried him away in vision and set him down among the captive Jews in the land of Chaldea. It seemed to Ezekiel a hard mission he was given, and his spirit rose against it. But at the touch of God he quieted and submitted himself to the will of the Almighty. So he became the third of the great prophets of that time to speak forth the will of God to a rebellious people. And by his meekness and yet his firmness he was to show them how they too should submit to God.

———

O seer of God, across the dim and blackened page
    Where men have traced the record of their doubt-
        filled span,
Bright shines the glory of thy faith from age to age,
    To fire the spirit of the fear-beleaguered man.

Wondering, I trace the splendor of thy visions rare,
    Wherein the glories of thy God thou didst behold;
Yet with a deeper thrill I guide mine eye to where
    The pen of God thy humble sufferings doth unfold.

And in mine hour of anguish, when I would despair,
    May I remember, and in fellowship with thee,
Before my God be able, answering to my prayer,
    To write the word, "I did as He commanded me."

Can This People Live?

2 Chronicles 36:14-16; Ezekiel 8; 11; 14; 18; 20; 29:17; 36; 37:1-14

FOR SEVENTEEN years after Ezekiel began to prophesy, the kingdom of Judah still stood. Jeremiah in Jerusalem was prophesying against their wickedness, while Ezekiel was prophesying both to the captives in Chaldea and to the people in Judah. He sent messages to these distant relatives; for he never returned to the land of Judah except in vision. After Jerusalem was taken and the last king and all the people carried captive, Ezekiel kept on prophesying to his people for at least ten years, or twenty-seven years in all, and perhaps more.

As Ezekiel sat in his house one day, the hand of the Lord fell upon him and took him in vision to Jerusalem. There he saw in the temple area altars set up to heathen gods. They were not in the temple itself; for the wicked worshipers dared not enter that place where God dwelt; but they made rooms in the buildings around the courts; and on the walls of those rooms they painted pictures of men and beasts and creeping things, all representing the false gods.

And in those rooms Ezekiel saw seventy men of the elders of Judah, leaders of the people, burning incense and worshiping the false gods. In another place he saw women "weeping for Tammuz." This Tammuz was a Babylonian god who, like Jezebel's Baal, represented the sun, and the weeping was a part of the worship. For when in the winter the day is shortened, and the sun is out of sight for so long a time, they pretended that the sun god had been slain, and they went about weeping and wailing and gashing themselves with knives.

Ezekiel was then shown another scene of sun worship. At the very door of the temple he saw twenty-five men with their backs turned to the temple of God, and looking to the east where the sun was rising, they worshiped the sun.

Then God said to Ezekiel: "Have you seen this, O son of man? The men of Judah turn their backs upon Me and worship false gods. And they go out and fill the land with crime. They have turned away from Me, and I will turn away from them. When they cry in their trouble, I cannot hear, because the gods they have chosen are not Me."

"Ah, Lord God!" cried Ezekiel, "they say to me, 'He is just telling stories.'"

Then in a vision the hand of the Lord picked up Ezekiel, and set him down in a valley which was filled with dead men's bones, dry bones, scattered and gleaming white.

"Can these bones live?" the Lord asked him.

What! Old dry bones of men long dead, could they become men again, with flesh and skin, and life blood flowing through their veins? Could these bones live? Ezekiel knew that God could do anything, and he answered, "Ah, Lord God, You know!"

Then the Lord said: "Prophesy, Ezekiel, prophesy to these bones, and say, 'I the Lord will cause breath to come into you, and you shall live.'"

So Ezekiel prophesied as he was told. And suddenly there was a rustling and a rattle, and a sound of moving. And as he looked, the bones came together, right bone to the right bone, till they made the skeletons of men, thousands of men; and then, as he watched, there came flesh upon the bones, and skin, and upon their shoulders heads, with eyes and ears and mouths. But there was no life in them.

Then the Lord said to Ezekiel, "Prophesy, O son of man, prophesy! Call to the four winds, 'Come, O breath, and breathe into these slain men, that they may live.'"

Ezekiel prophesied and called to the four winds. And breath came into the men, and they lived, and stood upon their feet, an exceeding great host.

Then said the Lord: "O son of man, these bones are the people of Israel. They keep saying, 'Our bones are dried up. Our hope is lost. We are cut off!' But say to them, 'I the Lord will open your graves, and cause your dry bones to live, and I will place you again in your own land. And then you shall know that I am the Lord, the God of Israel.'"

Such was the mercy and such was the love of God, the God of Israel, the God of all the earth, the God of the heavens above, who would take His sinful children and cleanse them and make them to live again in Him.

"Have I any pleasure at all that the wicked should die? saith the Lord God; and not that he should return from his ways, and live? . . . Therefore I will judge you, O house of Israel, every one according to his ways, saith the Lord God. Repent, and turn yourselves from all your transgressions; so iniquity shall not be your ruin. . . . Make you a new heart and a new spirit; for why will ye die, O house of Israel?"

The End of the Road

2 Kings 25:1-26; 2 Chronicles 36:11-21; Jeremiah
39 to 43; 52; Ezekiel 21:1-27

IT CAME to pass, as the prophets foretold, even Jeremiah and
Ezekiel, that because of the evil which the children of Judah did
and because of the wickedness of their kings, the mercy of the Lord
was withheld, and Judah came to the end of the road.

In the ninth year of Zedekiah the army of Nebuchadnezzar came
and besieged Jerusalem. For two years they besieged it, while the
famine grew in the city, and many were slain, and many died of
hunger. In the eleventh year of Zedekiah they could no longer resist.
The Chaldeans broke through the city walls and poured in, slaughtering and taking captive the people of Jerusalem.

Zedekiah with a few men fled through a secret gate, and escaped
as far as the plains of Jordan by Jericho. But there the Chaldeans
caught up with him. They scattered his men, and they took Zedekiah
captive and led him before Nebuchadnezzar. Nebuchadnezzar slew his
sons before his eyes, and that was the last thing that Zedekiah ever
saw. For Nebuchadnezzar put out his eyes and sent him to Babylon,
where he was put in prison, and stayed there till he died.

Nebuchadnezzar sent his captain, Nebuzar-adan, back to Jerusalem. His men broke down all the city walls and burned the king's
houses and every great man's house. Most terrible of all, they burned
the beautiful temple which Solomon had built. They broke down its
walls of stone and smashed them to pieces. They took all the gold that
had covered the walls and the holy things in the temple, and all the
brass that had made the laver and the altar of sacrifice in the court,
and all the vessels and instruments of gold and silver and brass, and
carried them away to Babylon.

But the sacred ark, with the tables of the law within it, they
never found. For before the city was taken, some of the devout priests,
with Jeremiah leading them, took the ark and hid it in a secret cave,
and there no doubt it is to this day, but no man knows where.

Away to the land of captivity, where their brethren had gone
before, the wretched remnant of the people were led. But Nebuchadnezzar left in the land some of the poor people and a few of the

king's family, that is, his daughters, and some of the lesser princes. Nebuchadnezzar put over these, and over the whole land, a man named Gedaliah. And he gave special orders to Nebuzar-adan that he should spare Jeremiah and treat him well and let him go wherever he wished.

So Nebuzar-adan sent to the prison where Jeremiah was kept and brought him out and said, "Go to Gedaliah, whom Nebuchadnezzar has set over the land and the people, and dwell with him. Or go anywhere you wish." What do you think Jeremiah chose to do? He chose to stay with the remnant of the people whom he had warned and for whom he had labored. So Nebuzar-adan gave him provisions and a reward and let him go.

There were Jews scattered around in the land and in the little nations nearby, Jews who had at one time or another escaped from the city or who had never gone into it. And when they heard that Gedaliah was made governor, they came to him at Mizpah, where he set up his headquarters. But one wicked man, named Ishmael, came with ten men and killed Gedaliah and many of his people, and took the rest who were there captive, and started with them to the land of the Ammonites. Then another captain, Johanan, overtook him and delivered the people, but Ishmael escaped to the king of Ammon.

Then Johanan and all the captains and the people with them were afraid that Nebuchadnezzar would kill them, because his governor, Gedaliah, had been slain. So they proposed to go down into Egypt. They came and asked Jeremiah to pray to the Lord for guidance, and they swore they would do what He said. But when the Lord through His prophet told them not to go down into Egypt, they said to Jeremiah, "You are telling lies. The Lord our God has not told you to say to us, 'Don't go down into Egypt.' But Baruch your helper sets you on against us, to deliver us into the hand of the Chaldeans, who will carry us to Babylon."

So to the very last they disobeyed the word of the Lord. The captains took all the people, men, women, and children, and they took Jeremiah, and carried them all into Egypt. But there they did not find the peace they sought; for Nebuchadnezzar carried the war into Egypt. And many of those who fled there were slain, and many more forgot God and worshiped the Egyptian gods. So they were lost to Israel and to God.

Jeremiah continued to prophesy to them, but they rejected his counsel. There at last in Egypt, Jeremiah died, a prophet of the Lord whose heart his people broke, as long afterward they broke the heart of their Redeemer, the Holy One of Israel.

266

Messiah's Kingdom

Ezekiel 40 to 48

THE VISION of the valley of dry bones encouraged Ezekiel. He thought: "Though the land of Israel and Judah is lost, and our city is taken and our temple destroyed, and we are captives in a strange land because of our sins, yet the Lord will save us, and revive us, and restore us, as He did the dry bones." He knew that could be only if the people turned with all their hearts to God as they never yet had done. But he saw some of those who were in captivity devoting themselves to the Lord in just that way. There were those four young men in Babylon who kept the law of God. And one of them was Daniel, already noted for his faith and courage and wisdom. So Ezekiel hoped the most of the people would be like Daniel. But he told them: "Though Noah, Daniel, and Job were in the land, they shall deliver neither son nor daughter; they shall but deliver their own souls by their righteousness."

So now Ezekiel's thoughts turned to the coming redemption. The Lord would be their Saviour, their Redeemer, their Messiah. And He would establish His kingdom of righteousness, and none should enter it but the righteous. As Ezekiel thought upon it, the Lord gave him a vision, a long vision, of what that kingdom would be like if His people should turn to Him.

In his vision the Lord took him again to Jerusalem. The city lay in ruins; but that was not what Ezekiel saw in his vision. He saw a new Jerusalem. And there was a man, an angel, who shone like brightest bronze, measuring it. And within the city was a new temple, and the man went on measuring every part of it, as the seer saw. "Note everything you see and hear," said the man to Ezekiel; "then go and tell it to the house of Israel."

They went through all the buildings around the courts, and through all the courts, and into the holy place of the temple, and into the most holy. All was in readiness for the coming of the King, the Messiah of God.

They went outside, and stood by the eastern gate. And as Ezekiel watched, lo, the glory of the God of Israel came from the east! The sound of His coming was like the sound of many waterfalls or like the booming of the ocean; and the earth shone with His glory. It was, Ezekiel saw, the same throne and the same glory and the same God that he had seen at the first by the river Chebar. And the glory of the Lord entered the house by the east gate. Messiah was come!

Then the Spirit lifted him up and took him into the inner court. And the glory of God filled the house. Then, as the man with the measuring rod stood by him, he heard the voice of God speaking to him from out the house, which said: "O son of man, this is the place of My throne, where I will dwell in the midst of the people of Israel. They shall nevermore defile My temple, but they shall be My people, and I will be their God. Go, show all this to the house of Israel."

Then the man took Ezekiel out of the temple, and they stood by the wall at the front. And lo, there came out waters from under the wall, and flowed through the court. So the man brought Ezekiel outside the court, to the outer wall. And there he saw the waters come out, just a little stream. The man with the measuring rod measured a thousand cubits down the stream and made the prophet wade across. The waters came up to his ankles. The man measured another thousand cubits downstream, and Ezekiel waded across. The waters came up to his knees. Another thousand, and the waters came up to his waist. Still another thousand downstream, and Ezekiel could not cross, for the waters were deep enough to swim in.

Then the angel and Ezekiel went down on the bank of the river, which was growing ever larger. And on either bank there were many fruit trees, whose leaves never faded nor fruit failed. For they bore fresh fruit every month, and their fruit was for food and their leaves for healing.

"Now," said the Lord, "I will show you the land which shall be divided among the twelve tribes of Israel. It is a larger land than Israel ever had, and it shall be divided equally among the tribes. Each one shall have a strip across, from east to west; and this is the order they shall be in: at the north, a portion for Dan. Next toward the south comes Asher, then Naphtali, then Manasseh, then Ephraim, then Reuben, then Judah.

"Now there is set apart, from east to west, a portion for the Lord" (who is the Prince, the King, the Lord's Anointed, the Messiah). "A part of the Prince's portion shall be given to the tribe of Levi, and a part to the priests. But the City of the Prince, and the sanctuary, the temple, shall be in the middle of the portion. And this is the capital of the land, the New Jerusalem. And they who work and serve in the City [that is, the priests] shall come out of all the tribes of Israel.

"Then on the south side of the King's portion, the remaining tribes shall have their portions: Benjamin first, then Simeon, then Issachar, then Zebulun, then Gad at the far south."

Ezekiel now was given a closer view of the City. The man with the measuring line went about it and measured it. He showed that the City was foursquare, each side the same length. There were twelve gates, three on each side, for the twelve tribes of people to enter through. They were placed most conveniently for the tribes, according to whether they were in the north or in the south. On the north side were the gates of Reuben, Judah, and Levi. On the west side were the gates of Gad, Asher, and Naphtali. On the south side were the gates of Simeon, Issachar, and Zebulun. And on the east side were the gates of Joseph, Benjamin, and Dan. Long afterward Dan was left out of the tribes of Israel (Revelation 7:4-6) because of his selfishness and idolatry. But his place was filled by one of Joseph's sons.

When God first made the earth, the river of life that ran out of the Garden of Eden was parted into four heads and went everywhere watering the earth. In Ezekiel's vision the river ran into the desert and the sea and healed them. Perhaps God meant it to be that way at first, and then afterwards to have it become as it was in Eden.

This was the kingdom that God planned for Israel, if they should turn and worship Him with all their hearts. Both Jeremiah and Ezekiel promised that if they would, then God would make a new covenant with them, writing the law on their hearts. So the law would be within them, and everything they did would be in accordance with it. And then, as Jeremiah prophesied, if they would keep in their hearts the Sabbath, which is the very center of the law of God, the kingdom of God would be theirs, and Jerusalem would stand forever. Then the kingdom would grow, as the river of life grew and healed the desert and the sea. And finally the kingdom would fill all the earth, with the wicked destroyed, and none but the righteous would live in it.

This was the vision of Ezekiel, this was the vision of God: that the people of Israel, the Jews, would become like Daniel and Ezekiel and Jeremiah and Isaiah and David and Moses and Abraham. And they would take in the Gentiles who would come to the light of their salvation, and these would become members of their tribes. All this depended on Israel's turning to God with all their hearts.

If only they had! If only they had! But the story goes on, beyond the Old Testament, into the New Testament, and on to the end of time and the glorious coming of Messiah, the Christ, the second time, when the kingdom of God shall fill all the earth.

The Prophet of Vision

Daniel 1

AMONG the captives who were carried away from Jerusalem by Nebuchadnezzar in the third year of the reign of Jehoiakim king of Judah were four young men, princes, whose parents had heeded the words of Jeremiah, and who had therefore been brought up to love the Lord God of Israel.

Nebuchadnezzar, king of Babylon, was on the lookout for bright young men, healthy and quick of mind, understanding science, and of good bearing. He wanted to teach them the language and the learning of the Chaldeans, so that when they were through with their schooling, he might enroll them among his wise men and counselors.

So he told Ashpenaz, the master of his household, to select from among the children of Judah, and especially from the royal family, such young men. They must be perfect in form and health, and they must be intelligent and keen. So Ashpenaz did as the king commanded. And among those whom he chose were these four: Daniel, Hananiah, Mishael, and Azariah.

About the first thing Ashpenaz did was to change their names. He said to Daniel: "Now you are starting a new career. You are not a Jew any more; you are a Chaldean. So your name shall not be Daniel [God is my judge], but Belteshazzar [prince of Bel]."

And to Hananiah he said, "Your name is Shadrach." And to Mishael, "Your name is Meshach." And to Azariah, "Your name is Abed-nego." These three thereafter went by their Chaldean names; but the first and chief of them is almost always called by his Hebrew name, Daniel.

Ashpenaz took a great liking to Daniel and would do almost anything for him that he could. But when Daniel came and asked for a change of diet for him and his three friends, because the meat and the wine given them not only were too rich but also had been offered to heathen gods for their blessing, why, Ashpenaz said: "But this is the same food that the king eats and the same wine that he drinks. It is a special favor to you to have it on the table. And if I should take it away from you, I'm afraid my lord the king, seeing you looking more pale and thin than the other students, would take my head off."

So Daniel said no more to Ashpenaz; but he said to the steward who set their food before them, "Please try us, Melzar, for ten days. Let us have just vegetables to eat and water to drink. And then compare us with the other students, and do as you see fit."

The steward also had a great liking for Daniel, and he tried the four of them on the vegetarian diet for ten days. At the end of that time they four looked better than the youths who had been eating the king's food and drinking his wine. So Melzar removed the meat and the wine, and gave them vegetables for a regular diet.

All the young men studied in the king's school for three years, and then they had their examination. And who do you suppose examined them? Nebuchadnezzar himself. He questioned them this and he questioned them that; he tried them here and he tried them there. And in every matter he found these four young men better educated than all the rest of the students, and even better than all his wise men, magicians, and enchanters. So he took them on at once as his attendants.

And Daniel, their leader, had understanding of all visions and dreams; so he became, in later years, the great prophet of vision.

Dream of Nebuchadnezzar

Daniel 2

ONE NIGHT God gave to Nebuchadnezzar the king a dream. Now there are dreams that are just dreams, which don't mean anything. But the dreams that God gives have a meaning. And by dreams He has often told the prophets what to say. And by dreams He has sometimes instructed kings, like the dreams of Pharaoh that Joseph interpreted, and this dream of Nebuchadnezzar.

In the morning Nebuchadnezzar was very sure he had dreamed a dream which was very important; but strange to say, he could not remember what the dream was. "Well," he thought, "I have wise men, magicians, and enchanters, who ought to know. They have often told me what they say is meant by the dreams I tell them. Now if they can tell the hidden meaning of a dream, they surely can tell the hidden dream."

So he called the wise men, the magicians, the enchanters, the sorcerers, and the teachers, and he said to them: "I have dreamed a dream, and my spirit was troubled to know the dream."

"O king, live forever!" they said. "Tell us the dream, and we will tell you what it means."

"That's just the trouble," said the king. "I can't remember the dream. Now tell me the dream, and I shall know that you can tell its meaning."

"O king," answered the wise men, "there's not a man on earth who can tell you what you dreamed if you can't tell the dream yourself. And no king ever asked any such thing of any of his wise men. No one can tell you the dream but the gods, who do not live with men."

Then King Nebuchadnezzar was very angry. He was a great king, with a big brain and great ability; but he had never learned to control his temper. Really he had a right to be angry at these men; for, as he said to them: "The gods! The gods! Haven't you said that the gods told you the meaning of dreams? If you know such secret things as the meaning of dreams, you must be able to know the secret dream. You have prepared lies to tell me all these years."

Then he showed what a heathen king would do to any who

The Fiery Furnace

Nebuchadnezzar's threat to have the three Hebrews thrown into the furnace did not force them to obey him. They told him that they must be true to God, and that they believed that He would deliver them. They knew that if they bowed to the image, the people would think that they were worshiping it.

ROBERT TEMPLE AYRES, ARTIST

crossed him. He said to them: "If you can tell me the dream, I'll give you great rewards and riches. But if you will not tell me the dream, then you shall be cut in pieces, and your houses shall be knocked down into a rubbish heap."

He shouted for Arioch, the captain of his guard. "Arioch," he said, "go out and slay all the wise men!"

Now the word came to Daniel, and he met Arioch and said, "Why is the king's commandment so hasty?"

"Because the king has dreamed a dream," said Arioch, "a dream he cannot remember. He asked the wise men to tell him what it was, and they couldn't. So the king was furious and commanded me to slay the wise men. I'm sorry, Daniel, but you're one of them."

"Wait a bit," said Daniel. "Let me see the king."

So Daniel went in before Nebuchadnezzar and said, "O king, I pray you give me time, and I will tell you both the dream and its interpretation."

Nebuchadnezzar was calmed down now. He had great respect for Daniel, and he said, "Go in peace. And when you have the answer, come and see me."

Daniel went to his house. He called his friends, Hananiah, Mishael, and Azariah, and told them all. They prayed to the Lord to give them the answer. No doubt they remembered Joseph, and how God gave him the meaning of Pharaoh's dream. Now here was a harder test; for Nebuchadnezzar did not even know what his dream was. So they prayed for the Lord to show His power and save them and magnify His name.

Then in a vision of the night the Lord told Daniel the dream and its meaning. And Daniel thanked the Lord: "I thank Thee, and praise Thee, O Thou God of my fathers, who hast given me wisdom and might, and hast made known unto me now what we desired of Thee: for Thou hast now made known unto us the king's matter."

So in the morning Daniel went to Arioch and said, "Do not slay the wise men of Babylon. Take me in before the king, and I will give him the dream and the interpretation."

Arioch brought Daniel in to the king and said, as though he had done it all: "I have found a man of the captives from Judah who will make known to the king what he wishes to know."

Then the king said to Daniel, "Are you able to make known to me the dream, and tell me what it means?"

Said Daniel: "The secret which the king wanted to know, the wise men of Babylon could not tell him. But there is a God in heaven

who reveals secrets, and He has shown me what it is. It is not in me, O king, because of any special wisdom I have, but God does it, to save the innocent and to satisfy the king. When you went to bed, O king, you kept thinking and wondering what was going to come to pass in the future. And God answered you in the dream and told you what to expect in the future.

"This is the dream that you dreamed. You saw a great image, exceedingly bright. Its head was made of gold, its arms and breast of silver, its waist and hips of brass, and its legs of iron, and the feet were partly of iron and partly of clay. You watched until a stone was cut out without anyone touching it, and it struck the image on the feet. Then the whole image, gold and silver and brass and iron and clay, crumbled to pieces, and became like the chaff of the summer threshing floor. And the wind carried them away, till no trace of them could be found. But the stone became a great mountain and filled the whole earth."

"That's it! That's it! That's the dream!" exclaimed the delighted king. "Now what does it mean?"

"This is the interpretation," went on the youthful prophet. "You, O king, are a king of kings; for the God of heaven has given you the kingdom, with power and glory. You are this head of gold.

"But after you there shall arise another kingdom, not so great; and that is the silver part. Then there shall be a third kingdom, worth still less; and that is the brass part.

"Then the fourth kingdom shall be strong as iron. And as iron breaks in pieces every other thing, so shall this kingdom do. But as you saw the toes to be iron mixed with clay, in the end this kingdom shall be partly strong and partly weak.

"Then the God of heaven will set up a kingdom, which shall never be destroyed. That is the stone you saw. It shall break in pieces all the kingdoms, and it shall stand forever. Now the great God has made known to Nebuchadnezzar what shall come to pass hereafter. The dream is true, and the interpretation is sure."

Then King Nebuchadnezzar stepped down from his throne and fell on his face before Daniel. He said, "True it is that your God is a God of gods and a Lord of kings and a revealer of secrets, seeing that you have been able to tell this dream and its interpretation."

Then he set Daniel at the head of all the wise men of Babylon. And when Daniel asked him to, he set his three friends over all the affairs of the province of Babylon. But Daniel remained in the king's council.

The Fiery Furnace

Daniel 3

NEBUCHADNEZZAR said: "I'll make a great image, like the one I saw in my dream. But I'll make it all of gold. Daniel said I was the head of gold. I'll make whatever comes after me to be gold, and that will mean my kingdom will last forever."

So he made a golden image ninety feet high and nine feet thick. Then he brought together a great company—princes and governors and captains and judges and treasurers and counselors and heads of the provinces, to dedicate his great image. And they stood before the image which Nebuchadnezzar had set up.

Then a herald cried aloud: "O you people! When the band plays, all of you fall down and worship the golden image which Nebuchadnezzar has set up. If any man fails to fall down and worship, he shall be cast into a burning fiery furnace."

So the band played, and the trumpets blew, and everybody fell down and worshiped the golden image. Everybody, that is, but Hananiah, Mishael, and Azariah, whom the king and his people called Shadrach, Meshach, and Abed-nego. They would not worship the image of Nebuchadnezzar, nor seem to deny the prophecy that God had made through their friend and leader, Daniel.

Then some Chaldeans came to the king, and they said: "Do you know there are certain Jews whom you have set over the province of Babylon, the most important province in your kingdom, namely, Shadrach, Meshach, and Abed-nego. These men pay no attention to what you command. They do not serve your gods, and they have not bowed down to the golden image which you have set up."

Nebuchadnezzar fell into a rage. "Bring them here!" he commanded. And when the three Hebrew youth were brought before him, he said, "Is it true, Shadrach, Meshach, and Abed-nego, that you do not serve my gods, nor worship the golden image I have set up? Now I will give you one more chance. The band will play again and the trumpets will blow, and if this time you bow down and worship, I will forgive you. But if not, you shall be cast into a burning fiery furnace. And what god can deliver you out of my hand?"

Shadrach, Meshach, and Abed-nego answered the king: "Our

God whom we serve is able to deliver us. But even if He does not, be sure, O king, that we will not serve your gods, nor worship your golden image."

Then Nebuchadnezzar was filled with fury. He commanded the furnace to be heated seven times hotter, if that could be, the hottest that was possible. And when it was ready, he had his soldiers bind the three young men with ropes, carry them to the mouth of the furnace, and throw them in.

His soldiers obeyed. They bound Shadrach, Meshach, and Abed-nego, carried them to the mouth of the furnace, and threw them in. But so hot were the flames that they killed the soldiers who did it.

Then into the midst of the burning fiery furnace fell Shadrach, Meshach, and Abed-nego. "That's the end," said Nebuchadnezzar. "I showed them!" And he looked at the blazing fire with satisfaction.

But suddenly he rose in panic. "Here! Here!" he cried to his courtiers. "Look! Didn't we cast three men bound into that furnace?"

"We certainly did, O king," they answered.

"But I see four men loose, walking around in it," said Nebuchadnezzar. "And the form of the fourth is like one of the gods!" His face, in spite of the fire, was as white as a sheet.

He went as near to the mouth of the furnace as he could, and he cried aloud: "Shadrach! Meshach! Abed-nego! Servants of the Most High God! Come out, and come here!"

Then Shadrach, Meshach, and Abed-nego came out of the fiery furnace, and stood before the king. Around him were all the princes and governors and captains and judges and sheriffs, the rulers of the provinces and the wise men of Babylon. They looked and they looked. Then they went near and touched the young men's clothes. They were not burned; only the ropes had been burned off. They smelled of them, but there was no smell of burning. They touched their skin; it was smooth and moist. They touched their hair; it was not singed.

Then Nebuchadnezzar spoke and said: "Blessed be the God of Shadrach, Meshach, and Abed-nego! Their God has sent His angel to deliver His servants who trusted in Him, giving themselves up to the fiery furnace rather than worship any other god!

"And now," said Nebuchadnezzar, "I make a decree that anyone who speaks a word against the God of Shadrach, Meshach, and Abed-nego shall be cut in pieces, and their houses shall be made a heap. For there is no other God who can deliver in such a way."

Then Nebuchadnezzar promoted Shadrach, Meshach, and Abed-nego, and made them higher than any others in Babylon.

Nebuchadnezzar Is Humbled

Daniel 4

NEBUCHADNEZZAR was a great warrior. He had conquered many kingdoms and peoples. He had slain his thousands and his tens of thousands. Sometimes he was cruel, as were all the heathen kings. But Nebuchadnezzar was more than a warrior. He was a great builder.

Babylon was a wonderful city. It was about fifteen miles square, and it had three walls around it, one inside the other. The outer wall was so broad that a chariot drawn by four horses could turn around on the top. The River Euphrates flowed through it, and on either side of the river there were walls with gates which could be shut, if ever any enemy should get in on the river. And he built great and beautiful palaces in the city and was very proud.

But God saw much good in Nebuchadnezzar, and He wanted to make that good better. To do this He had to humble him. He sent to him His servants, Daniel and his three friends; and Nebuchadnezzar listened to them sometimes. But then he would go back to his pride. This is the way God humbled him.

Nebuchadnezzar dreamed another dream. This time it was not of a great image of a man. He dreamed that he saw a great high tree. It grew and was strong, until it seemed to reach to heaven. The leaves were fair and the fruit much, so that all the birds and beasts of earth came and rested in it or under it and fed from it.

But Nebuchadnezzar dreamed that a Watcher, a Holy One, came down from heaven and cried: "Cut down that tree, cut off its branches, shake off its leaves, scatter its fruit. Let all the beasts and the birds get away from it. But leave the stump, with a band of iron and brass about it. Let it be drenched with the dew, and share with the beasts the grass of the field. Let his mind be changed from a man's to the mind of a beast, until seven years pass over him, until he knows that the Most High rules in the kingdoms of men, and gives them to whomever He will."

No wonder this dream alarmed Nebuchadnezzar; for in the midst of it the Watcher stopped talking about it as though it were a tree, and spoke of it as though it were a man. What did it mean? He called in his wise men again, and this time he told them the dream. But even then they could not give the meaning. At last he called in Daniel and told the dream to him.

Daniel saw at once what it meant; for God told him. And it was such woeful news for Nebuchadnezzar that Daniel felt stunned and said nothing. At last the king urged him, and he said:

"O King Nebuchadnezzar, may the dream and its interpretation be for your enemies. But this is what it means. The tree is you, who have grown so great and your pride so high that God now must humble you. There is a decision of God against you, that you shall lose your mind and think you are a beast. And you shall go out and live in the field, and be drenched with the evening dews, and eat grass like an ox, until seven years pass over you, and until you know that the Most High rules in the kingdoms of men and gives them to whomever He will.

"Now, O king, take my advice. Break off your sins by showing mercy to the poor. Then perhaps your prosperity may be lengthened."

Nebuchadnezzar listened, and he felt humble, a little. But it did not last long. At the end of twelve months, he was walking one evening on the flat roof of his palace, and he said to himself: "Is not this great Babylon, which I have built as a royal home and for my glorious majesty?"

Immediately a voice fell from heaven: "O King Nebuchadnezzar, judgment is passed upon you! Your kingdom is gone. You shall be driven from among men, and live with the beasts in the field, and eat grass like an ox, until seven years pass over you, until you learn that the Most High rules in the kingdom of men, giving it to whomever He will."

And that was what was done. Nebuchadnezzar lost his mind. He thought he was a beast. They let him go out into the field and eat grass. His hair grew as long as an eagle's feathers, and his nails were like the claws of a bird. Year after year went by, till seven years were gone. Then, suddenly, Nebuchadnezzar's senses came back to him. He woke up, and he said, "Truly the Most High rules in the kingdom of men. Not I, but God!"

So then he came back to his palace. His ministers and his lords came in to consult with him. They put him on the throne again, and he was Nebuchadnezzar once more. But oh, how changed!

He sent out a proclamation to all in his kingdom, praising and honoring the King of heaven, saying: "For all His works are right, and His ways just. And those who walk in pride He is able to abase."

The Feast of Death

Daniel 5

WHEN Nebuchadnezzar died, his son Nabonidus sat on the throne. He is not mentioned in the Bible, but his son Belshazzar, Nebuchadnezzar's grandson, is. At this time Nebuchadnezzar's empire had become very weak, and another nation, or really two nations together, had begun to conquer it. These nations were the Medes and the Persians, and they are usually called the Medo-Persian kingdom or empire. Their king was Cyrus. He conquered Nabonidus in the field, and took him captive.

But Nabonidus had made his son, Belshazzar, to reign alongside him. And Belshazzar shut himself up in the great city, Babylon, with his soldiers and people, and he thought that Cyrus could never take the city. Nebuchadnezzar had made it so strong with its great walls that nothing known in those days could enter its gates or knock down its walls, when defended by an army within.

There came a day and a night when Belshazzar, in honor of his gods, made a great feast for a thousand of his lords. And he and his lords and women drank wine so heavily that they were drunk. In the midst of the feast the drunken Belshazzar ordered the holy vessels of silver and gold, which Nebuchadnezzar had taken from the temple at Jerusalem, to be brought in. And they drank wine from them, and praised their gods of gold and silver and brass and iron and wood and stone. For they said their idol gods had conquered the God of the Jews, and now they would use the holy vessels of Jehovah as cups for the wine they drank to the praise of their gods.

Loud rang the shouts and the boasts and the drunken laughter of those thousand lords and thousand ladies in the palace of King Belshazzar. But suddenly every voice was hushed, every eye was strained, every hand that lifted the goblets of wine shook. For on the palace wall there appeared a hand of fire, writing, writing, tracing the words of an awful doom! Silently, silently, but in blazing light, it wrote. No man's hand was it, but the hand of an unseen God. Not a god of gold or of silver or of graven stone, but a God unseen and un-seeable, the only true God, whose holy vessels were being polluted in that hour of riot. The tumult died, and the drunken cries ceased.

279

Behold! the hand disappeared; but there, written in letters of fire, were four fateful words, gleaming on the wall:

MENE, MENE, TEKEL, UPHARSIN.

What did they mean? None knew. The revelers gazed in terror at the blazing line. Though the hand was gone, the writing did not fade away, but gleamed with an unearthly light:

MENE, MENE, TEKEL, UPHARSIN.

"Call the wise men!" at last croaked the frightened Belshazzar. "Call the astrologers, the Chaldeans, the soothsayers. Quick! Quick! The wise men!"

The wise men of Babylon came in. "Read me that writing," cried the king. "Tell me its meaning."

But the wise men could not read it. The words were Chaldean, yet they were hidden to them. Perhaps they were written in Hebrew letters, perhaps in the ancient letters of the law of God given on Sinai. Perhaps they were written in letters that only God knew. However that was, the wise men of Babylon could not read the words. And the terror sank ever deeper and deeper in that once drunken but now sobered throng.

MENE, MENE, TEKEL, UPHARSIN.

Belshazzar trembled and shook; the joints of his bones were loosened, and his knees shook together. He trembled with a dreadful chill, the chill of death and doom.

Then came in the queen mother. Perhaps she was the queen of Nebuchadnezzar, and Belshazzar's grandmother; perhaps she was the queen of Nabonidus, and Belshazzar's own mother. And she said to the king: "Do not be terrified. There is a man in your kingdom who in the days of Nebuchadnezzar showed wisdom like the wisdom of the gods; and your grandfather made him head of all the wise men of Babylon. He could interpret any dream, and make known any hidden meaning. His name is Daniel."

"Go!" cried Belshazzar to his servants. "Go and call this Daniel."

Then Daniel was brought in before the king, who said to him: "Are you that Daniel, of the captivity of Judah, whom my father Nebuchadnezzar brought out of Jewry? I have heard of you, that the spirit of the gods is in you, making you wise above all wise men. I have heard that you can make interpretations and settle doubts. See yonder writing of fire on the wall! My wise men cannot read it or interpret it.

If you will read that writing and tell me its meaning, I will make you the third ruler in the kingdom and clothe you with scarlet, and put a chain of gold about your neck."

Then said Daniel to the king: "Let your gifts be to yourself, and give your rewards to another. Yet I will read the writing, and give the interpretation. O king, the Most High God gave to Nebuchadnezzar your father power over nations and peoples and languages; and none is so great as He. But when his heart was lifted up in pride, he was cast down from his throne and made to eat grass. And you, Belshazzar, though you knew all this, have not humbled your heart. You have lifted up yourself against the God of heaven, and have brought the holy vessels of His temple before you; and you, your lords, and their women have drunk wine from them, praising your idol gods, which can neither see nor hear nor know. And you have not glorified the God of heaven, in whose hand is your breath.

"Then was this hand sent from Him, and this writing was written. This is the writing, and this is what it means:

MENE, MENE, TEKEL, UPHARSIN.

"MENE: God has numbered your kingdom, and finished it.
"TEKEL: You are weighed in the balances, and found wanting.
"PERES [another word for UPHARSIN]: Your kingdom is divided, and given to the Medes and Persians."

Then the king commanded, and they robed Daniel with the royal robe, and put the chain of gold about his neck, and proclaimed him the third ruler in the kingdom. That meant that he was next after Belshazzar, for Belshazzar was second. His father, Nabonidus, out with the army on the land, had been the king, the first. But he had surrendered; and now that Belshazzar was about to go, Daniel would really be the first in the falling kingdom.

The banquet hall was hushed, waiting the stroke of doom. Outside there rose the shouts of the conquering host and the cries of the conquered. The Medes and the Persians rushed in; and King Belshazzar with his lords, vainly fighting, was slain.

But towering above them all stood the figure of the Hebrew prophet, clothed indeed with the royal robe and signs, but majestic rather in the power of his righteousness and the light of his eye, the only sober man in the great festive hall. The power of God preserved him among the fighting men. Soon word of his office as spokesman for God must have reached the new ruler, Darius the Mede, who began to seek him as his chief adviser.

Delivered From the Lions

Daniel 6

WHEN Darius the Mede took the throne, it pleased him to set over the kingdom one hundred twenty princes, who should rule the whole realm. Over these were three presidents, of whom Daniel was one, and the chief.

The presidents and the princes were jealous of Daniel, because he was a foreigner and had been in third place in the kingdom of Babylon. Perhaps they were not all Medes and Persians; but anyway they all worshiped false gods, and they hated the true God and Daniel who worshiped Him. So they sought to find some fault in Daniel, that they might accuse him to the king. But he was so able and so careful and so successful in all the business that came to his hand, that they could find nothing amiss.

Then they said among themselves, "We shall not find any fault in this Daniel, except we find it in the law of his God." And they conspired together to ruin him. They went to the king and said:

"King Darius, live forever! All the presidents and princes and the counselors and the captains have decided we should have a law that whoever shall ask anything of any god or man, except of you, for the next thirty days shall be cast into the den of lions. Now, O king, make the law, according to the law of the Medes and Persians, which cannot be changed."

King Darius was a rather simple soul, and he did not see through their scheme. He was pretty vain, too, and it flattered him to think that no one could ask anything of anybody but him for a whole month. So he made the law. And a law of the Medes and Persians, once it was made, could not be changed.

When Daniel heard of the law, he did not obey. For it was his custom to pray three times a day to the true God, with his window open toward Jerusalem. So he kept on praying three times a day at his open window. Of course that was just what his enemies expected. They came around and saw him praying, as they knew he would do. And then they flew to the king and reminded him he had made such a law. Yes, he said, he had.

Then they said: "That Daniel, who is of the captives of Judah, cares not a fig for you, O king, or for the law you have made. He goes and prays to his God three times a day."

Darius saw at last the trap they had made for him. He was very fond of Daniel, and he surely did not want him thrown to the lions. But there was the law, which could not be changed. He thought and he thought, he labored and he labored, all day, to find some way to deliver Daniel, but he could not find it.

The presidents and the princes came to him at evening and said: "Just you note this, O king, that a law of the Medes and Persians can't be changed. What about it?" They had him fast and tight. "How foolish," he thought, "how foolish I have been to put Daniel in this fix." But he could not help it now, and so he gave orders to throw Daniel into the lions' den. He went along, and he said to Daniel, "Your God, whom you serve continually, He will save you."

Of course Daniel knew that. He remembered how God had saved his three friends from the fiery furnace. But like them, he could say, "He can deliver me; but if not, nevertheless I will serve Him."

The two presidents and the princes went home, saying, "Now that Daniel is finished. We shall not be troubled with him any more."

And the king went home. But, oh, what a night he passed, tossing and turning and never able to sleep a wink! He arose very early in the morning and went in all haste to the den of lions. He called in a sorrowful voice, "O Daniel! Has your God whom you serve been able to deliver you from the lions?"

And from the depths of the den came back Daniel's voice: "O king, live forever! My God has sent His angel, and has shut the mouths of the lions, so they have not hurt me, because He found me innocent. And before you also, O king, I have done nothing wrong."

Then the king was very glad, and he gave orders to take Daniel out of the den. And not a scratch was found on him, because he had trusted in God.

Then the king gave orders, and the men who had accused Daniel were brought forth and cast into the den of lions. And before they had reached the bottom, the lions leaped upon them and crushed the life out of them.

Then King Darius wrote to all the peoples, nations, and tongues that made up his empire: "Peace be multiplied to you! I hereby make a decree, that all men shall tremble in reverence before the God of Daniel. For He is the living God, eternal. His kingdom shall never be overthrown. He saves and delivers as none other can. For He has saved Daniel from the power of the lions."

The Visions
of Daniel

Daniel 7; 8; 11:1-4

MANY have been the prophets of the Lord, who have spoken for Him His word to kings and rulers and to priests and people. They have counseled in war and in peace. They have withstood the mighty and comforted the weak. They have foretold what should come to pass in the future. But to none of them has been given greater wisdom and power and honor by the God of heaven than to Daniel. For to him was given understanding in all visions and dreams.

Not only did Daniel, like Joseph, interpret the dreams of a king, but he was given dreams and visions which, with signs and symbols, foretold what should come to pass in the future, even to the end of the world.

In the first year of Belshazzar, king of Babylon, one night, when Daniel had lain down on his bed, God gave him a vision. The first thing he saw was a lion. But such a strange lion! It had two wings of an eagle. But suddenly its wings were plucked off, it stood up like a man, and a man's heart was given to it.

Then there came a bear, which stood with one side higher than the other. It had three ribs in its mouth, crunching them, and someone said to it, "Up! Eat and eat and eat."

Then there came a leopard, with four heads and four wings of a bird, and this strange creature took the place of those that had gone before.

But last there was a horrible beast, like nothing on earth, dreadful and terrible, and strong exceedingly. It had great iron teeth and brass claws. It devoured and broke in pieces everything it met, and stamped upon what was left. It had ten horns; but as Daniel watched, three of the horns were plucked up, and in their place came another horn, little at first, but which grew and grew; and in it were eyes, and a mouth speaking great things.

And after them all appeared the King of kings, the Ancient of Days, whose garment was white as snow, and the hair of His head like pure wool. His throne was like the fiery flame, and its wheels as burning fire. A fiery stream issued and came forth before Him; thousand thousands ministered to Him, and ten thousand times ten thou-

284

sand stood before Him. The judgment was set, and the books were opened.

Seeing all this, Daniel was greatly perplexed, because he could not understand it. So he asked one of the angels who stood by what it all meant. And the angel told him: "These four beasts are four kingdoms which shall rise in the earth. But in the end, the saints of the Most High shall take the kingdom forever and ever."

"But what about the fourth beast," Daniel asked, "the great and terrible beast? And what about the ten horns, and the little horn that grew so great, and warred against the Most High?"

And the angel said: "The fourth beast shall be the fourth kingdom upon the earth. It shall be different from all kingdoms before it, and it shall devour the earth. The ten horns are ten kingdoms that shall come out of it. And the little horn is one that shall arise in place of the three that were plucked up. It shall speak great words against the Most High, and shall try to change His laws. But the judgment shall sit, and his power shall be taken away forever. And the kingdom shall be given to the people of the Most High."

Daniel knew that the first kingdom was Babylon, now about to pass away. And the second, he could guess, was the kingdom of the Medes and Persians, who were conquering everywhere. The next kingdom he did not know until he was told in a later vision. And the fourth and greatest kingdom was not yet even heard of. So Daniel awoke; but he thought much about the vision, and what it told, and he wished to know more.

In the third year of Belshazzar God gave him another vision, much like the first, but with more action in it. In this vision, since the first kingdom, Babylon, was about to be destroyed, there was no beast representing it. But in his vision Daniel saw a ram with two horns, and the littler of the horns grew to be the greater. The ram was pushing westward, northward, and southward. Then with the speed of the wind there came a he-goat out of the west. He had one great horn between his eyes. He came so fast he seemed not to touch the ground. And he ran to the ram and knocked him down and trampled on him. That finished the ram.

Then Daniel watched until he saw the he-goat's great horn broken, and in its place came up four horns. Then after a while, out of one of the horns came a little horn, which grew and grew and grew, toward the south, and toward the east, and toward the Holy Land. And it grew up even to the host of heaven, and cast down some of the stars, and trampled on them. That little-big horn imagined itself to be

285

as great as the Prince, who is the King of kings; and it polluted His sanctuary.

Then the angel told Daniel what these symbols meant. "The ram with two horns," he said, "represents the kings of Media and Persia. The rough he-goat is the king of Grecia, and the notable horn between his eyes is the first king. When that horn is broken, four kings will stand up in his place. As for the little horn, at the close of these kingdoms, when crimes have reached their height, there shall arise a king of fierce countenance, who shall grow to great power. He shall even rise up against the Prince of princes, but he shall be broken by no human hand."

After these visions, Daniel had others; and the principal thing revealed in them will be told in the next story.

Visions of the nighttime! God's great picture show!
Daniel, seer beloved, did you go? Did you go?
Nay! I lay adreaming in my slumber on my bed;
And the vision came before me, in my head, in my head.
Daniel, tell us truly what the vision said.

Oh, I lay adreaming, and the storm upon the sea
Blew its spume against me. Woe to me! Woe to me!
Then there rose a lion, like a fury from the deep;
Wings like eagle's bore him in his leap, every leap.
Daniel, did the vision drive away your sleep?

Nay! I dreamed still further; and there rose a shaggy bear,
Raging, crunching, rushing from his lair, from his lair.
Then a leopard, hydra-headed, four wings like a fowl;
And behind him came a demon, with a growl, a fearful growl.
Daniel, did you fear that demon on the prowl?

Yea! I quaked and trembled. Then I saw a little horn
Rise and rage and blaspheme, till the morn, the heavenly morn,
Rose in splendor and destroyed those black and fiendish things,
And the Son of man in glory reigned as King, the King of kings.
Daniel, was there aught within that dream to give your spirit wings?

List! I asked an angel what the fearful vision meant.
He said, "O Daniel, for to tell you I am sent, by Heaven sent:
Four great kingdoms shall successive rule the earth in crime;
Then your God Almighty shall call time, the end of time.
This the meaning of the vision, this the theme sublime."

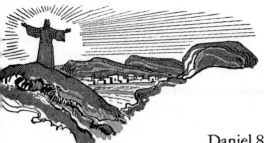

The Time of Messiah

Daniel 8:14; 9

MORE than anything else, the truehearted people of God looked and longed for the coming of the Messiah, who was to restore peace and purity in the earth. "Messiah" in the Hebrew language and "Christ" in the Greek language are the same word as "anointed" in the English language. And that is what they mean. Men used to anoint (that is, pour oil on the head of) a priest when he was made priest and a king when he was made king. So he was called the Lord's anointed, which is the same as saying the Lord's messiah. But as the great prophets came forth and prophesied of the coming of the great King who had been told of long and long before, the King who should sit on the throne of David and be the Saviour of His people, the name Messiah came to be used only for Him.

So when Daniel began to see visions and prophesy about coming events, he meant by the coming of Messiah, God's Anointed, the coming of the Christ. And first of all the prophets, Daniel was told just when Messiah should come. This knowledge he gave to his people in language which used words or objects that meant something else. For instance, when Nebuchadnezzar saw a great image, made in four parts, of gold, and silver, and brass, and iron, Daniel told him that meant four kingdoms. When Daniel in vision saw four beasts, lion, bear, leopard, and terrible beast, he was told they meant four nations.

So when Daniel was told that God's sanctuary was to be cleansed in two thousand three hundred days, the days meant years. And when he was told that seventy weeks were to be given to his people the Jews, it meant seventy times seven days, or 490 days, and the days meant years.

Well, in his second vision, about the ram and the he-goat and the little horn, which thought itself greater even than the Prince of princes and which polluted His sanctuary, Daniel was anxious to know how long that would last. He got his answer when, in vision, he heard one saint ask, "How long shall be the vision about treading down the sanctuary?" and another saint answered, "Unto two thousand three hundred days; then shall the sanctuary be cleansed." That is, two thousand three hundred years.

But when did those 2300 years begin? Daniel did not know, and he was not told until the next year. Then the Medes and Persians had taken Babylon and slain Belshazzar, and this was the first year of Darius the Mede. Daniel was now thinking much about God's promise through Jeremiah, that in seventy years He would bring back His people from captivity, and make them to dwell again in Jerusalem and Judah. Daniel knew very well that they had been taken captive because of their sins. And now he began to pray that they might all repent so thoroughly that God could fulfill His promise. So he set himself to praying earnestly, fasting, and pleading with God to forgive them their sins and in mercy save them.

In praying for his people, Daniel did not separate himself from them, as though he were better than they. He said, "We have sinned. We have rebelled."

Then the angel Gabriel was sent to him with a message from the Lord: "I have heard your prayers, and I am going to answer them. Your people who seek Me truly shall find Me, and I will be gracious to them. And I will cut off seventy weeks of years in which I will still seek them and let them know My will." Those seventy weeks, or seventy times seven days, or 490 days, are years. They were cut off, or set apart, for the Jews from the first of the 2300 years of which we heard in Daniel's vision of the year before.

"And now," said the angel, "the starting point of those seventy weeks of years shall be when the decree goes forth to restore and to build Jerusalem. In the first week of the seventy, or forty-nine years, the wall and the streets of Jerusalem will be rebuilt. The next sixty-two weeks, or 434 years, will reach to the coming of Messiah. There remains one week, or seven years. In the midst of this week the Messiah shall be cut off, not for Himself but for His people."

And so it was that the time when the Messiah should come was made known. For when the seventy years of captivity foretold by Jeremiah should come to an end, and the king of Persia should decree the restoring and rebuilding of Jerusalem, the people of God would know that then those years of prophecy were to begin. And in sixty-nine weeks of years, or 483 years, Messiah, the Christ, would come. The remaining week of seven years was to be given to the Jews to accept their Messiah, if they would.

So the learned men of the Jews knew the time when the Messiah, the Christ, was to come. And all the people, instructed by their learned men, looked for Him to come at that time. And, as we shall see, He did come then.

STORIES OF THE REMNANT

Daniel to Malachi

To Restore and to Build

2 Chronicles 36:22, 23; Ezra 1 to 6; Haggai; Zechariah

A REMNANT is the last small piece of a thing. And that is what the prophets Isaiah, Jeremiah, and Ezekiel called those who were left of Judah; for the Lord promised: "Yet will I leave a remnant, . . . and they that escape of you shall remember Me."

Through all the long years of captivity, Daniel had kept in mind God's promise that He would restore them to their land, and they should rebuild the city and the temple. Jeremiah had prophesied that in seventy years, God would punish Babylon and rescue His people. More than that, over a hundred years before, Isaiah had spoken a prophecy of the Lord, that He would use a king named Cyrus to start this work. (Isaiah 45:1-13.)

After the fall of Babylon and the short reign of Darius the Mede, Cyrus, who had taken the city, became king. He greatly admired Daniel for his uprightness and his ability. So Daniel had a good opportunity to influence Cyrus in favor of the Jews. He showed him that prophecy of Isaiah where, long before he was born, God had chosen him and led him by the right hand, to subdue nations, to open the gates of Babylon, and to restore His people to their land. Cyrus believed, and he made a proclamation that, as God had commanded him to build the house of the Lord in Jerusalem, all the people of God who wished might now go back there and build, and live on the land.

Then there rose up some of the chief men of Judah, and gathered together those who desired to go. Daniel was now too old to return to the land he had left seventy years before; and besides, he was needed by the king. But there was a young man, a prince of the line of David, who took the lead. Sheshbazzar was his Hebrew name, but he was also called Zerubbabel, which means, "born in Babylon," and he is mostly known by this name.

Zerubbabel gathered together the people of Judah who wished to return; and there were about fifty thousand of them. Of course there were a great many more than these in the land; for they had multiplied during the years of their captivity. But they had become used to living there, and indeed that was the only home the younger ones had ever known. Some of them had grown rich, and they did not wish to break up and go back where they would have toil and hardship in a ruined land. But many of them did give rich gifts to the pilgrims to be used in building the house of God. King Cyrus also gave great sums from his treasury; and he brought out the holy vessels of gold and silver and brass that Nebuchadnezzar had taken away from God's temple, and he gave them into the keeping of Zerubbabel.

At last the company was ready, and they traveled up the valley of the Euphrates until they came to the point where Abraham had turned toward Canaan. This was the great caravan route that all travelers took. They marched westward on this road to Jerusalem.

But, oh, what a sad sight! The city was all broken down. The temple was no more. Could they ever hope to build it again? They decided to settle first in the country and the little towns, so that they could make a living. This they did, and soon the land began to thrive.

When the seventh month came, the month of the great Day of Atonement, they gathered again at Jerusalem. Up on Mount Moriah, where the temple had been, they cleared away the rubbish on the spot where the altar of burnt offering had stood in the temple court. There they built again the altar of the God of Israel, and offered sacrifices on it, with many prayers.

They gave offerings, too, the gold and the silver that had been sent for the building of the temple, and they added what they could from their own store, to hire carpenters and masons. They dug out from the rubbish the great stones that were left from the ruin of Solomon's temple, and used them. And they sent to Mount Lebanon for cedar wood, and they began to build.

Now there came to them the Samaritans and said, "Let us build with you; for we seek your God, and sacrifice to Him, even from the time the king of Assyria brought us here."

But Zerubbabel and Joshua the high priest and all the elders of Judah said to the Samaritans: "You have nothing to do with building this temple. King Cyrus commanded us to build it, and we will." They knew that if they let the Samaritans join them, there would be a mixture of heathen worship with the true worship.

Then the Samaritans were angry. They went away and wrote letters, and hired lawyers to go to the court of Cyrus and carry false tales, and try to stop the work. There was great conflict in the king's court; but God kept His hand over it all. That is why the angel Gabriel told Daniel that he was delayed because he had to fight with the king of Persia, who withstood him for some time; but in the end Cyrus continued to obey the word of the Lord.

However, in the short reign of a king who followed Cyrus, called in the Bible Artaxerxes, the enemies of the Jews were successful in getting him to forbid the work on the temple to continue. Artaxerxes, means "great king," and the name is given to a number of kings. This one is not the same Artaxerxes who afterwards sent Ezra to Jerusalem with orders for the work to go on.

Building the temple stopped for about a year. But then God sent two prophets, Haggai and Zechariah, who called upon Zerubbabel and Joshua and all the people to start it up again. The people believed the prophets and began to build. Then their adversaries tried again to stop them. The governor of all those parts came with other men and said, "Who gave you a permit to build this house?"

Zerubbabel and the elders told them that Cyrus had given the commandment. So the governor wrote to the king to ask if that was so. Now a new king had come to the throne, whose name was Darius, the same as the name of Daniel's friend, Darius the Mede. But this one was called Darius Hystaspes. When the governor's letter came to him, he caused a search to be made, and they found the decree of Cyrus. So the king wrote the governor to let those Jews alone; and more than that, he ordered him to give them help, with supplies and money. And so, under the blessing of the Lord, the temple was finished at last, about twenty years after it was begun.

It was not so magnificent as Solomon's temple; for even with all the help given them, they did not have the immense wealth that David and Solomon poured into the first temple. When the exiles came back from their captivity and laid the foundations of this temple, there were old men among them who had seen the splendor of Solomon's temple, and they wept because this second temple was so much poorer.

And besides, it did not have the sacred ark within it; for that had been hidden and was lost forever. In its place was put a marble block. The glory of the Lord did not come down upon the temple, as it had upon Moses' tabernacle and Solomon's temple. There was no light of glory within the most holy place. So the old men wept.

But the prophet Haggai was sent with a message from God. "The glory of this latter house shall be greater than that of the former," He declared; "and in this place will I give peace."

That prophecy was fulfilled when, nearly 500 years afterward, the Messiah, the Christ, stood in the temple and taught and worked His miracles. Not in the splendor of the work of men's hands, but in the glory of the presence of God, even though veiled in human form, was this temple to be greater than the one before it.

Esther Saves Her People

Esther

THE JEWS who chose to stay in the land of their captivity, instead of returning to Jerusalem, were to have great trials. They wanted an easy time, but they were not left in peace. Upon the death of Darius Hystaspes, his son, Xerxes, became king. But in the Book of Esther he is called Ahasuerus. He was the richest of the kings of Persia, and his kingdom, or empire, was the biggest; but he was not the best king, nor the most successful. Like all the kings of the East in those times, he had many wives, and he was always having his servants search out the most attractive maidens in his realm for more wives.

Now there was a beautiful Jewish girl named Esther, who was an orphan, her father and mother having died. But her cousin, Mordecai, who was much older than she, brought her up as his own daughter, and he taught her the ways of the Lord. Being so beautiful and intelligent, she was found by the king's servants and taken to his house. Among all the maidens brought there, the king loved Esther the best, and he made her queen. Everybody who knew her loved her, because she was not only lovely, but kind and gracious. But she did not tell the king, nor anyone else, that she was a Jew.

Esther's cousin Mordecai became one of the king's counselors. But there was another man whom the king favored above all the rest. This man's name was Haman, and he was a descendant of that Amalekite king Agag whom Samuel slew. So he hated the Jews. He especially hated Mordecai, because he would not bow down to him and worship him, as all the other men in the king's palace did.

Haman decided to kill not only Mordecai, but also all his people the Jews. So he went to King Ahasuerus and said: "There is a people in your kingdom different from all others. They are called Jews. They do not keep your laws or worship your gods. So you had better get rid of them. I propose that you make a decree that they be destroyed, all on a certain day. And if you do, I will pay ten thousand talents of silver into your treasury."

"Oh, never mind the money, Haman; keep it," said the king. "But here's my signet ring. Write the decree, and stamp it with my ring, and send it out to all parts of my kingdom."

Haman made haste and did that. And the decree was sent by swift messengers to all parts of the kingdom that on a certain day all the Jews, young and old, should be slain. The news was cried aloud in every province and city and in the capital, Shushan.

Of course Mordecai heard it at once, and he saw that it meant the death of all the Jews in the world. So he sent word in to Esther the queen to plead with the king to stop it. But Esther sent back word that it was death for anyone to go in before the king unless the king called him or held out his golden scepter.

Said Mordecai to that: "Don't think you will escape when the killing begins, any more than other Jews. And who knows but that God has brought you to be queen for just such a time as this?"

Then Esther said: "Let all the Jews fast and pray for me, and I and my maidens will fast and pray. Then I will go in to the king; and if I perish, I perish."

On the third day Esther put on her royal robes and went in and stood in the court of the king's house. And when the king saw her standing there, he called her in and held out his golden scepter for her to touch. And he said, "What would you like, Queen Esther? You shall have it, even if it is half my kingdom."

Now Esther proved that she was not a simple-minded girl, to ask right off for what she wanted. She knew she had to please the king first. And what would please him better than a feast? So she said, "I would like for the king and Haman to come today to the banquet I have prepared."

"Thank you, Queen Esther! We will," said the king. And he sent orders for Haman to get ready and come. Haman was delighted, and of course he came and went with the king to the queen's banquet.

But the king thought Esther had something in mind besides that feast. So he said, "Really, what is it that you want, Esther?"

And she said, "Please do me this favor, that you and Haman come to my banquet tomorrow also. And then I will answer the king."

Now Haman went home proud and happy. But as he passed out of the gate, there he saw Mordecai, not bowing down to him, and he hated him more and more. So he told his wife and friends how proud he was to be invited with the king to the queen's banquet. "But," he said, "I can't be happy while that Mordecai sits there without doing me honor."

And his wife said, "Well, have a gallows made, fifty cubits high. Then ask the king to hang Mordecai on it." So Haman had the gallows made, and he went in high spirits with the king to Esther's banquet.

When the feast was over, the king said again: "Queen Esther, tell me what you really want. Tell me, and it shall be given to you, even to the half of my kingdom."

Then Esther said: "If I have found favor in your sight, O king, grant me my life, and the life of my people. For we are sold, I and my people, to be destroyed, and slain, and perish!"

"What!" cried the king. "Who dares propose such a thing?"

And Esther pointed her finger across the table at her wretched guest and said, "The enemy is this wicked Haman!"

The king rose in anger and walked out into the garden. He saw now how Haman had fooled him. He had not known much if anything about the Jews, and so he had readily believed what Haman told him. And now, suddenly, he found that his beloved Esther was one of those Jews. Higher and higher mounted his wrath. He strode back into the banquet room, determined to take vengeance on Haman.

Inside, he came to a sudden halt, and stared. What did he see? Haman, horrified to find that Esther was his enemy, had gone and fallen down before the queen and clasped her feet, begging for his life. The king, seeing him, roared: "Hola! Does he dare to touch my queen?"

Then one of the king's servants spoke up: "Yes, O king! And this Haman has made a gallows fifty cubits high to hang Mordecai on. And Mordecai is the queen's foster father."

"Hang Haman on his own gallows!" commanded the king. And they took Haman out.

But any law of the Medes and Persians, once it was made, could not be taken back. Esther told the king all about the wicked Haman's plan, and how the word had gone out to destroy all the Jews. And she begged him to undo the mischief.

The king called in Mordecai and put him in Haman's place. And he said to him: "Here's my signet ring. Write another decree, and seal it with my ring, and send it out by swift messengers to all my provinces and cities. Say in it that the Jews are told by their king to defend themselves and to slay all who would do them harm."

Mordecai saw to that at once. And when this second word came to all the cities and all the provinces, the enemies of the Jews were afraid. Now the rulers in those places helped the Jews. And instead of being cut off, man, woman, and child, the Jews got the upper hand of their enemies, and made the day a day of thanksgiving rather than of sorrow.

Thus was the young and beautiful and gracious Queen Esther the means of saving her people.

295

Ezra Leads His People

Ezra 7 to 10

THE DANGER into which the Jews had come, and their deliverance by the good services of Esther the queen, had a great effect all through the kingdom of Medo-Persia. People everywhere saw that the God of the Jews was able to defend His people, and the name of the true God was glorified throughout the realm.

More than that, it waked up the Jews to repent of their ease and carelessness, and it turned many of them to thinking that they had better go back to the land of Judah and help in building up the temple and its service.

Soon after this Ahasuerus, or Xerxes, died, and his son Artaxerxes reigned in his place. This son was called Artaxerxes Longimanus. "Longimanus" means "long-handed," or really "long-armed," because when he stood upright, his arms were so long he could touch his knees with his hands. But he was a good king, and he favored the Jews. No doubt he had taken to heart the lesson of Esther and Haman.

There was in the city of Shushan, the Persian capital, a Jew named Ezra. He was a priest and a scribe. The scribes were learned men, who could read and write; and in those days there were not many who could do that. The scribes read and studied the law of God and the Scriptures, and they also copied the books. After Ezra, the scribes became an important part of the Jewish leadership.

Ezra was the very best type of scribe; for he was not only learned, but he was also pious, a lover of the Lord, and wholly given to doing good to his people. He gathered together all the copies of the law of God that he could find, and had them multiplied by the hands of all his helping scribes, and given to those who wanted them. So Ezra did a great service, even to us, in preserving the Bible.

Now Ezra decided that he should go back to Jerusalem. Ezra himself had never lived there, for he was born in Babylon-land, and this was over seventy years after Zerubbabel had led the first company back. But Ezra talked to the Jews in Babylon and Medo-Persia, and got many of them to agree to go with him and strengthen the work in their homeland. During the captivity, when the temple at Jerusalem lay in ruins, the Jews made in the different cities where they were scattered, meeting places called synagogues. These were especially increased after Ezra provided copies of the Bible. In these synagogues the people were instructed, especially on the Sabbath day. The law of God was read to them, and the prophets, and the histories, and they were taught to sing the psalms. But God still intended to make the temple at Jerusalem the center of His worship.

Ezra was greatly respected and honored by King Artaxerxes. And when he told the king what was in his heart, to help to build up the land of Israel and the city of Jerusalem and the people of God, Artaxerxes encouraged him and gave much help to the work. He made a proclamation that all the Jews who wanted to go with Ezra should do so. And he gave great treasure of gold and silver and other precious things. And he ordered the governors of the provinces near Jerusalem to help also.

This decree of Artaxerxes, given in the year 457 B.C. (B.C. means "before Christ"), was the last of three which all together fulfilled the prophecy of restoring and building Jerusalem: first, Cyrus; second, Darius; third, Artaxerxes. And from this year, 457, the seventy weeks of years told to Daniel were to commence. They reached to the very year that Messiah the Christ began His teaching, and on for three and a half years, when He suffered for the sins of the world, and three and a half more years while the gospel went to the Jews.

So Ezra gathered the people together on the river of Ahava, some distance from Babylon. He took all the gold and the silver and the precious things which the king and the people had given, and started for Jerusalem. The company were four months on the way, and they went without any soldiers of the king to guard them, for Ezra trusted in God and led his people to trust in Him. And God brought them safely through to Jerusalem.

Ezra found a good deal of disorder there. The first leaders had died, and those who came after them were careless. Though the temple had been completed, and its services were going on, many of the Jews were backsliding and doing the bad things their fathers had done. Especially did they transgress God's commandment by taking wives from among the Samaritans and the heathen about them.

With fasting and prayer and exhortations, Ezra stopped this and had the men put away their foreign wives. He gathered all the men of the land together in Jerusalem, read them the law, and received their confessions and promises. There was a great reformation wrought under the teaching of Ezra. And the Jews in Jerusalem and in Judah began to prosper in the ways of the Lord.

Nehemiah
Reforms the People

Nehemiah

THIRTEEN years after Ezra led his company to Jerusalem and began to teach the people the law, another Jew, a young man, was high in favor with Artaxerxes. This young man was Nehemiah. He was cupbearer to the king. Now the cupbearer was a very important person in the courts of those kings. The king and the nobles all drank a great deal of wine, and it might have been easy for an enemy in the household to put poison in the cup of the king, and so poison him to death. So the kings, every one, appointed an officer who was responsible to see that no poison ever got into the wine; and to prove it, when he gave a cup of wine to the king, he first tasted it before him, to show that it was harmless. So the cupbearer was very close to the king, and was often held by him in great affection.

Now Nehemiah, one day, had a visit from his brother Hanani and some other Jews, who had just come from Jerusalem. Nehemiah asked his brother how things stood there, and Hanani said they looked very bad; for the walls were broken down and the gates were burned, and all the Jews were in great reproach among the people around them.

This made Nehemiah feel very sad, and he looked so woebegone when he went in to do his duty as cupbearer that the king asked him what was the matter. Nehemiah told him about Jerusalem and its sad state, and said that was why he felt so sad.

Artaxerxes had a great interest in Jerusalem, for he had sent Ezra there, and he had encouraged the Jews to go back and build it up. It seemed they had not done very well, and Artaxerxes shared his cupbearer's grief. So he said, "What do you want to do, Nehemiah?"

And Nehemiah answered, "I pray that the king may send me to Jerusalem, that I may rebuild it."

Now the king knew that Nehemiah, though a young man, was very capable and energetic. And though he would miss him, he thought that to grant his request would be a good thing for Jerusalem. So he said, "How long will you be gone?" And Nehemiah set him a time. He also asked the king to give him letters to the governors over in those parts, that they should help by giving supplies. And this the king did.

Nehemiah traveled to Jerusalem with some of his brethren and with an armed guard which the king furnished. When he reached the city, he did not tell anyone at first that the king had given him authority. But by night, taking a few of his men with him, he rode out and all around the walls of Jerusalem, and saw how they were broken down. In the morning he called the rulers together and said: "You see how Jerusalem's walls are broken down, and many of the houses inside are still not built. Come, let us build the walls of Jerusalem."

They just looked at him, thinking, no doubt, "Here all these years we have lived in this way, and there is just no hope of anything better. We haven't the money or the strength to rebuild the city."

But then Nehemiah told them that he was the king's high officer, and the king had told him to come and build the city, and had given letters to the governors to help. So they brightened up, and they said, "All right! Let's get to work and build." And they did.

But there were enemies who did not like to hear that Jerusalem was to be made strong. There were the Samaritans, who had hindered the work under Zerubbabel, and there were others around, like the Ammonites, and the Moabites, and the Ashdodites who were Philistines. Samaria was the center of the opposition. There were living there Sanballat, a Moabite, and Tobiah, an Ammonite, and they made fun of the Jews who were trying to rebuild Jerusalem. They said: "What do these feeble Jews think they are doing? Why, if a fox should go up against their walls, he would knock them down!" They mocked, and they conspired, trying to frighten Nehemiah. They tried to ambush him and to kill him, and they threatened to come up with an army and fight the Jews.

Then Nehemiah armed his people, and set half of them to stand guard while the others built. And so their enemies were frightened, and left them alone. In fifty-two days the wall was finished and the gates were set up. Most of the houses, though, were not rebuilt, and there were really few people living in the city.

More than that, the people complained that their rulers, their own Jewish princes and elders, oppressed them, taking great toll of the grain and produce they raised, and of money. The people had sold their land, and some of them had sold their sons and daughters to be servants, to raise money to pay the taxes and the interest the rulers charged.

At this Nehemiah was very angry with the rulers. Most of them had helped build the wall, for that seemed a good thing for their safety; but at the same time they were acting selfishly and cruelly

toward their people. Nehemiah called them together and reproached them for treating the people so. They were afraid of him, because the king had given him authority. And then they saw, too, that he was a very just man, and generous; for all the time he lived there he had not taken anything of the governor's salary, though he was governor, but he paid his own expenses and the expenses of his servants. So the nobles promised they would give back the lands and the children and would treat the people so no more. And they gathered more of the people into the city and built it up.

Now Nehemiah had found Ezra, the scribe, there; for he was still living and working for the people. But Ezra did not have the authority that the king had given Nehemiah, and the wayward ones among the Jews had disregarded him and made all this bad state of things. Now, however, he joined with Nehemiah, and the two of them brought the people up to a better state.

In the seventh month they called the people together for the great Feast of Tabernacles and the Day of Atonement. There was a great gathering in the square just inside the water gate. And there Ezra, standing on a wooden platform, read from daylight to noon the book of the law of God. You see, the people did not have the book, and what they might hear once in a while from the priests and Levites was easily forgotten. So now they found out they had been transgressing the law in many ways, and they mourned. But Nehemiah and Ezra told them to rejoice; for the Lord forgave them, and this was to be a glad day. So they all listened, and pledged themselves to obey the law. And then they made a holiday of it.

Nehemiah stayed there for twelve years as governor, and he wrought great reforms. Then he went back to be the king's cupbearer for a while. But within a few years he came back to Jerusalem. Again he found the people and even the priests in a backslidden state. Once more he set to work to bring them up to the mark. Great were the toils, earnest were the prayers, mighty were the labors of this man of God, Nehemiah. He was not a prophet, and neither was Ezra, but they were great servants of the Lord. Ezra taught the law of God, he multiplied copies of the Scriptures, and he set up schools to teach young and old. Nehemiah established the government and created respect for the law. They fixed the nation of the Jews as with a nail in a sure place. For though the people and their rulers were often backsliding, beyond one point they never again backslid. Nevermore did the Jews worship idols or false gods. And so the labors of Ezra and Nehemiah were not in vain.

The Messenger of the Lord

Malachi

THE LAST of the Old Testament prophets was Malachi, whose name means "the messenger of the Lord." Exactly when he lived we are not sure, but it was either in the time of Nehemiah or just after.

The Jews had been cured of the worship of graven images, those senseless idols that could not see or hear or feel, who knew nothing, and who were but the work of men's hands. They knew that their worship of false gods and their doing the things that worship commanded had been the reason they lost their home, their city, their temple, and were carried into captivity. Their prophets continually hammered this into their minds. So they set their faces against worshiping idols. That was made easier for them by the fact that in the latter days of their captivity they were under the Persians; and while the Persians worshiped false gods, they did not make images and bow down to them. Instead, they worshiped fire, because fire was the symbol of the sun, the moon, and the stars, which were their gods.

The Second Commandment of the Ten Commandments which God gave Israel from Mount Sinai forbids the making and the worshiping of images. After a thousand years of sinning against this commandment, the Jews at last came to obey it. But before the Second Commandment is the First, which says, "I am the Lord thy God. Thou shalt have no other gods before Me." Breaking the First Commandment leads to breaking the Second and all the rest. Obeying the First Commandment leads to obeying all the commandments. If we keep God in our hearts, we have love in our hearts, for God is love. And love keeps us from sinning against God.

The great Jews, the true Jews, like Daniel and Zerubbabel and Ezra and Nehemiah, kept the love of God in their hearts. But most of the Jews wore their religion outside. Because they did not worship graven images, they said, "We are the people of God." But yet they broke other commandments, and so they were guilty of breaking the whole law.

It was against this idolatry of the heart that Malachi prophesied. His prophecy is largely an answering of the questions the Jews asked, questions about the worship of the Lord.

301

"I have loved you," said the Lord through Malachi, His faithful prophet.

"How have You loved us?" asked the Jews.

"I have been to you like a father. But you have despised My name."

"How have we despised Your name?"

"Your offerings at My altar have been polluted."

"How have we polluted them?"

"You have said, 'Oh, what a weariness it is!' And you offer it as a duty, not from love."

"Return to Me," said the Lord, "and I will return to you."

"What do You mean, 'Return'?" said the people. "What have we done that is wrong?"

"You have robbed Me," said the Lord. "Will a man rob God?"

"How have we robbed You?"

"In tithes and offerings. Bring now the whole tithe into the storehouse, and prove Me," said the Lord, "if I will not open for you the windows of heaven, and pour you out a blessing until there is no more need."

And finally Malachi prophesied that the day of the Lord's judgment was coming, in which all the proud and all that do wickedly shall be as stubble which shall be burned up. But for those who love the Lord, the Sun of Righteousness shall arise, with healing in His wings.

And moreover: "Behold, I will send you Elijah the prophet before the coming of the great and dreadful day of the Lord. And he shall turn the heart of the fathers to the children, and the heart of the children to their fathers, lest I come and smite the earth with a curse."

With these words close the prophecies of Malachi and the messages of the Old Testament of the Bible.

Book of the ages! Book wherein God wrote
    Through holy penmen messages of love;
Book of the law; book of the deeds of note;
    Book of the music caught from choirs above;
Book of the dim sweet symbol of the lamb,
    Foreshadowing Christ, atoning sacrifice,
Incarnate Presence of the great I AM,
    Paying for sin the deep and awful price.
O sacred Book! Thy clear prophetic ring
Peals like the trumpet of the eternal King!

THE IN-BETWEEN

Malachi to Matthew

How Fared the Jews?

Hebrews 11:33-40

THE LAST book of the Old Testament is Malachi, and the first book of the New Testament is Matthew. But do you think that Malachi and Matthew knew each other? Were they neighbors? Or perhaps father and son? Could you just leave Malachi's home in the Old Testament, walk over a little hill, and there find the house of Matthew in the New Testament? No, indeed! They were years and years and ages and ages apart. Four hundred years! That is maybe seven or ten times as long as your father and mother have lived, and—let me see—maybe fifty or even a hundred times as long as you have lived.

That's a long, long time, isn't it? And the Bible does not tell us anything about what happened to the people of God, the Jews, during those four hundred years. We have to go to other books to find out. Well, there are such books. And so that we may link the Old Testament to the New Testament, we will ask those books, "How fared the Jews?"

They tell us that the Jews often had a hard time. Just as it had always been, they had their good men and their bad men, their strong men and their weak men. The good and the strong were those who loved and obeyed God. Their bad and their weak were those who disobeyed God. Yet through it all, their good and strong men prevailed over their bad and weak men, and they kept the knowledge of God alive in the hearts of the people.

The eleventh chapter of Hebrews tells of the heroes of faith, beginning with Abel in the first age of the world and coming on down to the time of Paul. And right there at the end, it tells of some men and women who endured great persecution, but who proved true and good and strong. That fits the good men and women who lived between the times of Malachi and Matthew. Such were they who "out of weakness were made strong, waxed valiant in fight, turned to flight the armies of the aliens." They "were tortured, not accepting deliverance; that they might obtain a better resurrection: and others had trial of cruel mockings and scourgings, yea, moreover, of bonds and imprisonment: they were stoned, they were sawn asunder, were tempted, were slain with the sword: they wandered about in sheepskins and

Nehemiah Rebuilds Jerusalem's Wall

The nobles of Tekoa accomplished little in their attempts to hinder the work of rebuilding the city. The presence of Nehemiah inspired the people to industry. Leading men of the land assumed responsibility for the building of specified sections of the wall and organized the willing people for the task.

ROBERT TEMPLE AYRES, ARTIST

goatskins, being destitute, afflicted, tormented; (of whom the world was not worthy)."

For about one hundred years after Nehemiah the Jews were under the Persians. Then, as Daniel saw in his vision, there came the armies of Grecia and conquered the Persians. Their first king was Alexander the Great.

At first he was angry with the Jews because they had loyally held to the Persian king, and he planned to destroy Jerusalem. But as he came near to the city, there met him a company of priests headed by the high priest, clothed in his priestly robes. When Alexander saw him, instead of being angry, he suddenly became very humble. He went forward and bowed down before him, as though worshiping.

"Why," said his generals, "what do you mean by bowing down to that priest?"

"Before we left Greece," said Alexander, "I had a dream of a Mighty One, robed as this priest is, who told me He would go before me, and I should conquer. So now I worship him as the priest of the Most High God." And he was ever afterward the friend of the Jews.

But Alexander did not live long. As Daniel saw in his vision, "the great horn was broken; and for it came up four notable ones toward the four winds." When Alexander died, his kingdom was divided into four parts; and the part in which Jerusalem and Judah were was the kingdom of Syria. The kings of Syria were Greeks, and very few of them were good men. They tried to make the Jews live and do and worship as they did, which meant to transgress the laws of God.

When some noble men and women resisted, they were slain. One mother, who had seven sons, young men grown, was forced to stand by while one by one they were horribly tortured and put to death. But instead of weeping and begging them to give in, she encouraged them to resist to the end. And then she, too, was put to death.

But not all of the Jews were so true. Some gave in and did as the Greeks wanted them to do. Some Jews were even glad to do it, because their hearts went astray from God and they loved evil things. There were also men among their rulers who did evil and destroyed the good.

But at last a priest named Mattathias not only refused to burn incense to heathen gods when all his townspeople were commanded to do it, but he slew some Jews who did. And then he took to the hills and called the truehearted Jews to join him in resisting the heathen. He had five sons, all true men, who joined with him. And because one of them, the most famous, was named Judas Maccabeus

305

(which means, "Judas the hammer," because in his battles he struck like a hammer), the whole family came to be called The Maccabees.

They fought great battles with their oppressors, and often with a few men they put to flight great armies sent against them. They made the nation of the Jews strong, and they won the right to keep and obey their own laws and customs. And when there arose in the West the nation of Rome, which began to enter into the affairs of the East, they made a treaty with the Romans, who helped them by finally destroying the Syrian kingdom.

Now, however, the Jews found themselves under the Romans. They were given the right to keep their religion, but they were not free in government. They had to submit to the Roman rule and pay the Romans tribute.

At last, when the four hundred years were drawing to a close, there came to be a king appointed by the Romans to rule the Jews whose name was Herod. Herod was not a Roman, and he was not a Jew. He was called an Idumean, which means an Edomite. If you will just juggle the first part of those words a little, you will see: Idum—Edom. Now Edom was another name for Esau, who was the brother of Jacob or Israel; and now, under the Romans, an Edomite was king over the Israelites.

Herod was a bad man, a very bad man, mean and cruel. He murdered many people, including some of his own family, and his wife. But he was very strong in war, and he had a smooth tongue that gained him the support of different Romans who came into power. So they kept him on the throne.

One thing he did, a few years before he died, was to rebuild the temple. Zerubbabel's temple was five hundred years old, and not being so strongly built as Solomon's temple, it was now going to pieces in some places. Herod told the Jews he would rebuild it; but they were so suspicious of him they would not allow him to tear it all down at once and start over, but made him do it part by part, as he rebuilt. So the temple that Haggai prophesied would have greater glory than the first temple really stood through this rebuilding, and it was never called the temple of Herod.

But now, though he knew it not, Herod, with all the people he ruled, and all the world, was come to—

The Holy Hour of History

Daniel 9:24, 25

GOD made the night, and God made the day. God is light, but sometimes He shrouds Himself in thick darkness. In the beginning there was darkness; but in the dark God spoke: "Let there be light!" And it was light. And the evening and the morning were the first day.

That men might not forget, God made another evening-morning, and another, and another, and another, until seven times had passed. And every time there was a night, there was a day to follow it. So the world was made, the beautiful, wonderful world, with God's name written in every flower and tree and bird and living creature, in the sun by day and the stars by night.

Would you have it always light? Then sight would grow weary, and eyelids would fall, and the light would hurt. So God made the night to rest us and to stop our work, that for a while we might look up and see the twinkling beauty of the stars, and fall asleep under the soft radiance of the moon, and be ready for another day.

Sometimes the night seems long to those who cannot sleep. Oh, when will the darkness cease? they ask. When will the sun rise? When will the day appear? For we cannot stand it to be dark so long. We wish and long for the morrow.

And the morrow always comes. Over in the east the sky begins to lighten. The stars pale in the sky. The dawn awakes, and we awake with it. The birds begin to peep and twitter. The dew sparkles on the grass. There is a scent of sweetness from the opening flowers. It is the holy hour of the day, when all is freshness and delight. The birds fly to the topmost branches of the trees and pour out their thanksgiving. The little four-footed creatures run here and there. The bigger animals stir to their duties. The sun arises to run his daily race. And we sing:

> "Lord, in the morning Thou shalt hear
>   My voice ascending high.
> To Thee will I direct my prayer,
>   To Thee lift up mine eye."

307

God turns the earth so often, makes light to follow dark, makes the night and the day, to teach us that His hand is upon the world, in its darkness as well as its light, and to make men know that "weeping may endure for a night, but joy cometh in the morning."

The world passed into darkness when Adam and Eve sinned. Troubles came, and death. The night fell upon men, and woe and wretchedness were their lot. Yet even in the night there was beauty and there was hope. Men looked up at the stars, and every star was a star of promise. For God said that He would send a Deliverer when the time should come, and light should follow darkness.

So through long ages men and women and little children, journeying through the night, watched the wheeling of the stars, the messages of the prophets, as they came up in the circle of the heavens, and passed overhead, and set. One by one they came in the order of God, and signaled the passing of the night. Some stars were dim, some stars were bright. But every star held on its appointed course, and God's hand was moving it.

Not many men remembered that God was over all. They chose to forget what was known in the beginning of time: that the world was made by the word of God, and that only by His power could life go on. Little men gave themselves up to feasting and drinking and enjoying silly pleasures. Great men thought only of pride and pomp and power. They lived in darkness, and they shunned the light. They loved the night because it hid their deeds of evil, and they thought that no eye could see them. The poor upon whom they laid their heavy hands wept their bitter tears. But in the shadows stood the Watcher of the heavens, making note of all men's deeds.

It is darkest just before dawn. It seemed to men in Herod's time that they could no longer live. Kings oppressed them, priests deceived them, disease fell heavily upon them. The rich hugged tight their wealth, and the poor begged for their crusts of bread. They lifted almost hopeless hands in prayer, longing for a Deliverer.

God did not forget them. In His plan the fullness of the time was come. There was a hush through all the world. Wars for a moment stopped. Men looked up in hope. And the sky lightened with a coming glory. It was the holy hour of history.

"Joy to the world! The Lord will come!
Let earth receive her King;
Let every heart prepare Him room,
And heaven and nature sing."

STORIES ABOUT JESUS

The Son of God, Our Saviour

The Voice in the Wilderness

Luke 1:5-25, 57-80; 3:1-18; Matthew 3:1-12;
Mark 1:1-8; John 1:19-28

SUCH a blessed baby! And so loved! Because he was the only child that Zacharias the priest and his wife Elizabeth had ever had or ever expected to have. For they were well along in years; and never having had any children, they had given up hope of ever having any.

But one day, as Zacharias was serving in the temple in Jerusalem, as it was his duty to do, he went into the holy place to offer incense on the altar. And there he saw a vision of an angel, who spoke to him and said: "You and your wife Elizabeth shall have a son born to you, who shall be great in the sight of the Lord. You shall call his name John. And he shall go before the Christ in the spirit and power of Elijah, and get a people ready to receive Him."

"How can I know this is true?" asked Zacharias. "I and my wife are old."

Said the angel: "I am Gabriel, who stand in the presence of God; and I am sent to tell you this. So now, since you do not believe me, you shall be dumb, and you cannot speak until this thing comes to pass." Then the angel left him.

Zacharias went out, and motioned to the people waiting for him. They saw that he could not speak, and they knew he had seen a vision. He wrote on a tablet what he had been told. And afterwards he told his wife in writing.

So now, what a happy time! When the baby was born, their friends said, "We'll call him Zacharias, after his father."

"No!" said the mother; "we'll call him John."

"Why," said they, "none of your relatives are called by that name. We'll ask his father."

So they asked him. He wrote on a tablet, "His name is John."

And immediately his tongue was loosed, and he praised God aloud. All through the hill country of Judea this marvel was told about; for it was in the hill country that they lived. And the people wondered what really lay before the little boy.

They could wonder for thirty years; for not until he was thirty years old did a priest begin his service. Little John was the son of a priest, and of course he would be a priest. But God had marked him

310

out to be the greatest of the prophets, the one who should prepare the way for the Messiah, the Christ. He was told of by Isaiah: "Hark! One calls, 'In the wilderness clear the way of the Lord!' " He was told of by Malachi: "Behold, I will send forth My messenger, and he shall prepare the way before Me." And in the last words of the Old Testament Bible: "Behold, I will send you Elijah the prophet, before the coming of the great and terrible day of the Lord; and he shall turn the heart of the fathers to the children, and the heart of the children to their fathers, lest I come and smite the earth with a curse."

All through his boyhood and his youth, John lived out there in the country, the wilderness of Judea. He lived very simply and dressed very roughly; but he was neither foolish nor rude. He studied the things God had made in nature, and he studied the Bible diligently, and he knew everything that was written in the Law and the Psalms and the Proverbs and the Prophets, and especially what was written about the Messiah.

His father and his mother taught him. They told him, too, about how he was born to be the messenger to go before the face of the Christ. And John, as he grew up, had no other thought or ambition than to do the will of God, in preparing the hearts of the people to receive their Lord. Just as the prophecy had told of him, he sought to turn the hearts of the fathers to their children and the hearts of the children to their fathers.

At last he came to his thirtieth birthday. And the Spirit of the Lord moved upon him to go out and preach the good news. So he went forth, and up and down the Jordan Valley, preaching: "Repent! For the kingdom of heaven is at hand!"

Those who repented of their sins came to him to be baptized. The baptism of John was to take the person to be baptized down with him into the river, dip him under, and lift him up. It signified the washing away of sin, as though the old sinful nature of the person died and was buried, and the new nature given by God was in the risen man. Of course baptism does not really wash away sin; it is only a sign. But when the sinner asks God to take away his sin and give him a new life, he shows his faith in God by going through the rite of baptism. This symbol or rite was started by John and taken over by Jesus and His disciples; so that now baptism is accounted the open way to show our love for Jesus and our faith in Him to cleanse us from our sins.

There were many and many who came to John to be baptized, repenting of their sins: priests and scribes and soldiers and merchants

311

and farmers and shepherds and others. John baptized them; and so he came to be known as John the Baptist.

"Who *are* you?" the people asked. "Who are you?" asked the soldiers. "Who are you?" asked the taxgatherers. "Who are you?" asked the priests. "Are you the Christ?"

"I am not the Christ," said John.

"Are you Elijah?"

"I am not," said John. For though Jesus afterwards said he was, John was too humble to claim to be.

"Are you the Prophet that Moses foretold?"

"No."

"Who are you, then?"

And John answered: "I am the voice of one crying in the wilderness, 'Make straight the way of the Lord.' Repent!" he cried, "and do the works that show that you sincerely repent, for the kingdom of God is at hand."

John came preaching in the wilderness,
    John the rugged Baptist, Heaven-sent,
Set to warn the wicked, and the good to bless,
    Crying, "Sinful people, turn, repent!"
John came preaching in the wilderness.

Pharisee and publican, soldier, sinners all,
    Came and at the Baptist's feet they bowed.
"Listen now, and heed," he said; "hear the kingdom's call."
    All they wept and prayed, that stricken crowd,
Pharisee and publican, soldier, sinners all.

Multitudes repented at his words, and were baptized.
    "For," he said, "the kingdom is at hand.
More than sacrifice and gift, the humble heart is prized;
    'Purify your hearts!' is the King's command."
Multitudes repented of their sins and were baptized.

"Is this not the Christ?" they asked. "Shall we place the thrones?"
    "Nay!" said John. "I am the herald's voice.
Build the desert highway, gather out the stones,
    And the wastes shall blossom and rejoice."
"Yokes," said John the Baptist, "come before the thrones."

An Angel Tells Mary

Luke 1:26-56; Matthew 1:18-25

THERE was a voice of singing heard in the hill town of Nazareth, in Galilee. It was the voice of Mary, a maiden sweet and pure and filled with happiness. Nazareth did not have a good name among the cities of Israel; for the people were sour and crabbed. The men were sly and hot of temper, and the women were given to gossip.

But there were some good people among them, and sweetest of all the girls in the town was Mary. She was not rich, yet she helped the poor from her little store, feeding the hungry and clothing the naked. She would not listen to the gossip of the women about her, but turned the tale of evil by her words of praise. She studied the words of God in the Scriptures, and she sang the psalms of David and the seers. Most of all, she loved the words of the prophets that told of the coming Messiah, and she learned that the time of His coming was very near. So she was happy, and she sang.

And especially now was she happy because she was going to be married. All the maidens of Israel, like maidens everywhere, were happy as their wedding day drew near. Every one of them loved children, and hoped that their children would be the best in the land. And Mary, like a good many others, had in her secret mind the hope that she might become the mother of the Messiah, that blessed Babe, that wonderful Boy, that kingly Man who was to deliver Israel from all its foes. But Mary little dreamed of how that King was to be born.

She was engaged to a man named Joseph. He was a carpenter, with a good trade in Nazareth; and all her friends thought Mary was very fortunate, and they thought that Joseph was even more fortunate, as indeed he was. He was much older than Mary, but a very kind and lovable man. He was the son of Heli and of the house and lineage of David. But above all else, Joseph had the well-earned reputation of being a just man. Other than this, the New Testament tells us very little of him. The wedding day was set, and Mary sang.

This morning the sun rose bright and glowing, and the day promised to be one of the best. As Mary went about her household duties, she meditated in her mind about the home she was going to help make, and about the adoring man she had taken into her warm

313

heart, and about the little son of her own she hoped to have. What if he should be the Messiah!

Suddenly the sun seemed brighter, and the sky bluer, and the earth more fair. She stopped, and put her hand upon her heart. For there, glowing in heavenly light, stood an angel. And he said:

"Good morning, Mary, happy maiden! The Lord bless you!"

Mary was startled. She was afraid. Of course she had never seen an angel before, and she wondered why he had come to her and what his greeting meant.

But the angel said: "Do not be afraid, Mary; for you are highly favored by God. You are to become a mother, and you will give birth to a Son and you shall call His name Jesus. He will be great, and He will be called the Son of the Most High. The Lord God will give Him the throne of His forefather David, and He will reign over the people of Israel forever."

But Mary said to the angel, "How can this be? I am not married yet."

And the angel said: "That is true, Mary. But the Holy Spirit of God will come upon you. And that holy Child that shall be born will be called the Son of God. More than that, I tell you God has prepared a messenger for Him. Your cousin Elizabeth, though she is so much older than you, is going to have a baby, who shall be the herald of your Son. Six months older he will be, and half a year ahead of Him he will begin to proclaim the kingdom of God."

And Mary did not doubt, as Zacharias had. She did not think of all the difficulties in the way. She just accepted what the angel told her. And she said, "I am the Lord's servant. Let it be as you say."

Then the angel left her. And after Mary had pondered this thing in her heart, she said, "I will go and see my cousin Elizabeth, away down there in the wilderness of Judea." So she arose and journeyed to the south. And when she came to Elizabeth, they were both so glad over the good news that they sang. Elizabeth sang:

"Blessed is Mary, and blessed her Son!
What a great marvel the Lord has done!
Blessed is Mary, who, hearing, believed;
And great is the honor she has received."

And Mary sang:

"My heart shall praise my glorious Lord,
My spirit leap with joy;

314

For blest according to His word
 Shall be my precious boy.

"The Lord has wrought a wondrous thing
 In strengthening the weak;
And all the world His praise shall sing
 Who lifted up the meek.

"According to His promise given
 To all our fathers past,
He crowns the earth with joy of heaven:
 Messiah comes at last!"

Mary stayed with Zacharias and Elizabeth for three months, then she went home. Now Joseph was troubled by all these things. But in a dream the Lord sent an angel to him, who said: "Joseph, do not be afraid! Mary is to have a Child who is the Son of God. Therefore marry her, and take care of her until He is born."

So when Joseph awoke from his sleep, he did as the angel of the Lord had told him to do. He and Mary were married. He took her to his home, and they waited with great expectation for the holy Child to be born.

———

A maid in graceless Nazareth, an angel in disguise,
 Who feeds the hungry, clothes the poor, and stops the wounds of
  strife,
With hand attentive to the task, and foot that swiftly flies
 Upon the errands of the Lord, in ministry of life.

Maiden betrothed, elate with love, her thoughts anticipate
 The glory and beatitude that Israel's mothers crave:
Would that in her the ancient promise be fulfilled—the great
 Deliverer and King her Son, to ransom and to save!

Lo! On her sight a radiance bursts, an angel clothed in light.
 "Hail, gracious lady! Blest art thou, above all women blest.
Thou shalt conceive and bear a Child, the Son of heaven's Might;
 In Him shall men salvation seek, and all the world find rest."

Now shall the song of Bethlehem rise over Nazareth:
 "Glory to God in the highest, and on earth good will to men!"
Now life shall be victorious, love triumph over death,
 Evil be conquered by righteousness, and Eden bloom again.

"Little Lord Jesus"

Luke 2:1-21

"FAREWELL! Farewell!" Joseph and Mary were departing from Nazareth to start on a journey far to the south. "Farewell! Farewell!" they called to their friends, as they joined a group of others going their way. For all the land was stirred to be on the move, because Augustus, emperor of Rome, had commanded all men to be enrolled in a list he was having made of everyone in the empire. Every man had to go to the city of his ancestors to have his name and the names of his household put on the list.

Now both Joseph and Mary were of the house of David; and the city of David, you know, was Bethlehem. Bethlehem was six miles south of Jerusalem, in Judea, and a long, long way from Nazareth in Galilee. But there Joseph had to go, and Mary went with him.

Perhaps, too, Mary remembered that the prophet Micah had written that the Messiah, the Christ, was to be born in Bethlehem. And she may have said to Joseph, "I'll go with you, because the Baby Jesus must be born, not in Nazareth, but in Bethlehem." So they two journeyed, along with many other people, south, over the great plain of Esdraelon, down through Samaria, beyond Jerusalem, until they came to the city of David, Bethlehem.

It was a little city, and the inn, or hotel, was crowded with all the people who had come in. When Joseph and Mary came and asked for a place to sleep, the innkeeper said, "No! I haven't a place left. All the room is taken up." But Mary looked so tired and worn with the long journey, that he said at last, "You can go and sleep in the stable, if you want to." And that was the only place they could find. So they lay down on the straw near the animals and went to sleep. No one paid them any attention. Nobody knew, or could even suppose, that these two humble travelers from Galilee were sent of heaven, and that that night would see the most important event in the history of the world, the birth of the Messiah, the Son of God.

But so it was; for in the night the Baby Jesus was born. O happy night and holy night! For this Babe was the Saviour of the world. And His mother wrapped Him in soft clothes and laid Him in a manger, where the cows and oxen were fed.

316

"Away in a manger, no crib for His bed,
The little Lord Jesus laid down His sweet head;
The stars in the sky looked down where He lay,
The little Lord Jesus, asleep on the hay."

Out on the hills of Bethlehem, where David used to shepherd his sheep, there were this night other shepherds keeping watch over their flocks. Perhaps they talked together about the coming King, the Messiah, who was to be born of the line of David, and in this very city; and the time of His coming, they had been told, was near at hand. The little fire around which they sat glowed red in the night and drove back the darkness for a few feet.

But suddenly it was light! What! Morning? No; it could not yet be morning. What was it then? Lighter and lighter it grew, till a glory greater than the sun shone round about them. They looked up, and there, come down from the sky, stood the angel of the Lord. The shepherds were terribly afraid.

But the angel said to them: "Do not be frightened. For I bring you good news of a great joy to all the people. For today, in the town of David, a Saviour for you has been born, who is your Messiah and the Lord. And this will prove it to you: you will find a baby wrapped up and lying in a manger."

And suddenly there were with the angel a throng of the heavenly host, praising God, and singing:

"Glory to God in the highest!
And on the earth peace!
Good will to men!"

Then all the angels rose toward heaven, taking with them the light and the glory. Fainter and fainter came back their song:

"Glory to God!
Glory to God!
And peace, good will to men!"

When the angels were quite gone away out of sight into heaven, the shepherds sat for a little while, stunned. Then they roused themselves and said to one another, "Come! Let us go now to Bethlehem, and see this thing which has come to pass, which the Lord has made known to us."

317

And they rose in haste, and left their sheep, and came into the city in the early morning. "A manger!" they said. "The angel told us we would find the Babe in a manger. Let us go now to the stable of the inn; for there the manger surely is." And they came to the door of the stable, and entered in.

In the dawning light they looked. And there, truly as the angel had told them, they found Mary, and Joseph, and the Babe lying in a manger. They told Mary and Joseph of the vision of the angels they had seen, and they knelt down before the manger and worshiped the Baby there. For this they knew was the Messiah, the Christ, this little Lord Jesus.

And the shepherds went out in the early day, where people were stirring in the morning. And to everyone they met and everyone they saw, they told the wondrous tale of the angels, saying, "To you is born this day in the city of David a Saviour, who is Christ the Lord." And everyone who heard it wondered at the story of the shepherds, but none believed it enough to search for the Baby lying there in the manger in the stable.

But Mary kept all these things in her heart and thought them over and over. Was not this a most wonderful thing that God in heaven had done, to give into her keeping the little Lord Jesus, the Son of God?

O little town of Bethlehem, how still we see thee lie!
Above thy deep and dreamless sleep the silent stars go by;
Yet in thy dark streets shineth the everlasting Light;
The hopes and fears of all the years are met in thee tonight.

For Christ is born of Mary; and gathered all above,
While mortals sleep, the angels keep their watch of wondering love.
O morning stars, together proclaim the holy birth!
And praises sing to God the King, and peace to men on earth.

How silently, how silently the wondrous gift is given!
So God imparts to human hearts the blessings of His heaven.
No ear may hear His coming; but in this world of sin,
Where meek souls will receive Him still, the dear Christ enters in.

Phillips Brooks.

Wise Men From the East

Matthew 2:1-12

SUCH a stir as there was in old Jerusalem! Every man asked his neighbor: "Have you heard? Have you heard? This morning there came Wise Men, stargazers, from the East, asking, 'Where is He that is born King of the Jews?' For they said, 'We have seen His star in the East, and have come to worship Him.' And Herod has called them in, to tell him what they have seen. And there they are now, in his palace."

And one said, and another said: "I warrant the old rascal is scared. He's been about to drop dead with disease and old age; but if he gets a whiff of a story that somebody threatens to be king, he'll murder him sure."

But the more thoughtful said: "The scribes tell us it is about time for the Messiah, the Christ, to come. Do you think this means He has been born? But where? Oh, if only it is the Messiah!"

It was true that Herod was near the end of his wicked reign. He was no Jew himself, but an Edomite whom the Romans had set up under them as king of the Jews, and the Jews hated him. For he had done many murders and other crimes, even killing his own wife, who was a Jewess of the noble family of the Maccabees; and he had killed her sons also, besides many, many other people. Now, filled with disease, he was near death.

But when these Wise Men from the East (that is, the country of old Babylonia and Persia) came in that morning and asked, "Where is He that is born King of the Jews?" Herod pricked up his ears and said, "What do they mean? Who is king of the Jews but I? Bring them in."

So they brought in the Wise Men. Probably they thought, "Now we are at the end of our journey. Of course the heir to the throne is born in the palace of King Herod." But Herod disappointed them. He did not know anything about the birth of a baby prince. "What have you seen?" he asked them. "His star? In the heavens? Tell me."

So they told him that as they were studying the heavens, they suddenly discovered a bright and blazing star which seemed to move toward the west. They remembered that in the old Jewish Scriptures another wise man from the East, named Balaam, had prophesied:

"There shall come a Star out of Jacob, and a Scepter shall arise out of Israel." That meant a King was to be born, and His birth would be signaled in the heavens by a new star. So they had watched it for some time; always it started from the same point and moved west. They knew much about the stars, and they knew that could not be a regular star, nor even a comet, moving like that. Was it a host of heavenly angels, so far up it looked like a star, beckoning them on to find the little King?

So after they had watched it for some time, always starting from the same place and moving west, they got ready to follow it, on camels or horses. And they got together many costly presents, which they might give to the King, and loaded them on the backs of animals to go with them. So now for many weeks they had traveled by night, following the star, and it had brought them to Jerusalem. "Where, now," they asked, "is the baby King? For you in Jerusalem must know."

Herod did not know, but he wanted to know, because in his secret black heart he was determined to kill that Baby if he could find Him. So he bade his servants make the Wise Men comfortable, while he called the chief priests and the scribes, who were learned in the Scriptures. And he said to them: "Have you been deceiving me? Did you know of a Baby that has been born to be King of the Jews? Where is He?"

The priests and the scribes knew nothing of the Baby Jesus, either; but they did know that according to Daniel the prophet, it was about time for Messiah to appear. And they did know that according to Micah the prophet, He was to be born in the city of David. So they answered: "We know not, neither have we heard, of any such Baby being born. But as to where Messiah is to be born, it is in Bethlehem of Judea. For thus it is written by the prophet: 'And thou, Bethlehem in the land of Judah, art not the least among the princes of Judah. For out of thee shall come a Governor that shall rule My people Israel.' "

Then Herod called the Wise Men in again, and he asked, "How long ago was it that you first saw the star?"

They told him it was some time ago; for at first they had taken time to watch the star, and then they had taken time to get ready for the journey, and then the journey had taken weeks. Maybe it was a year.

"Well," said Herod, "the Scriptures say He is to be born in Bethlehem. I have not heard of His being born. But you go to Bethlehem and search diligently for the young Child. And when you have found Him,

320

The Nativity of Our Lord

One of the most hopeful sights of all history was cherished by the shepherds. "The shepherds said one to another, Let us now go even unto Bethlehem, and see this thing which is come to pass, which the Lord hath made known unto us. And they came with haste, and found Mary, and Joseph, and the babe."

CLYDE N. PROVONSHA, ARTIST

come bring me word of where He is, so that I may go and worship Him too."

The Wise Men were pleased with this word, and sometime that night they set out to go to Bethlehem, which was only six miles south. When they were outside the city, they looked up, and lo! there was the star again. And were they glad to see it! It moved, and they moved below it, until it came and stood over the place where the young Child was.

Now Joseph and Mary, no doubt, were not in the stable where Jesus was born. For after His birth, as soon as the crowd of pilgrims had gone, Joseph had probably found a house and rented it. Perhaps he found work at his trade, too, and they settled down in Bethlehem to see what God would yet have them do. So it was in a house that the Wise Men found the young Child Jesus, who perhaps was a year old by this time.

The Wise Men came with their train of camels and stood at the door. Probably it was early morning. They knocked, and the door was opened. What a sight for Joseph and Mary: the Wise Men, the stargazers, clad in their rich robes; and the camels and horses in their gay trappings, filling the street! What did this mean?

The Wise Men said: "We have come to worship the little King of the Jews. For we have seen His star in the east and have brought our tribute to the King."

So they came in. And when they saw the young Child, with His mother, they fell down and worshiped Him. And then they brought in their packs, and opened them, and gave Him their gifts. What were the presents they gave? Oh, gold, much gold, in money and in ornaments. And frankincense, sweet-smelling, such as the priests burned in their censers in the temple. And myrrh, which also was sweet-smelling. And probably also they gave Him garments fit for a little child. Why, the house was filled with the wealth they gave; and if Joseph and Mary had wondered what they were going to live on, this was the answer, at least for a while.

The Wise Men stayed over that night. And in the night they had a dream. Maybe all of them had the same dream, or maybe only one of them had it, and told it to the others. In the dream God warned them never to go back to Herod, for he was a wicked old man who meant, not to worship, but to murder the little King.

So the Wise Men arose, and instead of going back to Jerusalem, they took another road and departed on their long journey into their own country.

God Cares for His Son

Matthew 2:13-23

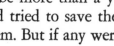

WHEN the Wise Men had departed, God came to Joseph in a dream and said, "Get up, Joseph! Take the young Child and His mother, and flee into Egypt, and stay there till I tell you to leave. For Herod will seek the young Child to kill Him."

You may believe that Joseph rose up in a hurry. That was a busy morning, packing up the gold and the other precious things the Wise Men had brought. And there were animals to be found to carry it all, and a specially gentle camel or donkey for Mary to ride on and carry the Baby. It may have taken all day, but certainly it was not long till Joseph and Mary and the Baby Jesus were on their way, out of Bethlehem, away from Jerusalem and Herod, going south, south and west, for days of travel into Egypt.

And there in Egypt they stayed, till they had other word from the Lord. Wasn't it fortunate that the Wise Men had come with their gifts in time to support the family? God planned it so, and sent the Wise Men just at the right time. It was probably not long that they stayed in Egypt, though, for it is reckoned that Herod died that year. But do you know what he did, as almost the last horrible thing in his life?

When he found that the Wise Men did not come back, but had departed by another way to their own country, he was filled with fury. "Of course they found the Child," he said, "and they have mocked me by leaving without notice. I'll see to it, though, that that Child shall not escape."

He called his guards, and he gave them a command which they dared not disobey. "Go to Bethlehem," he said, "and kill every child there from two years old down to the littlest baby."

Oh, what a terrible time when the soldiers of Herod came to the little city and went into every house and killed the children, be they boys or girls, every child from the baby up to the two-year-old; for Herod was determined not to miss the little King, if he should happen to be more than a year old. Oh, how the mothers wept and pleaded and tried to save their children, as the cruel soldiers came in to slay them. But if any were saved, it is not told us.

322

Herod slew the children, but he did not slay the Child. For far away was the little family of three, traveling toward a place of refuge in Egypt.

Very soon Herod died, hating all men and hated of all men. The day of his death was made a day of rejoicing in his kingdom. Then the Lord sent an angel to Joseph in Egypt in a dream, and he said: "Arise! Take the young Child and His mother and go into the land of Israel. For they are dead who sought the little Boy's life."

Gladly Joseph arose and prepared for the journey. He took Mary and Jesus, now not more than two years old, and journeyed back to Judea. But when he came into the land, he inquired who had taken Herod's place. And the people told him, "Herod's son, Archelaus."

Then Joseph was afraid to go to Bethlehem or to stay anywhere in Judea; for he thought the son might be as cruel as his father. So when he and Mary had talked the matter over, they decided to go back to Nazareth in Galilee. And back to Nazareth they went. Gone two years they had been, perhaps, but they were welcomed back to the little hill town, and there for the rest of His childhood and His youth the Boy Jesus was to live and grow and learn, until the time should come for Him to be revealed as the Messiah, the Saviour of the world.

Little Jesus, when You went to Egypt, did You cry?
Did You shut your eyes against the idols You passed by?
Did You close Your ears against the heathens' silly talk?
Did You cling to Mother Mary on each morning walk?

Little Jesus, did You ever know You played the part
Of Abraham and Jacob and of Joseph's broken heart,
Going into Egypt, all of them, against their will;
All their love and longing for the land of Canaan still?

Little Jesus, did the angels sometimes whisper sweet:
"Turn You this way; turn You that," to guide Your infant feet?
Did You put Your tiny hand in theirs, and walk along,
Listening in Your happy heart to their inspiring song?

Little Jesus, when Your stay in Egypt-land was done,
And the Lord in heaven out of Egypt called His Son,
Though the parting with Your little friends perhaps was sad,
When You went to Nazareth, were You glad? Were You glad?

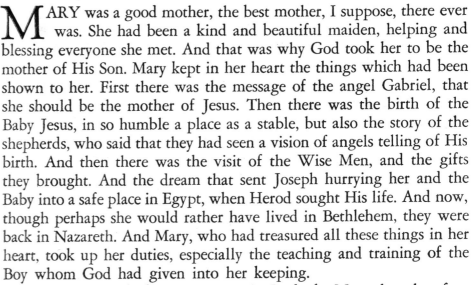

The Visit to Jerusalem

Luke 2:39-52

MARY was a good mother, the best mother, I suppose, there ever was. She had been a kind and beautiful maiden, helping and blessing everyone she met. And that was why God took her to be the mother of His Son. Mary kept in her heart the things which had been shown to her. First there was the message of the angel Gabriel, that she should be the mother of Jesus. Then was the birth of the Baby Jesus, in so humble a place as a stable, but also the story of the shepherds, who said that they had seen a vision of angels telling of His birth. And then there was the visit of the Wise Men, and the gifts they brought. And the dream that sent Joseph hurrying her and the Baby into a safe place in Egypt, when Herod sought His life. And now, though perhaps she would rather have lived in Bethlehem, they were back in Nazareth. And Mary, who had treasured all these things in her heart, took up her duties, especially the teaching and training of the Boy whom God had given into her keeping.

What a wonderful Boy He was! No doubt Mary thought often of Jochebed, the mother of Moses, who had her boy only twelve years before he was taken to the court of Pharaoh; but in those twelve years how she filled his mind and heart with the stories of his fathers and the truth of God. And Mary would do as much, and if possible even more, for her Boy.

So she taught Him from the Holy Scriptures, and He learned so quickly and so happily the stories that Moses and Samuel and all the prophets had written, and the wisdom of the righteous, and the songs of David. Every day and every year Jesus grew in height and in wisdom, and the grace of God was upon Him.

Every year the heads of the families of Israel were to go up to Jerusalem for the great feast of the Passover, and often some of them took their families with them. They did not all go, however, but Joseph and Mary did. And they promised Jesus that when He should reach His twelfth birthday, the very next feast He might go with them. What are called the feasts of the Jews were not just eating times, though of course they did eat; but the feasts are better called festivals, or holidays; for the principal things were something besides the meals they ate. They met their friends from far away; they learned lessons from great teachers; they heard and took part in wonderful singing; they had pageants and ceremonies that delighted and taught the children; and at the Feast of the Passover there was a rehearsing of the events of the first great Passover in Egypt, then a thousand and half a thousand years gone. It was a very impressive festival, especially for a twelve-year-old boy. So how the Boy Jesus looked forward to the time when He would be twelve years old! And when the day came for them to leave on their journey, with that rejoicing did He make ready and join the throng!

And what a happy journey! The little family was not alone; for there were multitudes of Jews going up to the feast, and they traveled with a great company. When the pilgrims came in sight of the holy city, they bowed with their faces to the ground and praised the Lord. And they sang songs of joy, like the 122nd Psalm:

> "I was glad when they said unto me,
> 'Let us go into the house of the Lord.'
> Our feet shall stand within thy gates,
> O Jerusalem!"

Then when they came to the wonderful temple and entered into the service there held day after day, and when they came to the solemn and beautiful night ceremony of the Passover, how the heart of the Boy was thrilled! The lamb was slain, the blood was sprinkled on the doorpost. In Egypt long ago that sign had turned away the angel of death. No doubt in the temple, and in the Passover supper, the mind of the Boy Jesus was awakening to the knowledge that He was to be the Lamb of God.

After the feast was over, Joseph and Mary, glad of heart, joined their friends on the homeward journey. All day the company journeyed, and Mary and Joseph gave scarcely a thought to the Boy Jesus. They supposed that, faithful and able to care for Himself, He was somewhere in the crowd. But when night came and they looked for Him, He could not be found. Oh, what had become of Jesus? Their hearts were heavy for fear they had lost the treasure that God had put in their care.

They arose and went back to Jerusalem. The next day and the next day and the next they searched for Him, but they could not find Him. Then after three days they went again to the temple. They had already looked through all its courts, but now, searching anxiously and asking everyone about Him, they were told there was a boy who was

sitting in the school of the doctors of the law, the teachers of Israel. If they would press on into the room where the school was held, they might see if that was the child they sought.

So into the school they went. And there, sitting in the midst of the doctors, they saw Jesus, answering the questions the teachers asked Him, and in turn asking them questions that made them think hard. No doubt they were questions about the work of the Messiah when He should come. Now the priests and the scribes and the doctors, the teachers of Israel, had thought much about the prophecies that told of the glorious reign of the Messiah, but they had thought little about the prophecies that told of His suffering and death for the sins of the world. And I suppose that the Boy Jesus, who had studied at His mother's knee and who had read and read again the Scriptures for Himself, had many questions to ask which would lead His teachers to better knowledge than they had.

As soon as Mary and Joseph could catch His eye, they beckoned Him out. And Mary said to Him: "Son, why have You treated us so? Your father and I have searched for You with fear and sorrow."

And Jesus said: "How is it that you were searching for Me?" That made them think. If they had taken the care of Him they should have, they would have been sure that He was with them when they left. And they would not have forgotten Him for a whole day.

But Jesus added, "Didn't you know I must be about My Father's business?" So He reminded them that Joseph was not His father, as they well knew, though everybody called him so. But Mary and Joseph too had been told that He was the Son of God, and Mary had told Jesus. This was God's temple, His Father's house. The business in this house was teaching the truth, getting a people ready to receive their Messiah. And Jesus, though yet a boy, had been doing just that. "Didn't you know that I must be about My Father's business?"

They fell silent, thinking. It is so easy to forget what God teaches us. And Mary and Joseph had forgotten much. So now they began to remember what they had learned from the angel: that Jesus was the Son of God, and that He had work to do for His heavenly Father. Jesus had had to remind them of that.

They started on their homeward journey, and Jesus went with them. Now on the journey, they three could be alone and meditate and talk together and learn. They had been His teachers; now He was their teacher. But, since He was yet a boy, He went home with them and was obedient to them in all things that were right; but first of all He was obedient to His Father in heaven.

326

The Days of Youth

Luke 2:40, 52; Mark 4:26-28

THE BIBLE tells us very little of the life of Jesus as a boy and young man. Two little verses tell all the tale. First: "And the Child grew, and waxed strong in spirit, filled with wisdom; and the grace of God was upon Him." Second: "And Jesus increased in wisdom and stature, and in favor with God and man." In a new translation, these are put in language more like that we speak today: "And the Child grew up, and became strong and thoughtful, with God's blessing resting on Him." And, "As Jesus grew older, He gained in wisdom, and won the approval of God and men."

Those two verses contain all that the Bible tells us about Him between His first year and His visit with His parents to Jerusalem at twelve years of age, and then between that time and the time of His baptism at thirty years of age. But, do you know, that tells a great deal more about Him than we might think. And then from the things He said when He went out to teach the people, we can gather much of what His boyhood and youth were; because what one learns in his early years comes out in his teaching when he is a man. These verses tell us that children should, like Jesus, grow up gradually and beautifully every day of their lives, but not try to be grown people before they are grown.

We want to learn from Jesus' example as a child and young man that it is good in our youthful days to be quiet and studious and thoughtful, and not try to attract attention to ourselves. Children are not to look for a great deal of notice and praise, though they are to have a great deal of love. They are not to go around boasting: "I can do that better than you can!" "Look at me!" "See what I can do!" Such children are like sickly sprouts trying to grow a bunch of oranges on a potato vine. Jesus lived for thirty years very quietly, doing good but not becoming famous for it.

And Jesus in His manhood told what He had learned in His childhood that made Him that way. He said (let me put it in words that you can easily understand): "A grain of wheat planted in the ground comes up first a little sprout; then it grows into a stalk; and then it has some flowers; and at last it is a ripe head of wheat. By that

327

time it is ready to be used, and so it helps to make the harvest." By that He meant: "The baby, like a tiny sprout, is full of promise of what he may become. Let him grow naturally, and pretty soon he will become stronger and wiser though not yet ready to preach or show himself in public. After he has grown up, he has become really wise and good, and then he is fit to go out and teach."

Some unwise parents want to make their little boys into preachers and their little girls into great musicians right away. That is trying to make the tiny sprout all at once a head of wheat. And these poor little ones think they are something great, when they are only pitiful. Jesus did not do that. He was kind and thoughtful, and always ready to help people. He did not think at all of Himself and how great He was; He thought of other people and how He could help them. He was not rich; but sometimes He would give His own dinner to hungry children, and give His own coat to one who was poorly clothed. He never grew angry or spoke harsh words, even when He was abused. He was growing up, "first the blade, then the ear, then the full corn in the ear." He studied the Bible so much and learned it so well that its teachings were always guiding Him in His speech and in His actions. He often quoted to Himself and to others from the 119th Psalm: "Wherewithal shall a young man cleanse his way? By taking heed thereto according to Thy Word."

He filled His mind and His heart with the Word of God. All about Him on the hills of Nazareth and in the valley below were the words of God in nature, which is the first book that God made. Everything in it—every blade of grass, every flower, every tree, every bird, every animal, sun, moon, star, mountain, river, sea—told Him something of His Father, God. He loved to go out and study the life of every living thing, and learn from it lessons that God taught Him. We see that in the stories He told when He was a teacher; for He could not have taught them if He had not learned them when He was young. What He taught was what He lived; and what He lived was what He was. He talked with God in prayer and song, and God talked to Him through nature and the Bible and the Holy Spirit. Every child today may learn as Jesus learned.

Nazareth was in a beautiful hill country, and no doubt the Boy Jesus walked all over the hills and through the valleys and ravines. He studied the flowers; He knew the lilies and the violets and the anemones and the roses, and how they lived and did their work of making seed. He knew the fruit trees and the forest trees, and no doubt He loved that first Psalm, which tells how the righteous man "shall be like a tree planted by the rivers of water, that bringeth forth his fruit in his season; his leaf also shall not wither; and whatsoever he doeth shall prosper." For it was by putting Bible and nature together that He learned the thoughts of God.

There were farmers and shepherds in that country, and from them Jesus learned many lessons which He afterward used in teaching. Wouldn't you think that as a boy He learned from a farmer friend how to get the ground ready for the sowing of the seed? And then can you see Him striding along behind the sower, and sometimes taking His place in broadcasting? And again, perhaps He went out with a shepherd who had lost a sheep, and they searched and searched through the hills and the gorges until they had found the poor sheep and brought it home. So many lessons did the Boy and Young Man Jesus learn that taught Him of the ways of God and the love of God, His heavenly Father.

And Jesus worked hard, too. Joseph was a carpenter, and he brought Jesus into his shop and took Him with him on his jobs, and taught Him the trade. Even before He was twelve years old and went to Jerusalem that time, He was first of all a great helper of His mother in the house and of Joseph in the shop. Joseph, being older than Mary, did not live so long. We do not know just when he died, but it was before Jesus became a man and went out to teach. Yet Joseph had done his part well, in taking care of Mary and of Jesus as a child, and in teaching Him some of the useful duties of life. And after Jesus grew up into a young man, He learned to be very skillful with tools and in building houses and their foundations, as His stories show; and every job He did was thoroughly finished.

God blessed Him abundantly and taught Him to be careful and skillful. And that is a reason men trusted Him and took Him into their favor. Another and even greater reason was that He was always so good and kind and helpful to them all, to the poor and the suffering and the afflicted and the sorrowing, to the good, and even to those who were bad.

So He spent all His childhood and young manhood learning quietly, and using what He learned to help other people. Wherever He went, there sprang up cheer and courage. No one ever said that He had worked a miracle, yet healing power went with Him in His cheerful spirit and His deeds of love. And when at last He had come to full manhood, like the full ear of wheat, God used Him for three and a half short years in the wondrous miracles and teachings that made Him our Saviour, our hope and our joy.

329

John Baptizes Jesus

Matthew 3:13-17; Mark 1:9-11; Luke 3:21, 22; John 1:29-34

DOWN in the valley of the Jordan a voice was sounding forth: "Repent! for the kingdom of heaven is at hand!" It was the voice of John the Baptist, the messenger of God going before the Christ in the spirit and power of Elijah, turning the hearts of the fathers to the children and the disobedient to the wisdom of the just, to make ready a people prepared for the Lord. His fame went out beyond Jordan, through all Judea and Samaria and Galilee. Hundreds and thousands heard of his thrilling word, and went down to John at the Jordan and were baptized by him, repenting of their sins.

In the little town of Nazareth in Galilee the news was told in the carpenter shop that had been Joseph's, and a young Man, thirty years old, knew that His time had come. Leaving His daily toil, Jesus bade farewell to His mother and followed in the steps of His neighbors who were flocking to the Jordan.

Jesus and John were cousins, but they had never met and did not know each other. John had been told by his parents about his own birth and about the birth of Jesus, and of His visit to Jerusalem and His talk with the doctors of the law. He knew of Jesus' sinless life, and he believed He was the Messiah; but Jesus had lived so quiet a life that most people would not have thought He was the Christ. "If He is," they would have said, "why doesn't He show Himself, and go about in pomp and glory, and sit on the throne of His father David?"

But when Jesus came among the crowds of people to be baptized, the Spirit of God told John who He was. The Sinless One had come to be baptized by one who was not sinless. For though John was a good man, above all the good men of that time, he was not the equal of Jesus, who had never sinned one sin.

So John drew back and said to Jesus, "I have need to be baptized by You; and do You come to me?"

Jesus did not argue. With gentle authority He said, "Let it be so now. For it is right for us to do everything that God requires." Not because He had sins to be washed away, but because He would set an example for every sinner who sought God's favor, Jesus went through the rite of baptism. John did not understand, but he did as Jesus asked.

330

Then, as Jesus came up out of the river, a wonderful thing happened. The heavens opened, and He saw the Spirit of God, in the form of a dove, come down and light upon Him; and a Voice from heaven said, "This is My beloved Son, in whom I am well pleased."

And John saw it too. Afterwards he testified: "I saw the Spirit come down from heaven like a dove, and it rested upon Him. I had not known Him; but He who sent me to baptize in water said to me, 'The One on whom you see the Spirit come down and remain is the One who is to baptize in the Holy Spirit.' And I did see it, and I testify that He is the Son of God."

It may be that others in the crowd saw and heard it too; but men have to be in the Spirit if they are to understand God. Years afterward the same Voice spoke the same words about Jesus in the presence of a multitude; but some of them said, "It thundered," and others, a little more wise, said, "An angel spoke to Him," but none knew what the Voice said. So, perhaps, it was at this baptismal scene. Yet perhaps some of the disciples of John heard and understood, as John did.

———

Andrew, did you see the dove?
   I was so surprised!
Dropped from heaven on that man
   John had just baptized.

Simon, yes! And then a sound
   As though an angel spake.
Like thunder was the heavenly voice;
   It made my heart to quake.

John, young John! Your ears are keen;
   What said that heavenly voice?
"This is My beloved Son,
   In whom I do rejoice."

Disciples of the Baptist now,
   Who saw the heavenly seal,
Tomorrow you shall know the Christ
   And follow Him with zeal.

Temptation in the Wilderness

Matthew 4:1-11; Mark 1:12, 13; Luke 4:1-13

NOW, at the very beginning of His work, Jesus was to be tested. The Spirit of God led Him into the wilderness, where John had grown up. It was a rough country, where only wild beasts lived. There for forty days and forty nights Jesus fasted, eating nothing. He was seeking for the power of the Spirit to go with Him on His mission, and His mind was so filled with this seeking that He could not think of eating. To go without food for even one day would make you very hungry. To go without eating for seven days would make you very weak. But to go with nothing to eat for over a month, for nearly six weeks—there have been very few men who could endure that. So Moses did; so Elijah did; and now so Jesus did. But when the forty days were past, He felt very hungry.

Then there came to Him one who seemed to be an angel from heaven, sent to minister to the starving Man. But his very first words betrayed who he was. He said, "If Thou be the Son of God." Every angel in heaven knew that Jesus was the Son of God; not one of them would cast doubt on it by saying "if." The seeming angel was the devil.

He pointed to the stones that strewed the desert floor, and he said, "If Thou be the Son of God, command these stones to be made bread." Of course the Son of God could do it, and satisfy His hunger. But would He do it at the command of Satan? No! As in all His life and experience, Jesus quoted the Bible. He said: "The Scripture says, 'Man shall not live by bread alone, but by every word that God speaks.'" It was through appetite that man first fell. It was Jesus' work to redeem men, and the first step was to conquer appetite. So He endured the hunger, because He would not sin by obeying Satan.

Then the devil took Him up to Jerusalem and stood with Him on the top of the temple; and he said: "If You are the Son of God, cast Yourself down; for the Scripture says:

" 'He will give His angels charge over You,
And they will lift You up in their hands,
Lest You strike Your foot against a stone.' "

Satan thought that by quoting Scripture, he would match Jesus' use of it. But he knew that the promise he quoted was not given to dare men to destroy themselves, so that God might save them. God would not tell His angels to save such a man; for he would be giving a dare to God.

Jesus answered him: "The Scripture says, 'You shall not dare the Lord your God.'"

Then the devil, no longer pretending to be an angel of light, took Jesus to a very high mountain and showed Him in a vision all the kingdoms of the world and their glory. And he said: "All this will I give You; for it has been turned over to me, and I can give it to anyone I please. If You will fall down on Your knees and worship me, I will give it all to You."

Jesus had come to win the world. Did not this seem an easy way to do it? He would not have to go through all the hard and painful things He must otherwise endure, and finally be crucified. Ah, but to gain the world this way He must worship Satan. And then He would lose everything, and the world—you and I—would be lost.

So Jesus answered: "Get out of My sight, Satan! For the Scripture says: 'Worship the Lord your God, and serve no one but Him.'"

And Satan had to obey. Having tried every kind of temptation, he was defeated. So he left Jesus. And then the angels came and waited on Him. They gave Him food, and they gave Him comfort. They brought the message, "Your Father is well pleased with You, His Son." And in the power of the Holy Spirit Jesus went forth to do His work, to conquer the world.

If You are the Son of God,
  Change these stones to bread!
Man shall not live by bread alone,
  But by God's word instead.

If You are the Son of God,
  Leap to an angel's arm!
You shall not tempt the Lord your God,
  By daring senseless harm.

If You would this kingdom win,
  Pay me homage now!
Out of My sight, O foe of good!
  To God alone I bow!

333

Jesus Begins His Work

John 1:35-51; 2:1-12

WHEN Jesus came out of the wilderness, having passed through the great temptation and having been ministered to by the angels, He was filled with the Spirit of God. He came again to the place where John was baptizing.

It was about four o'clock in the afternoon. John was standing with two of his disciples, one of them also named John, and the other one Andrew. And seeing Jesus passing by, John the Baptist said to his disciples, "Look! There is the Lamb of God!"

Andrew and John quickly left him and hastened after Jesus. Turning around, He said to them, "What are you looking for?"

They said, "Teacher, where are You staying?"

"Come and see," He invited them.

So they did; and they spent the rest of the day with Him. But first Andrew said, "I want my brother Simon to be in on this." And he hurried away to find him. When Andrew brought Simon, Jesus looked upon him and said, "You are Simon, son of Jonas. You shall be called Cephas." That is a Greek name which in Latin is Peter, and in English it means "rock," or "stone." Ever after that he was called Simon Peter, more often just Peter.

The next day Jesus determined to leave and go to Galilee. But first He found Philip and said to him, "Come with Me." And Philip did. But right away he went and found a friend named Nathanael.

Now all of these men were from Galilee. Andrew, Peter, John, and Philip lived in Bethsaida, though some of them also had property in Capernaum. Nathanael's home was in Cana, a little town near Nazareth.

Philip said to Nathanael: "We have found the One about whom Moses and the prophets wrote. It is Jesus, the son of Joseph, who comes from Nazareth."

Nathanael, like everybody else up there, did not think very much of that town, and he said: "Can any good thing come out of Nazareth?"

Philip said, "Come and see."

So Nathanael went with him, and when Jesus saw him coming, He greeted him: "Here is really an Israelite, true and honest."

334

Nathanael was surprised. "How do you know me?" he asked.

Jesus said, "While you were still under that fig tree, before Philip called you, I saw you."

Now Nathanael had been praying in secret under the drooping branches of the fig tree; and he knew that, hidden there, no one could see him but God. So he exclaimed: "Master, you are the Son of God! You are the King of Israel!" That was how quickly he was converted. He had found that the purest and best could come out of wicked Nazareth.

Jesus said: "Because I said that, do you believe? You shall see greater things. I tell you truly, you shall yet see heaven open, and the angels of God ascending and descending on the Son of man."

That made Nathanael think of Jacob's dream, away back eighteen hundred years before. In his dream Jacob saw a ladder or stairway reaching from heaven to earth, and angels going up and down on it. Now Nathanael had called Jesus the Son of God; but Jesus called Himself the Son of man. That made a connection between heaven and earth. Nathanael was a very thoughtful man, and his mind dwelt long on what Jesus had said. "Why," he thought, "Jesus is the ladder reaching from heaven to earth: Son of God, Son of man. And by Him God sends the angels from heaven to earth to care for us." And he loved Him more and more.

Soon they all took their journey into Galilee. They went right to Cana, Nathanael's home. On the third day there was a wedding there. And whom should they find but Mary, Jesus' mother, attending the wedding! It seems to have been an open wedding, everybody welcome. There were more people there than had been expected, perhaps because they had heard the fame of Mary's Son. Before long the refreshments gave out. The drink they had was grape juice, fresh wine. And the bridegroom was quite embarrassed. But Mary said quietly to Jesus, "They have no wine." As much as to say, "Now is Your chance to show them what You can do."

Jesus said to her, "Do not try to direct Me. It is not yet time for Me to act."

But His mother said to the servants, "Do whatever He tells you to do."

Jesus loved His mother, and He would not disappoint her when He could help it. The servants stood looking at Him, and waited. There were six big stone jars standing there. Perhaps they had held the wine which had now been drunk; perhaps they had only been filled with water for household use. Now they were empty.

Jesus said then to the servants, "Fill all these jars with water."

The servants hastened to the well and drew the water, bucket after bucket, and poured it into the six big jars. Soon they had filled them full.

Then Jesus said to them, "Now draw some out, and take it to the master of the feast."

They did so, and the master of the feast tasted it. Then he called to the bridegroom: "Everyone else serves his good wine first, and his poorer wine after the guests have drunk deeply. But you have kept back your good wine until now!"

The master of the feast did not know, the bridegroom did not know, and all the guests did not know where that good wine came from. But the servants knew, and it didn't take long to let all the people know that Jesus, the Son of Mary, had turned six big jars of water into wine. So His fame grew greater.

This, the first of the signs of His mission, Jesus showed in Cana of Galilee. And it added to His disciples' faith in Him.

After this, Jesus went down to Capernaum, the chief city on the Sea of Galilee. There went with Him His mother and His brothers and His disciples, and they stayed there a few days.

Who were the lovers that bright day?
    Who were the groom and bride?
Did they know that the fame of their wedding day
    Would forever abide?

Who was the master of the feast?
    What was the governor's name?
Did he know that the wine at that wedding feast
    Would give him a deathless fame?

Who were the guests that drank the wine?
    And would they ever forget?
Or did they know they were drinking a wine
    That would live in our memories yet?

The Boy Christ With the Doctors

Jesus came to the doctors longing for knowledge. His queries brought to their minds truths which had been neglected, but which were essential to salvation. The doctors, questioning Jesus in turn, were startled by His answers. Simply He quoted Scripture, giving to the Holy Word meaning new to them.

ROBERT TEMPLE AYRES, ARTIST

Jesus Cleanses the Temple

John 2:13-25

JESUS did not stay long in Capernaum or in Galilee. For the time of the Passover soon came, and with His disciples He went up to Jerusalem.

A great part of the temple service was the offering of animals as sacrifices. All these sacrificial animals were meant by God to represent the coming Messiah, who should die for the sins of the world. But there were very few if any of the worshipers who understood this. Even the priests did not, and so they could not teach the people. They did tell them their sins could not be forgiven unless they made the sacrifices. And so the poor people dumbly sacrificed animals, supposing that somehow the blood of bulls and goats would pay for their sins.

Most of the pilgrims could not bring their own animals for sacrifice, because they came from such distances. So they had to buy them after they reached Jerusalem. Some men who were dealers in animals saw a great chance here to make money. They went to the priests and bargained with them to lease a part of the lower temple court for a market, and paid them well for it. Then they brought in the doves and the lambs and the goats and the bullocks which were used in sacrifice, and sold them for high prices to the pilgrims. And they made a great deal of money that way.

Then besides, the pilgrims usually paid their tithes and offerings in money. But the priests would not take the money of the various countries from which the pilgrims came. They would accept only a special kind called the temple money. So there were other merchants who were called money-changers, because they would take the foreign money and give the pilgrims temple money for it. In doing this, they paid out far less than the worth of the money they took in. And so they too grew rich.

With all the buying and selling and bargaining, and the lowing of cattle and the bleating of sheep and goats, and the trampling of feet, and the loud voices of the buyers and sellers, there was great confusion in the temple courts. This was not what the house of God was meant to be. Some of the good men of the Jews were sorry for this state of things, but they could not seem to change it, because the

337

chief priests, who had charge of the temple, wanted it so, for they as well as the merchants made a great deal of money by it.

When Jesus came into the temple court and saw this evil state of things, His pity and anger rose up. He gathered together some small cords that had been tied around bundles brought in, and then thrown away. He walked through the crowds, making the cords into a whip, until He came to the steps that went into the upper court. He went up these steps till He was above the crowd, and there He stood for a moment, silently looking over the scene.

Quickly there ran a chill and a hush through the babbling crowd. All eyes were drawn to the figure of Jesus standing above them. His eyes seemed to burn into the souls of the priests and the merchants and the money-changers and all the people. In the silence His voice rang out: "Take these things away! Do not make My Father's house a market!"

He walked down the steps, raising His whip of cords. The money-changers and the merchants fell back, and then turned and ran. The cattle and the other beasts broke loose and rushed away with them. And Jesus pressed on. He did not strike anyone with His little whip of cords; they did not wait for that. But He overthrew the tables of the money-changers, and He emptied the stalls of the merchants of animals. Out of the temple streamed the unholy crowd.

Even the disciples were awed. They had never before seen their Master look like the thunder of God. No wonder the priests were scared and the merchants frightened out of their wits. So will the eyes of the Lord look upon the wicked ones in the last judgment day.

But soon some of the priests and rulers gathered courage to come back. And yet they were afraid of Him, too. "Perhaps," they thought, "He may be one of the prophets raised from the dead, or He may be a new prophet sent to make the temple service pure."

So they came to Him and said, "What sign do You show us that You are given authority to act this way?"

That was absurd, because in driving them all out, He had given the greatest sign of His authority. As the prophet Malachi had said of Him, "The Lord whom ye seek shall suddenly come to His temple." There stood before them the Holy One, the Messiah, whose coming to the temple made true the words of the prophet Haggai to those who were mourning because the temple of Zerubbabel seemed so much poorer than the temple of Solomon. He said: "The glory of this latter house shall be greater than that of the former, saith the Lord of hosts."

338

There was now in this temple, in the most holy place, no ark and no glory of God resting upon it. But there was standing in the court, in the midst of the priests who questioned Him, the very One who had commanded the making of the tabernacle and the building of the temple, and who in glory had filled each of them with His presence. He stood there, the glory of His life closed within the temple of a human body, as the glory of God had once been enclosed in the walls of Solomon's temple. His glory had flashed forth for a moment, and they had fled in terror from it; but now it was veiled again. A sign? He would give them a sign. Pointing to Himself, He said, "Destroy this temple, and in three days I will raise it up." He meant the temple of His body, which they would yet destroy, but in three days He would rise from the tomb.

They did not understand. They said scornfully: "This temple was forty-six years in building, and will You raise it up in three days?"

Yet the words of Jesus troubled them. There seemed to be in them a hidden meaning, and they could not face Him longer. So they turned away and left Him. They turned their backs upon their only hope, their Anointed One, the Messiah, the Christ. Said John: "He came unto His own, and His own received Him not."

O haughty priests with scornful glance,
    Who spurn the Light divine,
How shall the temple radiance
    Upon your dark minds shine?

Here, standing in your midst, is He
    Whose presence blessed this place.
Your eyes are blind; you cannot see
    The glory in His face.

Oh, lift the veil, and let the light,
    Shekinah's radiant flame,
Burst through the barriers of your night,
    And blaze the holy name!

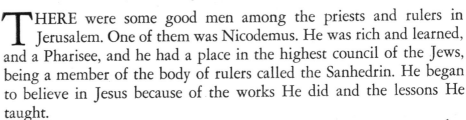

A Ruler Came by Night

John 3:1-21

THERE were some good men among the priests and rulers in Jerusalem. One of them was Nicodemus. He was rich and learned, and a Pharisee, and he had a place in the highest council of the Jews, being a member of the body of rulers called the Sanhedrin. He began to believe in Jesus because of the works He did and the lessons He taught.

But Nicodemus was afraid to confess his faith before men, because he might be put out of the Sanhedrin and be condemned by his fellow Pharisees. So he came to Jesus by night, when no one would see him. He was a teacher in Israel, very highly regarded, and he thought he would have a friendly visit with this young Man from Galilee who showed such promise of becoming a prophet. Perhaps, he thought, He could teach him something.

So he opened the conversation with a compliment. He said, "Master, we know that You are a teacher come from God, for no one can show the signs that You do unless God is with him."

But Jesus was not flattered. He was not going to give compliment for compliment. He looked behind this Pharisee's pride and fear, and He saw there a poor soul who was really reaching out for truth. And He went right to the point. He said to Nicodemus, "I tell you, no one can go into the kingdom of God unless he is born over again."

Nicodemus knew what Jesus meant, in a way; but it offended him to be thought of as one whose life needed to be made over. And he answered, a little sarcastically, "How can a man be born when he is old? Can he become a baby?"

Jesus did not argue. He knew that Nicodemus understood what He meant, partly, and He just put it more strongly, with a little explanation: "I tell you, a man must be born again, through baptism by water and by the Spirit of God, or he cannot get into the kingdom of God. There is a natural birth, and there is a spiritual birth. Do not wonder at My telling you that you must be born again from above. Listen! You hear the wind blow, but you do not know where it comes from or where it is going. That is the way with everyone who is born of the Spirit."

340

Jesus meant that just as we cannot see the wind, or call it up, or stop it, yet can see how it waves the grass and flutters the leaves, and how it turns windmills and pushes against the sails of ships, and sometimes cools us and sometimes warms us, and does many other wonderful things beyond our power—so we cannot see the Spirit of God, or control it, but we can see and feel how it moves men and makes them over, and lifts burdens and comforts the sorrowing, and opens minds to the light of truth. Think of this whenever you hear the wind or see what it does. It is through the influence of the Holy Spirit that a man is born again.

Nicodemus was very serious now. Jesus had been telling him things that he ought to have learned from the Bible and from nature, and he felt humble. But yet he had not been used to thinking like that, and it sounded strange to him. He said, "How can these things be?"

Jesus exclaimed, "Are you a teacher of Israel, and do not know these things? I have taught the things I know about, and I have seen the things I teach; but your class turn away from it. No one has been in heaven and come down to teach except the Son of man; but He must be lifted up, as Moses in the wilderness lifted up the brazen serpent. And everyone who believes in Him will have eternal life."

It was when the children of Israel, journeying through the wilderness, were attacked by fiery serpents, whose bite was poisonous, and many of the people died, that God told Moses to make a serpent of brass and lift it up on a pole. Then everyone who looked at it, with faith in God, would be cured of the serpent's bite.

The usual symbol of the Redeemer, the Sacrifice for sin, was a lamb; and that represented His innocence, His freedom from sin. But the brazen serpent represented the Saviour, too. Jesus was made in the likeness of sinful men, yet without sin. The brazen serpent was made in the likeness of poisonous snakes which had bitten the people, yet it never bit anyone; and looking upon it in faith cured them. Here was something for Nicodemus to think about, and he went away thinking very deeply. Still he did not have courage to tell everyone or anyone that he believed in Jesus. He just kept it to himself. But twice in the Sanhedrin he defended Jesus; and after the Lord was crucified, Nicodemus came forward and helped to bury Him. And thereafter he became an open disciple of Jesus.

After all Jesus' words, the Bible writer adds: "For God so loved the world, that He gave His only begotten Son, that whosoever believeth in Him might not perish, but have everlasting life." It is the sweetest verse in the Bible, John 3:16.

Jesus and John the Baptist

John 3:22-30; 4:1-3; Luke 3:19, 20; Mark 6:17-20

FOR SOME TIME Jesus stayed in Judea; for He wanted to give the rulers of the Jews, first of all, the opportunity to receive Him as their Saviour, their Messiah. He did many good works before them, healing and blessing the poor, whom they should have helped but whom instead they despised. And He taught some great truths. But they were blinded by their pride and would not listen.

They had listened more or less to John the Baptist, because the people believed he was the messenger of the Christ. Many of them had been baptized by him, though very few had really repented of their sins, as John asked them to do. He had said to them, "Do the things that will show you really repent." More and more they turned against John, but openly they professed to believe in him, for fear of the people, who said that John was a prophet. John had told them: "I baptize in water, but there comes One who is greater than I; He will baptize you in the Holy Spirit and in fire." And that was Jesus of Nazareth.

Now Jesus, having started His work in Galilee, had come to Jerusalem and Judea and was in the country where John was still preaching and baptizing. Jesus was preaching that the kingdom of God had come, while John had been preaching that it was about to come. But the kingdom that Jesus was preaching about was not the kingdom that the Jews looked for and wanted. They wanted their Messiah to go at the head of an army and overthrow the Romans and sit in glory on the throne of David. That, they said, would be the kingdom of God. But Jesus was teaching that first of all, love, which is the basis of the kingdom of God, must come into the hearts of everyone, and the love of God must fill them all before the outward showing of the kingdom could come. Jesus taught, but He did not baptize, as John did. His disciples did the baptizing.

John knew that his work in preparing the way for the Christ was done. And when his disciples came to him and complained, "Master, the Man who was with you at the Jordan, to whom you gave witness, is baptizing, and everyone is going to Him," John said, "You know that I said, 'I am not the Christ, but I have been sent in advance

342

of Him.' I am happy that He has come. He must grow greater and greater, but I less and less."

That was John the Baptist, wonderful in power, but meek as the lowliest. Many people wanted him to be the Christ, but he was faithful to his mission, and he set the Lord Jesus up on high, while he was content to be more and more forgotten. And so he was of the greatest, and he has never been forgotten, but he is next in honor to the Lord Jesus Himself.

The Pharisees and rulers tried to split the two apart, and they made much of the discontent of John's disciples. But John stopped that. And Jesus, when He heard what the Pharisees were trying to do, decided to leave the country and go back to Galilee. So there, with His disciples, He went.

John had not much longer to preach in the wilderness. There was ruling at that time in Galilee and the country beyond Jordan a son of Herod the Great, named Herod Antipas. He was a wicked man, like his father, and John rebuked him for his sins. Herod heard him respectfully and really tried to change some of his bad ways. But then he fell into the snares of a woman as evil as Jezebel of old. She was Herodias, a granddaughter of the first Herod and a niece of Antipas. All but one of the sons and grandsons of the first Herod were evil men. And though none of them were quite the monster he was, they were so bad that to say, "Herod," is almost like saying, "the devil." The women of Herod's family, too, were wayward and most of them very evil. Two of them, Drusilla and Bernice, were sisters and nieces of Herodias. They are mentioned in the Bible (Acts 24 and 25), and they were bad.

But Herodias certainly was the worst. She first married one of her uncles, Philip, and then left him and lived with Herod Antipas, who finally married her. The Herods were all mixed up, marrying and divorcing and joining and leaving one another, and helping one another to commit murder and do evil to their people. Though Herod the First married ten wives and had nine sons and five daughters, he put some of them to death; and it is a relief to know that in a hundred years, though there had been five or six generations of Herods, there was not one left alive.

When this Herodias went and lived with Herod Antipas, John reproved him, and this made Herodias hate John so much that she tried to have Herod kill him. But Herod would not; yet to halfway please her, he shut up John in prison. And there he was to stay for many a long day, till—but you shall hear that story later.

The Woman at the Well

John 4:1-42

BETWEEN Judea and Galilee lay the country of Samaria. The Samaritans were people descended from a mixture of Israelites and heathen, whom the king of Assyria had brought in over seven hundred years before, after he had carried Israel into captivity. There were some of the poorest of the Israelites left in the land, and in time these intermarried with the foreigners, and so they made the Samaritans. Their religion was a mixture of truth and error.

When the Jews returned from captivity under Zerubbabel and Ezra and Nehemiah, the Samaritans asked them to let them help build the temple in Jerusalem, but the Jews would not let them. So the Samaritans built a temple of their own in Samaria, and there they worshiped. There was hatred between the Samaritans and the Jews, and they had no dealings with one another if they could help it. They would, however, sell food and other things to each other, because that meant money, and who would pass up the chance to make money?

When Jesus left Judea with His disciples to go to Galilee, they had to pass through Samaria. So they came to a city there called Sychar. There was Jacob's well, which he had dug eighteen hundred years before, when he lived there. It was a very good well, and all the people in the city drew their water there.

Jesus was weary with His journey, and He sat down by the well while His disciples went into the city to buy food. Then there came a woman of Samaria to draw water. She paid no attention to Jesus, because she saw He was a Jew. But Jesus spoke to her, asking, "Please give Me a drink."

She said to Him, "How is it that a Jew like You asks a Samaritan woman like me for a drink?"

"If you knew," answered Jesus, "who it is that asked you for a drink, you would have asked Him for a drink, and He would have given you living water."

"Is that so?" said the woman scornfully. "Mister, You have no bucket nor rope to draw the water up, and the well is deep. Where can You get your living water? Are You a greater man than our forefather Jacob, who dug this well and drank from it and gave it to us?"

344

This was the opening Jesus wanted to teach her the spiritual truth He was aiming at. He said: "Anyone who drinks this water will be thirsty again; but anyone who drinks the water I will give him will become a spring of water himself, bubbling up for eternal life."

The woman was puzzled and attracted, but she was not going to show it. She was a sinful woman, and she did not want to have any spiritual talk, as she saw this was aiming to be. So she said, sarcastically: "Give me this water, Sir, so that I may never be thirsty again, or have to come all this way to draw water."

That seemed to put an end to their talk. But no! Jesus took another tack. He said to her, "Go, call your husband, and come back."

She was startled by this change of subject, but she had a ready answer. "I have no husband," she said.

"You are right," said Jesus; "you have no husband, for you have had five husbands, and the man you are now living with is not your husband. You told the truth that time!"

The woman was astonished and a little frightened. How did this Jew know about her? He must know the secrets of God. Well, then, let's argue religion.

"Sir," she said to Him, "I see that You are a prophet. Our forefathers worshiped God in this mountain, yet you Jews say that Jerusalem is the place where people must worship. What about it?"

Jesus answered, "Believe Me, the time is coming when you will worship the Father neither here nor at Jerusalem. In fact, the time has now come! The true worshipers will worship the Father in spirit and in truth; for He wants such worshipers. God is a Spirit, and His worshipers must worship Him in spirit and in truth."

Now the woman listened intently. This did not sound just like a Jew. Perhaps He was a prophet, bringing in a new order. She said: "I know that the Messiah is coming, He who is called the Christ. When He comes, He will tell us everything!"

Jesus said to her, "I who am talking to you am He!"

Just then His disciples came back, and they were surprised to find Him talking with a Samaritan woman, but they did not say anything. The woman suddenly turned, left her pitcher, and fled as fast as her feet could carry her back to the city. When she got there, she called to the people: "Come! Come see a Man who has told me everything I ever did! Is not this the Christ?" She started back, and they followed her.

Meanwhile His disciples begged Him to eat some of the food they had brought. But Jesus was happy; His spirit was lifted up. And

He said to them, "I have food to eat of which you know nothing."

They said, "Has any man brought Him something to eat?"

"My food," Jesus answered them, "is to do the will of Him who sent Me, and to finish His work. Look there!" He exclaimed. "You say it is four months till harvesttime. Look, I tell you." He pointed to the crowd of people coming toward them. "There are the fields, white already for the harvest."

When the Samaritans reached Him, they begged Him to stay with them, something Samaritans had never before asked of a Jew. And He, with His disciples, stayed with them for two days and taught them. And then the Samaritans said to the woman, "Now we believe, not for what you told us, but because we have heard Him ourselves. And we know that this is indeed the Christ, the Saviour of the world."

Then Jesus went on to Galilee, where the people received Him gladly, because of the reports they had of what He had done in Jerusalem. And after He had healed and blessed some sick here in Galilee, it was time for Him to return to Judea.

Sweet wells! Sweet wells! Wells of the water of life!
  A woman went down from Sychar hill
  With a pitcher at Jacob's well to fill;
  And she found there springs she never had known;
  For the river of life to her there was shown,
And she entered the garden of God and drank of the wells of the
    water of life.

Deep wells! Deep wells! Wells that will never go dry!
  For he who drinks of Jacob's well
  Will thirst again in a little spell;
  But he will escape from a world of strife
  Who drinks from the wells of the water of life,
And never again will he famish from thirst; for those wells they
    never go dry!

Eternal wells! Eternal wells! Wells of the love of God!
  The woman ran back to Sychar town
  And called to her friends, "Come down! Come down!
  And see a Man who knows everything.
  Is not this Messiah, the Lord, the King?
He will give you the water that ever shall flow from the wells
    of the love of God!"

Healing on the Sabbath

John 5

AFTER this there was a feast of the Jews, and Jesus went up to Jerusalem to attend it. Now there was in Jerusalem by the sheep market a pool called Bethesda, which means "house of mercy." This pool was fed by water that came through a pipe or tunnel from a spring far away; and it would every once in a while bubble up as though it were being stirred. The people had a story that this was done by an angel coming down and stirring the water, and they believed that whoever was sick and got into the pool first after the troubling of the water would be cured.

There had been built around the pool five covered porches, and here a great many sick people lay, waiting for the troubling of the water. But of course they could not every one get in first, and so there were more disappointed than happy.

Jesus went down to the pool one Sabbath day and walked among the sick people. He found one man who had been sick for thirty-eight years. He could not walk, but lay on a mat. Jesus said to him, "Do you want to get well?"

"Oh, Sir," said the man, "I have nobody to put me into the pool when the water stirs; but while I am creeping down, someone else steps in ahead of me."

Jesus said to him suddenly, "Get up! Pick up your mat and walk!"

The man leaped to his feet. How did he get the strength to do it, when he had not stood up for almost forty years? Why, he just trusted Jesus; and when He told him to walk, he could! He walked and he walked, and he never went near the pool. He forgot the Man who had cured him, and he went right on walking through the streets of Jerusalem, carrying his bed. He didn't stop to think that it was the Sabbath day.

Now the Jews had made Sabbathkeeping a very hard and disagreeable task. While the commandment forbids unnecessary work, in order to give people time to think of God and of His great works and of His love, the Jews had made it a heavy yoke. They said no one could carry a burden, not so much as a pin, on the Sabbath day; for that

would be work. And many other foolish laws they made. And now when they saw this man carrying his bed or mat through the streets, they stopped him and said, "It is the Sabbath day. It is not lawful for you to carry your bed."

"Why," he said, "the Man that cured me said, 'Take up your bed and walk.'"

"Who was it told you that?" they asked.

"I don't know," he answered. For he had never seen Jesus before, and Jesus had not told His name.

But by and by the man went up to the temple to give thanks for being cured. He knew it was God who had cured him through the Man. And there Jesus found him and said to him: "Now you are well again. Sin no more, or something worse may happen to you."

He found out then that it was Jesus, and he went and told the Jews. He did not know they would find fault with Jesus; he just thought they wanted to know who had done this wonderful thing. But the Jews came up to Jesus and accused Him of breaking the Sabbath by healing the man on that day.

Jesus said, "My Father is still at work, and I work too."

They understood that He claimed God as His Father. They had to admit that God works all the while, keeping creation going. He rested on the seventh day, but nevertheless He was working; for the sun came up, and the plants kept growing, and the flowers bloomed, and even man breathed and lived; and all this is done by God's life acting upon them. It was a mystery to them, for they thought keeping the Sabbath meant just doing nothing. But Jesus was teaching them that keeping the Sabbath is an act of love, and we are not only to worship and study, but to do the necessary things to keep life going and to bless others, even as the heavenly Father does.

"The Sabbath," said Jesus, "was made for man, and not man for the Sabbath." Only when the love of God fills us can we truly keep the Sabbath. All the works of God tell us of His love; and the more we study them and read God's lessons in them, the more we shall love Him. And we shall be filled with the love of Jesus, who went about doing good and healing all that were oppressed of the devil. That was what He was doing when He healed the sick man on the Sabbath day.

But the Jews hated Jesus for this, and were ready to kill Him, because, they said, He had not only broken the Sabbath but also had claimed God for His Father. But He had not broken the Sabbath, and God *was* His Father. They were so blind they could not know this.

"More Than a Prophet"

Matthew 11:2-15; 14:1-12; Mark 6:14-29; Luke 9:7-9

JOHN the Baptist was shut up in prison. He had always been a man of the open air, growing up in the wilderness, preaching up and down the Jordan Valley, looking to the mountaintops and the deep blue sky. Now the four walls of his dungeon shut him in. He could not see the sunsets and the rainbows; he could not hear the songs of the birds or the roll of the thunder; he could not walk and run and climb; he could not preach.

He remembered how he had proclaimed the dawn of the kingdom of God and had testified that Jesus was the Messiah. But now it seemed that Jesus was not doing what John had preached He would. John had not wholly understood what Messiah was to do. With the rest of the Jews, he had thought that the Christ would strike their enemy down and reign on the throne of David. He had seen that clean lives and good deeds and loving hearts must first come in his people, but he expected that this would be done by his preaching, and that then Messiah would declare himself King. If true repentance had come to all his people, he would have been right; but they were a long way from that yet.

John's disciples came to him in prison and told him how Jesus was drawing all the crowds, while He seemed to forget that John was shut up in prison. Why, they asked, should Messiah forget His messenger? Jesus had not forgotten John; but He was letting him taste a little of the trouble and trial that Jesus was to undergo; and He knew that, like thousands of other witnesses for Him, John would be true.

At last John sent two of his disciples to find Jesus and ask Him: "Are you the One who should come? Or do we look for another?"

They came to Jesus while He was healing many sick folks. He did not answer their question at once, but kept on healing and teaching. John's disciples stayed and watched. They saw the blind receive their sight, they saw the lame walk and the deaf hear, they saw lepers cleansed, they saw evil spirits cast out, they even saw the dead raised to life, and they heard the gospel preached to the poor. And then Jesus said to them, "Go tell John what you have seen and heard. And blessed is he who finds in Me nothing to drive him away."

349

John's disciples were deeply impressed by what they saw and heard; and they took Jesus' word back to their master. It was enough for John. He saw that Jesus was doing the work of the Messiah, as Isaiah had prophesied of Him, and he could wait for the crowning of the King. His faith grew strong again, and he waited patiently for what God had in store for him.

After the disciples had left, Jesus spoke to the people about John. He said: "What did you go out in the wilderness to see? A reed shaken in the wind? A man clothed in soft raiment? No; you would go to kings' palaces to see that. What did you see? A prophet? Yes, I tell you, and much more than a prophet. John is the one of whom the prophets told, the messenger who should go before Messiah's face, to prepare His way. And I tell you that among men born of mothers, there is none greater than John."

But John had not much longer thereafter to live. Herodias had not forgotten him. She hated him with all her wicked soul, and she wanted to kill him. Soon her chance came. On Herod's birthday he made a feast for his lords and captains and chief men. They ate and drank till they were drunk. Then Herodias sent in her young daughter to dance. Her name, Salome, is not told in the Bible, but we know it from other books. Salome was a great dancer, and she could dance the shameless dances of the heathen. She danced before Herod and his drunken guests until they were enchanted. And Herod said to her, "Ask anything you want, and I will give it to you."

"Will you?" she asked archly. "Swear to me that you will."

And Herod swore with an oath that he would give her anything, anything, even to the half of his kingdom. Salome slipped out and asked her mother what she should say. She had a pretty good idea of what her mother wanted, because Herodias had more than hinted it to her before she danced; but it was so terrible a thing that Salome wanted her mother to give her the exact words. "What shall I say?" she asked her mother.

And Herodias said savagely, "Say, 'Give me the head of John the Baptist on a platter.' "

Salome went back in, and all the guests stilled their clamor to hear her as she stood before Herod, a beautiful young girl. They thought that perhaps she would ask for a jeweled crown or necklace, or maybe even half of the kingdom.

"Give me the head of John the Baptist on a platter!"

Dead silence in the banquet hall. Herod paled. His guests were stricken dumb. Such a request from the lips of a girl! Herod waited for someone to say, "No!" What an honor it would have been for some man to stand up and thunder, "No! It shall not be!" But not a man spoke. They were all drunk, too drunk to think, too drunk to stop a murder. Herod waited and waited. And the girl stood there, waiting too. He had promised to give her anything she should ask. Would he go back on his word?

At last Herod spoke. In a hoarse voice he gave a command. A soldier went out to the prison. And shortly he came back, carrying on a platter the head of John the Baptist. Forever sealed were those lips which had told those men of their sins and pointed the way to salvation. The ghastly sight turned those hardened men sick. The feast was over.

Salome, almost fainting, carried the head on the platter out to her mother. Herodias was delighted. She danced and sang. This was the head that had told of her sin and had rebuked Herod for her sake. John the Baptist was dead! But in the books of heaven his name was written high; and when Christ comes in glory and sits on the everlasting throne of His Father, John will be there to see the King crowned.

In the murky light of the dungeon-keep
   That crept through the slitted stone,
The prophet bent down his noble head
   And studied the Word alone.

"He has come," he said. "Messiah has come!
   My faith no doubt can shake.
He heals the sick; He comforts the poor;
   He soon will the kingdom take.

"My work is done; let the Lord decide
   When my life shall be offered up.
I have finished the work He gave me to do;
   I will drink of the bitter cup."

A step on the flag, a hand on the sword;
And the Baptist hath yielded his life to his Lord.

"His Own Received Him Not"

Matthew 13:54-58; Mark 6:1-6; Luke 4:16-30

JESUS had spent His boyhood and youth in Nazareth, and now that He was a man and a teacher famed through all the land, you might suppose the people of Nazareth would be proud of Him. But they were a crabbed lot. They went to church, or the synagogue, on Sabbath. They paid their tithe; they prayed long prayers. They had their school, where the Scriptures were taught after the manner of the scribes and Pharisees. So they thought they were pretty good. And as for what the rest of the country thought of them, which was not good, they just put that down to jealousy.

So when Jesus came back to visit His home town, they looked at Him very critically. Yes, they said, He had been a good boy; He took care of His mother all right; and when you came to think of it, He was kind to other people. But wasn't He just a carpenter? Had He ever been to the rabbis' school? No; He never would go. And you couldn't expect a carpenter who was not trained in the rabbis' school to be anything much. However, they would give Him a show.

On the Sabbath day He went to the synagogue, where as a boy He had attended. And there, even in His youth, He was often asked to read aloud to the people the Scripture for the day. It was a pleasure to hear Him, He had such a clear and beautiful voice.

Now He sat down in the audience, and the elder or rabbi preached a sermon. Then they thought: "Well, we'd better honor the young Man a little. Really, He has made His mark." So they asked Him to read. He went to the front and stood up to read. And there was given Him the book, or roll, of the prophet Isaiah. He found the place He wanted, and He began to read: "The Spirit of the Lord is upon Me, because He hath anointed Me to preach the gospel to the poor; He hath sent Me to heal the brokenhearted, to preach deliverance to the captives, and recovering of sight to the blind, to set at liberty them that are bruised, to preach the acceptable year of the Lord."

Then He rolled up the book and gave it back to the minister and sat down to teach; for the teacher and preacher of those days sat and did not stand to preach. And the eyes of everyone in the synagogue were fastened upon Him.

The Raising of Jairus's Daughter

What rejoicing there was when Jesus took Jairus's daughter by the hand and brought her back to life! When Jesus arrived at the house, everyone was weeping. Now everyone, most of all the little girl's father and mother, was happy again because she was raised.

ROBERT TEMPLE AYRES, ARTIST

He began by saying, "This day is this Scripture fulfilled before you." As He went on in His musical voice to speak gracious words to them, they were all astonished and charmed, at first. They said, "What a Man the Lad has become! Just think! This is Joseph's Son. Where did He get this wisdom?"

"Yes," whispered another, "He's a carpenter's Son, no rabbi."

And another said: "Isn't His mother Mary? And His brothers James, Joseph, Simon, and Judas? And all His sisters live among us. Where did He get all this?" And they turned their minds against Him.

Then He said to them: "No doubt you are saying, 'Doctor, cure Yourself! Do the things here in Your own country that we hear You did in Capernaum.' But I tell you, No prophet is welcome in his own country. And I tell you there were plenty of widows in Israel in Elijah's time, when there was no rain for three years and a half, and there was a famine; but Elijah was not sent to one of them, but to a widow of Sidon. And there were plenty of lepers in Elisha's time, and none of them was cured, but only Naaman the Syrian."

They had been thinking: "Of all places in the land, He ought to favor Nazareth the most. Why, down there at Capernaum half the people are heathen, and yet He chooses to work His miracles there instead of here!" That is why He reminded them of Elijah and Elisha.

But that made them furious. They rose up, took hold of Him, rushed Him out of the synagogue and up to the top of the high hill above their town, and were going to throw Him down from the cliff.

But, lo, when they reached there, their ugly hands were empty! Jesus was not in their grasp. He was not in their midst at all. Unseen, He passed through the crowd and went on His way. He had not been able to do much there, except to heal a few sick people. The men of Nazareth rejected their Messiah because He had been one of them. "He came unto His own, and His own received Him not."

Phylacteries and frontlets, garment purple-fringed,
Miter high and costly, cheeks with henna tinged—
Not a single symbol His attire doth trim;
Who can be so simple as to follow Him?

Labels of the rabbis, not a single one
Is there seen on Jesus, simple Joseph's Son.
They are earned in study in a priestly school.
Why, this Carpenter Fellow is just a common fool!

353

The Call by the Sea

Matthew 4:18-22; Mark 1:16-20; Luke 5:1-11

SOME young men had followed Jesus as His disciples. Disciple is an old-time word for pupil or student. It means a learner, and also a follower. Jesus' school was not shut up in a building, though oftentimes He taught in a synagogue or in a house. But He loved to teach outdoors. The hills and the lake and the birds and the flowers and the sky were His textbooks. And He did not stay in just one place, but wherever He was, He taught.

His disciples were men who worked for a living. Some of them were fishermen; one of them was a publican or tax collector; others had trades that we do not know about. And so at first, while some of them went with Him on His trips to Judea and around in Galilee, they did not all go, nor any of them go all the time. Three of those who were the disciples of John the Baptist, and who followed Jesus from the first, were Andrew, Peter, and John. All three were fishermen, and it may be that Philip was too; for he lived in Bethsaida, the town of Andrew and Peter. John had an older brother named James. Their father was Zebedee, who seems to have had a very prosperous fish business. Their mother's name was Salome, but she was not the same one as Herodias' daughter. They probably lived in the same town as Andrew and Peter, for they were all partners in the fishing business. But their home may have been in Capernaum. Peter had a house there.

Well, I suppose they said among themselves, "We are truly disciples of Jesus, who is the Christ; but still we have to make a living." So they would go back to fishing. Zebedee ran the business when they were away, and he had to hire men to help him; but as much as they could they came back and worked with him.

Now one day Jesus, whom they had left to go fishing, came along by the Sea of Galilee. A great crowd went along with Him and pressed upon Him to hear the word of God. He found the two ships of the fishermen on the shore, and the fishermen washing their nets. So He asked Simon Peter to row Him out a little way; and Peter and Andrew did. There He sat and taught the people on the shore. When He had finished, He said to Peter, "Launch out into the lake, and let down your net for a haul."

"O Master," said Peter, "we have toiled all night and have caught no fish. Nevertheless, because You ask it, I will let down the net."

So he and Andrew let down their net and rowed along. And suddenly they found the net was full of fish, and it began to break. So they called to James and John, their partners, to come in their ship and help them. When they did, they all hauled on the net, and filled both ships with the fish, till they almost sank.

Then Peter, who was always impulsive, fell down at Jesus' knees, and prayed, "Depart from me, O Lord, for I am a sinful man!" And he was, too. He was used to cursing and swearing and using rough language, and probably he was just as ready with his fists. He certainly was ready to use a sword when he had one. Andrew, his older brother, was calm and perhaps slow; but he loved his fiery younger brother. And you know that down at the Jordan, with John the Baptist, it was Andrew who hunted up Simon Peter and brought him to Jesus. Now Peter knew he was not worthy to be with Jesus; and yet, though he prayed Him to depart from him, he did not really want Him to. For Peter felt he wanted to follow Jesus forever. And Jesus said to Peter: "Don't be afraid. From this time forth you shall catch men."

When they came to shore, Jesus said to all four, "Follow Me." And they left their boats and their nets and their wonderful haul of fishes; they left them with Zebedee and followed Jesus. They did not ask now how they could make a living; they just loved Jesus and followed Him. And though Jesus did not make them rich, their wants were all provided for, and they really went to school. For after this they were with Him everywhere—in the house, in the field, in the place of prayer, in His healing the sick and feeding the hungry and teaching the people.

Do you think they went to school? Yes; and to the greatest school there ever was. For they learned, or they were set to learn, that love is the greatest thing in the world; that to be humble is to be great; that to give is more blessed than to receive; that to minister to others, instead of asking others for service, is the greatest and noblest mark of the Master's disciples.

Zebedee stayed with the business. He hired men to take the place of his sons and of the other two brothers. And when his wife, Salome, the mother of James and John, after a while wanted to go with Jesus, along with some other women, Zebedee let her go, and through her he gave much money to the cause. Zebedee surely was a giver. And don't you think that when the Lord Jesus comes in His kingdom, Zebedee will be rewarded as much as his wife and his famous sons?

He Chose Twelve

Matthew 5 to 7; 8:19, 20; 10; Mark 3:13-19;
Luke 6:12-49; John 6:64, 70, 71

THE TIME had come for Jesus to lay out His plan for His kingdom of righteousness. One evening He went up on a mountain alone to pray, and all night He continued in prayer. He prayed for His disciples, that they might understand and have courage. He prayed for the multitude who pressed upon Him daily, that they might not only receive healing, but also receive knowledge of the truth and obey. He prayed for Himself, that His heavenly Father would fill Him with love and compassion and power, to show the truth in Himself, that all men might know it.

When daylight came, He rose and called to Him His disciples. They came, many of them. Out of their number He chose twelve, whom He named apostles; that is, "those who are sent." First of these were the five who had followed Him at the time of His baptism, and the brother of one of them: Simon Peter, Andrew, James and John, Philip, and Bartholomew (another name for Nathanael); then came one whom He had called from his business as taxgatherer, Matthew. He added these others: Thomas, James the son of Alphaeus, Simon the Zealot, Judas the brother of James (whom Matthew calls Lebbaeus and Thaddaeus), and at last Judas Iscariot.

Some think that Judas Iscariot pushed himself in, and that he was the scribe who said to Jesus, "Master, I will follow You wherever You are going," and to whom Jesus said, "Foxes have holes, and wild birds have nests; but the Son of man has nowhere to lay His head." Still Judas pressed in; for he thought there was a great reward in the end, even if they were now poor. He was more learned than the others, and he was pleasing in manners; and the disciples wanted him to be one of them, for they thought he would have influence with the scribes and rulers. Jesus knew him inside and out, and He knew from the beginning that he would betray Him. But Judas had no greater faults than some of the others, like Peter and James and John; and Jesus knew he could overcome his faults if he would. So He gave him the very best chance, by drawing him into His circle of apostles.

Jesus prayed for these apostles whom He had chosen, putting His

356

hands upon their heads and blessing them. A little later He sent them out two by two to prepare the way for Him in many cities.

Now when He had finished choosing them and binding them together in a little band of His closest disciples, He went down the mountain a little way with them and preached to the multitude of people.

And He sat down and taught them the foundation of His kingdom of grace. This discourse of His is called the Sermon on the Mount. It sets forth the nature and traits that will be in all who enter into the kingdom of heaven. These sayings of Jesus are given in part in both the gospels of Mark and Luke; but they are given most fully in Matthew 5, 6, and 7. You want to study these and make them a part of your life. And certainly you can memorize the first of these sayings, which are called the Beatitudes. That means "the happy things," for "blessed" means "happy." The familiar words are found in the first verses of Matthew 5; and probably your Bible is like my favorite version of the Bible. But to make the meaning clearer, I will give you the Beatitudes as they are told in a translation that has been recently made:

"Blessed are those who feel their spiritual need; for the kingdom of heaven belongs to them.

"Blessed are the mourners; for they will be consoled.

"Blessed are the humble-minded; for they will possess the land.

"Blessed are those who are hungry and thirsty for uprightness; for they will be satisfied.

"Blessed are the merciful; for they will be shown mercy.

"Blessed are the pure in heart; for they will see God.

"Blessed are the peacemakers; for they will be called God's sons.

"Blessed are they who have endured persecution for their uprightness; for the kingdom of heaven belongs to them.

"Blessed are you when people abuse you, and falsely say everything bad of you, on My account. Be glad and exult over it; for you will be richly rewarded in heaven; for that is the way they persecuted the prophets who went before you.

———————

Blessed are they who pray; for theirs is the kingdom of heaven.
Blessed are they that mourn; for comfort to them shall be given.
Blessed are they who are meek; for they shall receive the earth.
Blessed are they who seek for truth; for they are of priceless
    worth.
Blessed are they who are pure; for they have Moses' rod.
Blessed are they who are makers of peace; for they are the chil-
    dren of God.

Jesus Stills the Sea

Matthew 8:23-27; Mark 4:35-41; Luke 8:22-25

LET US go over to the other side of the lake," said Jesus one time to His disciples. And He stepped into one of their boats. They followed Him, rowed out a little way, and put up the sail. Seeing this, other people got into little boats and followed them. A brisk breeze sailed them gaily over the sea. Jesus was weary, and back in the stern of the boat He fell asleep.

But the breeze grew into a wind, and the wind brought a storm. Down from the mountain gorges on the eastern shore came the gale, and lashed the water of the lake into huge waves that swept over the boat. The night came down and added to the terror of the storm. Those hardy fishermen were used to storms, and they had great skill in the management of their boat; but their boat was filling and was about to sink.

"Master! Master!" they called; but the fury of the storm drowned their voices. Then a flash of lightning showed them Jesus peacefully sleeping in the end of the boat. In despair they shouted and called to Him, "Master! Don't You care that we are sinking?"

Then Jesus awoke. He saw the great waves towering over them and dashing into the boat. He heard the fierce wind howling. He saw His dear disciples now struggling in vain, or crouching in fear, and calling to Him to save them.

Then Jesus stood up, balanced and sure in the pitching boat. And He said to the waves and the storm, "Hush! Be still!"

And suddenly there was a calm. No more the waves, no more the wind, no more the storm! Upon the waters there was peace. The clouds parted, and the stars shone down in blessing upon them. The little boats that had followed them and struggled in the storm, shared in the salvation. It was a blessed moment, and they sat in awe as in the presence of God.

And Jesus said to them: "Why were you afraid? Have you yet no faith?"

The disciples sat amazed. "What sort of Man is this," they said, "that even the winds and the waves obey Him?"

Then they were at the other side of the sea; and they landed.

The Life-giver

Matthew 9:18, 19, 23-26; Mark 5:21-24, 35-43;
Luke 8:41, 42, 49-56

JESUS and His disciples sailed back again to the western shore. And as He stepped on shore, a great crowd began gathering to see and hear Him. But pushing through the crowd there came an important man, a ruler of the synagogue, named Jairus. He pressed his way in, not to show himself off, but because he was in deep trouble; he wanted Jesus' help.

His little daughter, twelve years old, was the only child her father and mother had. She had fallen ill with a fever, which had grown worse and worse every hour, until her mother said to her father, "You must get a doctor."

There was just one doctor, Jairus felt, who could save the little girl from death. That was Jesus. He didn't know where Jesus was, but he went out to find Him. And someone said, "He went to the other side of the lake." But someone else said, "Yes, but He is back. See! He is there, just getting out of the boat."

So down to the lake went Jairus. And he pushed his way through the crowd, saying to everybody, "Let me through, please. My little girl is dying!" They made way for him, though many were wanting to get next to Jesus; but they saw how troubled the ruler was. So when he reached Jesus, he cast himself down at His feet and sobbed, "O Master, my little girl is dying! Come, lay Your hands on her, so that she will get well and live."

"I'll go with you," said Jesus. And they started, Jairus pushing his way through eagerly, and Jesus with him. But the crowd pressed so hard upon Him, some wanting to be healed, some wanting to ask Him questions, some just wanting to be near Him, and they were stopped so often, Jairus feared they would not get to his house in time.

And so it was. For soon one came from his house and said to him, "Trouble the Master no more. Your little daughter is dead."

Then, oh, how bad the father felt! It was too late! His little girl was dead!

But Jesus said, "Don't worry. Have faith, and she will get well."

So they went on to the house of Jairus. And there were all the

359

friends making a great outcry, mourning for the little girl. They were in the house and around the house, making a great uproar, as it was the custom then when anyone died. Jesus said to them, "Why all this confusion and crying? The little girl is not dead; she is asleep." He said this because He knew what He was going to do, and it would be just as though she had been asleep.

But they knew she was dead, and they sneered at Him.

Then He took just Peter and James and John, and the father and mother of the little girl, and went into her room.

Jesus took her hand, "Little girl, I am speaking to you. Get up!"

And the little girl opened her eyes. The breath came into her body; the roses came into her cheeks. She was alive! And she got up and walked about. Jesus knew she was hungry, for she had had no food for some time; and He told them to get her something to eat.

And I think—don't you?—that that little girl was a disciple of the Lord Jesus forever after.

———

O little girl of summers twelve,
    And lily-white your brow,
And roses painted on your cheeks,
    What is the matter now?

You stop your play, and, languishing,
    You seek your bed and sigh.
Your head is hot; your eyes are wild—
    We cannot let you die!

Oh, shorter, shorter comes her breath,
    And fainter beats her heart.
O precious little daughter ours,
    How can we bear to part?

Lo, there is one Physician who
    Can fill again life's cup.
And Jesus speaks, "Come, little girl;
    I want you to wake up!"

O little maid, how glad we are
    Again you breathe your breath!
And glory be to Christ the Lord,
    Who wakened you from death!

Five Loaves and Two Small Fishes

Matthew 14:13-21; Mark 6:30-44; Luke 9:10-17; John 6:1-14

WHEN Jesus was told that Herod had put John the Baptist to death, He was very sorrowful. He had sent out His twelve apostles to teach, saying, "The kingdom of God is come to you." Now they came back and told Him all that they had done.

And Jesus said to them, "Come away with Me to some quiet place, and rest awhile." For people were coming and going in great numbers, and they had not time even for meals. So they set off by themselves in their boat to go to some quiet place on the eastern shore.

But the people saw them start and knew where they were going. And they started off on foot to go around the lake to get there too. So when Jesus landed from the boat, He found a great crowd waiting for Him. No quiet here! But He was sorry for them, because they were like sheep who have no shepherd. And He began to teach them and to heal their sick, and all the rest of the day He waited on them.

When it grew late, His disciples came to Him and said: "This is a lonely place, and it is getting late. Send the people off to the farms and villages around to get something for themselves to eat."

But He said to them, "You give them something to eat."

"We!" they exclaimed. And Philip said, "Why, forty dollars' worth of bread would not be enough to feed them all. There must be five thousand men here, besides women and children."

"How many loaves have you?" He asked them.

Philip had no answer, but Andrew said, "There is a boy here who has five barley loaves and a couple of fishes, but what is that among so many people?"

I suppose this boy was trying to make some money by selling some food, just as perhaps you would by selling popcorn and lemonade. Perhaps his mother had kissed him good-by that morning and said, "Samuel [if that was his name], be a good boy, and do whatever Jesus would want you to do." And probably he had said, "Mother, I think I know where Jesus is going to be today, and there will be big crowds, and some of them will surely be hungry. I will take as many loaves of bread and as many little fishes as I can carry, and maybe I'll have a good sale. Yes, I'll be good. I love Jesus."

Now the loaves of bread they baked in those times and in that country were not big, fat loaves like ours. They were flat, more like big pancakes. So the boy could stack them up and carry a lot of them in his basket. And then he probably had another basket which he filled with fishes. Whether the fish were cooked or not I don't know, but many people in those days ate little fishes raw.

So the boy went along and followed the crowds, and he sold some of his loaves and some of his fishes. And by the time evening came, he had left only five loaves and two small fishes. Maybe he came from Bethsaida, Andrew's town, and maybe Andrew knew him. And, because Andrew was kind and thoughtful, maybe he said, "Sonny, have you had a good day?" And the boy said, "Pretty good, Andrew. Only five loaves and two fishes left." And that is how Andrew knew.

And Jesus said, "Bring the lad here." And they brought him. I don't know, but I suppose Jesus said, "Laddie, I'll pay you for what loaves and fishes you have left." And it would be just like the boy to answer, "O Master, take them. I don't want any pay. They are so few, and anyway I've had a good day." That was a gift to Jesus that He multiplied a thousandfold, and brought a blessing to the little boy.

Jesus said to His disciples, "Make the people sit down on the grass in order." And they did. Then Jesus took the five loaves and the two fishes, and looking up to heaven, He blessed them. And then He handed out some bread and two fishes to Andrew and said, "Go give it."

But then—what do you think? He still had five loaves and two fishes, and there was Peter waiting. And the other disciples. And Jesus handed out more bread and more fishes, and the disciples kept giving them out. So all the men and women and children ate all they wanted, maybe six or eight thousand all fed from five loaves and two fishes.

And when they had finished eating, Jesus said, "Gather up the fragments, so that nothing may be lost." And they took the little lad's baskets and maybe some other baskets they found, and they filled twelve baskets with the food that was left, and the disciples carried it away. All out of the little boy's thank offering!

What a miracle! And yet, you know, that's just what God does all the while, even for us, though He may take a little longer to do it. But He gives us seeds, say a bean seed, and we plant it; and God makes it grow and flower and set seed; and there at last are a hundred beans for one! And just so with corn and wheat and potatoes and all the food we eat. Jesus works miracles every day and every year for us. Shall we, like the little boy and the five thousand men and the women and children, shall we thank Him?

Jesus Walks on the Water

Matthew 14:22-33; Mark 6:45-52; John 6:14-21

THE GREAT multitude whom Jesus fed were astonished. They said: "Just think! He had only five loaves of bread and two little fishes to begin with. And we all ate our fill. And then they took up the fragments that were left, and there were twelve baskets full! Think how He could feed His armies! And if He could feed them by a miracle, He could defeat their enemies by miracles. Who could do such miracles but the Messiah? It is He! It is He! It is the Christ! Come, let us lift Him up on high and make Him king!"

The disciples heard the people saying this, and they were glad. "Now is the time," they said. "Jesus is certainly the Christ, but yet He will not declare Himself king. Well, the people will do it. And we will go along. And when He sits on the throne, we will be next to Him, the highest in the kingdom."

But when Jesus saw that the people would take Him and make Him king, He met them and firmly dismissed them. They could not do what they meant to do. They had to obey Jesus. So reluctantly they left. Probably some of them traveled home that night, while others waited for the morning.

Jesus then commanded His disciples to get into their ship and row for the other side, while He went up on the mountain alone to pray. The disciples were greatly disappointed, and they were really angry, because they thought Jesus had passed by the greatest opportunity of His life. They got into the boat and rowed away in the gathering darkness, but their hearts were rebellious.

They had not gone very far till a great wind swept down out of the mountain gorges and blew up a terrible storm. It was like that night not long before, when they were overtaken by a storm on the lake and Jesus stilled the wind and the waves. But now Jesus was not with them. Oh, what could they do? They rowed hard to come to shore, but they could do nothing. Oh, if Jesus were with them! They were sorry that they had been so bad in their hearts and in their words. They began to see, a little, that the kingdom of God must come into their hearts before it could appear in glory. Oh, if Jesus would only come to them! But how could He? He had no boat. They had left

363

Him on the shore. Now they were about to perish, and there was no Jesus to save them.

The storm roared on. The waves dashed high. The lightning flashed, and the thunder crashed. A bolt of lightning zigzagged across the sky, lighting up the great, high waves on which their boat was tossed. But look! What is that? The lightning had shown a form walking on the water! O merciful God, save us! It is a spirit! A ghost! O Lord! O Jesus!

And then a cheering Voice came out of the dark: "It is I! Be not afraid!" It was Jesus! He was coming to them, walking on the water! Could it be? A soft light shone around Him, and they saw that it was really Jesus.

Peter called out, "If it is You, Master, tell me to come to You on the water." That was Peter! Always thinking up some new adventure. And here could be proved, not only that this was Jesus and that Jesus was the Christ, but also that Peter could do something great.

Jesus said, "Come!"

Peter jumped out of the boat, and he really walked on the water toward Jesus. "Aha!" thought Peter, "No one else could do this." And he looked around at his fellow disciples in the boat. Then, oh, horror! He found he was sinking. A terrible fear came over him. He could never swim in this awful sea.

"Oh, Master, save me!" he cried.

Jesus stretched out His hand and caught Peter and lifted him up. "Why did you waver?" He said. "You have so little faith!" But when pride comes in, faith goes out.

So they came together and got into the boat. And the wind went down. And all the men in the boat fell down and worshiped Jesus and said, "You are certainly the Son of God!"

And immediately they were at the shore.

Vanity goes before a fall,
    Pride before a sinking.
It is not you that's great at all,
    If that is what you're thinking.

Look upon Jesus, not upon men
    Who try to flatter and please us;
You can walk safely on billows when
    You keep your eyes on Jesus.

An Hour of Glory

Matthew 16:13-28; 17:1-13; Mark 8:27-38; 9:1-13; Luke 9:18-36

AS JESUS and His disciples were going along toward some towns on the northern side of the Sea of Galilee, He asked them, "Who do people say that I am?"

They answered: "Some say you are John the Baptist risen from the dead. Others say you are Elijah who was promised. And still others say you are Jeremiah, or one of the prophets."

"But who do you say that I am?" asked Jesus.

And Peter answered, "You are the Christ, the Son of God."

"Don't tell anyone that," said Jesus. He knew that if His disciples began preaching that He was the Messiah, the Christ, people would at once expect Him to be king and go forth with armies to fight their enemies. But He had come to set the kingdom of God in their hearts; and until a people are ready, with pure lives, to make up the kingdom of God, it cannot come in glory.

Then Jesus began to tell His disciples how He must go through much suffering and be rejected by the elders and priests and scribes and be killed and rise again the third day. He told them this plainly.

But they did not want to hear it. And Peter took Him and began to reprove Him for saying it. "God bless You, Master!" he exclaimed. "That can never happen to You!" They all agreed with Peter; for they wanted the Christ to reign as king, and then they might have great things for themselves.

Jesus turned and looked on His disciples. Then He rebuked Peter with burning words: "Get out of My sight, Satan! You hinder Me; for you do not side with God, but with men!"

And He said to them all: "If anyone wants to go with Me, he must forget himself, and take up his cross, and follow Me. For whoever wants to save his life will lose it; but whoever loses his life for Me will find it. And what good will it do a man if he gains the whole world, and loses his life?"

His disciples felt very downcast at that. All their hopes of glory fell into ashes. Where would they be if Jesus' words came true, that the Jews would reject Him and kill Him? The cross? That did not mean to them what it means to us. It meant to die, crucified on the

365

terrible cross, just as bad men were put to death by the Romans. And Jesus was not bad. He was all good, above all other men. How could these words of His come true?

So Jesus sought to cheer them up. After the cross, the crown! After death, life eternal! He said, "The Son of man is going to come with His angels, in His Father's glory; and then He will repay everyone for what he has done. I tell you, some of you who stand here will certainly live to see the Son of man in His glory."

Six days after this Jesus took Peter, James, and John, and went up on the mountain to pray. And as He was praying, the look of His face changed, and His clothes turned dazzling white. The three disciples, though at first they had followed His prayer, grew weary, and fell asleep. But now they woke up to a wonderful vision. Their Lord was in glory! And there were two glorious men with Him. They were Moses, whom God had raised from the dead, and Elijah, who went to heaven without ever seeing death. And they talked there with Jesus about His coming trials at Jerusalem.

Just as the two were leaving Jesus, Peter exclaimed: "Master, it is good for us to be here. Let us put up three booths, one for You, one for Moses, and one for Elijah!" He was dazed and did not know what he was saying. But he and the others all saw that the kingdom of glory was there represented: Jesus, the King; Moses, the resurrected; and Elijah, the translated.

Just then a bright cloud descended upon them, the cloud that had appeared at Sinai and that had descended upon the tabernacle and the temple. It was the cloud in which God hid Himself so that men should not die by seeing Him. And out of the cloud came a Voice, the Voice that had been heard at Jesus' baptism, the Voice of God: "This is My beloved Son, in whom I am well pleased."

The disciples fell on their faces, terribly afraid. How long they lay there dazed they did not know. But then they felt Jesus' hand upon them and heard His voice saying, "Get up, and do not be afraid." And, looking up, they saw only Jesus there. The glory had passed. But they had seen the kingdom of God.

As they were going down the mountain, Jesus said to them: "Keep this to yourselves. Tell no one, till I am risen from the dead."

They did not forget what He said; but they talked among themselves about what "rising from the dead" meant. They had set their minds so hard against the thought that He would die, that they did not remember what He had told them about it. But they told no man what they had seen and heard.

366

"Who Is the Greatest?"

Matthew 18:1-6; 20:20-28; Mark 9:33-37; 10:35-45; Luke 9:46-48

WHO DO you think is the greatest among you? The boy or girl who brags the most? Listen to what Jesus taught:

As they were going along the way to Capernaum one day, the disciples fell behind and let Jesus go ahead alone. For they wanted to settle among themselves who of them was the greatest. I don't suppose they came right out and said, each one: "I'm the greatest. I know more than you do. I can do greater things than you can. Jesus loves me more than He does you." That would be just too childish. But they began to tell what powers each one had and to compare them with others. Peter and James and John could say that Jesus took them more often to pray—and they did not tell that they fell asleep. Matthew could say that he had more business experience than any other of them— and he did not tell how he sometimes cheated. Thomas could say that he was not headlong like Peter, but would stop and think first—and he did not tell that he was often filled with doubts. And so they all could boast of what they had, and not of what they lacked. And they disputed among themselves who was the greatest.

When they were come into the house, Jesus asked them, "What were you discussing among yourselves on the way?" They were ashamed to tell Him; but after a while one of them asked, "Master, who is really the greatest in the kingdom of heaven?"

Then Jesus took a little child in His arms, there in their midst. And like any little child, he cuddled close to Jesus because he loved Him. And Jesus said to His disciples: "Except you change, and become as little children, you shall not even get into the kingdom of God. But whoever humbles himself as this little child, he is the greatest in the kingdom. For it is the lowliest among you who is really great."

But that did not cure them. For while they all loved Jesus, they loved themselves more; and everyone was thinking that when Jesus should be king, he would like to be next to Him, the highest in the kingdom.

Salome, the mother of James and John, was in the company. She and Zebedee, her husband, had given a great deal to Jesus—money and service and even their two sons. And she thought they ought to be rewarded with the highest places. So she took James and John with her and went to Jesus. And they said, "Master, will You give us whatever we ask of You?"

"What is it you want?" He asked.

"Why," said Salome, "that my two sons may sit on Your right hand and on Your left when You take the throne as king." That meant that one of them would be prime minister, the top man, and the other maybe secretary of the treasury, and handle all the money. So they would have more power than their fellow disciples or anyone else.

Jesus said, "You do not know what you are asking. Can you drink what I am drinking and go through the baptism that I am going through?"

They did not know what He meant; but they said, "Yes, we can."

"Well, you shall so drink and so be baptized," said Jesus. "But as for sitting on My right hand and My left, that is not Mine to give, but it belongs to them who are fit for it." So they were disappointed.

Pretty soon the other ten disciples heard what James and John had done, and they were very indignant. "To think," they said, "that those two hotheads should suppose they are the greatest and should have the highest places in the kingdom!"

But Jesus called them all to Him, and He said: "You know that those who are supposed to rule the heathen call themselves the great, and lord it over their subjects. But that is not so among you. Whoever wants to be great among you must be servant to everybody else. And whoever wants to hold the first place among you must make himself everybody's slave. For the Son of man Himself has come, not to be waited on, but to wait on other people and to give His life to free many men."

It took a long time for the disciples to learn that lesson. They did not learn it well until after Jesus had been put to death and had risen again. One of them never learned it, and so he cut himself out from among the disciples. That was Judas Iscariot, the most brilliant, the best educated, the keenest of them all, but the most selfish. No doubt it was he who kept stirring up among them this question of who was the greatest, always trying to show that he was the one. But for all his talents, he was not great at all, because he did not give himself to serve others.

This is the great lesson that Jesus taught to His disciples and to us: He that is greatest in the kingdom of God is the one who does not think himself great, but loves the Lord and his fellow men and gives himself to their service.

That the Blind May See

John 9

JESUS and His disciples were again in Jerusalem. The disciples still hoped that the rulers of the Jews would take Jesus as their Messiah; but Jesus knew that the rulers had shut their hearts against Him and only sought a chance to kill Him. This was very sad to Him, not because He was afraid for His life or because He was unwilling to die, but because He loved them and wanted to save them. But they would not be saved.

One Sabbath day as Jesus with His disciples walked along, they came to a blind man who sat and begged for money from the passersby. He was well known in Jerusalem as the blind beggar who had never seen, for he was born blind.

Now the Jews all thought that a man who was afflicted was being punished for his sins. But because this man was born blind, before he had lived and could have sinned, the disciples thought he must either be receiving punishment for his parents' sins or else punishment for sins he had not yet sinned but was going to sin. That did not seem right, either.

It puzzled them; so they asked Jesus, "Master, why was this man born blind? Because his parents had sinned, or because he was going to sin?"

Jesus answered, "Neither one. He was born blind to let you see what God can do. He has never seen light; but I am the Light of the world, and I will shine into his eyes and his heart."

Then He spat on the ground and made wet clay. This He plastered over the man's eyelids and said to him, "Go and wash them in the pool of Siloam."

So the blind man got to his feet and went tap-tapping with his cane to the pool of Siloam, which was outside the walls and below Jerusalem. He went in faith that he would see; for he had heard what Jesus said, and he believed that He was the Light of the world.

So he washed the clay from his eyelids and opened them. And he could see! What a wonderful miracle! All the world, everything in it, all the people that he had never seen, were there before his eyes. He walked home and told his parents how he had been cured.

And all the neighbors and everyone who had known him said, "Isn't this the man who used to sit and beg?"

Some said, "Yes, it is."

Others said, "It can't be. But he looks like him."

But he said, "I am the man."

So they asked, "Then how does it happen that you can see?"

He answered: "The man they call Jesus made some clay and rubbed it on my eyes and said to me, 'Go to Siloam and wash them.' So I went, and when I had washed them, I could see."

They asked, "Where is He?"

He said, "I don't know."

So they took him to the Pharisees and told them about him. They asked him again how he had been cured, and he told them the story.

Some of the Pharisees said, "This Jesus does not come from God; for He does not keep the Sabbath."

But others of them said, "How can a sinful man do such miracles as this?" Even the Pharisees did not agree among themselves about Jesus. So they asked the man who had been given sight, "What do you say about Him, since He has made you to see?"

He said, "He is a prophet."

But the Pharisees said, "Give God the praise. This man we know is a sinner."

He answered: "I don't know about His being a sinner. All I know is that I was blind, but now I see."

They said, "What did He do to you? How did He cure you?"

Back he came with this: "I have told you once, and you would not listen. Why do you want to hear it again? Do you want to become disciples of His, too?"

They sneered at him. They said: "You are a disciple of His, but we are disciples of Moses. We know that God spoke to Moses; but as for this fellow, we do not know where He came from."

He said: "There is something very strange about this! You do not know where He came from, and yet He has made me able to see! If this Man were not from God, He could do nothing!"

The Pharisees were enraged. "You were born in utter sin, and are you trying to teach us?" Then they shut him out of the synagogue.

Jesus found him and said, "Do you believe in the Son of God?"

"Who is He, sir? Tell me, that I may believe in Him."

"It is He who is now talking to you," said Jesus.

"I believe, Sir!" exclaimed the man. And he fell on his knees before Jesus and worshiped Him.

Let the Little Children Come

Matthew 19:13-15; Mark 10:13-16; Luke 18:15-17

ONE DAY some mothers came with their children to ask Jesus to lay His hands on their heads and pray and bless them. Wouldn't you have liked to see that company of mothers and children coming to Jesus? One mother started out that morning because she had heard that Jesus was in the neighborhood, and it came into her mind that her little boy and girl should see Him and hear Him and be blessed by Him. Going by a neighbor's house, leading her little boy in one hand and her little girl in the other, she was hailed by that neighbor: "Where are you going this bright and early morning, Mary?"

"I'm going to find Jesus and have Him bless my children."

"Wait a minute. I want to go with you." And she picked up her baby and carried him in her arms.

They two met another mother. "Where are you going, neighbors?"

"Going to find Jesus and have Him bless our children."

"Oh, I want to go too!" And she came with her children. And then they met another, and another, and another, who joined them. Pretty soon there were a whole company, trudging along the road to the grove by the brookside where Jesus was. Close about Him were the disciples, and all around them a great crowd of people, pressing in to see and hear Jesus. Some of them were sick and wanted to be healed. Some were weary of heart and wanted to be comforted. Some were proud and wanted to find fault. There were farmers and merchants and fishermen and scribes and Pharisees and young people and old people and men and women.

"Oh, Mary, how can we ever get to Jesus?" sighed a mother holding her baby.

"Have courage, Dorcas. And follow me." And Mary pressed into the crowd. "Please let us through," she said. "We want Jesus to bless our children." The crowd made way for the mothers, little by little, until they came up almost to Jesus. They could see Him, and they could hear Him.

But between them and Jesus were the apostles. And one of them —I think it must have been Judas Iscariot—said roughly to the moth-

ers: "Here! Why are you crowding in so rudely, and pushing everybody out of the way?"

"We want Jesus to bless our children."

"No! He's too busy. Don't you see He's talking with those Pharisees? They are important people, and He can't take time for your kids."

And then another disciple joined in. And another. And another. "Oh," said one more gentle than the others, "we are sorry. But really this is no time to come to Jesus with your children. You ought to have an appointment at some quieter hour. But surely you can't take His time now."

The mothers were downcast. Some of them were weary with carrying their little ones along the dusty road. All of them were anxious. But what could they do against Jesus' disciples?

Then Jesus changed it all. He stopped His talking to important people, some of whom were just faultfinders. And He said to His apostles, "Let the little children come to Me, and don't try to stop them. For the kingdom of God belongs to them. I tell you, whoever does not come to the kingdom of God like a little child will never get in."

Then the disciples were ashamed that Jesus had rebuked them before the people. And the Pharisees and scribes stood aside. And all the people in the crowd were pleased. Jesus made a circle around Him, and now the disciples helped the mothers come in with their children, so that they were the closest of all to Him. And that was the kingdom of heaven.

The children crowded around Jesus and looked up into His face and laughed, and then were quiet and listened. Even the babies were soothed as Jesus blessed them. Perhaps He told the children one of His stories. He took them up in His arms and held them close. Oh, how happy the children were! And how happy the mothers!

We hardly want to think that visit ever ended, do we? But finally the mothers took their children, blessed forever, and went home with joy. And I think it very likely that in after years the children on whom Jesus laid His hands that day became His loving followers and disciples and apostles.

"Lazarus, Come Forth!"

John 11

IN BETHANY, about two miles from Jerusalem, on the other side of the Mount of Olives, lived three friends of Jesus, Lazarus and his two sisters, Martha and Mary. They were always glad to see Him and took care that no one should disturb Him. Martha was a busy, bustling young woman, who always took charge of things, while Mary was a quiet, lovable soul who would rather listen to Jesus' teaching than anything else.

One day when Jesus was with His apostles away over the Jordan River, word came to Him from Martha and Mary: "Lord, Your friend, whom You love, is sick." They hoped that when Jesus heard this, He would hasten to Bethany and make Lazarus well.

But Jesus stayed for two days where He was. Then He said to His disciples, "Let us go back to Judea."

They said, "Master, the Jews have just been trying to stone You, and are You going back there again?"

He answered, "Our friend Lazarus has fallen asleep, but I am going there to wake him."

"Why, if he has fallen asleep," they said, "he will get well."

Then Jesus told them plainly: "Lazarus is dead. And I am glad for your sakes that I was not there, so that you may learn to believe in Me. But let us go to him."

So they went. When they came to Bethany, they found that Lazarus had been dead and buried for four days. Many friends of the family had come out from Jerusalem to comfort Martha and Mary, and they were with them in the house. While Jesus was yet outside the town, Martha heard of His coming, and she went out to meet Him, but Mary remained at home. When Martha saw Jesus, she exclaimed, "Master, if You had been here, my brother would not have died. But I know that even now, anything you ask of God, He will give You."

Jesus said to her, "Your brother will rise."

"I know that he will rise at the resurrection," she said.

Jesus answered: "I am the resurrection and the life. He who believes in Me will live even if he dies, and no one who is alive and believes on Me will ever die. Do you believe that?"

"Yes, Master, I do indeed believe that You are the Christ, the Son of God." With these words she went and called her sister Mary, whispering to her, "The Master has come, and calls for you."

Mary sprang up and started to meet Him. And her friends who were with her in the house followed. When Mary saw Jesus, she fell at His feet and said, like Martha, "Master, if You had been here, my brother would not have died."

When Jesus saw her weeping and her friends weeping, He was deeply troubled. He asked, "Where have you laid him?"

They said, "Come and see, Master."

Jesus wept. So the Jews said, "See how He loved him!" Others said, "Could not this Man, who opened the eyes of the blind, have kept Lazarus from dying?"

They took Jesus to the tomb, which was a cave with a stone rolled against the mouth. Jesus said, "Move the stone away."

But Martha said, "Master, by this time he is decaying. For he has been dead four days."

Jesus answered, "Have I not promised you that if you will believe Me, you will see the glory of God?"

So they moved the stone away. And Jesus looked upward and said: "Father, I thank You for listening to Me. You always listen. Now make the people who stand by believe that You have made Me Your messenger."

Then Jesus, standing by the open tomb, called out in a loud voice, "Lazarus, come forth!"

The dead man came out, bound hand and foot with wrappings, and his face covered with a handkerchief.

Jesus said to them, "Loose him, and let him go."

Marveling, they moved toward Lazarus and unwound the wrappings. And Lazarus, who had been dead four days, Lazarus was alive! Oh, what a happy family then! And how the news flew over the land! Thousands shouted the praise of Jesus, and many who had doubted and waited now believed in Him.

But when the news reached the Pharisees and priests, they were angry. They said: "What are we going to do about this Man who is doing such miracles? If we let Him go on, everybody will believe in Him, and the Romans will come and put an end to our holy place and our people." And they plotted to put Him to death. They even planned to do away with Lazarus, because he was a living witness that Jesus was the Master of life and could raise the dead. But God put His hand over them; for Jesus' time to die was not yet come.

The Feast at Simon's House

Matthew 26:6-13; Mark 14:3-9; Luke 7:36-50; John 12:1-11

SIX DAYS before the Passover, Jesus came again to Bethany and to the home of Lazarus, Martha, and Mary. There was a Pharisee in that town named Simon, whom Jesus had cured of the leprosy. Simon was grateful and called himself a disciple of Jesus, but his heart had not been fully changed. However, he planned a dinner to honor Jesus and invited Lazarus and many notable people from Jerusalem. Of course Jesus and His disciples, along with Lazarus, were the chief guests. With Jesus in the center, and Simon the healed leper and Lazarus the man raised from the dead on either side of Him, that was a great occasion indeed.

Sometimes at their feasts they had both men and women as guests, but more often among the Jews just men. This was a feast for men only; but Martha and Mary, Lazarus' sisters, were there. Martha, we are told, served the dinner; probably she had others helping her.

Mary, however, had something else in mind. More than His disciples, she had hung on every word she heard Jesus speak. She believed everything He said, and she understood better than the men who were closest to Him. So when He told that He was to be put to death here in Jerusalem, though she did not quite understand why, she made preparation for His burial. It was the custom then to anoint the body of a dead person with sweet-smelling ointments or oil. Mary took her savings and bought a very costly alabaster box of spikenard.

Now, however, she heard everybody saying that Jesus was going to be crowned king, and that made her very happy. She thought, "Instead of keeping my box of spikenard for His burial, I will pour it on Him while He is living. I am not the one to anoint Him as the King, the Messiah, but I will anoint Him King of my heart. And this dinner is the best opportunity I shall have to do it."

So while the feast was going on, she came in softly and sat at the feet of Jesus. In their feasts then, men did not sit up at table, but lay on a couch, with their heads at the table and their feet stretched out behind. So Mary came in and stood at Jesus' feet with her precious box of fragrant oil. She was so grateful to Jesus for saving her and for being her Friend that her tears flowed for very happiness.

375

We are told that she had been a great sinner. Who has not been? Everybody at that feast had been a great sinner, though, not like Mary, some of them thought they were pretty good. Mary sat quietly for a time, weeping. She bent over and kissed Jesus' feet, and her tears wet them. Then she wiped them with her long hair. And breaking the seal on her alabaster box, she poured some of the perfume on Jesus' feet.

The sweet odor filled the room, and everyone looked at Jesus and Mary. Judas Iscariot said to the disciples near him: "What a waste of money! That perfume could have been sold for sixty dollars, and the money could have been given to the poor." He said this not because he pitied the poor, but because he carried the purse of the little band, and he stole money out of it for himself. The other disciples took up the cry and began to say, "What a pity! What a waste!"

Simon heard the murmur of the disciples. He looked around and saw Mary, and he thought in his heart, "If this Man were a prophet, He would have known that this woman is a sinner."

Mary shrank back, but Jesus spoke up and said: "Let her alone! Why do you bother her? It is a fine thing she has done to Me. In pouring this perfume on Me, she has done something to prepare Me for My burial. And I tell you that wherever the gospel is preached in all the world, what she has done will be told in memory of her."

Then Mary was encouraged, and having some of the oil left, she poured it on the head of Jesus, as kings and priests were anointed.

Jesus said, "Simon, there is something I want to say to you."

Simon answered, "Do so, Master."

"Two men were in debt to a money lender. One owed him a hundred dollars and the other ten. As neither could pay him, he forgave both debts. Now which of them will be more grateful to him?"

"I suppose," said Simon, "the one whom he forgave the most."

"You are right," said Jesus. "Do you see this woman? I came to your house; you gave Me no water for My feet, but she has wet My feet with her tears and wiped them with her hair. You gave Me no kiss, but she has kissed My feet from the moment she came in. You put no oil on My head, but she has put perfume on My feet. So her sins, though many, are forgiven, for she loved Me much. But the man who thinks his debt which has been forgiven is little loves Me little."

But Judas Iscariot, feeling himself rebuked, went away to the priests and rulers, and offered to betray Jesus into their hands. They bargained to pay him thirty pieces of silver, and he took it. Oh, what a traitor! But no one except himself and the priests knew of it yet, and he stayed in the company of the other disciples and of Jesus.

"Thy King Cometh!"

Matthew 21:1-17; Mark 11:1-11; Luke 19:28-46; John 12:12-19

JESUS loved His people the Jews. He longed to cleanse their hearts of sin and make them fit to enter the kingdom of heaven. He had healed their sick, comforted their sorrowing, fed their hungry, cleansed their lepers, raised their dead. He had taught them the way of life, and He was all the while giving them His life. If they would receive Him, He would put His righteousness within them and make them all His apostles to the world.

But their rulers wanted none of His righteousness. They did not want to change their evil lives into good lives. They wanted power without purity, honor without honesty, a Messiah of might without mercy. They would take from the devil the offer which Jesus had rejected, of having all the kingdoms of the world at the price of worshiping Satan. Jesus could not please them. They wanted to kill Him.

All that the prophets had foretold of Messiah's mission, in healing and teaching, Jesus had done before them. The last great sign He had given was raising Lazarus from the dead after he had lain in the tomb for four days. This sign of His power the priests and rulers could not deny, but it made them so angry they wanted to kill not only Jesus but Lazarus too. One more sign which the prophets had foretold would be given them. Would it convince them and convert them? The prophet Zechariah had prophesied: "Rejoice greatly, O daughter of Zion! Shout, O daughter of Jerusalem! Behold, thy King cometh unto thee. He is just, and having salvation; lowly, and riding upon an ass and upon a colt the foal of an ass." If they should see their King coming in such manner, would they believe?

Jesus with His company prepared to leave Bethany for Jerusalem. Then Jesus said to two of His disciples: "Go into the village ahead of you, and you will find an ass tied, and a colt with her. Untie her, and bring them to Me. If anyone says anything to you, say, 'The Master needs them,' and they will let them go."

So the two disciples went and found the ass and her colt, and began to untie her. Then some of the bystanders said, "What are you doing?" And they answered as Jesus had instructed them. Then the men let them go.

377

They brought the two little animals to Jesus. He took the smaller of the two, the colt, which had never been ridden. The disciples threw their coats over its back, and Jesus sat on it, and started toward Jerusalem.

Then the disciples remembered the prophecy. They saw their Master for the first time seeming to declare Himself King. And they said to the crowd that was gathering, "See! The King is coming into His own!"

Then the crowd went wild. They took off their coats and spread them in the road for the colt to walk over. They cut down branches of palm trees and waved them, and then cast them in the road. And the crowds that went before and that followed Him shouted: "God bless the Son of David! Blessed be He who comes in the name of the Lord! Hosanna in the highest!"

Now they reached the top of the Mount of Olives, and the beautiful city and temple came to view below. Jesus stopped, and the procession stopped, held by the loveliness of the scene. But while the shouts were rising in His praise, the people were astonished to see Jesus burst into tears and sobs. What could be the matter? The crowd, awed and silent, now heard Him saying to the proud city:

"If you only knew today what you need for your peace! But it is hidden from you! The time is coming when your enemies will surround you and shut you in on every side. And they will throw you, and your children within you, to the ground, and not leave one stone upon another; because you did not know when God visited you." The fate of Jerusalem and of the Jews was being sealed.

Recovering His calm, He rode on. And the crowds grew, and they shouted more and more, crying: "Rejoice, O Zion! For your King comes to you, lowly, and riding on a colt the foal of an ass, as the prophet declared!"

But some of the Pharisees in the crowd were greatly displeased. They saw they could not stop the people from shouting the praises of Jesus; so they pressed in close to Him and said, "Master, rebuke Your disciples!"

But Jesus said to them, "I tell you, if they should keep still, the very stones would cry out!"

The procession passed within the gates of Jerusalem. And all the city was stirred. People asked, "Who is this that comes in such fashion, with crowds acclaiming Him?" And some answered, "It is Jesus, the prophet of Nazareth." But His disciples proclaimed, "It is Jesus, the Christ, the King of Israel!"

As they came to the gates of the court of the temple, the procession halted; for they could not go in with tumult. Jesus then walked into the temple court and looked around. What did He see? The same traffic from which He had cleansed the temple three years before at the beginning of His work.

Now the wrath of God blazed forth from Him. He said to the buyers and sellers and the money-changers: "It is written, 'My house shall be called the house of prayer,' but you have made it a den of thieves. Take these things out!" And He drove them out of the temple. They fled in terror from His face.

Now from the crowd outside there came in those who wanted to be near Jesus, those who wanted to be healed. There were blind men there and lame men and people with many troubles. They came to Jesus; and He who a moment before had been an avenging God became at once a healing Saviour. As He had done in the beginning, so He did at the close of His work. The sick and the maimed were cured.

Now the temple court was filled with the exultant throng. Foremost among them were children, who waved the palm branches they had brought in, and cried in a chorus of voices, "God bless the Son of David!"

The chief priests and the scribes, who at first had fled with the merchants, now returned. And when they heard the children praising Jesus in the temple, they were angry. And they said to Jesus, "Do you hear what these are saying?" Their anger choked them; so they could not even say, "these children," or, "these little ones"; for they had no love in their hearts. They just said, "these!" as they would say, "these brats!"

And Jesus answered: "Yes. Did you never read in the Scriptures, 'Thou hast drawn praise from the mouths of children and babies'?"

So ended the great day of the triumphal entry in the familiar scene of Jesus healing and teaching. He was the King of their hearts. The shades of eventide descended upon them like the covering hand of God.

Jesus left them and with His disciples went out to Bethany.

———

Hosanna, hosanna! Messiah comes!
   Let Israel hail the King!
Blow the great trumpets; beat the loud drums!
   Let men and angels sing.
Today shall the throne of David be filled,
And righteousness reign, as the Lord has willed.

Jesus Tells the Future

Matthew 23:37-39; 24; Mark 13; Luke 21:5-38

FOR TWO or three days after this, Jesus taught in the temple, meeting the enmity of the priests and rulers, who tried to trip Him up with hard questions. But they were always defeated by His wisdom. He taught much in parables, which told His lessons in story; but sometimes He met their questions with straight answers.

He knew that the rulers had rejected Him, and that there was now no hope for the Jews' taking the kingdom of God into their hearts. So He could not be their King. And they could not be His people. He would die for the sins of the world, but He would be raised from the dead. But instead then of becoming King of the Jews and reigning in a new Jerusalem over a people who would be missionaries to all the world, He would go to heaven, and His kingdom of glory would be put off till the gospel had gone to all the world.

How hard it was for Jesus to give up His cherished people, whom He had guided and helped and blessed from the time of Abraham, none of us can know. He was cheered by the knowledge that men from every nation on earth would accept Him; but how sad that the people to whom He had given so much should now return nothing.

Mournfully Jesus cried: "O Jerusalem! Jerusalem! Thou that killest the prophets and stonest them which are sent unto thee, how often would I have gathered thy children together, even as a hen gathereth her chickens under her wings, and ye would not."

He turned away, casting His last sorrowful glance upon the temple, which was no longer to be the house of God. Gathering His disciples about Him, He said this last word to the priests and rulers:

"Behold, your house is left unto you desolate. For I tell you, You will never see Me again until you say, 'Blessed is He who comes in the name of the Lord!' " He was the Messiah, the Christ, and He was now leaving His temple forever; but they saw Him only as a man, a Galilean. They would put Him to death, seeing in Him not the Christ but a mere man; but in the day when He shall come in His glory, as King of kings, they shall see Him and mourn, while all His faithful ones will be shouting, "Blessed is He that comes in the name of the Lord!"

As He and His disciples passed out of the temple and around its base in the valley of the Kidron, they called His attention to the stones which made its foundation. These were of great size, and so closely joined together they seemed like the living rock.

But Jesus said: "Do you see all this? I tell you, not one stone will be left here upon another, but shall be torn down."

The disciples were silent, thinking upon these words, and so they climbed the slopes of Mount Olivet on their way to Bethany. But before they went over the crest, Jesus stopped, and sat down with His disciples around Him, looking back upon the city.

Alone now, with no crowds around them, the disciples thought it a good time to hear the secrets of Jesus. They asked Him: "Tell us, when shall all these things happen, and what will be the sign of Your coming, and of the end of the world?" It seemed to them that the temple could not be destroyed except in the last great judgment day.

Jesus knew that His disciples could not at this time take into their minds all the years and hundreds of years that would follow before His second coming. Their minds were fixed upon His prophecy that Jerusalem and the temple should be destroyed. So He told them of the coming destruction of Jerusalem, and made it the sign of the end of the world, when He should come the second time, in glory.

"Let no one deceive you," He said; "for many will come in My name, saying, 'I am the Christ,' and many people will be deceived. You will hear of wars and rumors of wars; do not be alarmed. They have to come, but that is not the end.

"All this will be but the beginning of sorrows. They will persecute you and put you to death, and you will be hated by all men, because you bear My name. Many will fall away and betray and hate one another. And because wickedness will increase, the love of many will grow cold. But he who holds out to the end will be saved.

"When you see the abomination of desolation, told of by Daniel, stand in the holy place, then you who are in Judea must flee to the mountains. And pray that your flight be not in the winter nor on the Sabbath day. For then will be greater troubles than have ever been since the beginning of creation."

Thirty-eight years afterward this prophecy was fulfilled when Titus, a Roman general, besieged and captured the city, slaughtering a million persons and carrying captive nearly a hundred thousand more. The temple was burned; and in searching for the melted gold and silver in the ruins, the Roman soldiers threw down the remainder of the walls.

But now, on the Mount of Olives, Jesus continued His prophecy. He looked far into the future, when such troubles as the people of His time should see would be felt by the followers of Jesus for years upon years and centuries upon centuries. And He said: "Immediately after the trouble of those days, the sun will be darkened, and the moon will not give its light, and the stars will fall from the sky, and all the powers of heaven will be shaken.

"And then," He said, "shall appear the sign of the Son of man in heaven. And then shall all the nations of the earth mourn, when they see Him coming in the clouds of heaven, in all His power and glory. And He shall send His angels with a great sound of a trumpet, and they shall gather together His chosen ones from the four winds, from one end of the sky to the other."

But of all the signs of His coming, the greatest Jesus told of was this: "This gospel of the kingdom shall be preached in all the world for a witness unto all nations; and then shall the end come."

And to make sure that none of His people should be deceived by false Christs who would arise, Jesus said: "If they say to you, 'There He is, in the desert,' do not go out there. Or, 'Here He is, in a room in here,' do not believe it. For just as the lightning starts in the east and flashes to the west, so the coming of the Son of man will be."

In the last book in the Bible, one who sat with Jesus on the Mount of Olives that day and heard this prophecy, even John the beloved, writes: "Behold, He cometh with clouds, and every eye shall see Him, and they also which pierced Him; and all kindreds of the earth shall wail because of Him." "Even so, come, Lord Jesus." Revelation 1:7; 22:20.

There shall be music and songs of joy
    Tomorrow!
There shall be nought of weeping or crying.
There in the Mountain nought shall destroy,
    And far forgotten shall be all sighing
    And sorrow!

O hope of the blessed! O promised word!
    God's story!
Shout, O ye ransomed, in ecstasy thrilling!
Lo, through the heavens appeareth our Lord,
    With angels descending, His promise fulfilling
    In glory!

Last Supper and First Supper

Matthew 26:17-30; Mark 14:12-25; Luke 22:1-38; John 13;
1 Corinthians 11:23-26

THE NIGHT of the Passover drew near, the last Passover which Jesus was to keep, and the last Passover that held any meaning. For the Passover lamb that was slain represented the Lamb of God, the Christ, who was to die for the sins of the world. And it was at this Passover that Jesus, the Lamb of God, was to die, the very next day after the Passover supper. And on that day, in God's mind, the sacrifice of animals stopped; for the Messiah to whom they pointed was Himself sacrificed. The Jews might go on sacrificing animals in the temple, but their sacrifice had no meaning.

Now Jesus sent Peter and John into the city to prepare the Passover supper. His disciples were His family. Of old time, the head of the family slew the lamb and sprinkled the blood on the doorpost; but since the temple was built, the lambs were all slain by the priests in the temple, and the blood was sprinkled on the altar. Then the lamb was taken to the house of the family for the supper.

"Where shall we prepare the supper?" asked the disciples; for Jesus had no house in Jerusalem.

"When you go into the city," He told them, "you will see a man carrying a pitcher of water. Follow him to the house where he goes, and say to the owner of the house, 'The Master says to you, "Where is the room where I can eat the Passover with My disciples?"' And he will show you a large upper room, all furnished. Make preparation there."

So they went and found everything just as He had told them, and they prepared the Passover supper. When evening came, Jesus went with His disciples to that upper room and sat down with them at the table. But there was something missing. Everyone then wore sandals, and so their feet became dusty. It was the custom then for the host to provide water and a basin and a towel, to wash their feet when they came in. A servant usually did this, but sometimes, as a great honor, the host did it. Now the disciples had provided the water and the basin and the towel, but there was no servant.

Who should play servant? Each one said to himself, "Not I! I

383

will not lower myself to be the servant of these others." Though Jesus had taught them that the greatest was the one who would be servant of all, every one of them felt that he could not be the servant; for did he not deserve to be the highest? So they sat there and waited.

Then Jesus arose, laid aside His coat, fastened a towel around His waist, took a basin and poured water in it, and came to wash their feet and wipe them with the towel, as a servant would. Now they were ashamed. They remembered that their Master had said He was a servant, and that they were to be servants like Him.

One by one Jesus washed their feet, till He came to Simon Peter. Peter said, "Master, are You going to wash my feet?"

"You cannot understand now what I am doing," said Jesus, "but you will learn by and by." That ceremony of washing feet meant deeper things than Peter or any of the disciples could then know; but when they had learned more of Jesus, they would know.

Peter said, "I will never let You wash my feet."

"You will have no share with Me," said Jesus, "unless I wash you."

Then Peter gave up. "O Master," he cried, "wash not only my feet, but my hands and my face too."

Jesus said, "Anyone who has bathed needs only to have his feet washed to be wholly clean." It was a sort of parable He spoke. The disciples had been with Jesus for three years, and they had learned to love Him. It was like taking a bath. But they had been on a journey through life, and they had some dust, as it were, on their manners. They were still selfish in wanting the highest place. So Jesus, in washing their feet, was also washing away that evil from their hearts. And Jesus went on, "You are clean now—but not all of you." For He knew who was going to betray Him.

He came to Judas and knelt to wash that traitor's feet. None in the room knew what Judas was going to do, none but Judas—and Jesus. At first Judas felt a rush of tenderness come over him. But then the evil spirit took possession of him, and he thought, "If this Man stoops to wash the feet of others, like a servant, He cannot be King." And he hardened his heart; for he had already bargained with the priests to betray Jesus.

When Jesus had finished washing all their feet, He said: "Do you understand what I have done to you? You call me Teacher and Master, and you are right, for I am. If then I, your Master and Teacher, have washed your feet, you ought to wash one another's feet. For I have set you an example, that you may do what I have done to you."

King Jesus Entering Jerusalem

The prophet Zechariah prophesied the entrance of Christ into Jerusalem five hundred years before it happened. The prophet wrote of Jesus as a King, and the common people of the city welcomed Him in that way. Even the children brought flowers and palm branches to give to Jesus and lay on the ground.

ROBERT TEMPLE AYRES, ARTIST

They sat and ate the Passover supper together. Jesus said to them: "I have greatly desired to eat this Passover supper with you before I suffer. I tell you, I will never eat one again till I eat with you in the kingdom of God."

Then Jesus, knowing that the Passover was no more, set up that which was to take its place among His disciples. He took a loaf of un-leavened bread, and blessed it. Breaking it, He gave a piece to each of His disciples, saying, "Take this; eat it. It is My body."

Then He took the cup of wine and gave thanks and gave it to them, saying: "You must all drink from it; for this is My blood of the new testament, which is to be poured out for many people, for the forgiveness of their sins."

This we call the Lord's Supper. And Paul tells us: "As often as ye eat this bread and drink this cup, ye do show the Lord's death, till He come."

Then Jesus became greatly distressed. And He said to them, "I tell you, one of you shall betray Me."

The disciples looked at one another, wondering whom He meant. And they began to ask Him, "Is it I? Master, is it I?" Peter motioned to John, who was next to Jesus, to ask Him. John did. And Jesus said: "It is the one to whom I am going to give this piece of bread, when I have dipped it in the dish." So He dipped it and gave it to Judas Iscariot. "Be quick about your business," He said to him. None of the disciples knew what business He meant, but Judas knew.

He quickly arose, for he saw he was discovered, and he went out. It was pitch dark; but nowhere was it so black as in Judas' heart. When he first had gone to the priests and offered to betray his Master, his motives were mixed. He was angry because Jesus had rebuked him at Simon's feast. But he had long thought about doing this, because he saw that Jesus would not make Himself King; and he thought that if he could put Him in a dangerous place, where His life was threatened, then Jesus would use His divine power to free Himself. Then, Judas reasoned, Jesus would take the throne, and Judas would be honored for having brought it about, and he would be given the highest place in the kingdom. He still thought so. And then, besides, he would be richer by thirty pieces of silver, and the priests would have cheated themselves. But now, having given himself over to Satan, he could think of nothing but pushing his plot through to deliver his Master to death. He went straight to the priests and said, "I will now show you where He is." For he knew where Jesus would go after the supper.

Jesus now held His last session of school with His eleven disciples. It is a wonderful and beautiful talk He gave them, which we find in the last of John 13, and in the 14th, 15th, and 16th chapters, with His closing prayer in the 17th. The central thought of it all is in His words: "A new commandment give I unto you, that ye love one another; as I have loved you, that ye also love one another."

And then: "Let not your heart be troubled. Ye believe in God, believe also in Me. In My Father's house are many mansions; if it were not so, I would have told you. I go to prepare a place for you. And if I go and prepare a place for you, I will come again, and receive you unto Myself; that where I am, there ye may be also. And whither I go ye know, and the way ye know."

But Thomas said, "Master, we do not know where You are going. How can we know the way?"

"I am the way," answered Jesus, "and I am the truth and the life. No man can come to the Father except through Me. If you had really known Me, you would have known My Father, too. From now on you do know Him and you have seen Him, because you have seen Me."

But Philip said, "Lord, show us the Father, and we shall be satisfied."

"Philip," said Jesus, "I have been a long time with you. Don't you recognize Me? Whoever has seen Me has seen the Father, for we are one."

And when they had sung the Passover hymn, they went out.

In the Garden of Woe

Matthew 26:31-46; Mark 14:27-42; Luke 22:39-46; John 18:1

THE GARDEN OF GETHSEMANE lay at the foot of the Mount of Olives, just over the brook Kidron. It was a quiet place, with large trees and much shrubbery; and here Jesus used often to go with His disciples to pray, especially in the quiet hours of the night. Now, after the supper in the upper room, He led the eleven to this familiar spot.

On the way Jesus said to them: "You will all desert Me tonight. But after I am raised to life, I will meet you in Galilee." They could not understand this; but they were grieved by His charge that they would desert Him. Peter said, "If they all leave You, I never will."

Jesus answered, "I tell you, Peter, that before the cock crows twice in the morning, you will have denied Me three times!"

"Even if I have to die with You," declared Peter, "I will never disown You." And so said all the disciples. They meant it, but they did not know themselves.

Then they came into the garden, and Jesus said, "Sit down here, while I go yonder and pray." He took Peter and James and John with Him a little way. He grew very sad and sorrowful, and He said to them, "My heart is almost breaking. Stay here and keep watch with Me." The sins of the world were pressing down upon Him, and they seemed to be shutting Him away from His Father, God.

He went on a little way and threw Himself on His face and prayed: "My Father, if it is possible, let this cup pass Me by. Yet not as I will, but as You will."

The weight was almost more than He could bear. He longed for the sympathy of His disciples, and He staggered up and went back to the three. But He found them asleep. He said to Peter: "Were you not able to watch with Me for one hour? You must all watch and pray, that you may not be overcome by temptation. Your spirit indeed is willing, but the flesh is weak."

He went away again and prayed: "My Father, if it cannot pass by Me without My drinking it, Thy will be done."

The disciples truly wanted to stay awake and pray with their Master, but heavy sleep overcame them. Satan pressed it upon them.

If they had struggled and prayed through, they would have gained the victory, and they would not have been so weak when they came to the test. But they slept.

Jesus came again and found them asleep. And when He spoke to them, they could scarcely wake up enough to know what He was saying or to answer Him.

The third time Jesus went away, staggering to His place of prayer. The agony of the world's sins pressed Him down. He fell to the ground. Satan was fighting his last fight to overcome Jesus. If now he could make Him give up, the battle for the world would be won. With all his evil power he pressed the question upon Jesus: "Is it worth it? The world does not want You or care for You. If You die, will You gain anything?"

Jesus was in agony. Great drops of sweat mingled with blood fell from His face and form. How could He, the Sinless One, bear the guilt of the whole world? The Father in heaven was not unmindful of His precious Son, struggling there under the burden of the world's sin. But He knew that He must bear this if He was to save the world. And the Father sent a mighty angel to Jesus. The angel bent over Him, lifting and pillowing His head, wiping the bloody sweat from His brow, and speaking the sweet message that His Father loved Him.

The struggle was over. Jesus rose to victory over Satan, ready to meet the great trial before Him. He came to His disciples and said: "Are you still sleeping? The time has come for Me to be handed over to wicked men! Arise! Let us be going! Here comes My betrayer!"

'Tis midnight; and on Olives' brow,
    The star is dimmed that lately shone.
'Tis midnight in the garden; now
    The suffering Saviour prays alone.

'Tis midnight; and from all removed,
    The Saviour wrestles lone with fears.
E'en that disciple whom He loved
    Heeds not His Master's grief and tears.

'Tis midnight, and from ether plains
    Is borne the song that angels know;
Unheard by mortals are the strains
    That sweetly soothe the Saviour's woe.

                    Tappan.

In the Hands of Wicked Men

Matthew 26:47-75; 27:1-10; Mark 14:43-72; Luke 22:47-62; John 18:2-27

THERE was a mob coming! The quiet peace of the garden was rent with the shouts and hoots of a rabble seeking Jesus. Priests and scribes mingled with criminals and with temple guards, armed with swords and clubs, and lighting the night with flaming torches. And they were led by Judas!

Jesus stepped forth before His disciples and said, "Who is it you are looking for?"

They answered, "Jesus of Nazareth."

"I am He."

As He said these words, they staggered and fell to the ground.

Again He asked, "Who is it you are looking for?" And again they said, "Jesus of Nazareth."

"I have told you that I am He. So if you are looking for Me, let these men go." Thus He gave a chance for His disciples to escape.

But seeing the danger, they asked Him, "Master, shall we use our swords?"

Peter did not wait for an answer. He drew his sword and struck at the nearest man, a servant of the high priest. He missed his head, but he cut off his ear.

Jesus said, "Let Me do this much." And He touched the man's ear and made it whole.

Judas had told the priests he would show them who was the Master by giving Him a kiss. Now, though they all knew, he went up to Jesus and kissed Him.

Jesus said, "Judas, do you betray the Son of man with a kiss?"

Then they seized Jesus and bound Him. When they saw that Jesus would not save Himself, all the disciples, struck with dismay and terror, forsook Him and fled.

The mob led Jesus away to the city to Annas, the father-in-law of Caiaphas the high priest. Annas had been high priest before, and he still had great influence. He was sometimes still called high priest.

Two of the disciples, John and Peter, followed at a little distance, and came at the tail of the procession to the house of Annas. John was

known to the high priest, and they let him in, while Peter stayed outside. Then John went back and got them to let Peter in, too.

The maid at the door said to Peter, "You are one of His disciples too?"

Peter was afraid. He answered roughly, "No; I am not!" He went and joined himself to a group who had built a fire in the courtyard, for it was cold.

Jesus' captors placed Him before Annas, who questioned Him about His disciples and His teaching.

Jesus answered: "I have spoken openly. I have always taught in the synagogues and the temple, and I have nothing secret. Ask those who have heard Me what I have said." It is one of the laws of justice everywhere, and it was a law of Moses, that a man cannot be made to testify against himself, but there must be at least two witnesses against him.

But now one of those standing by struck Jesus on the mouth and said, "Is that the way You answer the high priest?"

Jesus said, "If I have said anything wrong, testify to it. But if what I have said is true, why do you strike Me?"

Then Annas sent Him bound to Caiaphas.

Peter still stood by the fire. And one of them there said to him, "You are surely a follower of this Galilean, for you talk like a Galilean."

"I am not a follower of this Man!" declared Peter.

But soon another man, a near relative of the servant whose ear Peter had cut off, said, "Didn't I see you with Him in the garden?"

Now Peter was really scared. He thought he might not only suffer for being Jesus' disciple, but he might be condemned because he had fought for Him. And he began to curse and swear as he had before he met Jesus. Again he swore, "I do not even know the Man!"

Just then Jesus was being led past. He turned and looked at Peter. It was not a look of scorn, but a look full of pity and love.

And then the cock crowed the second time. And Peter remembered what his Lord had told him: "Before the cock crows twice, you will deny Me thrice."

Peter went out and wept bitterly. Now he knew himself as Jesus knew him. He hated himself for what he had done, and he longed to know that God would forgive him.

But it was far worse with Judas Iscariot. For when he saw that Jesus would not deliver Himself from His enemies, he went out and hanged himself.

Jesus Is Condemned

Matthew 27:11-31; Mark 15:1-20; Luke 22:63-71; 23:1-25;
John 18:28-40; 19:1-16

IN THE early morning the Sanhedrin was called together, and Caiaphas the high priest sat as its head. But they had carefully left out two of their number who were known to favor Jesus: Nicodemus and Joseph of Arimathea.

Now they brought Jesus before the council. Witnesses against Him stood up and told all sorts of false things, but they did not agree in their testimony. Some said: "We have heard Him say, 'I will tear down this temple built by men's hands, and in three days I will build another made without hands.' " But not one of them told it the same way as another, and none of them told truly what He said.

Then the high priest stood up and came forward face to face with Jesus. "Have You no answer to make?" he said. "What about the testimony of these witnesses?"

But Jesus said never a word.

Then the high priest raised his hand toward heaven and said: "I charge You, on Your oath, by the living God, tell us whether You are the Christ, the Son of God."

Jesus said, "It is true. But I tell you, you will soon see the Son of man seated at the right hand of God, and coming upon the clouds of the sky."

In pretended horror, Caiaphas tore his robe and cried out: "He has uttered blasphemy! What do we want of witnesses now? Here you have heard His blasphemy. What do you say?"

They all answered, "He deserves death!"

Then they spat in His face and struck Him. They blindfolded Him and slapped Him and said, "Show us that You are a prophet, You Christ! Who was it that struck You?"

But the Romans did not let the Jews put any man to death. They might say that a man should die, but they had to ask the Romans to put him to death. The Roman governor at that time was Pontius Pilate. And the Sanhedrin, though they had condemned Jesus, knew that they must get Pilate to pass the sentence of death. The priests who hated Jesus knew that Pilate would not sentence a man because they said he had blasphemed God; for he did not care about that. They must bring some charge of treason. And so they fixed up a charge that Jesus was a rebel against the Roman rule and was trying to make Himself a King.

In the morning they took Jesus to the governor's palace and called Pilate out to the porch before the court, because, they said, to go into the palace would defile them, and then they could not keep the Passover. Once Jesus had told them that it is not the things from without that defile a man, but the things which come from within. But they had not received His lesson, and now they could not see that they were already defiled by the blackness of their hearts.

Pilate came out and sat in the judgment seat which was on the porch. The mob filled the courtyard in tumult and noise. Most of the people in the mob were the worst kind in the land, whom the priests had gathered together. The priests knew that multitudes believed in Jesus, and they took care not to call all the people together. Jesus' enemies, the priests, even the high priests, went at the head of the mob with the soldiers who guarded and kept the prisoner, Jesus.

They said to Pilate: "Here is a Man whom we have found misleading our nation and forbidding the payment of taxes to the emperor and claiming to be an anointed King Himself."

Pilate took Jesus inside and asked Him, "Are You the King of the Jews?"

Jesus said: "My kingdom is not a kingdom of this world. If it were, My men would have fought for Me. But My kingdom is not of that kind."

"Then You are a King?" asked Pilate.

"As you say, I am a King," answered Jesus. "For this I was born, and for this I came into the world, to witness to the truth. Everyone who is on the side of truth listens to My voice."

"Truth!" said Pilate. "What is truth?" For he knew force as a Roman would, but he did not know love, and so he did not know truth.

Still he was so impressed by Jesus and what He had said that he went outside and declared to the mob, "I find no fault in this Man."

But they shouted: "He is stirring up the people everywhere by His teaching. He began in Galilee, and He has come here."

When Pilate heard that Jesus was from Galilee, he thought he would get rid of the case by sending Him to Herod, who was governor of Galilee, but who was just then at Jerusalem attending the feast. So Pilate sent Jesus under guard to Herod.

Now this was that Herod who had killed John the Baptist. He had long wished to see Jesus, whom he had at first supposed must be

John risen from the dead. Now he questioned Jesus a long while, but Jesus made him no answer. The priests and scribes stood by, shouting charges.

When Herod found that Jesus would not talk to him, he led His guards in making sport of Him. They clothed Him in an old, showy robe and pretended to honor Him as a king, but they only clowned about Him. They jostled Him and dragged Him this way and that. If the Roman soldiers had not stopped them, they would have torn Him in pieces. Then Herod sent Him back to Pilate.

The Romans at Passover time, as a special favor to the Jews, released some prisoner, the one they might choose. Now the mob began to clamor for Pilate to do that. He said to them and to the priests and rulers: "Well, here are two prisoners: this Jesus who is called King of the Jews, in whom I have found no fault at all; and there is Barabbas, that wicked robber, who has committed murder. Choose between them."

He sat down again on the judgment seat, as though he would give the final judgment. Just then a messenger came in with a message from his wife. She wrote: "Have nothing to do with that good Man. For I have had a dream this night about Him. It was indeed sad, and gave me much pain."

But the priests stirred up the mob, and they were shouting, "Not this Man, but Barabbas! Release Barabbas!"

Pilate said, "What then shall I do with Jesus who is called Christ?"

They shouted, "Crucify Him!"

"Why? What evil has He done?"

But they only shouted the louder, "Crucify Him! Crucify Him!"

Pilate said: "I find no fault in Him. But I will have Him whipped, and then I will release Him."

Jesus was taken back into the governor's palace. They bared His back, and He was cruelly lashed with a Roman whip. Then the soldiers put on Him a purple robe, such as kings wear. They took a thorny vine and made of it a crown, and pressed the crown of thorns down on His head. They took a reed and placed it in His hands as a scepter. Then they passed before Him, bowing in mockery and saying, "Long live the King of the Jews!" as each one gave Him a blow.

Pilate went out to the crowd and said, "I will bring Him before you, that you may see what an innocent Man He is."

They brought Jesus out, wearing the crown of thorns and the purple robe. And Pilate exclaimed, "Look at the Man!"

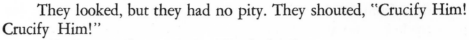

They looked, but they had no pity. They shouted, "Crucify Him! Crucify Him!"

"Shall I crucify your King?" asked Pilate.

And they shouted back, "We have no king but Caesar!"

"I find no fault in Him," Pilate repeated. "I have had Him flogged, and now I will let Him go."

The priests shouted: "If you let Him go, you are no friend of Caesar's. Anyone who calls himself a king is a traitor to the emperor."

That frightened Pilate; for he was afraid they would accuse him to the emperor, and he would be removed from being governor, and perhaps he would be put to death. Why throw away his life for this Galilean? Against what conscience he had, he gave the sentence that Jesus should be crucified.

He took a basin of water and washed his hands before them, saying: "I am innocent of the blood of this good Man. See to it yourselves!" But all the water in the world could not wash away his guilt.

We should remember that only a part of the Jewish people hated Jesus, and Pilate and the Roman government could have saved His life.

When I survey the wondrous cross
    On which the Prince of glory died,
My richest gain I count but loss,
    And pour contempt on all my pride.

See, from His head, His hands, His feet,
    Sorrow and love flowed mingled down;
Did e'er such love and sorrow meet?
    Or thorns compose so rich a crown?

Since I, who was undone and lost,
    Have pardon through His name and word;
Forbid it, then, that I should boast,
    Save in the cross of Christ, my Lord.

Were the whole realm of nature mine,
    That were a tribute far too small;
Love so amazing, so divine,
    Demands my life, my soul, my all.

                                        Watts.

394

"The Lamb of God"

Matthew 27:31-66; Mark 15:20-47; Luke 23:26-56; John 19: 16-42; Hebrews 13:12

AT THE beginning of Jesus' work, three and a half years before this, John the Baptist, seeing Him coming, had said to Andrew and John, "Behold the Lamb of God!"

Long ages ago, nineteen hundred years before, on the same Mount Moriah where the temple now stood, Abraham with Isaac at his side was climbing to the top, at the command of God, to offer his son as a burnt offering. And the young man said to Abraham, "Father, here is the fire and the wood, but where is the lamb for a burnt offering?" And Abraham had replied, "My son, God will provide Himself a lamb." God did that day provide a sheep for the sacrifice in place of Isaac; but Abraham's words went far beyond, even to this hour.

For all these years and centuries the Israelites had offered as burnt sacrifices lambs and other animals. But most of the people never knew that these sacrifices pointed to the coming Messiah, the Lamb of God, who should die for the sins of the world. Yet Isaiah had prophesied of Him: "He is brought as a lamb to the slaughter." And now God had provided for Himself the Lamb, even His Son, Jesus. And, like Isaac, Jesus gave Himself willingly. "For this cause came I into the world." Jesus was going as a lamb to the sacrifice.

It was the rule of the Romans that the man who was to be crucified should carry his cross from the judgment place to the place of crucifixion. So they laid upon Jesus His cross, and bearing it, He went forth to death. But He had been so badly used and He was so weak that He could not stand up under it. And as He staggered and fell under its weight, they seized upon a man named Simon, who came from the country of Cyrene, in northern Africa. And they laid the cross upon him, that he might bear it after Jesus.

Now many of the Jews in Jerusalem believed on Jesus, and they began to gather along the way, and some cried out against the priests and rulers who had condemned Him to death. There were many women who wept and cried, their tears falling for Him who had blessed their children and healed their sick and taught them love. But Jesus turned to them and said: "Daughters of Jerusalem, weep not

395

for Me, but weep for yourselves and for your children. For the days are coming when they will say, 'Happy are they who have no children.' And they will cry to the mountains, 'Fall on us and cover us!' "

The dire procession, led by the soldiers and Jesus and followed by the crowd, went through the gate in the wall of the city to the place called Calvary. Calvary is the Latin word for the Hebrew Golgotha, which means "the place of the skull." It was outside the northern wall of Jerusalem, and it was called Skull Hill because the south side was a cliff, in which, high up, were two small caves. At a distance this looked like a human skull, with the caves as the eye-holes.

Here on Calvary they nailed Jesus to the cross, and lifting it up, they thrust it into a hole they had dug in the rocky soil. The cruel nails tore His hands as the cross thudded into the hole. They offered Him sour wine mixed with gall to deaden the pain; but when He had tasted it, He would not drink it. For not so was the lamb slain; and Jesus would keep His senses to the end.

On top of the cross, over His head, was a writing by Pilate, telling why He was crucified. It said, "Jesus, the King of the Jews."

The soldiers who crucified Him parted His raiment among them; but when they came to His outer robe, which loving hands had woven for Him without a seam, it was too fair a garment for them to cut in pieces and divide among them; so they cast lots for it, and it was given whole to one of them, we know not whom. Thus was fulfilled the scripture which says, "They parted My raiment among them, and for My vesture did they cast lots." (Psalm 22:18.)

On either side of Him they crucified a thief; and so was fulfilled the prophecy that said, "He was numbered with the transgressors." (Isaiah 53:12.)

The passers-by jeered at Him, wagging their heads and saying: "You who would tear down the temple and build one in three days, save Yourself! If You are the Son of God, come down from the cross." Others who had come out to see Him die mocked Him, saying, "He saved others; Himself He cannot save! If He is the Christ, let Him come down from the cross, and we will believe on Him. He said, 'I am the Son of God'; let God now save Him."

But Jesus said no word of anger or reproach. He did not curse His enemies or the soldiers who had nailed Him to the cross. He patiently suffered. And He prayed, "Father, forgive them; for they know not what they do."

At first both of the thieves who were being crucified with Him joined in cursing Him and saying, "If You are the Christ, save Your-

396

self and us!" But after a while one of them, seeing how patiently Jesus suffered, and doubtless remembering something of His life, began to repent. He said to his fellow thief: "Have you no fear of God? We are suffering justly for our crimes, but this Man has done nothing wrong." And turning his head, he said, "Jesus, remember me when You come into Your kingdom."

Then Jesus said to him, "I tell you this day, you shall be with Me in Paradise."

There were also in the crowd some of Jesus' disciples. The only one who is certainly mentioned is John. But there were gentle women there, who had been in Jesus' company and helped Him as He gave His loving ministry to the sick and suffering. There were three named Mary: first, Mary the mother of Jesus, fainting with grief, and supported by the disciple whom Jesus loved; and Mary the mother of James and Joses; and Mary Magdalene; and there was also Salome, the wife of Zebedee and mother of James and John.

And Jesus, through all His suffering, looked down and saw His mother with His disciple, and He said to her, "There is your son!" And to John He said, "There is your mother!" From that hour John took Mary the mother of his Lord to his home and cared for her.

It had been late in the forenoon when they brought Jesus and nailed Him to the cross. And now at noon, when the sun was high in the heavens, there suddenly fell a terrible darkness upon the earth, a darkness that could be felt. For three hours it continued, while Jesus wrestled with the powers of darkness. The Lord of glory was dying. God's Lamb was being offered for the sins of the world. He felt the weight of the world's evil-doing resting down upon Him and shutting Him away from His heavenly Father, as the darkness hid the sun. It was not the cruel cross that killed the Christ; it was the sins of the world.

Yet in that darkness God was merciful to His Son. In the sunlight He had been jeered and mocked; now God hid Him in His cloud. The mad cries of the mob ceased. In fear and trembling they waited to see what would come.

At the ninth hour (that is, three o'clock) the voice of Jesus rang forth in agony and appeal: "My God, My God, why hast Thou forsaken Me?" The darkness lifted and moved off to city and temple.

Jesus awoke to His physical suffering. He said, "I thirst." A Roman soldier, moved by pity, filled a sponge with sour wine and lifted it on a reed to His parched lips. But the priests mocked. They said, "Stop! Leave Him alone. Let us see if Elijah will come and save Him."

397

Then came the end. With a triumphant cry, "It is finished! Father, into Thy hands I commit My spirit," Jesus died.

His work on earth indeed was finished. He was victorious over Satan. The Lamb of God had given His life; and the world, if it would be, was saved.

At that moment, in the temple, the great veil that hung between the holy place and the most holy was torn from top to bottom, showing that the temple service and all the ceremonies that went with it were at an end.

And there was a great earthquake which rent the hills and spilled the dead from many tombs. Some of those were of good men, who were brought to life, and later, upon Jesus' resurrection, were seen in the city. The captain of the Roman soldiers, seeing all this, exclaimed, "Truly this was the Son of God!"

There were two good men at the scene of the crucifixion, Jews, who had been disciples, but secretly for fear of those who hated Jesus. Now they were no longer afraid. They were Nicodemus and Joseph of Arimathea, both of them members of the Sanhedrin, but who had not been there when Jesus was condemned. Joseph went to Pilate and begged for the body of Jesus. Pilate was astonished that Jesus was dead; for men crucified usually lived on the cross for several days. But he called the captain, who told him that Jesus was indeed dead, and it was proved because a soldier had thrust a spear into His side, and there came out blood and water. Then Pilate gave permission to Joseph to take the body.

Joseph and Nicodemus brought linen cloth and spices. When Jesus' body had been taken down from the cross, they, with His disciples and the women, wrapped it in the linen cloth with spices; and they took Him to His burial.

There was in the garden below a new tomb, carved out of the rock. It belonged to Joseph. No body had ever been laid in it. There they laid Jesus.

The next day, though it was the Sabbath, the Jews went to Pilate and said: "We remember that this Man, while He was yet living, said that He would rise the third day. Now, lest His disciples come and steal the body away, we ask you to seal the great stone which closes the tomb, and set a guard of soldiers about it."

And Pilate said: "Go your way. You have the seal and the soldiers. Make it as sure as you can."

The tomb was sealed, and the Roman soldiers took up their watch.

"He Is Risen"

Matthew 28:1-15; Mark 16:1-14; Luke 23:54-56;
24:1-12; John 20:1-29

IT WAS a Sabbath of Sabbaths; for on this Sabbath day the Son of God rested in triumph. He had created the world, and when He had finished His work of creation, He had rested on the first Sabbath day in the joy of life. He was now the Redeemer of the world, and when He had finished His work of redemption, again He rested, but in the quiet of death.

To His disciples it was a sad Sabbath day; for He was dead, and they did not remember that He had told them He would rise again. But to the angels in heaven it was a glad Sabbath day; for they knew that their Lord had triumphed over Satan, and that His Father would not leave Him in the tomb. So in joy they prepared for the glorious morning.

It was now the darkest hour of the night, just before the dawn of the first day of the week. The tomb of Joseph, where Jesus lay, was closed by the great stone, sealed with the Roman seal. Before it watched the Roman guard. Brave men they were, who never feared a human foe. Rough, cruel men they were, who may have been among the mockers and scourgers of Jesus in the judgment hall, and the guard that took Jesus to Calvary and crucified Him there. They were Roman soldiers, and Rome ruled the world.

But suddenly there came a rumbling and a trembling of the earth. An earthquake had marked the death of Jesus; another earthquake now thundered as His resurrection dawned.

A dazzling light burst upon the eyes of the soldiers. No rising sun was this! In blazing light the angel of the Lord descended from heaven. His appearance was like the lightning, and his form was garbed in glory. Before him the keepers of the tomb were smitten as though dead, yet they saw and heard what happened then.

The angel came, and with a touch of his finger rolled away the stone. No Roman seal could keep it there. The door was open, and the angel form filled the entrance. In the thunderous tones of the earthquake and the storm he called forth the Son of God. He entered and unwrapped the form of the Lord of life.

399

And Jesus, whom those soldiers had seen dying upon the cross, came forth and stood in glory before their eyes. "I am the Resurrection and the Life!" Before the tomb of Lazarus those words had first been spoken, and they brought forth the dead; now from the emptied tomb of Joseph the blessed truth was proclaimed in the person of the Life-giver Himself.

Suddenly the light was gone. The form of the risen Christ, the Son of God, was there no more. The soldiers staggered to their feet and gazed in dumb terror at the opened tomb. Then they fled away as fast as their trembling limbs could carry them to tell Pilate.

But the news they carried flew ahead of them, and before they reached the city, the high priests knew it. They almost died from fear. But they called the guards in before they reached Pilate, and they paid them much money to tell that while they slept, the disciples of Jesus had come and stolen His body away. For a Roman soldier to sleep on guard was punishable by death; but the priests said, "If this comes to the ears of Pilate, we will fix it up with him." So they bought the guards.

The women who had seen where Jesus was laid had gone home that sad evening to prepare more spices and ointments for the body of Jesus, because in the fading day it had been but hastily prepared by Joseph and Nicodemus. Now early in the morning they came, bringing their precious spices. They did not know that Pilate and the Jews had sealed the tomb and set a guard of soldiers there. As they came through the darkness, they said to one another, "Who shall roll away for us the stone from the door of the tomb?"

But one of their number came before them. Mary Magdalene, alone but unafraid, approached the place just after the angel of God had rolled away the stone and the Master had come forth in glory. The Roman soldiers, white and trembling, had fled from the scene. All was still when Mary came.

But lo, in the early dawn she saw that the stone was rolled away from the door of the tomb. In great fear she turned and ran to find the disciples. She found Peter and John, and she said to them breathlessly: "They have taken the Master out of the tomb, and where they have laid Him I do not know."

At once Peter and John started running for the tomb.

Meanwhile the other women came to the tomb and found the stone rolled back from the door. They ventured in, but found no body of Jesus where they had seen Him laid two days before. They knew not what to think.

"The Lord Is Risen"

Jesus did not remain dead in the tomb. On the morning of the first day of the week a mighty angel came and rolled the stone away from the door of the tomb. Then Jesus, strong and joyous, came out of the tomb as the Father in heaven and all the angels rejoiced. Thus the Saviour conquered death.

CLYDE N. PROVONSHA, ARTIST

But suddenly there stood by them two angels in dazzling white. They were frightened, but the angel said to them: "Why do you look among the dead for Him who is alive? Remember what He told you while He was still in Galilee, that He must suffer death, but that He would rise the third day?"

Then they remembered, and leaving the angels, they fled back to the city. They found the disciples, with others of the company, and they said to them, "The Lord is risen!" And they told them what they had seen and heard. But the disciples would not believe them.

Peter and John, however, were running as fast as they could to the tomb. John outran Peter, and came to the open door; and stooping down, he saw the linen cloths lying there folded; but he did not go in. Peter, coming up, passed him and entered. John then joined him, and they stood looking in wonder and awe. Then they remembered what Jesus had told them, and they believed. And they went back home.

Mary had followed them, but she could not go so fast as they. And now she stood alone at the mouth of the tomb. She wept. Stooping down, she looked into it. And there through her tears she saw two angels in white, one sitting where Jesus' head had lain, and the other at the place of His feet. And they said to her, "Why are you weeping?"

She answered, "They have taken my Master away, and I do not know where they have laid Him."

As she said this, she turned around and saw Jesus standing there. But she did not know it was Jesus. He said to her, "Why are you weeping? Who are you looking for?"

She thought it was the gardener, and she said: "If it was You, Sir, who carried Him away, tell me where You have put Him, and I will take Him away."

"Mary!" said Jesus.

She turned and said, "Master!" and fell at His feet.

But He said to her: "Do not detain Me; for I have not yet gone up to My Father. But go and tell My brethren, 'I am going up to My Father and your Father, My God and your God.'" Then He disappeared.

Mary turned and hastened again to the city. She found all the remaining disciples and others who were with them, and she said, "I have seen the Master!" And she told them all she had seen. But still they did not believe.

The Road to Emmaus

Luke 24:13-49; John 20:19-29

NOW on that day, a little later, two disciples who were not of the twelve started to go to their home in Emmaus, about seven miles from Jerusalem. One of them was named Cleopas. They walked along, talking together about all these things that had happened. And as they walked, Jesus Himself joined them, but they did not know it was Jesus.

"What is it you are talking about?" He asked them.

And Cleopas said, "Are You the only visitor to Jerusalem who does not know what has happened there lately?"

"What things?" asked Jesus.

"About Jesus of Nazareth," they said, "who was a great prophet. But the high priests and rulers had Him crucified. But we were hoping He was the Messiah. And besides all this, it is now the third day since it happened, and some women of our number have astonished us. For they went to the tomb this morning and could not find His body, and they came back and said some angels had told them that He was alive. Some of our men went to the tomb and found it empty, but they did not see Him."

Then He said to them: "How foolish you are, and how slow to believe all that the prophets have said! Did not Christ have to suffer thus before entering into His glory?" And He began teaching them from Moses' writings and the prophets that which referred to Himself.

When they reached the village and their house, Jesus made as though He would go on. But they begged Him to stay with them. So He went in, and they prepared the evening meal. As they sat down to it, Jesus took the bread and blessed it. He broke it in pieces and handed it to them. At that familiar act their eyes were opened and they knew Him. But He vanished out of their sight.

They said to each other, "Did not our hearts glow when He was talking to us on the road, explaining the Scriptures to us?" They rose at once and went back to Jerusalem and found the eleven disciples and their party all together. They told what had happened on the road, and how they had known Jesus when He broke the bread in pieces after He had blessed it.

While they were still talking of these things, Jesus Himself suddenly stood among them. They were startled and panic-stricken; for they thought they saw a spirit. But He said to them: "Why are you so disturbed, and why do doubts rise in your minds? Look at My hands and My feet, for it is I indeed! Feel of Me and see; for a spirit has not flesh and bones, as you see I have."

We can see by this that since He had met Mary in the morning, He had gone to heaven and come back. For He said to Mary, "Do not touch Me, for I have not yet gone up to My Father." But now He said to the disciples, "Feel of Me, and see." Though heaven is so far away we cannot even imagine how far, Jesus could go and come in a moment of time, or any time.

Jesus had reported to heaven to His Father. His sacrifice had been accepted amid the joyful songs and harping of the angels, and He had entered into the glory of His Father, God. Then He had come back to earth to make His disciples know that He was risen.

But while the disciples could not yet believe for sheer joy, Jesus said, "Have you anything here to eat?" They gave Him a piece of broiled fish and an honeycomb, and He ate it before their eyes. Then He said, "This is what I told you when I was still with you." Then He opened their minds to the Scriptures and what they told about the Christ, how He should suffer death for sin and be raised to life again. And He told them that this gospel should be preached in His name to all nations.

Now one of the eleven, Thomas, was not with them that night when Jesus appeared to them. The other disciples told him of it the next day. But he said, "Unless I see the marks of the nails in His hands, and put my finger in them, and put my hand into His side, I will never believe it."

Then eight days after this, they were all together, and Thomas with them. Although the doors were locked, Jesus came in and stood among them and said, "Peace be with you!" Then He said to Thomas, "Put your finger here on the nail prints in My hands, and feel My side, and be no longer doubtful, but believing."

Thomas exclaimed, "My Master and my God!"

Jesus said to him: "Because you have seen Me, you believe. Blessed are they who believe without having seen Me!"

Jesus appointed a day when He would meet them in Galilee, that land where the happiest days of His ministry had been spent, and where they had had the sweetest companionship with Him.

Then He left them.

They Meet in Galilee

Matthew 28:16-20; John 21:1-23; 1 Corinthians 15:6

"MEET Me in Galilee," said Jesus to His eleven apostles, when He met with them in Jerusalem after His resurrection. And He named a certain day and a certain mountain where they were to meet Him. We do not know what that day was, nor what the mountain was. It may have been that high mountain where He was transfigured, or it may have been the mountain where He spoke the Beatitudes. We do not know. But surely it must have been some mountain rich in memories to Jesus and His disciples.

It seems that seven of them went to Galilee together, awhile before the appointed day: Peter and John and James, Thomas and Nathanael, and two others. Probably they were Andrew and Philip; for these all were from the city of Bethsaida. Nathanael was from Cana, and Thomas from we know not where.

Peter was never one to stay idle. So, soon he said to the others, "I am going fishing." That had been his business before Jesus called him to be His disciple, and so it had been of Andrew, James, and John, and probably Philip.

They all said, "We will go with you."

They went out and got into the boat and fished all night, but they caught nothing. Just as the day was breaking, Jesus stood on the beach. They saw Him, but they did not know it was Jesus.

He said to them, "Children, have you any fish?"

They answered, "No."

"Throw your net in on the other side of the boat," He said, "and you will find them."

They did so, and they found their net so full of fishes they could not haul it in. Oh, what a memory swept over them of the same miracle Jesus had done when He first called them! And John said to Peter, "It is the Master!"

When Simon Peter heard that, he put on his clothes, for he had taken them off so he could fish better. Then he sprang into the sea, and swam to shore to be with Jesus. The rest of the disciples followed in the boat, for they were only about a hundred yards from land, and they dragged in the net full of fishes.

404

When they landed, they saw a charcoal fire burning, with a fish laid on it, and some bread. Oh, what a holy, happy picnic was this! Alone with Jesus on the shore in the early dawn, and He had started breakfast for them! A simple breakfast, but it looked good to hungry men. Three and a half years ago He had called them. It seemed an age now, with such great deeds and such terrible and glorious things happening in between. But here alone with their beloved Master it all rolled off their shoulders, and they were young again.

Jesus said to them, "Bring some of the fish you have just caught."

Peter went and drew the net on the shore, the others helping him; and they found a hundred and fifty-three great fishes they had caught.

"Come and have breakfast," said Jesus. He went and got some more bread and gave it to them, and more fish too, when they were cooked. Their Master waited on them again, reminding them of what He had said: "The Son of man has come, not to be served, but to serve." They sat and ate and talked.

When they had finished, Jesus said to Peter, "Simon, son of Jonas, do you love Me more than these others?"

The other disciples looked at Peter—Peter, who had boasted that he would never desert Jesus, and then had gone and denied Him before men with cursing and swearing. Once Peter, like all of them, had said he was the greatest. What would he say now?

Peter knew that he was being examined, and he searched his heart. He had most deeply repented, and he knew that he loved Jesus. But did he love more than the others? Once Peter would have said he did; but now he was more humble. He said, "Yes, Master, You know that I love You."

Jesus said, "Then feed My lambs."

Soon Jesus said to him again, "Simon, son of Jonas, do you love Me?"

"Yes, Master; You know that I love You."

"Then feed My sheep."

Once more Jesus asked, "Simon, son of Jonas, do you love Me?"

Peter was hurt because the third time Jesus asked him if he loved Him. But he remembered, too, that it was three times that he had denied his Lord. And he said, "Master, You know everything! You can see that I love You."

Jesus said, "Then feed My sheep."

Three times: "Feed My lambs and My sheep!" Peter was a fisherman; he knew how to catch fish. And Jesus had said, when He called them from their fish nets, "From henceforth you shall catch men." But

catching fish and even catching men was rough business. Peter had never been a shepherd, and he did not know how to care for sheep, how to save the lost ones and how carefully and tenderly to feed the little ones. He had been a man's man, ready to deal with grown people as he would haul in fish, but knowing little and caring less for children. Lambs were so different from fish! Hadn't he rebuked the mothers for bringing their children to Jesus to be blessed? Now he was told to help and bless and teach the little ones.

He had been learning through the years that he lived and worked with Jesus. He remembered that Jesus had said, "I am the Good Shepherd; the Good Shepherd giveth His life for the sheep." But still at heart Peter was a fisherman. Now he was no more to catch fish; he was to feed the lambs. What a changed life for Peter! But so he would become more like his Lord.

Jesus went on: "Peter, when you were young, you used to dress yourself and go where you pleased; but when you grow old, you will stretch out your hands, and someone else will dress you and take you where you do not wish to go." He said this to show how Peter's spirit was to be made submissive, and the kind of death by which he would honor God. And afterward He said to Peter, "Follow Me."

It was time now for the meeting that Jesus had appointed. Probably they took time to sell the fish, or else old Zebedee attended to it; for Jesus never let anything go to waste. But soon they went to the mountain, and there the other disciples came on the day appointed. The others were James the Less and his brother Jude, and Matthew, and Simon the Zealot.

Paul tells us that Jesus met with more than five hundred disciples at one time. And this was doubtless the time; for the word of this appointment had gone out from the disciples at Jerusalem; and the faithful ones who had kept their hope in Jesus made their way by this road and that to the place of the meeting.

Jesus had given instruction to the eleven when He met them on that first night after His resurrection, telling them that they should go into all the world and preach the gospel. Now He repeated it in full, not only to the apostles, but also to all the company:

"All power is given to Me in heaven and in earth. Go, then, to all the world, and carry the gospel to everyone. Baptize them in the name of the Father, the Son, and the Holy Spirit, and teach them to keep all the commandments I have given you. Whoever believes and is baptized will be saved, but he who does not believe will be condemned. And I will always be with you, even to the end of the world."

406

Jesus Goes to Heaven

Mark 16:19, 20; Luke 24:49-53; Acts 1:1-14

JESUS was back in Jerusalem, and His disciples were with Him. The time had now come for Him to go to His Father in glory. He had been born in Bethlehem of Judea. He had died at Jerusalem in Judea. He had been raised to life again from Joseph's tomb in Judea. And now from a mountain in Judea He was to ascend into the courts of heaven. He had finished the work His Father gave Him to do on the earth. He had sealed His testimony with His blood on the cross. He had entered the tomb, and from it He had risen triumphant over death. Then He had tarried with His disciples for a while, to make them sure it was really He, and to give them instruction.

Their disappointment had been turned into joy. They thought of Him no longer as defeated and buried in the grave, but as the conqueror of death, a living, almighty Saviour.

As the place of His departure into heaven, Jesus chose the Mount of Olives, or Olivet. Not Mount Zion, the place of kings' palaces, not Mount Moriah, where the temple stood, was to receive that honor. There He had been mocked and rejected and spit upon and condemned to die. There His words of love and mercy had fallen upon the hard rock of evil hearts. From that city Jesus had often gone to find rest on the Mount of Olives. On its heights, in its groves, in its sheltering home in Bethany, Jesus had found refuge. In the garden of Gethsemane at its foot He had fought the last battle, and had won. Now from this mountain He was to rise and go to His heavenly home and His Father, God.

He had said to His disciples on the last night before His crucifixion: "In My Father's house are many mansions. . . . I go to prepare a place for you. And . . . I will come again, and receive you unto Myself." Now they were to see His words fulfilled.

He led them out of the city, on the well-worn road to Bethany. Down into the valley of the Kidron, past the gate of Gethsemane, up the slope of Olivet they passed, and over the crest near to Bethany. They did not know that this was their last time with Him. They knew that they loved Him as they never had loved before. They knew that He was their divine Master, and they knew that they were brethren in

heart and soul. There was now no strife among them as to who was the greatest. Everyone was willing to be the servant, because such was their Master.

In cheerful conversation Jesus talked with them on the way that bright and sunny spring morning. They were at peace, and gladness filled their hearts. And, knowing that His sacrifice as the Lamb of God was completed, the minds of some turned to the other part of the prophecies concerning Him, and they asked Him, "Master, is this the time when you are going to restore the kingdom to Israel?"

It was not; for the Jews had rejected the Messiah, and God had rejected them. Their disobedience had broken the pledge God had given them. No longer were they, as a people, chosen to be the missionaries of Christ. Some from among them, like the apostles and disciples, were chosen because they had chosen Him; but the nation as a whole was lost.

But Jesus knew that the disciples could not yet take in all the mystery of this; and He only answered them: "It is not for you to know times and dates, which the Father has fixed. But you will be given power, when the Holy Spirit comes upon you; and you will be witnesses for Me in Jerusalem, and all over Judea, and Samaria, and to the very ends of the earth."

As He said this, He raised His hands above their heads and blessed them. And, drawn by the power of God's love, He was lifted up from their midst, up, up into the sky. The disciples followed Him with their eyes, straining to catch the last glimpse of their beloved Lord. At last a cloud, a cloud of holy angels, received Him out of their sight. And did not the angels, who had sung to the shepherds at His birth, now sound forth their glorious melody again to His faithful disciples at His ascension?

While they were gazing after Him, two men dressed in white raiment stood by them. They were two angels, sent back by Jesus to give them His last word. And the angels said:

"Ye men of Galilee, why stand ye gazing up into heaven? This same Jesus, who has been caught up from you into heaven, will come again, in just the way you have seen Him go into heaven." Blessed assurance: Jesus will come again!

Then the disciples went back to Jerusalem. Not downcast, but full of cheer and hope, they went to the upper room where they had last communed with Jesus. As Jesus had told them to do, they waited—studying, praying, singing—for the coming of the Holy Spirit to give them power and wisdom in their witnessing for Jesus.

STORIES JESUS TOLD

His Parables

Why Jesus Taught in Parables

Matthew 13:10-15, 34, 35; Mark 4:11, 12; Luke 8:9, 10

THE STORIES Jesus told are called parables. A parable is a story meant to teach some lesson. It may be a story of what actually happened, or it may be a story imagined. But every person in it stands for something else, and everything that happens in it is to be understood according to the lesson meant. It is great fun to try to interpret a parable so as to get its meaning.

Jesus liked to teach in parables for three reasons. First, everybody likes to hear a story, and so a parable will be listened to by young and old. Second, when He wished, He could hide His meaning from His enemies in a parable; and since everyone must tell for himself what it means, no one could say that Jesus said so-and-so. Third, since a story sticks in the mind better than a saying, it would remain long in memory and keep its lesson ever before the hearer. Even today Jesus' parables have as fresh meaning to us as when they were spoken to the people two thousand years ago.

Sometimes Jesus' disciples asked Him to interpret a parable He had told, because they could not get His meaning for sure. He would explain it, but He always told them they should learn how to interpret them for themselves. And this they could do only if they gave their minds wholly to God and let His Spirit shine the light of His understanding upon it. So Jesus says to us too.

Jesus' parables always had to do with common things. Either they were of nature, which lies all about us, or they were about the dealings with one another of men and women and children. If we learn them thoroughly and think of them as we go about our work or our play, we shall be taught by Jesus as much today as when He lived and talked with His disciples in Judea and Galilee of old.

In this book we do not give all the parables Jesus told, but about two thirds of them. You can find the others in Matthew, Mark, Luke, or John. Would you like to make a list of all His parables for yourself?

410

Built on the Rock

Matthew 7:24-27

ONE of the first of Jesus' parables that we find is the parable of the two houses. It was the last part of His Sermon on the Mount. It is not exactly a parable, either, but it is what parables are made of. Parables, like trees, grow from seed, and the seed of parables is what we call figures of speech. There are different kinds of figures of speech, but the simplest kind is a simile (*sim*-i-lee).

We may say, for instance, "A man is like a tree." That is a simile. So every time you see a tree you think of a man, and often when you see a man you think of a tree, and you begin to think of what ways they are alike.

Or we may say, "A good man is a tree of righteousness." There is no word "like" in there, but it says the man "is" the tree. That kind of figure of speech is called a metaphor (*met*-a-for). You know a man is not really a tree, but you know that it means a tree may represent a man, and some of its ways may teach you of the ways of a man. And so when you see a good man, you think of a fruitful tree, and every time you see a tree filled with fruit, you think of a good man.

Now when we make such a figure of speech into a story, we make an allegory or parable. For instance, Jesus might tell a very short parable like this: "There was an apple tree that never bore any apples. The farmer had planted it in good soil, and he enriched it, and he cultivated it, and he pruned it. And every year he came looking for apples. But it never bore any apples at all. So finally what do you think he did with it?"

And you say, "Why, he cut it down. For why should it take up the ground and have all that care, and never give the man any apples?"

Then Jesus looks at you. And you stop and think. And you begin to interpret the parable for yourself. You say: "A tree is like a man. The business of a fruit tree is to bear fruit, so that people may eat of it. And the business of a man, or a boy or a girl, is to do good deeds, which are the fruit of righteousness, so that people may be helped by them. Am I that tree?" Do you see how a parable grows from a seed?

Well, after Jesus had spoken to the people all the wonderful words of the Sermon on the Mount, He finished with this simile:

411

*   *   *

So everyone who hears these sayings of Mine, and does them, I will liken him to a wise man, who built his house on a rock. And the rain fell, and the rivers rose, and the winds blew, and beat upon that house. And it did not fall, for it was built upon a rock.

And everyone who hears these sayings of Mine, and does not do them, I will liken him to a foolish man, who built his house upon the sand. And the rain fell, and the rivers rose, and the winds blew, and beat upon that house. And it fell, and great was the fall of it.

*   *   *

I like to think that Jesus called up that picture of the two houses and the storm from having seen it happen when He was a boy. Suppose He was out on one of His long walks one day, when He came to the brink of the valley of the Kishon River, flowing to the sea. Down there on the bank of the river He saw two houses: one great house built on a ledge of rock around which the river flowed, and the other built of reeds and plastered with mud, on a low sandy place right where the people forded the stream. And because He was being taught the builder's trade, Jesus would say, "That house built on a rock is safe; that's where Joseph would build it. But that house down there on the sandy shore, built of reeds and mud, is not safe, for any flood will wash it away."

And suppose, then, a big thunderstorm came up, and the Boy found shelter under an overhanging cliff; while He watched, the lightnings played, the thunders crashed, the winds blew, and the rain came down in sheets. Suppose it kept this up for a long time. But finally it stopped.

And then the Boy looked down in the valley, and He saw the swollen stream wash up against the rock on which the good house was built. But there it stood, and it did not fall, for it was built on a rock, and the rock would not move. But when He looked for the other house, built of reeds and mud on the sand, behold, it was washed away! And He thought, and He thought, and He thought.

Maybe!

Built on the rock, or built on the sand;
   What is the difference here?
A little mud hut, or a palace grand,
Is going to fall or going to stand.
   Now how will you build, my dear?

412

"A Sower Went Forth to Sow"

Matthew 13:1-9, 18-23; Mark 4:1-10, 13-20;
Luke 5:1-3; 8:4-8, 11-15

JESUS had much work to do every day. People were eager to hear
Him; the sick were waiting to be healed; there were proud Pharisees
and scribes to meet and correct. He was often weary and could find no
place to rest. He spent whole nights in prayer, on the mountain, in the
garden, under the stars, talking with His heavenly Father. And it was
from these times of prayer that He drew more strength and more love
for the poor people who were so needy and who were so wrong in
their thinking. But He wanted time to rest, too, in the sunlight and
the woods and on the hills.

So one morning He started out toward the lake. But as He went,
the people saw Him, and a great crowd soon pressed around Him.
There were sick there, and He cured them. There were questions to
answer and lessons to teach. But the people crowded against Him so
tight He could not get room, and He could not see them all very well.
So He got into the disciples' boat, and asked to be rowed out a little
way. They did so, and held the boat there, while Jesus sat and talked
to the people.

Now He could see all the crowd, and He could see beyond them,
up on the hills that rose a little way behind. Up there He saw a farmer
sowing his wheat. The way they sowed then was not by machine, for
they did not have any; but they sowed by hand, what we call broadcasting. A man hangs a bag of seed about his neck; he starts in at the
edge of his field, and as he walks along he takes a fistful of seed and
slings it in a broad, sweeping motion. He has learned how to do it just
right and to time it just right, so the seed falls evenly over the field.
When he has come to the end of the field, he starts back on another
row, and he keeps going back and forth until all the field is sowed.
Then he drags a harrow or rake or a bushy branch over it to cover it
with earth.

While he has been doing all this, some birds have found their
breakfast there, and he hurries to cover it so that it will not all be eaten
up. No doubt Jesus, when a boy, had seen many a field sowed in this
way, and maybe He had even helped to sow it. He Himself lived in

413

a carpenter's home in the village, but He was a friendly lad, and knew some farmers as well as other people. And because He was such a cheerful boy, and bright, they were always glad when He came around; they taught Him many things, and let Him help when He wanted to.

Now, as He looked up from the boat and saw the farmer swinging along, casting his seed, probably a scene of His boyhood came up before His mind, and He could see the field with the hard path running through it and a rocky patch and the corners where the brush had been left and the birds following in the farmer's track. And He made this story from it all, while the people listened and could see the very thing He was telling:

*   *   *

A sower went out to sow, and as he was sowing, some of the seed fell by the path, and the birds came and ate it up. And some fell on rocky ground, where there was not much soil, and it sprang up at once, because the soil was not deep. But when the sun came up, it was scorched and soon withered away, because it had no root. And some of it fell among the thorns, and the thorns grew up and choked it out. And some fell on good soil, and some of it yielded a hundredfold, and some sixty, and some thirtyfold. Pay attention to this, and think!

*   *   *

What did the parable mean? Maybe—yes, I think very likely—there were a boy and a girl back there in the crowd, with their father and mother, listening for all they were worth to this charming young Teacher of Nazareth, and quickly catching up in their minds the meaning of the story He told. Of course, when they could not quite understand, they would ask their father and mother; and it put those parents to the stretch to answer their questions. If they were wise parents, and learned in the Scriptures, they would put story and Bible together, and often they could find in the Scriptures the secret of the lesson Jesus taught from nature. It's a good thing to try.

The disciples were not very used yet to this kind of teaching. Most of them were rough fishermen, who had not yet studied the Scriptures very much. In Jesus' school they would come to know them very well, and they would then be able to understand Jesus' parables pretty well for themselves. But now they were perplexed, and maybe a little vexed. They came to Jesus and said, "Why do You teach in parables?"

Jesus soothed them by answering: "You may know the secret of the kingdom of heaven, but not they. I have to teach them in parables because they could not take in the truth if I should tell it in plain

414

words, just as the prophets foretold of them. But blessed are your eyes and ears, for they see and hear what the prophets longed to know.

"Don't you understand this parable? You must listen closely and set your minds to thinking when I tell a parable. And the better you know the Scriptures, the better will you be able to interpret it. I'll explain this one to you. Listen now. What the sower sows is the word of God. The ones by the hard path are those who hear, and then the devil comes and carries the message away from their hearts. The ones on the rocky ground are those who receive the message joyfully when they first hear it, but it takes no real root. They believe for a little while, and then in the time of trial they draw back. And what falls among the thorns means those who listen and pass on, and the worries and the riches and the pleasures of life creep in and choke out the message, and it yields nothing. But the seed in the good soil means those who listen to the message and keep it in good and true hearts, and yield much seed to give to others. Some of them are the best and truest, who yield a hundred times as much. Some others may not be quite so gifted, but they give all they have, and they make sixty times as much. Some, perhaps, are very common people, but they have good hearts, and they yield thirty times what they received. They are all good ground."

The disciples thought and thought and thought, as the word of God fell upon their ears. And I don't doubt that the boy and the girl whom their parents helped to understand, thought too, and thought and thought and thought. So they all took the seed into good ground, and yielded a bountiful harvest.

The crowd was the field. There were hard hearts there, in which the seed did not bury itself at all, and it was soon taken away. There were minds too shallow to think very deeply; and when persecution came, they had no root, and the word withered away. There were souls filled with cares and pleasures, who let these choke out the good words of Jesus. But, oh, joy! there were men and women and boys and girls who were good ground, and they yielded fruit in their lives.

Sowing the seed on the hard path,
  Or where the rocks are found,
Sowing the seed in the brier patch,
  Sowing it in good ground.
Dear Sower, I pledge You on my part,
To give You good soil in my garden heart.

415

Weeds in the Field

Matthew 13:24-30

THAT same morning, right there in the boat, Jesus told another farm story. It was about a farmer who sowed good seed in his field, but something happened so that a lot of weeds came up with the wheat. I wonder if Jesus, when He was a boy, heard of such a thing. Maybe they told it in the village of Nazareth, and He heard it. To them it just meant a tale, a story of an evil which an enemy had done to the farmer; but to Jesus it meant something more. I wonder if it will to you.

In your Bible you will probably see this story about "tares." Tares is an old-time word for weeds; so you will understand better if you read "weeds" for "tares." This is the story Jesus told:

* * *

The kingdom of heaven is like a man who sowed good seed in his field; but in the night, when people were asleep, his enemy came and sowed weed seed among the wheat and went away. And when the wheat came up, the weeds came up too. And the man's servants came to him and said, "Wasn't the seed you sowed good seed? So where did these weeds come from?"

He went and looked, and he said, "Some enemy has done this."

They asked him, "Do you want us to go and pull them up?"

"No," he said; "if you do, you may uproot the wheat. Let them both grow together till harvesttime; and when we reap, I'll tell the reapers to gather out the weeds and tie them up in bundles to be burned, but get the wheat into my barn."

* * *

Can you think of any weeds that an enemy of Jesus could sow in your minds after your parents and teachers have sown the Word?

Not weeds and tares, dear Master,
　　Shall any wicked foe
Within the good field of my heart
　　Come stealing in to sow.
For I will keep it night and day
Against the enemy of Thy way.

416

"A Grain of Mustard Seed"

Matthew 13:31, 32; Mark 4:30-32; Luke 13:18, 19

JESUS' mind was rich in knowledge of growing things. Even as a boy He had studied the life that He saw all about Him—men and animals and birds and insects and trees and plants. And this knowledge which He gained was like seed planted in good ground; so as He became a young man, and at last a teacher, it brought forth good fruit, surely a hundredfold.

There was one tree which did not grow right in His part of the country, but He learned about it, and probably He found it before He was grown. Maybe some merchants traveling through to Egypt brought some seeds and sold them in the market. They were stingy seeds, like pepper, and they were very small, smaller than the seeds of black pepper. But the merchants said that out in the hot and dry places where they came from, these little seeds grew on a bush or small tree big enough to make shade. And maybe Jesus planted a seed and watched it grow.

They called it sinapi, but the men who translated our Bible called it mustard. Now you know we grow a mustard in our gardens which is not a tree but only a plant, the leaves of which we eat for greens. But this mustard, or sinapi, which made Jesus' parable was a little seed and a big bush or tree. While He was still in the boat that morning, and using figures of farm things to illustrate His lessons, He thought of this mustard, and He said:

* * *

What shall I say the kingdom of God is like? What figure can I use to describe it? It is like a grain of mustard seed, which is the smallest of all seeds in the world. But when it is sown, it comes up and grows to be the largest of all garden plants, and grows branches so big that the wild birds can roost under its shelter.

* * *

That was a short little story, wasn't it? Just about as big as a grain of mustard seed. But suppose you had been a boy or a girl back there, listening to Jesus, and this story of His had entered your ears. Would it have found a hard path, or rocky ground, or a thorny corner? Or would it have fallen into good ground?

417

Like Yeast

Matthew 13:33; Luke 13:20, 21

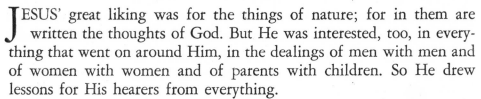

JESUS' great liking was for the things of nature; for in them are written the thoughts of God. But He was interested, too, in everything that went on around Him, in the dealings of men with men and of women with women and of parents with children. So He drew lessons for His hearers from everything.

In the crowds that daily thronged Him and listened to His teachings there were always women as well as men. And Jesus did not forget them when He told His stories. Happenings in the house made up some of them. One was about making bread. You know your mother and the bakers, in all their breadmaking, really make just two kinds of bread, hard breads and soft breads. The hard breads are what are called, in some parts of the country, crackers, and in other parts, biscuits. The soft breads are what are called light bread or raised bread, and a good many other names.

Now the difference between these two kinds is made by yeast. In olden time yeast was called leaven, and so in the Bible we read of leaven where now we say yeast. Leavened bread is raised bread, and unleavened bread is crackers or other hard bread. Maybe you do not know that yeast, which nowadays your mother gets from the grocery in little cakes or packages, is a plant. It isn't like the plants we grow in our gardens, with green leaves and flowers and fruit, but it is a plant just the same. When it is given warmth and moisture and something to feed on, like starch or sugar, it grows; and as it grows it gives off a gas that lifts all the flour or meal in which it is placed, so that there are little spaces or air bubbles in it, and that, when the dough is baked, makes raised bread.

Now Jesus looked into the faces of some women in the crowd who were interested in what He was teaching. They were interested when He told about sowing and cultivating and reaping, and when He told about fishing and building and buying and selling; for they knew about all these things. But to come right down to their everyday duties, Jesus told some stories about what happened in the house, cooking and sweeping and mending. And this is one story He told, about breadmaking and yeast. Probably in your Bible it says "leaven"; but in some

418

Bibles that have been translated since ours, it says "yeast," which is the same thing. Jesus said:

*   *   *

The kingdom of heaven is like yeast, which a woman took and buried in a bushel of flour, until it had all risen.

*   *   *

Little short story that is, isn't it? But you know, that little story is like yeast, which Jesus took and put in the mind of the cook, whether baker, or mother, or you. Give it the right warmth of interest and the right moisture of thinking, and it rises and rises, until the whole of you is leavened, made into a good big loaf of a Christian, to feed the hungry and heal the sick and teach those who do not know.

Every time any woman who heard Jesus then and anybody who hears His parable now put some yeast in the moist flour and set it aside in a warm place to rise, well, if they do what Jesus means for them to do, they think of the Word of God hidden in their hearts.

Maybe, since you like to read the Bible, you will think of a text that says, "Thy word have I hid in my heart, that I might not sin against Thee." Psalm 119:11. Yeast! And then: "Thy words were found, and I did eat them; and Thy word was unto me the joy and rejoicing of mine heart." Jeremiah 15:16. Bread! And then: "Jesus said unto them, I am the Bread of Life." John 6:35.

So every time we pray in the Lord's Prayer, "Give us this day our daily bread" (Matthew 6:11), and when we eat the bread which God gives us, we will think of Jesus who is the Bread of Life. Especially so in the Lord's Supper.

What's the matter with this sad bread—
    Soggy, and heavy, and gray?
Why, mother forgot to put any yeast
    Into the dough today.
What's the matter with my sad heart?
Oh, I left out the Bible, the very best part.

What do you think of this beautiful bread—
    Risen, and baken, and brown?
Why, it's raised with the leaven that mother put in;
    'Tis the beautifulest bread in town.
What makes me happy, my spirits gay?
Why, I put in the Morning Watch today.

419

The Proud Man; the Humble Man

Luke 18:9-14

THE PHARISEES were a class of Jews who claimed to be more righteous than the rest of the people, because they made a great show of keeping the Commandments and of praying in public and of paying tithe and giving money to the poor. There were really good men among them, but most of them were vain and proud, and in secret they did many evil things, though they made such an outward show of goodness.

They despised Jesus, because He came from a humble home in Galilee, while they taught that Judea and Jerusalem were the most holy. But mostly they hated Him because He taught the righteousness that comes from having God dwell in the heart, rather than in making an outward show.

There was another party opposed to them who were called Sadducees. There were not so many Sadducees as Pharisees, and they did not have so much influence with the people, but they were very powerful nevertheless. In Jesus' time, both the high priests, Annas and Caiaphas, were Sadducees. The Sadducees were not any better than the Pharisees, and they were wrong in much of what they believed. They did not believe there were angels; they did not believe there would be a judgment day; they did not believe that the dead would be raised to life. Jesus had sometimes to meet their opposition and their hatred. And it was both Pharisees and Sadducees who combined at the last to sentence Him to death.

Quite opposite in life to both these sects were the publicans. They were a class of Jews who served the Romans by gathering their taxes for them. For doing this they were allowed to pay themselves by taking a commission, or part of the taxes. The other Jews, and especially the Pharisees and Sadducees, hated them and called them "the sinners." They despised them first because they were the agents of the Romans who held rule over the Jews. And in the second place, the publicans were really crooked and bad. When they gathered the taxes, they charged a great deal more than their commission and they kept it; so generally they grew rich at the expense of the rest of the people.

But the publicans, more than the Pharisees, listened to Jesus, because they knew they were bad, and some of them wanted to be turned into good men. Jesus had more followers from among them than He had from among the Pharisees. One of His apostles, Matthew, had been a publican, but he turned to Jesus and His truth and became a very good man and a worthy apostle.

Jesus did not hate either the Pharisees or the Sadducees, and He did not despise the publicans. But He had to teach truth which ran right against them. And especially did He teach men to be humble and true, and not to pretend to goodness which they did not have. So He warned the people against such ways and deeds as the Pharisees especially did. One time He told this parable to some who trusted in themselves that they were righteous and despised others:

*　　*　　*

Two men went up to the temple to pray. One was a Pharisee and the other a publican. The Pharisee stood up and prayed this prayer to himself: "O God, I thank You that I am not like other men, greedy, dishonest, adulterous, like that publican yonder. I fast two days in the week. I pay tithe on everything I get."

But the publican stood off at a distance, and would not even lift his eyes to heaven, but struck his breast and said, "O God, have mercy on a sinner like me!" I tell you, it was he who went back to his house made righteous, and not the proud man. Everyone who exalts himself will be humbled, but he who humbles himself will be exalted.

*　　*　　*

I hope that the Pharisees took that parable to heart, and the publicans learned how to act before God. Don't you?

————————

Are there any publicans here today?
　　Or Pharisees abroad?
The publican is a sinner, of course,
　　And the Pharisee is a fraud.
But if they both confess their sin,
God will put righteousness within.

If I am a Pharisee, let me pray:
　　"God, forgive Thy son!"
If I am a publican, let me resolve
　　I will right the wrong I have done.
And we each shall go down to his house forgiven,
Children of God in the kingdom of heaven.

421

The Lost Sheep

Matthew 18:10-14; Luke 5:27-32; 15:1-7

"LOOK at Him!" cried the Pharisees, pointing at Jesus. "He receives sinners, and even eats with them!" They would no more think of eating with a publican or those they called sinners than they would think of cutting off their heads. They washed their hands every time they had to take change from a publican. They washed their clothes every time they brushed against one. And to go into their houses and sit down to eat with them, why, they thought that would take them right out of the kingdom of God.

But here was Jesus letting the publicans and sinners come close to Him, and He would touch them and never think He was defiled by it. He even took a publican, Matthew, to be one of His apostles. And Matthew made a feast for Jesus, and called his friends, other publicans, to come to it. No, said the Pharisees, this Jesus could not be a prophet, or He would not go in the company of sinners. He must be a sinner Himself.

And yet Jesus was the only man who never sinned a single sin! So He told them this parable:

*   *   *

What man among you, if he has a hundred sheep and loses one of them, does not leave the ninety and nine in the sheepfold and go search for the lost sheep till he finds it? And when he finds it, he puts it on his shoulders and joyfully carries it home. Then he calls to his friends and neighbors and says to them, "Rejoice with me; for I have found my sheep that was lost!"

I tell you, in just that way there will be more joy in heaven over one sinner who repents than over ninety-nine good people who do not need any repentance.

*   *   *

Did you ever lose a pet of yours that you loved very much? Maybe it was your dog Frisky, who ran away and could not be found for days and days and days. Didn't you search everywhere for him, and ask everybody if they had seen him? And maybe your daddy put an ad in the paper and even offered a reward to anyone who would bring him back.

Or maybe, if you lived on a farm, maybe it was a calf or a colt your daddy had given you for your very own. There might be a dozen horses and a hundred cows on the farm, and everyone of them worth a good deal. But if your own calf or colt strayed away, how you mourned for it and searched for it and told your friends what a great loss you had. And when it was found, how glad you were! And when you told all your friends, they were glad with you.

I knew of a family in which there were thirteen children. And their father and mother loved every one of them. But one day the youngest got lost at a picnic, and nobody knew where he was. The father and the mother said to the oldest girl, "Take care of all these little children, while we go searching through the grounds and the woods to find our boy." And they left them and went searching. Of course the older children went searching too, but the littlest ones were kept together under the care of their sister. The father and mother called their friends and neighbors to search for the lost boy, too. At last they found him, pretty wet and muddied where he had been playing in the creek. But his daddy just picked him up, all sopping wet as he was, and carried him to the family. And didn't they make over him though! And all the friends rejoiced, and everybody, even the little sinner, was happy.

That's just a sample of how Jesus loves the littlest and the naughtiest and the wildest persons in the world, to say nothing of how He loves those who do not go astray.

———

There were ninety and nine that safely lay
    In the shelter of the fold,
But one was out on the hills away,
    Far, far from the gates of gold—
Away on the mountains wild and bare,
Away from the tender Shepherd's care.

"Lord, Thou hast here Thy ninety and nine;
    Are they not enough for Thee?"
But the Shepherd made answer: "One of Mine
    Has wandered away from Me,
And although the road be rough and steep,
I go to the desert to find My sheep."

Elizabeth Clephane.

The Father's Love

Luke 15:11-24

RIGHT after Jesus had told the parable of the lost sheep, He told another story that illustrates God's love for the wayward and the wicked. He loves the good and obedient wondrously well; but if anyone goes astray, He does not say, "Well, just let him go!" He says —but just listen to Jesus' parable of the Father's love:

    *   *   *

There was a man who had two sons. Naturally, when the father should die, his sons would inherit all he had and divide it between them. But the younger boy of these two wanted his part right away. So he said to his father, "Father, give me now my share of the property." So he divided his property and gave his younger son his share.

But the young man was restless. And not many days afterward he gathered together all that was his, turned it into money, and went off to a far country. There he threw it all away in feasting and gambling and playing, until at last he had not a cent left. Then all his gay companions fell away, and he was pretty sad and did not have much fun.

He had to go to work then to get something to eat. But no one wanted to hire him, because he seemed to be no good. Finally a man who had a number of hogs said, "You can go out in the field and tend the pigs." He did. But there came on a famine just then, and his master would neither pay him nor feed him. He got so hungry he could have eaten the garbage he fed the pigs. But even the pigs would not let him have any.

At last he woke up to what he was and what he might have been. And he said: "Here I am, without a cent or a bite to eat. And my father has plenty of hired men who have more than enough to eat. I will get up and go to my father and say to him, 'Father, I have sinned against heaven and against you. I am no longer fit to be called your son. Treat me as one of your hired men.'"

And he got up and traveled back that long way to his father. Now his father had always been looking and watching for him, for he thought he would come back. And now he saw him while he was yet a long way off, and he knew him. He ran to him and threw his arms around him and kissed him.

424

His son said to him: "Father, I have sinned against heaven and against you. I am no longer fit to be called your son. Treat me as one of your hired men."

But his father said to the servants who came around them, "Hurry up, and get the best robe and put it on him. And put a ring on his hand and shoes on his feet. And get the calf we are fattening, and kill it and cook it, and let us have a big dinner and celebrate! For my son here was dead, and he has come to life. He was lost, and he is found!"

*   *   *

That is how our heavenly Father loves us, even when we go astray.

You might expect that the older son would join in the welcome of his brother, but he did not. And when we think about it, and remember what most folks are like, we can understand how he felt jealous rather than glad. Here was this younger brother, who took half his father's property and went and gambled and played it away. And now he comes back in rags, and their father throws his arms around him and kisses him and covers up his rags with the best clothes he has in the house, and makes a feast for him.

"Well," says the older brother, "what do you think of that? Here I have stayed by and done the work and have never thrown away a dollar. But is the feast for me? It is not. Is the best robe in the house for me? No, indeed. And the welcome! When I come in from a hard day's work, does my father throw his arms around me and kiss me and tell me how glad he is to see me? No; that is kept for this young scamp who has wasted his father's money. I will have nothing to do with the celebration." And he just went off by himself.

But his father came out to him and said, "Dear Son, come in and welcome your brother. It is just as though he had been dead, and now is alive."

"No!" said the older son. "You never gave me even a kid to make a feast for my friends. But let this young scamp return, and you kill for him the fatted calf."

"Why, Son," said his father, "all that I have is yours. You never gave me a kid, either; but I know you love me, just as I love you. But you never were lost, while this brother of yours was lost and now is found."

A Dinner That Was Different

Luke 14:1-24

YOU could not be around Jesus much without hearing a story. Whatever He saw brought a lesson to His mind, and He taught His lessons, very often, in stories. Down by the lake it was a fish story. Out in the fields it was a flower story. In the market place it was a story about a pearl. In the house it was a story about biscuits or brooms or brides. And all His stories had to do with the kingdom of God.

One Sabbath day a Pharisee took Him home to dinner with some of his friends. You see, some of the Pharisees believed on Him, at least a little. But they found it hard to understand Him. And because they could not understand Him, they were likely to turn against Him. They thought that no sick person ought to be healed on the Sabbath day. And they thought that they were to be the first ones in the kingdom of God, and all the poor people and the foreigners were to be shut out.

Well, during the meal a poor man who had the dropsy, all swollen up, somehow got into the room and stood before Jesus. All the Pharisees watched Jesus to see what He would do.

He asked His host and the doctors of the law who were present, "Is it right to cure people on the Sabbath day, or not?"

They made no answer. They just watched. He took hold of the man and cured him and sent him away. Then He said to them, "What one of you, if his child or even his ox should fall into a ditch on the Sabbath day, would not at once pull him out?"

They could say nothing to that, because they knew they would pull either one out. And here was a man, a child of God, whom Jesus had pulled out.

Then Jesus, seeing that the guests had all picked out the best places at the table they could find, gave them a lesson on manners. He said: "When someone invites you to a wedding supper, don't take the best place at the table; for someone more notable than you may have been invited, and your host will come and say to you, 'Make room for this man'; and then you will be ashamed when you go to take the poorest place. But when you are invited, go and take the poorest place. So when your host comes in, he will say to you, 'My friend, come to a better place'; and then you will be honored by all the other guests." Don't you think that is good advice for us today?

And then Jesus gave His host a lesson on selecting his guests. He said: "When you give a luncheon or a dinner, don't invite your friends, or your brothers, or your rich neighbors; for of course they will invite you in return, and you will be paid back. But go and invite people who are poor, maimed, lame, or blind. Then you will be blessed because they cannot repay you, but you will be repaid in the resurrection of the righteous." That is good counsel, too; but not many people will follow it.

One of the guests, to change the subject, said, "Blessed is the man who shall eat dinner in the kingdom of God." He said this very smugly, for he thought he would surely be there. True enough he, along with his friends the Jews, had been invited. But Jesus knew that pride, and the seeking of riches, and the pleasures of this life, were keeping many of them from accepting the invitation. Yet even if they failed to go in, the kingdom of God would be filled. So He told them this parable:

*　　*　　*

A man once gave a great dinner and invited many guests. When the day for the dinner came, he sent around his servant to say to them: "Come! for dinner is now ready." But what! Every one of them began to make excuse why he could not come. One of them said, "I have bought a piece of land, and I must go and look at it." Another said, "I have bought five yoke of oxen, and I am going to see how they work. Please excuse me." And another said, "I have married a wife, and so I cannot come!"

The servant came back and told his master. Then the man was angry, because he had been insulted. And he said to his servant, "Hurry out into the streets and squares of the city, and bring in the poor, the crippled, the blind, and the lame." The servant did so, and reported, "What you ordered, master, has been done, and still there is room."

And the master said to him, "Go out on the roads and among the hedges, and make everyone come in that you meet, so that my house may be full. For I tell you that none of those men who refused my invitation, if they get around and come late, shall have any of my dinner."

*　　*　　*

Do you think those guests with Jesus at the table got the lesson?

427

Forgiven Servant Forgives Not

Matthew 18:23-35

SIMON PETER may sometimes have wished that people would call him by his first name, Simon, instead of the second name which Jesus gave him. There were four languages known by the Jews in those days. One was Aramaic, the common speech of the people. One was Hebrew, the language in which their Scriptures were first written. One was Greek, which the Greeks brought in and which was the tongue of the learned. And the last was Latin, spoken by the Romans, who ruled the world.

Now Simon is the same name as the Hebrew Simeon, and it means "happy hearing." Simon Peter liked that. But Jesus had called him, in Greek, "Cephas," and in Latin, "Peter," which both mean "a stone." Simon came to be called Peter more than Simon; and maybe sometimes, when the disciples got into an argument about who was the greatest, they twitted Peter about his name, saying that Jesus must have known his head was as hard as a stone, and maybe his heart was too.

Very likely James and John, his closest friends, would needle him in this way, for they three seemed highest in favor—but which one of them should be the very highest? Or perhaps Judas Iscariot was the teaser; for Judas clearly wanted to be highest in the kingdom. However, Peter tried hard to be forgiving, as Jesus taught them to be. But he wondered how many times he must forgive. So one day he came to Jesus and asked: "Master, how many times am I to forgive my brother when he wrongs me? Seven times?"

Jesus said, "Not seven times, but seventy times seven."

"Whew!" thought Peter, "that means almost five hundred times, and I don't believe I could keep track of that. I suppose He means forgive forever and ever."

Jesus did mean that, but He meant something more. And what He meant by what He said, He showed in the way He acted. He always forgave, even when He was nailed to the cross; for there He cried, "Father, forgive them, for they know not what they do!" Now He meant to show Peter that love must rule in his heart, and then he would always be ready to forgive. So He told this parable:

428

*　　*　　*

The kingdom of heaven is like a king who made up his mind to settle accounts with his servants who owed him money. He soon found one man who owed him ten million dollars. As he could not pay it, the king gave orders that he and his wife and his children should all be sold as slaves, to pay the debt. Then the servant came and threw himself at his master's feet, and begged, "Give me time, and I will pay all of it."

The king knew the man could never do it; he said, "I forgive you all. Your debt is paid. Go in peace."

But this man, who had been forgiven so much, went out and found a fellow servant who owed him twenty dollars. And he took his fellow servant by the throat and said, "Pay me what you owe me!" "Oh," cried the poor fellow, "give me time, and I will pay you!" But he refused and had him put in prison till he should pay the debt.

Then his fellow servants were very sorry, and they went and told the king. The king called in this man he had forgiven so much, and said to him: "You wicked slave! I forgave you all that debt of yours when you begged me for time. Why did you not take pity on your fellow servant, as I did on you?" Then he handed him over to the jailers, until he should pay all that ten million dollars, which he never could.

*　　*　　*

"So," said Jesus to His disciples, "your heavenly Father has forgiven you a huge debt. If you do not forgive the little debts your brothers owe you, the greater punishment will be yours."

"That Judas," said Peter to James and John,
　　"Is always sneering at me.
He thinks he's a right to stare me down
　　Because I have fished in the sea.
A scribe is he, a fisherman I,
But I know the Master will set me on high."

"But the Master," said John, the gentle and wise,
　　"Has forgiven again and again.
Have you noticed how Judas would supervise
　　The affairs of the Master of men?
But always our Lord, with a high-minded grace,
By forgiving the man, puts him down in his place."

429

The Rich Man's Barns

Luke 12:13-21

SOMEONE in the crowd that was about Jesus called out to Him: "Master, tell my brother to give me my share of the inheritance!" I suppose the father of these two brothers had died, and the older one had gotten all the property and would not give his brother any. Or maybe he had just taken more than half, and the younger brother wanted his half, or even more. Anyway, he called on Jesus to be the judge and get him what he wanted.

But Jesus said: "Who made Me a judge between you two? Take care," He said then to all the multitude. "You must guard against being selfish. For a man's life is not made up of the things he owns, no matter how rich he is."

Then He told them this story:

*   *   *

A certain man's lands bore heavy crops. And he said to himself, "What am I going to do? for I have nowhere to store my crops." Then he said: "I know what I will do. I will tear down my barns and build larger ones, and in them I will store all my grain and my goods. And I will say to myself, 'Good man! You now have great riches stored up for years to come. Now take your ease, eat, drink, and enjoy yourself!' "

But God said to him, "You fool! This very night your life will be taken from you; then who will have all you have laid up?" That is what happens to the man who lays up money for himself, and is not rich with God.

*   *   *

I don't know whether or not the young man stayed to hear this lesson. He seems to have been all wrapped up in his own interests, and he may have thought that Jesus was very unkind to refuse to help him out, when anything He would say would settle the matter. Sometimes we get that way, too.

But on the other hand, the young man may have been sensible enough to look at the other side of the question. Let's hope he took the parable to heart, and went away more unselfish and better. And let's pray that we do.

The Last First and the First Last

Matthew 20:1-16

MOST of the apostles, and perhaps all of them, thought they would get a great reward by following Jesus. And the reward they meant was honor and riches and power. That was the main purpose of Judas Iscariot, and it showed up in John and James too. Peter at first, and even to Gethsemane, was all for fighting to make Jesus King. And probably Peter thought, since he was the best fighter among them, he would be made general of the army, which sometimes is more important than being prime minister or treasurer.

One day a rich young ruler came to Jesus to ask what he could do to get eternal life. He said he had kept all the Commandments, but still he thought there must be something greater for him to do. Jesus told him to go and sell all he had, and give help to the poor, and to come and follow Him. Then the young man turned away sorrowful, for he had great riches and he did not want to give them up.

"How hard it is," said Jesus, "for a rich man to enter into the kingdom of heaven."

Peter spoke up and said, "Now we have left everything we had to follow you. What shall we have for it?"

Jesus pitied him and his fellow disciples for being so selfish and greedy. But He also knew that they had grown to be much better than they were, and He had high hopes that all of them would come through—except Judas Iscariot, who He knew was going to betray Him. So He said something to encourage them, though really, with the ideas they had, they could not quite understand what He meant.

"In the new world," He said, "when the Son of man takes His seat on His glorious throne, you who have followed Me will also sit on twelve thrones, governing the twelve tribes of Israel. But many who are first now will be last then, and many who are now last will be first. Listen to a parable":

*　　*　　*

A man who had a big vineyard went out early in the morning to hire laborers. The grapes were ripe, and needed many hands to gather them before they should rot. So he hired some men at a dollar a day and sent them into his vineyard. About nine o'clock he went out again

431

and found some men standing idle in the market place. And he said to them, "You go to my vineyard too, and I will pay you whatever is right." So they went. Then at noon he went out again and found some men. And then he went at three o'clock in the afternoon and found still more. And he sent both these groups into the vineyard. It came five o'clock, just an hour before the workday closed. Then he went out and found still more men standing idle. And he said, "Why do you stand here all day without doing anything?"

"Because no man has hired us," they said.

"Go into my vineyard, and whatever is right I will pay you."

So when evening came, the laborers all flocked in to get their pay. The owner said to his foreman, "Start with the last lot of laborers, and pay them a dollar—even the very first who went in."

So the foreman paid them off. And the last to be paid, who were the first to go in to work, grumbled. They said, "Those men who were hired last worked only one hour, and you have paid them as much as you paid us who worked through the heat of the day."

But the owner said to one of them: "Friend, I am doing you no wrong. Didn't you agree with me to work for a dollar a day? There it is; take it and go. I have hired these later ones in the pressure of the work, to get it done. If I wish to give them a dollar, may I not do what I please with my own? Are you angry because I am generous?"

*   *   *

No doubt the owner had watched them all, and he knew what each one was worth, but it was the spirit in which the workers labored that interested the owner more.

Take heed and beware of covetousness,
  For that is idolatry.
To be jealous of others is wickedness,
  And envy iniquity.

The law of God as a chain is cast,
  Each link in the forge above.
The last is first and the first is last,
  In a perfect circle of love.

Love the Lord thy God with all thy soul,
  Thy neighbor with heart and hand;
And all the law will make a whole,
  From the first to the tenth command.

The Pharisee and the Publican

The Pharisee went up to worship hoping to win commendation because of his imagined righteousness. The publican knew himself to be a great sinner and despaired of forgiveness and pardon. He cried, "God be merciful to me, a sinner." It was his humility and sorrow that brought him peace with God.

CLYDE N. PROVONSHA, ARTIST

Talents

Matthew 25:14-30

PERHAPS you have heard someone say of a young man, "He has great talent," or of a young woman, "She's very talented." And maybe at first you didn't know just what that meant. But by this time you have learned that it means "gift," as much as to say, "He has many gifts," and, "She's very gifted." But even that needs to be explained.

Well, let's say you are a poor little boy without a penny in your piggy bank; or a poor little girl without even a rag doll. Some good uncle comes along and gives you fifty pennies, and you drop them one by one, clink, clank, clink, clank, into your bank. That's a gift, and it makes you feel rich, doesn't it?

Or Christmas comes, and the poor little girl whose only dolly was a corn-cob or a stick wrapped in a piece of calico, gets a present of a bee-yu-ti-ful doll with curly hair and rosy cheeks and eyes that open and shut and a voice that says, "Ma-ma." 'Cause some dear maiden aunt has just found out you need it. What a gift! Nobody is so rich as you!

Well, the word "talent," and all that it means, comes from a story Jesus told about a man who gave gifts to three of his servants which made them rich, but which were meant for them to use so that they would have twice as much. Now "talent" back there meant money, a large sum of money; in fact, a thousand dollars. And anybody who was given a thousand dollars was "gifted" or "talented."

Jesus told this story to teach that God gives us gifts which we are to use so that we will be even more gifted and we can help people with the riches we make. Some people are more gifted or talented than others, but everybody has some talent; and if we use what we are given as well as we can, our Lord will say, "Well done!" no matter whether our talent is big or little.

Everyone has the talent of time. Nobody has more time than anyone else. Did you ever think of that? For there are just twenty-four hours in the day, and the day is as long for you as for me and no longer. Whether the time is well used depends on what we do with it. And everybody has strength, some more and some less. The baby has a little strength, and if he uses it he will come to have much more. Everybody has health, so long as he is living, though some have more

health than others. But mostly it depends on how you use your gift of health whether you have more or less. And everybody or nearly everybody can sing. I am sure if you count up you will find that you have ten talents or even a hundred. Now listen to Jesus' story:

* * *

A rich man was going on a long journey, and he called in his servants and put his money in their hands. He gave one of them five talents, and another two talents, and another one talent.

The man who had received the five talents quickly went into business with the money, and made five talents more. In the same way the man who had received the two talents made two talents more. But the man who had received but one talent went away and dug a hole in the ground and hid his lord's money there.

Long afterward their master came back and called them in to see what they had done with his gifts. The man who had received the five talents came bringing ten talents, and said, "Master, you put five talents in my hands, and I have made five talents more." His master said to him, "Well done, good and faithful servant. You have been faithful about a small amount, and I will put a larger one in your keeping. Come, be happy with me!"

And the man who had received the two talents came in with four talents. And he said, "Master, you put two talents in my hands, and I have made two talents more." And his master said to him: "Well done, good and faithful servant! You have been faithful about a small amount; I will give you a larger one. Come, be happy with me!"

But the man who had received the one talent came in and said: "Sir, I knew that you were a hard man, who reaped where you had not sown and gathered where you had not threshed; and I was scared, and I went and hid your talent in the ground. Here is your money." His master said: "You wicked, lazy servant! You have just been doing nothing. If you thought I was so unjust, and you were scared, you could at least have put your talent in the bank, and then when I came back I should have gotten my money and the interest too." Then he said to his guards: "Take the one talent away from him, and give it to the man who has ten thousand dollars; for the man who has used his talents well will have more given to him, but the man who has gained nothing will have even his little taken away from him."

* * *

Talents! Who does not have talents? And how are you using yours?

The Good Samaritan

Luke 10:25-37

LIKE a good many other people, the Jews liked to argue and show off their learning and wit. And they liked to ask Jesus puzzling questions to see if they could trip Him up sometime.

So one day a lawyer stood up and asked Jesus the familiar question: "Master, what must I do to make sure of eternal life?"

Jesus answered, "What does the law say? How does it read?"

And the lawyer quoted from the law: "You must love the Lord your God with your whole heart, your whole soul, your whole strength, and your whole mind, and your neighbor as yourself."

Jesus said, "You are right. Do that, and you will live."

But the lawyer did not want the argument to end there. So he asked another question: "Who is my neighbor?"

So then Jesus told this story:

*　　*　　*

A man was on his way down from Jerusalem to Jericho, when he fell among thieves. And they stripped him, and beat him, and went off leaving him half dead. Now, a priest happened to be going that way, but when he saw him he went by on the other side of the road. And a Levite also came to the place, and when he saw him he went by on the other side too. But a Samaritan who was traveling that way came upon him, and when he saw him he pitied him. And he went to him and dressed his wounds with oil and wine and bound them up. And he put him on his own mule and brought him to an inn, and took care of him. The next day he took out a dollar and gave it to the innkeeper and said, "Take care of him, and whatever more you spend I will give you on my way back."

*　　*　　*

"Which of these three," Jesus asked, "do you think proved himself a neighbor to the man who had fallen among robbers?"

The lawyer was cornered. He was not asked to be a neighbor to a Samaritan; he was told of a Samaritan who acted as a neighbor to a Jew. He thought all Samaritans were bad, but here Jesus told of a good Samaritan. The lawyer did not want even to say, "Samaritan," he hated them so. But he answered Jesus, "He that took pity on him."

Jesus said, "Go and do so yourself."

Ten Bridesmaids

Matthew 25:1-13

ONE of the last stories Jesus told was given to His disciples as they sat with Him on the Mount of Olives two or three days before His crucifixion. He had just spoken His great prophecy of the end of the world and the signs of His second coming.

As the day wore away, the sun set behind the mountains and the shades of night began to fall. Twinkling lights began to appear in houses; yet it was still light enough to see outside. Down below was a house all lighted up; and outside, in the yard, were a company of people standing around, waiting for something. It was the scene of a wedding, and that was the house of the bride. The way they staged it was for the bridegroom to come with his friends to the bride's home and take her in procession to his own home. The bride had her own bridesmaids, and there they were all robed in white, with lamps in their hands already lighted. They were waiting for the bridegroom to come.

It made Jesus think of His own coming by and by to receive His waiting church. And He told this story:

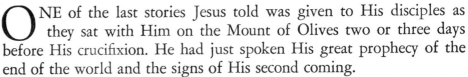

Then the kingdom of heaven will be like ten bridesmaids who took their lamps and went out to meet the bridegroom. Now five of them were foolish, and five of them were wise. The foolish ones brought their lamps but brought no extra oil. But the wise ones, besides the oil in their lamps, brought flasks of extra oil.

The bridegroom was slow in coming, and they all grew sleepy and fell asleep. But at midnight there was a shout: "Here is the bridegroom! Come out and meet him!" Then all the bridesmaids awoke and trimmed their lamps. And the foolish ones said to the wise ones, "Give us some of your oil, for our lamps are going out." But the wise ones answered, "There may not be enough for us and you. You had better go to the store and buy some for yourselves."

The foolish bridesmaids hurried away to buy more oil. But while they were gone, the bridegroom came, and the ones that were ready went with him in the procession to the wedding banquet, and the door of the bridegroom's house was shut and locked.

By and by the foolish bridesmaids came back. They hurried along the road to the bridegroom's house and knocked on the door and called: "Lord! Lord! Open the door for us!"

They made so much fuss the doorkeepers called the bridegroom, and he heard their plea. But all he knew was that the bride's party was waiting for him when he reached her house, and had come in with him before the door was shut. And so he answered them: "I don't know you! I tell you I don't know you!" They seemed to him to be just a party trying to get in without an invitation, and he would not open the door.

*　　*　　*

When Jesus had finished the story, He said to His disciples: "So I tell you, you must be on the watch; for you do not know either the day or the hour when the Son of man will come."

"Watch, ye saints, with eyelids waking!
Lo, the powers of heaven are shaking.
Keep your lamps all trimmed and burning,
Ready for your Lord's returning.
Lo, He comes! Lo, Jesus comes!
Lo, He comes, He comes all glorious,
Jesus comes to reign victorious,
Lo, He comes! Yes, Jesus comes!"

STORIES ABOUT THE APOSTLES

Peter, John, and Paul

Our Great High Priest

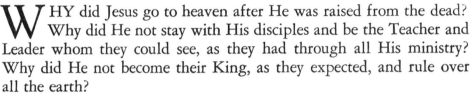

John 14; 16:11-16; 1 Corinthians
11:23-26; Hebrews 4:15, 16; 8 to 10

WHY did Jesus go to heaven after He was raised from the dead? Why did He not stay with His disciples and be the Teacher and Leader whom they could see, as they had through all His ministry? Why did He not become their King, as they expected, and rule over all the earth?

Because His people rejected Him, and thereby they rejected all the good things that the prophets had spoken about them. The prophets had told of a Christ who would bring righteousness and purity into the hearts of His people, who would suffer death for the sins of the world, but whom God would raise from the dead, and who would then reign in a new Jerusalem over His beloved people, and finally over a new earth in which there would be no sin and no sinners. But most of the Jews did not want purity of heart. They wanted a king of glory without the purity that made the glory. And at last they turned against the Christ and crucified Him.

So, as the Lamb of God He suffered death. He was raised from the dead; but He had no people ready to receive Him, and so He could not be their King. That had to be put off until there should be gathered out of all nations a people who would truly take Jesus into their hearts, and so prepare the way for His glorious coming as King of kings and Lord of lords.

The night before His crucifixion, Jesus comforted His disciples. He told them He was to die, and to be raised from the dead, and that He would then go to His Father in heaven. But He said He would not leave them without comfort. He would send the Holy Spirit to be with them always while He was away. He told them it was better for them that He should go away, because then the Comforter would come to them, and be everywhere at once, guiding them into all truth. And He said that He would come again and receive them and all who believe in Him, into glory.

All the sacrifices and the services in the temple, and before the temple, for those hundreds and thousands of years, had only pointed to the sacrifice and service of Jesus, the Messiah, the Christ. And the high priests who served in the tabernacle and the temple represented Jesus, who is not only the Lamb of God, but the Priest of His people. Jesus had a work to do as High Priest before He should be crowned as King. The high priest stood between the people and God, offering the sacrifices that in symbol atoned for their sins, and at the end of the year he did a work of cleansing the sanctuary of the forgiven sins. Jesus as High Priest offers His own sacrifice on the cross, and with it the incense of His prayers that God will forgive the sins of His people.

If His people the Jews had accepted Him, He would have done His work right there. As the prophets had promised, Jerusalem would never have been destroyed, but would have been made over into a beautiful new Jerusalem. And the sanctuary, the temple, would have been not one made with hands, but one made by Jesus without hands. The earthly tabernacle and temple were made after a pattern which God showed Moses at Mount Sinai, but the real temple is in heaven.

Jesus went to heaven to act as our High Priest while the gospel goes in the earth to prepare a people for His kingdom.

But though Jesus is in heaven, He is never far from any one of us. By His Holy Spirit He is always working in our midst and in every heart. And He is still an ever-present help in time of trouble.

"For we have not an high priest which cannot be touched with the feeling of our infirmities; but was in all points tempted like as we are, yet without sin. Let us therefore come boldly unto the throne of grace, that we may obtain mercy, and find grace to help in time of need."

———

"Now the main point in what I am saying is this: We have such a high priest as this, and he has taken his seat in heaven at the right hand of God's Majesty, to officiate as priest in the sanctuary and in that true tent of worship which not man but the Lord himself set up. But every high priest is appointed to offer gifts and sacrifices, and so this high priest also must have some sacrifice to offer. Further, if he were still on earth, he would not be a priest at all, for there are priests enough provided to offer the gifts the Law prescribes—though the service they engage in is only a shadow and imitation of that in heaven. For when Moses was going to make the tent of worship, he was warned, 'Be sure to make it all just like the pattern you were shown on the mountain.' But, as it is, the priestly service to which Christ has been appointed is as much better than the old as the agreement established by him and the promises on which it is based are superior to the former ones." Hebrews 8:1-6, Goodspeed.

441

The Holy Spirit Comes

Luke 24:49-53; Acts 1:12-14; 2

FROM the Mount of Olives, where they had seen Jesus go to heaven, the disciples returned to Jerusalem. They were not sorrowful now; they were filled with joy. Their eyes had been opened, so that they knew what the kingdom of Jesus was—hearts filled with purity and peace. They had seen their Lord taken from them into heaven, but they had His promise that He would come again in glory. And they had His other promise, that He would send the Comforter, the Holy Spirit, to be with them and guide them into all truth. They had been given a mission to carry the gospel of Jesus to all the world. But they had been told to wait in Jerusalem until that promise should be kept, and they should be filled with power from on high.

They went back to an upper room where they lived. They went up to the temple day by day, to pray and to praise, and no doubt they witnessed there for Jesus. But in the upper room they studied the Scriptures, and they prayed and sang.

They had not many days to wait. Fifty days after Passover came the Feast of Harvest Ingathering, called in the New Testament Pentecost, which means "fiftieth." On that day, in the Jewish law, it was ordained that of the first fruits of the harvest an offering should be made to God. This finished the great feast of the spring, which began with Passover and ended with Pentecost.

Now Jesus was crucified on the day of Passover and was raised on the third day afterward. Then He spent forty days on earth with His disciples, so that there were only seven or eight days left until Pentecost. These were the days the disciples spent in prayer and praise, preparing their hearts for the coming of the Holy Spirit.

And when the day of Pentecost was fully come, they were all meeting together, when suddenly there came from the sky a rushing sound like a great wind, and it filled the whole house where they were sitting. And they saw split tongues of fire, which came and rested on everyone's head. Then they were all filled with the Holy Spirit, and began to speak in foreign languages, whatever the Spirit told them to say.

The Holy Spirit, Jesus told Nicodemus, is like the wind, which

442

you cannot see, but you can see what it does. No man has ever seen the Holy Spirit, but we can see and we can feel what He does, as we see the trees moved by the wind and feel the breeze upon our faces. The Holy Spirit is represented, too, by other things, like the dove that alighted on Jesus' head at His baptism, like the oil with which the priest and the king were anointed, like the rain that refreshes the earth, and like fire that purifies gold. On Pentecost the Holy Spirit appeared as cloven tongues of fire.

As you grow older, there will be much for you to learn of what these symbols mean. The Father, the Son, and the Holy Spirit are one God. (1 John 5:7.) We cannot understand this, but it is true, and someday we shall understand.

Now at the Feast of Pentecost there were good men, Jews and converts, gathered from many countries in Asia and Africa and Europe, who spoke more than a dozen languages. When the sound of the Holy Spirit's coming was heard, there came a crowd to the house where the apostles were. And the apostles stood forth, speaking in the various languages, I suppose taking turns.

Then the people in the crowd from these many countries were amazed. They said, "Are not all these men who are speaking Galileans? How is it, then, that every one of us hears his own native tongue?"

Some others in the crowd jeered, "Oh, they are drunk!"

Then Peter stood forth and preached his first sermon. He said: "Men of Judea, and all of you, pay attention. These men are not drunk. This is what the prophet Joel foretold, that in these days God would pour out His Spirit, and the young men should prophesy, and everyone who calls on the name of the Lord shall be saved."

Then he went on to preach to them Jesus, whom they had slain, but whom God had raised from the dead. And he quoted from the Scriptures to show that it was so prophesied. "Therefore," he said, "the whole nation of Israel must know that this same Jesus, whom you crucified, God has made both Lord and Christ."

When they had heard Peter through, they were stung to the heart, and they said to the apostles, "Brothers, what shall we do?"

"You must repent," answered Peter, "and be baptized in the name of Jesus Christ, that you may have your sins forgiven." And he went on to tell them more.

Then they who received his word gave themselves for baptism. And about three thousand people joined them that day. They clung to the apostles, as they had to Jesus, and they were blessed by the Holy Spirit, and made the first church of Christians.

At the Beautiful Gate

Acts 3; 4

NOW, every day the apostles went from house to house, teaching those who believed. They and all their converts also went up to the temple every day; for that was the house which had been built for God, and it was the only church building they had. And God added to the church every day more and more people who wanted to be saved. Many of these new converts were people who had known and believed in Jesus when He taught and healed among them, and now the Holy Spirit spoke to their hearts, and they became the first to believe the gospel.

There came a day when Peter and John went up together into the temple for the three o'clock hour of prayer. And as they arrived, there was carried by them a man who had been lame all his life and had never walked. His friends were used to carrying him in and putting him down at the principal gate of the temple, which was called the Beautiful Gate. There he sat and begged the passers-by for money.

As he saw Peter and John coming, he held out his hand and begged for a gift. The two apostles stopped and looked pityingly upon him and said, "Look on us." He fastened his eyes upon them, supposing they were about to give him something. And Peter said: "Silver and gold have I none; but such as I have I give to you. In the name of Jesus Christ of Nazareth, rise up and walk!"

Then he took him by the right hand and lifted him up. His feet and ankles at once grew strong. Finding that he could stand, he began to walk. He went into the temple with them, so happy he leaped and ran and turned about, praising God in a loud voice. And all the people who had seen him begging at the Beautiful Gate were perfectly astonished at what had happened to him.

He held Peter and John while he told everybody that they had cured him. When Peter saw this, he said: "Men of Israel, why do you stare at us, as though by our own power and goodness we had done this? The God of our fathers has done this, through His Son Jesus, whom you betrayed and disowned before Pilate, when he had decided to let Him go." And Peter went on and preached a sermon.

Now the priests and the Sadducees, seeing and hearing this, came with the captain of the temple guards, and arrested Peter and John and put them in prison. The next morning they were brought before Annas and Caiaphas and other priests to be tried. How Peter must have thought of that night, so short a time before, when Jesus stood as the prisoner before these two high priests, and Peter had denied Him! But now he was forgiven, and he was no longer a coward. He stood before the council and declared his faith in Jesus.

The priests asked, "By what power or authority have men like you done this?"

And they answered, "Through the power of Jesus Christ, whom you crucified, but whom God raised from the dead, has this man been healed. There is no salvation through anyone else; for He is the only One in the world through whom men must be saved."

Caiaphas and Annas were astonished and dismayed. They knew that Peter and John had been disciples of Jesus. And they saw before them the man who had been healed from his lameness. They set the apostles outside, while they talked it over. They called them back in and ordered them not to speak again in the name of Jesus.

But Peter and John said, "Tell us whether it is right to obey you rather than God. As for us, we cannot keep from telling what we have seen and heard."

The priests turned the two men loose, and they went on teaching while more and more of the people believed and joined the church.

Through the rosy portals of morning
  Now the tides of sunshine flow;
O'er the blossoming earth and the glistening sea
The praise Thou inspirest rolls back to Thee;
Its tones through the infinite arches go;
Yet, crippled and dumb, behold me wait,
  Dear Lord, at the Beautiful Gate.

I wait for Thy hand of healing,
  For vigor and hope in Thee.
Open wide the door—let me feel the sun!
Let me touch Thy robes!—I shall rise and run
Through Thy happy universe, safe and free,
Where in and out Thy beloved go,
  Nor want nor wandering know.

Lucy Larcom.

445

The First Christian Martyr

Acts 6; 7

MULTITUDES and multitudes of people began to believe in Jesus and to join the church in Jerusalem. First there were three thousand on the day of Pentecost, then five thousand on the day that Peter and John healed the lame man; and after that it just says, "The number of the disciples multiplied in Jerusalem greatly."

Now, in those days of brotherly love, the believers held everything in common. For those who had property sold it, and with the money helped those who had none. But it was sort of hit and miss, because there were so many, and no one was exactly in charge. And the Greek-speaking disciples complained that the widows among them were neglected in the daily giving out of food.

So the apostles called the whole body together, probably in the court of the temple, and said to them: "It is not a good thing that we give up preaching the gospel to keep accounts. You, brothers, must pick out seven men of good standing who are wise and filled with the Spirit of God. And we will put them in charge of this matter, while we give ourselves to prayer and delivering the message."

They all said that was good, and they chose seven, of whom Stephen was first. The second was Philip, and the last was Nicholas, a Greek who had been converted to the Jewish religion and then had become a Christian. They brought these men to the apostles, who prayed and laid their hands upon them, so ordaining them as the first deacons the church ever had.

Now these seven deacons were not only men of business, but good workers for Jesus. They straightened things out and put in order the business they had been appointed to see to, but they also gave the message of salvation everywhere they went. And Stephen, full of faith and power, did great wonders and miracles among the people.

The Jews who opposed them could not answer Stephen's teachings; so they hired some men to bear false witness. These false witnesses said, "We have heard him speak wicked words against Moses and against God." They stirred up the mob, with the elders and the scribes, and they came upon him and caught him and brought him to the Sanhedrin. There they testified that he had said that Jesus of

Nazareth would tear down the temple and change the religion which Moses had taught.

Everyone who sat in the council fixed his eyes on Stephen, and they saw his face as though it had been the face of an angel. The high priest said to him, "Is all this true?"

Then Stephen arose and spoke, telling the history of the Israelites from Abraham on. They all listened with rapt attention; for this was what they liked to hear. He spoke on, through the history of Moses to David and Solomon who built the temple. Then he said: "But the Most High does not live in houses made by human hands, as the prophet Isaiah has said: ' "Heaven is My throne, and earth is My footstool; what house will you build for Me?" says the Lord.' "

Though Stephen quoted from their own Scriptures, they said he was speaking against the temple. And they loved the temple more than they loved the Bible and the God who was the Maker of all. The temple was their idol. So now they rose in anger against Stephen.

But Stephen stood like a rock against them. He said in their faces: "You are always opposing the Holy Spirit, just as your fathers did. Which of the prophets did not your fathers persecute? And they slew those who told beforehand of the coming of the righteous One, whom you have now betrayed and killed—you who had the law given to you by angels, and did not obey it!"

When they heard him say that, they were furious, and gnashed their teeth at him. But he, full of the Holy Spirit, looked up toward the sky and said, "Behold! I see heaven opened, and the Son of man standing on the right hand of God."

Then they gave a great shout, and rushed upon him all together, and dragged him out of the city, and stoned him. They were breaking the Roman law in putting a man to death, but there was no Roman governor just then in Jerusalem, and they did what they pleased. However, the law of Moses said that a man could not be put to death unless there were at least two or three witnesses against him. They had their witnesses, false witnesses, who told lies. They took off their coats, and laid them down at the feet of a young man named Saul, and then turned to throw the first stones.

As they stoned Stephen, he prayed, "Lord Jesus, receive my spirit!" Then, falling upon his knees, he cried, as Jesus had, "Lord, do not lay this sin up against them!" With these words he fell asleep. So died the first Christian martyr.

And the young man Saul steeled his heart against the terrible sight and consented to his death.

Philip and the Ethiopian

Acts 8

UPON the death of Stephen there arose a fierce persecution against the church in Jerusalem. And the church members scattered out through Judea and Samaria. Only the apostles stayed in Jerusalem.

Philip the deacon went to Samaria, and preached Christ there, and did many miracles of healing and casting out of devils. And many Samaritans believed and were baptized. Then the apostles, hearing of this, sent Peter and John, who finished the work and returned to Jerusalem.

Now an angel of the Lord said to Philip, "Get up and go south by the road that runs from Jerusalem to Gaza." So he got up and went. As he was going along the road, there went riding by, with his attendants, an Ethiopian officer, a member of the court of Candace, queen of Ethiopia, and her chief treasurer. But he was a convert to the Jewish religion, and had been to Jerusalem to worship. Now as he rode along in the chariot, driven by his charioteer, he was reading in the roll of the prophets from the Book of Isaiah.

And the Spirit said to Philip, "Go and join that chariot." So Philip ran, and heard him reading aloud from Isaiah the part that says, "He was led as a sheep to the slaughter; and like a lamb dumb before his shearer, so opened He not His mouth."

And Philip said, "Do you understand what you are reading?"

"Why, how can I," he answered, "unless someone explains it to me? Tell me, of whom is the prophet speaking? of himself, or of someone else?"

Then Philip began from that scripture and told him the good news of Jesus. It was natural, then, for the officer to invite him into his chariot, and so they rode along for a great way, while Philip told him all about Jesus, who died to save the world, who rose from the dead, and passed into heaven, where He lives as the great High Priest of His people. The officer received it all with joy and was converted then and there.

Pretty soon they came to some water, perhaps a stream that crossed their road. And the officer said to Philip, "See! Here is some water! What stands in the way of my being baptized?"

The Story of the Beautiful Gate

Peter said, "Look on us. And he gave heed unto them, expecting to receive something of them. Then Peter said, Silver and gold have I none; but such as I have give I thee: In the name of Jesus Christ of Nazareth rise up and walk. And he took him by the right hand, and lifted him up: and immediately his feet and ankle bones received strength. And he . . . entered with them into the temple."

ROBERT TEMPLE AYRES, ARTIST

And Philip said, "If you believe with all your heart, you may."
"I believe that Jesus Christ is the Son of God."

So he commanded the charioteer to stop, and the chariot stood still. Then they both got out and went down into the water, and Philip baptized him.

Then the Spirit of God caught Philip away, and the officer never saw him again. But he went on his way rejoicing and carried the gospel of Jesus to Ethiopia.

There was a Philip who was one of Jesus' twelve apostles, but this Philip was not he. He was one of the seven deacons, of whom Stephen was first. Though the deacons were chosen as businessmen, to see that the widows and orphans were not neglected, that did not stop them from preaching the gospel of Jesus; and some of them at least were good teachers and missionaries. That was true of Stephen, and it was true of Philip.

When his work as deacon in Jerusalem was ended, and the believers were scattered abroad because of persecution, Philip went to Samaria, preaching the Word. Then God sent him to instruct the Ethiopian officer. And when he had done that, the Spirit of the Lord caught him up and set him down at Azotus, or Ashdod, on the coast between Gaza and Joppa. Later he lived in Caesarea. And Philip went on preaching and drawing people to Christ, so he came to be known as Philip the Evangelist.

Philip was a good father, too, and his wife must have been a good mother; for their children grew up in the Christian faith. Whether they had any boys I don't know, but anyway they had four girls. When these girls had grown up to be young women, God gave them the gift of prophecy. And when Paul went through on his last visit to Jerusalem, these young prophetesses told him the message of God, as you will read in the twenty-first chapter of Acts.

On the Road to Damascus

Acts 8:1-3; 9:1-22; 22:3-16, 20; Philippians 3:4, 5

THE YOUNG man Saul had been born in Tarsus, which was a long way from Jerusalem, and not in Judea at all. But the Jews were spread abroad in foreign lands, as well as in their homeland; and Saul's family were away up here in Cilicia and Tarsus, its chief city. Tarsus was well known for its learning and its schools; and the boy Saul, son of a Pharisee, of the tribe of Benjamin, was a studious lad, and learned a great deal. When he was perhaps fourteen or fifteen years old, his father sent him to Jerusalem, where he entered the school of Gamaliel, who was one of the most famous teachers the Jews ever had. Saul became learned in the law, and while still young was a favorite with the high priests and elders.

Led by his teachers, the Pharisees, he was very zealous against the followers of Jesus, and was determined to root them out. So it came about that when the council had condemned Stephen, and he was rushed outside the city walls to his death, Saul was there taking part, and he kept the clothes of those who stoned him. The scene of Stephen's heroic death haunted Saul's mind; but he tried to drown out the thoughts that arose by being more furious against the disciples. He went from house to house, dragging out men and women, and putting them in prison. None were so furious about this as Saul, so he grew more and more in favor with the priests.

When the church was scattered by this persecution, many went to Damascus, about two hundred and fifty miles northeast of Jerusalem, in the province of Syria, and there they formed another church. When Saul heard of this company in Damascus, he made up his mind to go there and bring them in chains to Jerusalem. So he went to the high priest and asked for letters to the rulers of the synagogues in Damascus; and the high priest gladly gave them to him.

So Saul got together a band of horsemen and rode forth on his quest. But as they came near to Damascus, suddenly a brilliant light flashed around him from heaven, and he fell to the ground. Then he heard a Voice saying to him, "Saul! Saul! Why do you persecute Me?"

Lying there flat on the ground, blinded by the light, he could only ask feebly, "Who are You, Lord?"

"I am Jesus, whom you persecute," said the Voice. "But get up and go into the city, and there you will be told what you should do."

Saul's companions stood speechless. They saw the light, but they did not see Jesus. They heard the Voice, but they did not understand what it said. Then the light went away. When Paul was helped to his feet, he could not see anything. But they led him by the hand into Damascus, and there he lay and fasted for three days, blind and helpless, praying and wondering.

There was in Damascus a disciple named Ananias, to whom God came in a dream and said, "Get up and go to the street called Straight, and ask there at the house of Judas for a man named Saul. He is there praying. And he has seen a vision of a man named Ananias coming in and laying his hands on him to restore his sight."

But Ananias said, "Lord, I have heard many people tell of this man and the harm he has done to Your people in Jerusalem. He is here with authority to arrest everyone who calls upon Your name."

But the Lord said to him, "Go! This man is the one I have chosen to carry My name to the heathen and their kings and among the children of Israel. I am going to show him how much he must suffer for My sake."

So Ananias set out and went to the house of Judas on Straight Street. He was let in, and going to Saul he laid his hands on him and said, "Saul, my brother, I have been sent by the Lord Jesus Christ, who showed Himself to you on your journey, so that you may receive your sight and be filled with the Holy Spirit."

Something like scales at once dropped from Saul's eyes, and his sight was restored. He looked up and saw the face of Ananias, God's messenger to him. And Ananias said: "The God of our fathers has chosen you, that you should know His will, and see and hear Him. You are to be His witness to all men of what you have seen and heard. And now why wait? Get up, and be baptized, and wash away your sins, calling on His name." So Saul got up and was baptized. And after taking some food, he regained his strength.

He stayed for some time with the disciples at Damascus and began at once to speak in the synagogues, declaring that Jesus was the Son of God. Everyone was astonished and said, "Isn't this the man who destroyed those who called on this Name in Jerusalem? And he came here just to arrest such people and take them before the high priests."

Saul grew more and more powerful and put to confusion the Jews who lived in Damascus, proving that Jesus is the very Christ. But many hardened their hearts and turned against his message. Soon they came to

451

hate him as they had hated Jesus, and Stephen His martyr. They grew so fierce that Paul felt he had to have time to study and prepare himself for the great conflict before him. And by the counsel of God he left Damascus and journeyed into the Arabian desert to the east. There he emptied his soul of the wrong ideas he had had, and filled it with the truths of the Scriptures, as he was taught by the Holy Spirit.

And so did Jesus choose His great apostle, and so did He ordain him. Like Judas Iscariot, he was learned in the law, and more learned. Like Judas, he was talented, and he did not hide his talent in the ground, but used it to make many more. Unlike Judas, he humbled himself and became a servant of servants, and so he became the greatest of all.

The young man Saul of Tarsus was a zealous young man;
 ("Saul, Saul, why persecutest thou Me?")
He rooted out the heretics according to the plan;
But everywhere he went, through his troubled mind there ran:
 "Saul, Saul, why persecutest thou Me?"

So he rode off north toward Damascus on the plain,
 ("Saul, Saul, why persecutest thou Me?")
For to catch more martyrs and see that they were slain;
But this word struck him down and made his mission vain:
 "Saul, Saul, why persecutest thou Me?"

"Who art Thou, Lord?" in anguish and in terror deep he cried.
 ("Saul, Saul, why persecutest thou Me?")
"I am Jesus, Lord and Saviour, who for you have died;
I will send you to the Gentiles, to proclaim the Crucified!
 Saul, Saul, why persecutest thou Me?"

Now this Saul of Tarsus could not stand the light;
 ("Saul, Saul, why persecutest thou Me?")
His natural eyes were blinded, and he lived in blackest night;
And, oh, how he prayed that he might be given sight.
 "Saul, Saul, why persecutest thou Me?"

And this Saul of Tarsus was nevermore the same;
 ("Saul, Saul, why persecutest thou Me?")
For he turned in his course to revere the holy name
And blaze through all the earth its glory and its fame—
 "This Paul I have chosen, who persecuted Me."

452

Gentle Lady of Joppa

Acts 9:36-43

AFTER the persecution that came with the death of Stephen, the churches in Jerusalem and throughout Judea and Samaria were left alone by their enemies, and they had peace. The believers were filled with the Spirit and worked and taught in the name of Jesus; so many were added to the church.

The apostles labored all through the country. And Peter, going here and there, came to a town called Lydda. It lay between Jerusalem and the seaport of Joppa. There he found a man named Aeneas, who had palsy and had kept his bed for eight years. Peter went in to him and said, "Aeneas, Jesus Christ cures you. Get up, and make your bed." At once he got up, and was well. And everybody who lived around there heard of it, and many turned to the Lord.

Now at Joppa, among the disciples, there lived a gentle lady named Tabitha, which in Greek is Dorcas, and both names mean "gazelle," which is a graceful animal much like a deer. And Dorcas was a dear. She was graceful and gentle, and more than that, she was good. She spent her time in helping the poor, and especially, since she was a good seamstress, she made coats and dresses, which she gave to the widows and orphans. So they all loved her very much.

But Dorcas fell ill, and suddenly she died. Her friends prepared her for burial and laid her in an upper room. Then someone said, "You know, Peter, the great apostle of the Lord Jesus, is at Lydda right now. That's only nine miles from here. He was with Jesus so long, and saw Him raise people from the dead. Do you suppose, maybe, he could raise Dorcas from the dead? Let's send for him."

So they sent and asked Peter to come down to Joppa. And when he came there, he found the widows and other people in the house crying and showing the garments that Dorcas had made for them. They had reason to mourn, and their sorrow was not put on. But it must have reminded Peter of that day long before, when, with James and John, Jesus had taken him into the house of Jairus, where a little girl lay dead, and where the mourners were making such a noise; and how Jesus put them all out of the house, except the three disciples and the father and mother; and how they went in where the little girl lay, and

Jesus raised her from the dead. Peter must have remembered, and now, oh, how he prayed!

He put all the mourners out of the room. He knew he was not so great as Jesus, but he remembered that Jesus had promised that His apostles should be able to raise the dead, when the Holy Spirit had come upon them. So he knelt down and prayed. Then he turned to the body of Dorcas and said, "Tabitha, stand up!"

She opened her eyes, and when she saw Peter, she sat up. He gave her his hand and raised her to her feet. Then he called in the believers and the widows, and gave her back to them alive. Oh, what a joyous time when Dorcas was with them once again!

What a miracle! The fame of it spread all over Joppa and the land round about, and many believed on Jesus and were added to the church. So Peter stayed awhile in Joppa to teach the new and old believers. He found lodging with a man named Simon, a tanner, who lived in a house by the seaside.

There is a sound of sobbing in Joppa by the sea,
Of sobbing and of crying and of mourning bitterly;
For Dorcas lies for burial on an upper-chamber bed;
And the blesser of the widows and the orphans, she is dead.

All the widows and the orphans, all the poor and friendless folk,
Showed the coats and garments Dorcas gave. And thus they spoke:
"Gone is she who marked our sorrows and our many wants supplied;
Who is there to heed and comfort us, since Dorcas died?"

Then there was a stirring of the crowd around her bed
As the elders brought in Peter. And he bowed his head,
Saying, "Leave, my friends, for that the Healer may come in
And rebuke the foul destroyer and his chains of death and sin."

Then he prayed, O mighty wrestler with the Christ he loved;
And the arm of the Almighty most wonderfully moved.
For when Peter prayed, believing, and commanded, "Dorcas, rise!"
Then the tide of life within her opened wide her eyes.

Oh, rejoice, ye saints and widows, and ye children, sing!
For to you again is given one for ministering.
Dorcas! Dorcas! loved and loving, take from God your breath,
And a thousandfold your service, since His life has conquered death.

454

Cornelius, the Centurion

Acts 10; 11:1-18

SOME thirty-five miles north of Joppa lay the city of Caesarea. It was a great city, which Herod the First had built and made the capital of the country. Here the Romans had their headquarters, though both Herod and the Romans had to pay much attention to Jerusalem, and often lived there.

Now there was stationed in Caesarea a band of Roman soldiers called the Italian band. Their centurion, or captain, was Cornelius. He was a good man, who was very kind to the poor and needy. And though not a Jew, he was a friend to them, and he worshiped God. He prayed to God every day, and he led all his household and some of his soldiers to do the same.

One afternoon, about three o'clock, as he was praying, he had a vision in which he saw an angel of God come into his room and say to him, "Cornelius!"

He stared at the angel, startled, and said, "What is it, sir?"

The angel answered, "Your prayers and good deeds have gone up and are remembered before God. Now send men to Joppa for a man named Simon, who is also called Peter. He is staying at the house of a tanner named Simon, which is close to the sea. He will tell you what you ought to do."

When the angel had gone, Cornelius called two of his servants, and after telling them the story of his dream, he sent them to Joppa.

While they were on the way, and near Joppa, Peter went up on the housetop, about noon, to pray. He grew very hungry and wanted something to eat. While they were getting it ready, he fell into a trance and saw the sky opened and a great sheet let down by its four corners, with all kinds of animals, reptiles, and birds in it. And a Voice said to him, "Get up, Peter! Kill something, and eat it."

Peter looked in disgust at the unclean animals, and he said, "Never! I have never eaten anything that the law says is unclean."

Then the Voice said, "What God has cleansed, do not call unclean."

This happened three times. And then the thing was taken up in the sky. Peter, now awake, was wondering what the vision could mean.

455

Just then the men whom Cornelius had sent reached the house, and called to ask if a man named Peter was there. And the Spirit said to Peter, "There are two men looking for you. Get up and go down, and go with them without any question; for I have sent them."

Peter went down and greeted the men and asked them what they wanted. They said: "Cornelius, a captain, and a God-fearing man, and well liked by all the Jews, was told by a holy angel to send for you and to listen to what you have to say."

So Peter invited them in and kept them overnight. Now Peter was a Jew, and like all the Jews in those days he had been brought up to think that all other people were unclean, or unfit for a Jew to company with or to eat with. But he had just been told by God not to think anything unclean when God had cleansed it. So he pondered and prayed that night, and he made up his mind this was what the vision meant.

In the morning, then, he and some of the brethren in Joppa went with the men; and the day after that they reached Caesarea. Cornelius had invited in his relatives and his close friends, and they were waiting for them. When Peter actually came in, Cornelius fell at his feet to worship him. But Peter lifted him up and said, "Get up! I am only a man myself!" So they went into the house together, talking with each other. And there was a great company gathered.

Peter said to them: "You know it is against the law for a Jew to company with a foreigner or to visit one; but God has taught me not to call anyone common or unclean. And now I ask why you sent for me."

Then Cornelius recited to him all his story, and added, "Now we are all here in God's presence, to hear everything that the Lord has told you to say."

Then Peter said: "Now I really understand that God has no favorites, but welcomes the man of any nation who worships Him. You know the story, as it has gone over all the land, about Jesus of Nazareth, whom God anointed to be the Saviour, and who went about doing good, and healing all that were oppressed of the devil. You know how He was condemned and put to death, but God raised Him the third day, and we are witnesses to this, because we were with Him after He had risen. He has appointed us to tell the good news to all the people, that whoever believes in Him will have his sins forgiven."

While Peter was speaking, his listeners drank in every word. And suddenly the Holy Spirit came in, as it had upon the apostles on the day of Pentecost. The Jewish believers who had come with Peter were amazed at this. Then Peter said, "Can any man forbid that these should be baptized, who have received the Holy Spirit as well as we?" And he commanded that they be baptized. After that he stayed with them a few days, and taught them.

Now when Peter and some of the brethren went back to Jerusalem, the Jewish believers there accused him, saying, "You went in to men who were not Jews, and ate with them."

Then Peter told them the whole story from the beginning, and said at the close, "I remembered what the Lord Jesus had said to us: 'John baptized in water, but you shall be baptized in the Holy Spirit.' So when I saw them receive the Holy Spirit, who was I, that I should interfere with God?"

Then they all agreed, and said, "So God has given even the heathen repentance and the hope of life!"

Thus did the Lord begin to break down the wall of separation between Jew and Gentile, to make of them all the Christian church.

"Arise, shine; for thy light is come,
  And the glory of the Lord is risen upon thee.
  For, behold, the darkness shall cover the earth,
  And gross darkness the people:
  But the Lord shall arise upon thee,
  And his glory shall be seen upon thee.
  And the Gentiles shall come to thy light,
  And kings to the brightness of thy rising.

"Lift up thine eyes round about, and see:
  All they gather themselves together, they come to thee:
  Thy sons shall come from far,
  And thy daughters shall be nursed at thy side.
  Then thou shalt see, and flow together,
  And thine heart shall fear, and be enlarged;
  Because the abundance of the sea shall be converted unto thee,
  The forces of the Gentiles shall come unto thee."
                                        Isaiah 60:1-5.

"And other sheep I have, which are not of this fold: them also I must bring, and they shall hear my voice; and there shall be one fold, and one shepherd." John 10:16.

Peter Delivered From Prison

Acts 12:1-17

NOW once again the church began to endure persecution. Herod the king stretched forth his hand to afflict them. This was not that Herod Antipas who put John the Baptist to death and mocked at Jesus. He had been put down from being king and was in exile far away. This was his nephew, Herod Agrippa I, who had become king in his place. But like almost all the Herods, he was bad.

He seized James the brother of John and had him beheaded. James was the first of the apostles to suffer death for Jesus' sake. When Herod saw that this pleased the Jews, he arrested Peter too, at the time of the Passover, and put him in prison, intending after the feast to kill him too. Peter was put down in the dungeon, chained to a soldier on either side, so that he could not get away.

But while Peter was in prison, many of the church members were gathered together in the house of Mary the mother of Mark, to pray that the Lord would save them from Herod, and that He would take Peter out of prison.

Along with all the grown people who came to that meeting was a little girl about twelve years old, named Rhoda. And all the grownups said, "Now Rhoda is just a little girl. She'll not want to come into the prayer meeting. We'll put her out there to tend the door." And they did. They said: "Rhoda, you sit there by the door and listen. And if anyone comes and raps, don't you let him in. Come and tell us."

But Rhoda was a little girl who loved Peter, as all the children did. And she said, "I'm not going to be kept from praying for Peter. I'll pray by myself out here by the door." And she did. She prayed that the Lord would send His angel from heaven that very night and let Peter out of prison.

So here was Peter, away down in the dungeon, chained to a soldier on this side and on that side so he could not get away. And while they were praying for him in the house of Mary the mother of Mark, Peter went to sleep. And the soldiers went to sleep.

Then the Lord sent His angel down from heaven, and he came and stood in the prison where Peter was. He struck Peter on the side and woke him up. But Peter thought he was dreaming.

458

The angel said to Peter, "Stand up!" Peter stood up, and the chains fell from his hands, but the soldiers never woke up or knew.

Then the angel said, "Put on your coat and your shoes." And Peter did. But still he thought he was dreaming.

Then the angel said, "Follow me." And he walked up the stairs and out of the prison into the prison yard, and Peter followed him. But still he thought he was dreaming. They came to the great iron gate that opened upon the street, and it opened of itself and let the angel and Peter through. But still Peter thought he was dreaming!

They went along one street into another, and suddenly the angel left Peter. And Peter came to himself, and he found he wasn't dreaming after all, but he was out of the prison; he was free. So he came to the house where inside the door was Rhoda, listening. Peter knocked on the door. And Rhoda said, "Who is it?"

And he said, "It's Peter. Let me in."

But Rhoda was so glad to hear his voice she didn't stop to open the door. She ran in where all the people were praying for the Lord to let Peter out of prison, and she cried, "Peter's here! Peter's here!"

They looked at her, and they said, "Ah! You're crazy!"

But she said, "No! No! I tell you, Peter's at the door!"

Then they said, "It must be his guardian angel."

"No!" cried Rhoda, "I tell you, it is Peter. You come and see!"

So at last they came to the door, where Peter still was knocking. They opened the door, and there, sure enough, stood Peter!

And when Rhoda heard Peter tell how the Lord had sent His angel that very night and had taken him out of prison, just as she had prayed He would do, Rhoda said to herself, "I just knew He would!"

*   *   *

This is the last the Bible tells us of Peter, except what Paul says of him in the Book of Galatians. But the Bible does contain two epistles or letters, which Peter wrote to Christians. They are called First Peter and Second Peter.

From other books we learn that Peter kept on preaching Christ and teaching the gospel, as all the apostles did. He had about thirty-five years to bear his witness. Then, in his old age, he was in Rome, where he was condemned to death for Christ's sake and was crucified like Jesus. But Peter remembered, in the hour of death, his shameful act of denying his Lord. He thought he was not worthy to die like Jesus, and so he asked to be crucified with his head down. They granted his request, and thus died Peter, the great apostle, about the year A.D. 68.

The Gospel Goes to the Gentiles

Acts 9:23-30; 11:19-30; 12:25; 13; 14; Galatians 1

G ENTILES" is a name that the Jews gave to all peoples who were not Jews. It really means just "nations," but it was used much as "heathen" has been used by Christians for all peoples who are not Christians, and as "infidel" is used by Mohammedans for all peoples who are not Mohammedans.

If the Jewish Christians had had their way, the Christians would have been just a branch of the Jews; but Jesus intended His message to go to all the world, and to contain people from every nation and kindred and tongue and people. Therefore God took Saul of Tarsus, who was later called Paul, to become the great Apostle to the Gentiles. Jesus converted Paul in such a thunderous fashion that it broke him all up. And then He took him into the desert, as He had taken Moses ages before, and there He taught him the gospel that should go not just to the Jews but to all the world.

He called on Saul (a name which means "asked for"), a man who was willing to be changed all over, who from being proud became humble, who from thinking himself great came to feel that he was nothing, but Christ was all; and He changed his name to Paul, which means "little." Three years in the Arabian Desert Saul spent studying the Scriptures, meditating, praying, and perhaps teaching the few people who came by. Then he went back to Damascus.

Three years had not been long enough to make either the Jews or the Christians forget how Saul had persecuted the church. The Jews in Damascus lay in wait for him to kill him, and the king guarded the gates so that he might not pass. But the disciples took him to a house on the wall of the city and let him down in a basket outside.

He journeyed then to Jerusalem and tried to join himself to the disciples. But they, remembering he had had a part in Stephen's death, and then had been a terrible scourge to the church, were nearly all afraid of him. But there was a good man there, named Joses, whom the apostles called Barnabas, which means "son of consolation," because he was so kind and helpful. Right after Pentecost he sold some land he had and gave the money to the apostles for the church. His sister was Mary the mother of Mark, and she had a house in Jerusalem which

460

she gave over to the church, and there the apostles and others made their home.

Now when Saul came back to Jerusalem, Barnabas alone welcomed him. He took him to Peter and James, and told them the story of Saul's conversion on the road to Damascus. So they received him, and for fifteen days he boldly taught in the synagogues of Jerusalem that Jesus is the Christ. But this enraged the Jews, and especially the high priests who had sent him to Damascus to root out the hated followers of Jesus; and they planned to kill him.

But as Saul was praying in the temple, God appeared to him in a vision and told him to leave Jerusalem, for they would not receive his word. "Depart!" He said. "For I will send you far away to the Gentiles." When the apostles heard of this, they took him to Caesarea, put him on a ship, and sent him to Tarsus.

Now when the persecution that arose about Stephen had taken place, some of the disciples who fled from Jerusalem traveled as far as Antioch, three hundred miles north, on the seacoast. There they converted not only many Jews but also many Gentiles to the faith. And since the whole company could not be called Jews, the people of Antioch called them Christians, and that was the first time the name "Christian" was given to the church.

When the word of all this came to the church in Jerusalem, they sent Barnabas to Antioch to organize things, and he taught and encouraged them. Finding that he needed help, he thought of Saul in Tarsus, about a hundred miles northwest, and he went there and invited him to go back with him to Antioch. So Saul was introduced to his great mission. They stayed together and taught in Antioch for a whole year, and the Lord greatly blessed their labors.

A great famine came in those days in the country around Jerusalem, and the church in Antioch gathered relief for them and sent it to Jerusalem by the hands of Barnabas and Saul. Then they came back to Antioch, bringing with them Barnabas' nephew, John Mark.

As they ministered there for the Lord, the Holy Spirit said to the church, "Set Barnabas and Saul apart for Me, for the work to which I have called them." So when the church had fasted and prayed, the elders laid their hands upon these two, and let them go. They took with them Mark as their servant and helper.

They first sailed to the island of Cyprus, and preached the gospel there. They wrought miracles, and converted many people. And there, in his first ministry especially for the Gentiles, Saul's name was changed to Paul, by which he was ever afterwards known.

After a while they returned to the mainland and took their journey up into the country to various cities. They came after a while to another Antioch, back in the country, where they were invited to address the Jews in their synagogue. They preached Jesus, and some of the Jews believed, and many of the proselytes followed them, eager to hear more.

The next Sabbath nearly the whole town gathered to hear God's message. But when the unbelieving Jews saw the crowd, they were very jealous and spoke against Paul and cursed him. Then Paul and Barnabas spoke out plainly and said: "God's message ought to be told to you Jews first; but since you throw it off, and think yourselves unworthy of eternal life, lo, we turn to the Gentiles." And when the Greeks heard this, they were very glad, and praised God. From this time on, while Paul labored for the Jews when they would listen, his great mission was to the Gentiles. And to him and those who worked with him was chiefly due the growth of the church outside the Jewish people and in all the world.

At Lystra, one of the cities they visited, they saw a man, like the one at the Beautiful Gate, who had been lame from his birth, and had never walked. Paul, seeing that this man had faith to believe, called on him to rise and walk. He did. When all the heathen saw this miracle, they cried, "The gods have come down to us in the likeness of men!" And the priest of Jupiter, the chief god of the Romans, brought oxen and flowers to sacrifice to them. But Barnabas and Paul ran in among the people, saying, "Friends, why do you do this? We are only human beings like you, and bring you the good news that you should turn from these follies to the living God, who made heaven and earth." So they stopped worshiping Paul and Barnabas.

But then some Jews came from towns they had already visited, and stirred up the people, both Jews and Gentiles, and turned them against the apostles. They made a riot, and stoned Paul, and dragged him out of the town and left him for dead. But as the brethren stood around lamenting, he rose up, and went back with them into the same town.

One of those who thus first saw Paul was a young man named Timothy, whose mother Eunice was a Jewish Christian, but his father was a Greek. On Paul's next visit, he took Timothy with him; and after this Timothy was one of his best helpers. Another young Greek whom Paul converted was Titus, who also came to be one of his chief helpers. Three of the books of the Bible are letters which Paul later wrote to Timothy and Titus.

462

The People of God

Acts 15:1-35; Galatians 2:1-10

WHEN Paul and Barnabas went back to Antioch, they found that some Jewish Christians from Jerusalem, who had been Pharisees, had come there and taught that all the Gentile converts must become Jewish proselytes and keep all the ceremonial laws of Moses. Paul and Barnabas had been freed from this wrong idea, and they stood up against it. After long discussion the brethren decided that these two, with several other men, should go up to Jerusalem and take the question to the apostles there. One of the young men whom they took with them was Titus. Remember, he was not a Jew, but a Greek; and I suppose Paul took him along as a sample of what fine young men could be converted straight from heathenism.

When they reached Jerusalem, they found the apostles. Whether all of the apostles were there we cannot be certain. Some of them may have been away on missions. But certainly the three chief ones were there. The first of these was James. This was not James the brother of John; for Herod had killed him. He was another James, the son of Alphaeus, whom Paul calls "the Lord's brother." (Galatians 1:19.) Back there in that time they often used the word "brother" to mean "cousin" or some other close relation; so many think that this James was a cousin of the Lord Jesus.

The other two chief apostles were Peter and John. Paul says these three "seemed to be pillars" of the church. They were the leaders. They received Paul and Barnabas and gladly listened to all they had to tell of how the Lord had blessed them in taking the gospel to the Gentiles; and they gave them the right hand of fellowship.

Then they went into council with the rest of the apostles and rulers. But some of the Pharisees who had accepted the gospel still held to their old ideas. It was some of their number who had gone to Antioch and made all the trouble there. Now they said the Gentile converts must be made Jews before they could be Christians.

At last Peter arose and said: "Brothers, you know that in the early days God chose me to take the gospel to the Gentiles. And He put His Holy Spirit upon them just as He did upon us. Now why do you try to provoke God by putting a yoke upon the necks of these

disciples? It is a yoke that neither our forefathers nor we have been able to bear. We believe that it is by the mercy of the Lord Jesus that we and they are saved."

That quieted them, and they listened to the report that Paul and Barnabas had to make. After that James, who seems to have been presiding, said: "Brothers, listen! Peter has told us how God first took Gentiles into His family. And so the prophets have foretold. Now in my opinion we ought not to put stumbling blocks in the path of these Gentile converts, but only tell them the necessary things to do, and leave the laws of Moses to the Jews in their synagogues."

So the apostles and the elders and the whole church agreed to send such a letter to the Gentile believers in Antioch. They wrote: "We have heard that some of our number, without any instruction from us, have troubled you by their teaching. We are sending our representatives, Judas and Silas, with our dear brothers, Barnabas and Paul, who will tell you what we advise. The Holy Spirit and we have decided not to lay any burden upon you other than these things: Avoid anything which has been offered to idols; eat nothing strangled, with the blood in it; and keep yourselves from the sins of the heathen. Live up to the ways of Jesus, and all will be well. Good-by."

So Judas and Silas strengthened Barnabas and Paul, and the Gentile believers were accepted as a part of the people of God. When their mission was over, Judas went back to Jerusalem, but Silas stayed on in Antioch, and he became a helper of Paul.

———————

Stumbling blocks! Stumbling blocks!
   How many people say
They're building walls with mighty rocks,
   When they're only in the way.
Be sure you build the walls of life,
   Nor strew your blocks around:
There is no temple where men strive,
   But only littered ground.

464

The Jailer Is Converted

The jailer was awakened by the earthquake that opened the doors of the prison where Paul and Silas were held. Thinking they had escaped, the jailer drew his sword and was about to kill himself when Paul called, "Do thyself no harm: for we are all here." The jailer went into the room to Paul and Silas and said, "Sirs, what must I do to be saved?"

ROBERT TEMPLE AYRES, ARTIST

Come Over and Help Us

Acts 15:36-41; 16

AFTER they had been in Antioch for some time, Paul and Barnabas decided to go out and visit the believers in the places where they had been before. Barnabas went one way, taking his nephew Mark with him. Paul went the other way, taking Silas as his helper. At Lystra Paul picked up Timothy, who went along with them as a student, and who finally became a great apostle himself. He was the chief of the young men whom Paul called his "sons in the faith."

They came at last to a seaside town called Troas. The Spirit of God had turned them away from the cities of Asia Minor, and brought them down to this seaport. Here they were joined by Luke, a physician, who after this traveled much with Paul, and who wrote the Gospel of Luke and the Book of Acts.

Across the waters, in Europe, lay the country of Macedonia, the upper part of Greece. And now the gospel was about to enter Europe.

In the night Paul had a vision. He saw a man of Macedonia standing and calling to him, "Come over into Macedonia, and help us."

Immediately they planned to go by ship to Macedonia; and into Macedonia they came. They soon reached the principal city, Philippi, and in this place they stayed some days. On the Sabbath day they went outside the gates to the bank of the river, where was a place of prayer. There they sat down and talked with the women who gathered there. One of them was a woman named Lydia, who was a merchant dealing in fine clothing. She believed in Jesus, and was baptized, with all her family. Then she opened her house to the apostles, and they stayed there.

As they passed down the streets, they were followed by a girl who was a fortuneteller, possessed by an evil spirit. This girl followed the apostles, crying out, "These men are servants of the Most High God, and they are making known to you a way of salvation." That was true, but they did not want to be advertised by such a person; and Paul turned to her and in the name of Jesus commanded the evil spirit to come out of her, which it did. Then she no longer told fortunes, and her masters were very angry, for they had made much money by her fortunetelling.

465

They seized Paul and Silas and dragged them before the judges. A mob gathered and joined in the attack. The rulers had them beaten and threw them into jail. But Paul and Silas prayed and sang hymns, rejoicing that they might suffer for Jesus' sake. And the prisoners listened to them.

At midnight there was such an earthquake that the prison was jarred to the foundations. All the doors flew open, and everyone's chains were unfastened. It woke up the jailer; and when he saw the doors open, he thought all the prisoners were escaped. As the law commanded death for any soldier or jailer who lost his prisoners, this jailer called for a sword and was going to kill himself. Paul shouted to him, "Do yourself no harm, for we are all here!"

Then the jailer called for lights and rushed in and fell trembling at the feet of Paul and Silas. He led them out of the prison and asked them, "What must I do to be saved?"

"Believe in the Lord Jesus," they answered, "and you and your household will be saved."

Then he washed their wounds, and he and all his household listened to the gospel, and were baptized. He took the apostles up to his house and gave them food, and he and all his family were very happy in their new faith in God.

In the morning the rulers of the city sent policemen to tell the jailer to let those men go. The jailer told them this and said, "Now you can go free."

But Paul answered: "They had us beaten in public without a trial, and put us in jail, though we are Roman citizens. And now will they turn us out in secret? No, indeed! Have them come here themselves and take us out."

The rulers were afraid when they heard that the men they had beaten were Roman citizens; for to be a Roman was greater than to be a king. They came in person and begged their forgiveness and asked them to leave town. When they were let out, they went to the house of Lydia and saw the new converts and encouraged them. Then they left town.

They went to the city of Thessalonica, and there they converted many. But being mobbed, they left for Berea, where they made many disciples of both the Jews and the Greeks. But the Jews of Thessalonica came there and stirred up a mob. Then the believers sent Paul away, but Silas and Timothy stayed behind to teach. Paul went on to Athens, the most famous and learned city of Greece, leaving word for Silas and Timothy to meet him there.

466

The Unknown God

Acts 17:14-34

ATHENS was the capital of Greece. Of old time it had been famous for its statesmen and warriors and most of all for its wise men and great artists. Its buildings were noble and its laws were just. But when the Romans conquered Greece, Athens lost much of its splendor. Still it had its schools and its wise men after the world, and the people were very proud of its history.

When Paul came to Athens, he did not seem to the men there to be much of anybody. Maybe those who noticed him said: "Well, here's another Jew, one of those queer people who do not worship the gods of Greece or Rome, nor even have any image of their own god. What's another Jew to us?"

While he waited in Athens for Timothy and Silas to come to him, he walked its beautiful streets filled with statues of men and gods. He entered the public square, where men high and low spent their time debating and arguing. He saw their magnificent temples, the work of the greatest builders and sculptors of all time. He went to the synagogue of the Jews, hoping to find there some open hearts. But everywhere he saw idolatry. And though the Jews did not worship idols, they were so filled with pride and selfishness that they too knew not God.

Paul began to talk with men of every kind, telling them of Jesus. He tried to teach the Jews in their synagogue, and he spoke to the Greeks in the public square. Some of the learned men of the city happened by. They were proud of their learning, and quite scornful of this seemingly humble man who was trying to be a teacher. "What is this gad-about trying to make out?" some idly asked. And others answered, "He seems to be recommending some foreign gods."

But what he was saying caught the attention of some of the more thoughtful of them, and they said to him: "Sir, we would like to hear more of your doctrine. Come with us to a quieter place, and talk with us."

So they took him to the council on Mars Hill, or Areopagus. This was a high court which dealt with all cases of great crimes as they thought of crime, like murder and blasphemy and immorality;

and they punished vices of all kinds. Its members were the most learned and influential of the men of Athens. Here the common crowd could not come. All was quiet and dignified. And they said to Paul, "May we know just what this new teaching of yours is? Some of the things you tell us seem strange, and we want to know just what they mean."

Then Paul stood up in their midst and said: "Men of Athens, everywhere I look I see that you are very religious. Not only do you worship all the gods you know; but as I looked at your devotions, I saw an altar on which was written, 'To the Unknown God.' Whom therefore you worship without knowing, I declare to you."

Then he went on to tell them of the true God, who made all things, and who made all men brothers, of whom He is the Father. And he said: "Since we are God's children, we ought not to think that He is like images of gold and silver and stone, made by men's hands. In past time God overlooked men's ignorance; but now He commands all men to repent, because He has fixed a day on which He will judge the world, through the Man He has appointed, a divine Man whom He raised from the dead."

As he told them of Jesus and of the resurrection from the dead, some of them sneered, but others said, "We would like to hear you again on this matter." Most of them were too much filled with the wisdom of the world to listen to the simple gospel. But one member of high standing in the council, a man named Dionysius, and a noble woman named Damaris, believed, as did some others. But Paul saw that the wisdom of God seemed foolishness to the Greeks, and as for the Jews, it was only a stumbling block. It was the more simple and unspoiled people who would listen.

Silas and Timothy did not come, being held in Thessalonica and Berea. And Paul departed from Athens.

O men of Athens! Men who learning boast,
　　You know so much of that which is not so;
Who now can teach you what is needed most,
　　The knowledge of the God you do not know?
Shall science reign? or faith? Shall Athens bow,
　　And Calvary teach to bend the suppliant knee
To One reject before, but Saviour now,
　　Elect to save the race and set men free?
This is your hour; but if you will transgress,
　　Your boasted wisdom will prove foolishness.

468

Christians in a Wicked City

Acts 18:1-18; 1 Corinthians 2:1-5; 1 Thessalonians; 2 Thessalonians

PAUL left Athens and went to Corinth. This was a beautiful and wealthy city, west of Athens. It was built on a neck of land between two arms of the sea, which almost cut Greece in two. The merchant ships of Asia on the east and of Italy on the west sailed up these gulfs and passed their goods across. Many of these things were sold in Corinth, and by this business the city grew rich.

But it was a very wicked city, given up not only to idolatry but to evil living. Athens was evil but cultured; Corinth was evil and vulgar. When Paul left Athens, he was disappointed by his visit there. He had used his best efforts to convince them, and he was a very good debater and orator. But very few of the Athenians had heeded his message and been converted. So now when he went to Corinth, where they were not especially brainy, he decided he would not try to show himself learned and brilliant, but he would just preach Christ.

We now think of the cross of Christ as the symbol of a glorious truth, the salvation of the world and of each one of us. But that is because Jesus died on the cross, and through dying saved the world. Back there in Paul's time the cross meant only a terrible and shameful death, as today we think of the gallows or the electric chair, by which criminals are put to death. Paul's great mission was to teach men that a humble Jew, Jesus, crucified, was yet the Saviour of the world, the Son of God. Think of the worst criminal you ever heard of, and try to tell men that he was the greatest of men and the lord of all, and you will see what a task Paul had. Nevertheless he says that he left behind his lofty teaching at Athens, and came to the Corinthians determined to know nothing among them but Christ, and Him crucified.

When he reached Corinth, he found there two Jews, husband and wife, named Aquila and Priscilla. They had but lately come from Rome, from which the emperor had banished all Jews, and they had set up shop in Corinth. They were tentmakers, and this was the trade in which Paul, in his boyhood and youth, had been trained. So he lived with them and worked at his trade. But every Sabbath he went with them to the synagogue and preached, trying to convince both the Jews and the Greek proselytes.

469

At last Silas and Timothy came and joined Paul, and he was very glad. By this time he was deep in his work of presenting Christ to the Jews in Corinth. But as they disputed and abused him, he said to them, "Your blood be upon your own heads"—just as the Jews had cried at the trial of Jesus before Pilate, "His blood be on us and on our children!" Paul said: "So be it! I am not to blame for your rejection. After this I will go to the Gentiles."

So he left the synagogue, and went to the house of a devout proselyte named Titus Justus, which was next door to the synagogue. But his work for the Jews had not all been in vain; for the leader of the synagogue, Crispus, with all his family, believed and joined the Christians. So did many of the others. And the Lord said to Paul in a night vision: "Do not be afraid! Go on speaking, and do not give up. For I am with you, and no man shall hurt you. For I have many people in this city."

So Paul stayed there for a year and a half, teaching. But the Jews made an attack upon him, and with a great mob brought him before the Roman governor of Greece, Gallio. "This fellow," they charged, "is trying to get people to worship God in ways that are against the law!"

Paul was about to answer, but Gallio stopped him, saying that he did not need to. Then he turned to the Jews and said: "If this man had done some evil thing, I would listen to you. But since it is only a matter of talking and names and your law, I will have nothing to do with it." And he drove them away from the judgment seat. Then the mob turned against the Jews, and beat up their leader, Sosthenes. And Gallio paid no attention to it because he was disgusted with what the Jews had done.

Silas and Timothy had brought good word about the believers in Macedonia, and especially in Thessalonica. But while they told of their faith and courage and devotion, they also told of some trouble among them. And now Paul began his great writings, which have come down to us in the Bible, by sending an epistle or letter to the Thessalonians.

There are fourteen epistles of Paul in the New Testament. Nine of them were written to churches, four of them to individual persons, and one, the Book of Hebrews, was general, to everybody.

Then he departed from Corinth, leaving a good strong church, and sailed away to Ephesus, in Asia Minor. He took Aquila and Priscilla with him; for they had proved to be good workers for Christ. And now to a great work in Asia.

470

A Stronghold in Asia

Acts 18:19-28; 19; 20; 1 Corinthians; 2 Corinthians;
Romans; Galatians

THE CITY in Asia where Paul stayed the longest and did the most to set Jesus in the hearts of men was Ephesus, the capital of the country. He first went to the Jewish synagogue, and for some time preached Jesus to them. But at last most of them turned against him, so Paul separated the believers from the unbelievers and carried on his meetings in the school of a teacher named Tyrannus. There he taught for two years, and the gospel was spread all through Asia Minor, that great peninsula which lies between the Black Sea and the Mediterranean.

Once while Paul was away, there came to Ephesus a man from Alexandria, in Egypt, whose name was Apollos. He had heard only the preaching of John the Baptist and did not know very much about the life of Jesus. Aquila and Priscilla, hearing him in the synagogue, took him home and taught him about the life and mission of Jesus. And after this he taught the way of life as they and Paul taught it. He crossed over to Greece and helped the believers much, especially at Corinth.

While here in Ephesus, Paul wrote a letter to the church in Corinth, to correct some faults they had. In the Bible it is called First Corinthians. Later he wrote Second Corinthians. And still a little later, he wrote the epistles to the Romans and the Galatians.

The Christian movement in Ephesus and the country round about grew so strong that the worship of idols fell off; and the men who made the little images they sold to persons found their business poorer and poorer. There was a great temple in Ephesus, in which Diana, the moon goddess, was worshiped. And in it was a great image of her which they said had fallen down from heaven. Silversmiths and others got a great deal of money by making and selling little copies of this image.

A silversmith named Demetrius grew very angry over Paul's work. He called together the other smiths, and said to them: "Gentlemen, you know that by this business we have our wealth. Now this Paul has won so many people, telling them that gods made by human

hands are no gods at all, that not only will our business be ruined, but the temple of Diana will be deserted."

Then they all rose up in anger and began shouting, "Great is Diana of the Ephesians! Great is Diana of the Ephesians!" The riot spread all through the city, and great crowds rushed to the outdoor theater, dragging with them some of Paul's helpers. Paul wanted to go in and reason with them, but the brethren would not let him. And some of the chief men of Asia who were his friends also sent word for him not to appear.

In the theater the Jews put forward one of their number, named Alexander, to have him talk to the mob and tell them they had nothing to do with Paul. But when the crowd saw that Alexander was a Jew, they drowned out his voice, shouting, "Great is Diana of the Ephesians!" And this went on for two hours.

The town clerk at last quieted them down, and he said to them: "Men of Ephesus, everybody knows that Ephesus guards the temple and image of Diana. So there is no need for you to be so riotous and reckless. You have brought these men here, who have said nothing against our goddess, and the Romans are likely to call us to account for this riot, since there is no cause for it. If Demetrius and his fellows have any grievance, there are the courts; let them bring their charges." And he sent them home.

After the uproar was over, Paul sent for the believers and encouraged them. Then he told them good-by and started for Macedonia. He first went to the seaport of Troas, expecting to meet Titus there, as he had directed; but Titus did not come. It was not so easy to travel then, and it was not so easy to get in touch with one another. There were no railway trains or busses to travel on. You had to walk or ride horseback, or once in a while in a chariot or wagon. And the ships had no timetable to sail by. They just went when they got a cargo to carry. And you couldn't call up your friends on long distance, for there were no telephones. And you couldn't send a wire, for there were no telegraphs. You couldn't even send an air-mail letter, for there were no airplanes, and there wasn't even a post office or a mail service. Letters had to be sent by private messengers or by someone going that way. So it is no surprise that Paul's friends sometimes failed to make connections.

Titus did not come to Troas, as Paul expected; so Paul sailed away to Philippi in Macedonia, where he met Timothy and received from him a good report. And soon Titus came with good news from Corinth. They had received Paul's letter, and it had taken effect. They

472

repented and reformed, and now, Titus said, they were pretty good and getting better. Paul was refreshed and encouraged by this news. And at once he wrote another letter to that church, filled with thanksgiving. That epistle we know as Second Corinthians.

After visiting the churches in Macedonia, such as Philippi, Thessalonica, and Berea, he went on down into Greece and came again to Corinth. And there he worked for three months.

Now it came time for Paul to leave for Jerusalem. Quite a company of workers were to go with him. He sent them ahead to Troas, and there they waited for him. A few, however, stayed with him, among them Luke; and in a few days they all sailed from Philippi to Troas. Then they all went by stages to Miletus, which was a seaport thirty-six miles south of Ephesus. Paul had no time to spend in Ephesus if he was to get to Jerusalem before Pentecost.

He therefore called to Miletus the elders of the Ephesus church, and there bade them farewell. He reminded them of all his labors with them, testifying of Jesus both before the Jews and the Greeks, both of which were in the church now. And he said: "I am now going to Jerusalem, and I do not know what awaits me there. Only, in every town I visit the Holy Spirit warns me that persecution and imprisonment will be my fate. But I do not count my life of value, if I can only finish my race and do the work the Lord has given me to do. Now I know that you among whom I have worked will never see my face again."

With that they all wept, and embraced him, and kissed him, sorrowing because of that word.

And then, with his companions, he sailed away.

———

My brethren beloved who dwell on the golden sea,
    Where merchandise of Rome and Asia meet,
    I, Paul, the merchant of the Lord, entreat
Within your ranks a greater harmony.

For that the gospel which to you I bore
    Was not a message of debate and strife,
    But peace and joy in Christ's immaculate life,
Take now the priceless gift, and strive no more.

473

Paul in Jerusalem

Acts 21; 22; 23:1-11

PAUL and his company sailed from Miletus, and after changing ships two or three times, they arrived at Caesarea. At every place they stopped and saw the brethren of the churches, Paul was warned not to go to Jerusalem, for there awaited him persecution and imprisonment. But he would not be turned back; he felt he had a mission to perform.

When they reached Jerusalem, the brethren there gave them a hearty welcome. The next day they went to see James, and all the elders came in. Paul greeted them warmly, and gave a full account of what God had done among the Gentiles through his efforts. They praised God when they heard it.

But it shows how much the Judaizing spirit had crept in among them, when they said to Paul: "You see, brother, how many thousands of Jews have believed on Jesus, all of them strong upholders of the law. Now they have been told that you teach the Gentiles to turn away from Moses, and not to observe the old customs. What then? Prove to them that this is not so. We have four men who have vowed a vow, according to Moses' law. And tomorrow they are finishing up at the temple the ceremonies their vow requires. You go with them, and be one of their party, and pay their expenses. That will show the Jews that the charges against you are false."

Paul wanted to please his brethren. He knew that the old ceremonies now had no force nor place in the Christian church; but since they meant nothing to him, he thought he could do this favor and keep the peace. So he did what they asked him to do. There were yet seven days during which the men of the vow had to perform ceremonies in the temple. The seven days were almost over when Jews from Asia caught sight of Paul in the temple and seized him, crying out: "Men of Israel, help! This is the man who teaches everybody everywhere against our people and the law and the temple. And besides, he has brought Greeks into the temple and profaned this holy place!"

That was false. The outer and largest court of the temple was open to Gentiles, but they must not go into the next court or beyond. The Jews called these inner courts a part of the temple, but the outer

474

court was the court of the Gentiles. They had seen Paul with Trophimus, an Ephesian Christian, in the outer court, and they supposed, or made out, that he had taken him into the inner court, which he had not.

Now a mob gathered. They seized Paul and drew him out of the temple and were about to kill him. When Claudius Lysias, the chief captain of the Roman guard who were in the castle right next to the temple, saw this riot, he took some soldiers and ran down to them. Then they left off beating Paul. The captain took him and had him bound with two chains, and demanded of the Jews to tell what he had done.

Some cried this and some cried that. And when the captain could get no clear answer, he commanded Paul to be carried into the castle. The mob surged around them, crying, "Kill him! Kill him!" So, because of their violence, the soldiers had to carry him. As they were going up the stairs, Paul said to the chief captain in Greek, "May I say something to you?"

"Do you know Greek?" exclaimed the captain. "Aren't you that Egyptian who some time ago raised four thousand cutthroats and led them out into the desert?"

"I am a Jew," answered Paul, "from Tarsus, a citizen of no little city. I beg you to let me speak to the people."

The captain gave him permission, and Paul, standing on the steps, motioned to the people. When they were quiet, he spoke to them in Hebrew. He began by telling them the story of his conversion on the road to Damascus and of God's directions to him since. He got as far as God's command for him to go to the Gentiles; but that maddened them, and they began to shout, "Kill him! Kill him, and get him out of the world! A creature like that ought not to live!"

As they were shouting and throwing their clothes about and flinging dust into the air, the captain ordered Paul to be brought into the castle and gave directions for him to be flogged while they questioned him, so that he might find out why the Jews demanded his death. But when they had strapped him up, Paul said to the officer standing by, "Is it lawful for you to flog a Roman citizen without giving him a trial?"

Upon hearing this, the officer went to Lysias and said, "Take care what you do! This man is a Roman citizen!"

Lysias came to Paul and asked, "Are you really a Roman citizen?"

"Yes," he said.

"I had to pay a large sum for my citizenship," said the captain.

475

As much as to say that Paul, judging from his appearance, could never have paid a penny.

"But I am a citizen by birth," said Paul. Tarsus, with all its citizens, had for some great service been given citizenship by the emperor.

Then the captain had Paul unbound; for he was alarmed when he learned that he had been about to flog a Roman citizen. The next day he ordered the chief priests and the whole Sanhedrin to assemble, and he took Paul down and put him before them. Now this, remember, was many years after the trial of Jesus, and the high priests Annas and Caiaphas had been removed. The high priest now was a man named Ananias. But Paul did not know him.

Paul said, "Brothers, I have done my duty to God with a perfectly clear conscience up to this very day."

Ananias ordered the people standing next to Paul to strike him on the mouth. But it was forbidden by the law of Moses to abuse a prisoner, or punish him uncondemned.

Paul said to him indignantly, "God will strike you, you white-washed wall! Do you sit there to try me by the law, and order them to strike me in violation of the law?"

The men next him said, "Will you insult God's high priest?"

Paul's anger stopped, and he said, "I did not know, brothers, that he was the high priest. The Scripture says, 'You shall not say anything against any ruler of your people.'"

But, knowing that the Sanhedrin was made up partly of Pharisees, of whom he had been one, and partly of Sadducees, who did not believe in angels and who denied that there was to be a resurrection, Paul called out:

"Brothers, I am a Pharisee, and the son of Pharisees! It is for my hope of the resurrection of the dead that I am on trial."

Immediately a dispute arose between the Pharisees and the Sadducees, and the meeting was divided. There was a great uproar. Some of the Pharisees got up and said, "We find nothing wrong with this man. Perhaps some spirit or angel really spoke to him!"

The council became riotous, and the chief captain, afraid they would pull Paul in pieces, sent his soldiers in and bore him out. And he kept him safe in the castle.

That night the Lord stood by him and said, "Be of good cheer, Paul! For just as you have testified for Me in Jerusalem, you must also testify in Rome." So Paul was going to Rome, as he had desired! But he had not thought that he was going as a prisoner.

476

Paul on Trial

Acts 23:12-35; 24 to 26

NOW what? Paul had been saved from the mob; but almost all Jerusalem now was a mob, following the high priest, and Paul was in the midst of it, although in the castle.

In the morning the Jews made a plot to do away with Paul. They got forty desperate fellows to swear that they would neither eat nor drink till they had killed him. They went to the priests and the elders and said: "Now you and the council must ask the chief captain to have Paul brought down to you, as though you mean to look into his case more carefully, and we will be ready to kill him before he gets there."

But Paul had some relatives in the city. One of them was a nephew, the son of his sister, who by some means got wind of this plot, and he went at once to the castle. He was let in to see Paul, and he told him about it. So Paul called one of the officers and said, "Take this young man to the chief captain, for he has something to tell him."

The officer took the young man to the captain, and Lysias took him by the arm and led him aside and asked, "What is it that you have to tell me?"

So he told him about the plot and said, "They are all ready now and only waiting to get you to promise."

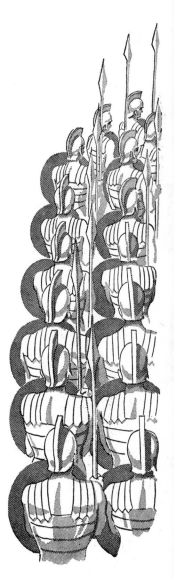

The captain sent the young man away, telling him to say no word of this to anyone else. Then he called for two of his officers and ordered them to get ready two hundred foot-soldiers, spearmen, and seventy horsemen by nine o'clock that night. And when they were ready, he sent them, with Paul in their midst, to Felix the governor, in Caesarea. He sent along a letter explaining the case. The soldiers took Paul to within thirty miles of Caesarea, and there the spearmen turned back to Jerusalem, leaving the horsemen to carry Paul to the governor.

When Felix read the letter of Claudius Lysias, he said to Paul: "What is your birthplace? In what province?"

Paul said, "Tarsus, in Cilicia."

Said the governor, "I will hear your case as soon as your accusers come." And he gave orders that Paul should be kept in Herod's palace.

Herod (who was Herod Agrippa II, the son of the Herod who had killed James) was away just then, traveling somewhere in his kingdom.

Five days later, the high priest Ananias came down, with some of the elders and with a lawyer named Tertullus. And when Paul had been brought in, Tertullus began to accuse him of being a pest and a disturber of the peace among Jews all over the world. Also, he said, they had caught him trying to profane the temple, but they stopped him. "But the chief captain Lysias," he complained, "came upon us with great violence and took him out of our hands." And all the Jews stood around saying this was so.

The governor made a sign to Paul to speak, and Paul began: "As I know that for many years you have acted as judge for this people, I cheerfully undertake my defense. It is not more than twelve days ago, as you can easily find out for yourself, that I went up to worship at Jerusalem. And they have never found me disputing with anyone in the temple, or creating any disturbance, and they cannot prove the charges they have just made against me. But this I confess, that in worshiping the God of our fathers I follow the way of life that they call a sect, holding that there is to be a resurrection of the good and the wicked.

"Having been away for several years, I came with gifts for my nation, and they found me in the temple with no crowd or disturbance at all. But there were some Jews from Asia, who ought to be here to testify against me, if they have any complaint. And the only offense I gave was that in the council I shouted through the tumult, 'It is because of the resurrection of the dead that I am called in question.'"

Then Felix, who already knew a good deal about the Christians, adjourned the trial, saying to the Jews, "When Lysias the chief captain comes down here, I will decide your case." He ordered the officer to keep Paul, but to allow his friends to come to him.

Felix's wife was Drusilla, a sister of Herod Agrippa II, and the great-granddaughter of the first Herod. A few days later the two of them sent for Paul and listened to what he had to say about faith in Christ Jesus. But as he talked of uprightness, self-control, and the coming judgment, Felix became alarmed and said, "You may go now. I will find time later to send for you."

Felix was not a noble Roman. He had been a slave in Caesar's household, but was freed by the emperor and rose to be governor of Palestine. He was a bad ruler, committing various crimes, and the Jews hated him. Now he thought Paul might bribe him with money to let him go. So he kept him in prison for two years, sending for him often

478

to talk with him. At the end of that time, however, Felix was removed from being governor. To please the Jews, he left Paul in prison. But however much that pleased them, it did not make them love Felix. They followed him to Rome and accused him of many crimes. Had it not been for his brother, who had influence in the royal court, he would have been put to death. As it was, he was removed from office, and that's the last we hear of him, though it is on record that his wife Drusilla and their son died in the volcanic eruption of Vesuvius a few years later.

The governor who took Felix's place was Porcius Festus. When he came into the province, he stopped at the capital, Caesarea, for three days, and then he went up to Jerusalem. There the high priests presented their charges against Paul and begged Festus to bring him to Jerusalem—but they plotted to kill him on the way. Festus answered that Paul was to be kept in Caesarea. "So have your chief men go down with me," he said, "and bring charges against the man, if there is anything wrong with him."

After eight or ten days he went down to Caesarea, and the next day sat in the judge's chair and ordered Paul to be brought in. When he came, the Jews from Jerusalem made a number of serious charges against him, which they could not prove.

Paul said in his own defense, "I have done nothing against the Jewish law, or the temple, or the emperor."

Then Festus, wishing to please the Jews, said to Paul, "Will you go up to Jerusalem and be tried there before me on these charges?"

That would be playing right into the hands of the Jews. Paul had been kept unjustly in prison for two years by one governor, and now he suspected that the new governor was going to treat him just as badly. There was just one thing to do: appeal to the highest court. He answered: "I stand at Caesar's judgment seat, where I ought to be judged. To the Jews I have done no wrong, as you can easily see. If I am guilty, I do not refuse to die; but if I am innocent, no man may deliver me to my enemies. I appeal to Caesar!"

Festus, nettled at this appeal over his head in the first case he had tried, said: "You appeal to Caesar, do you? To Caesar you shall go!" That sounded like, "You'll be sorry!" And no wonder. For the emperor who sat in the seat of Caesar at that time was the worst ruler that ever lived. His name was Nero; and Nero has become a byword for the meanest, lowest, vilest, wickedest person imaginable. All of that was Nero Caesar, emperor of Rome, to whom Paul had appealed.

Some time after this, King Herod Agrippa and Bernice came back

to Caesarea. Bernice was another daughter of Herod Agrippa I, and the sister both of this Agrippa and of Drusilla. Festus said to them: "There is a man left here in prison by Felix, against whom the Jews have made charges, not such as I had expected, but about things in their law, and about a certain Jesus, who had died, but who Paul said was alive. I did not know how to judge such matters, and I asked him if he would go up to Jerusalem for trial. But he appealed his case to Caesar, and I have kept him a prisoner until I can send him to the emperor."

"I should like to hear the man myself," said Agrippa.

"Tomorrow you shall," promised Festus.

So the next day Agrippa and Bernice came with great pomp into the judgment hall, attended by officers and leading citizens. At the command of Festus, Paul was brought in. Festus introduced him to Agrippa, and Agrippa said to Paul, "Be free to speak in your own behalf."

So Paul began his defense, reciting his conversion on the road to Damascus, and his experience since, up to the time the Jews seized him in the temple. As he spoke of the salvation that is in Jesus Christ, Festus called out: "You are raving, Paul! Your great learning is driving you mad!"

Paul said: "I am not raving, most noble Festus. I am telling the sober truth. The king knows about this. I do not believe he missed any of it, for it was not done in a corner. King Agrippa, do you believe the prophets? I know you do!"

Agrippa answered, "Almost you persuade me to be a Christian."

Paul said: "I wish to God that not only you but all who hear me today, might be what I am—except for these chains." And he lifted his fettered hands.

Then the king rose, with the governor and Bernice, and they left the room. After talking it over among themselves, they said, "This man has not done anything to deserve imprisonment or death." And Agrippa added to Festus, "He might have been set free if he had not appealed to Caesar."

But he had appealed, and he was therefore sentenced to be sent to Rome as a prisoner, there to be judged by the emperor.

480

The Shipwreck of Paul

The centurion in charge of the ship "commanded that they which could swim should cast themselves first into the sea, and get to land: and the rest, some on boards, and some on broken pieces of the ship. And so it came to pass, that they escaped. . . ."

CLYDE N. PROVONSHA, ARTIST

Shipwreck

Acts 27; 28:1-10

PAUL, with some other prisoners, was turned over to Julius, a captain of the imperial band of soldiers. Two of Paul's companions, Luke, the physician, and Aristarchus, a believer from Thessalonica, were allowed to go with him. The captain and his soldiers put the prisoners on a ship sailing to a port in Asia Minor. Almost never was there a ship sailing from Palestine directly to Italy, so they had to change ships.

At the end of this short trip they got off, and the captain found a ship from Alexandria, Egypt, which was going to Italy, and he put them in it. It was nearing winter, a season when ships in those days did not usually make long voyages. They had to steer by sight of the sun and stars, and when winter storm and clouds covered these, they were lost. Now, with slow sailing, they got as far as the island of Crete, and came to a harbor called Fair Havens.

As a good deal of time had now passed and voyages had become dangerous, Paul warned them. "Gentlemen," he said, "I see that this voyage is likely to end in ruin and heavy loss, not only of the ship and cargo, but of our own lives too."

But the officer, trusting more to the judgment of the pilot and the owner than to what Paul had to say, decided to go on. The harbor where they lay was small and not very good to winter in; so they thought they would try for Phenice, on the western end of Crete. And when a south wind blew softly, they judged it was the time, weighed anchor, and ran close along the shore.

But very soon a violent wind rushed down upon them. The ship was caught by it and could not bear up, so they gave way and ran before the wind wherever it would take them. The ships of those days were so small they seldom carried on deck a lifeboat or small boat. They let it trail behind. Now, as they passed under the lee of a small island named Clauda, with great difficulty they secured the little boat and hauled it on deck. And then they passed ropes around the ship and pulled them tight to strengthen it. Afraid of being cast on the quicksands, they struck their sails and let the ship drift.

For many days neither sun nor stars appeared, and the storm continued to rage, until they gave up all hope of being saved. They

tossed out the cargo, and then the tackling of the ship. Now they had gone a long time without any food. Paul stood up among them and said: "Gentlemen, you ought to have listened to me, and not have sailed from Crete and come into all this ruin and loss. But I beg you to keep up your courage, for there will be no loss of life, but only of the ship. For last night an angel of the God I belong to and serve stood before me and said, 'Do not be afraid, Paul! You must stand before the emperor, and God has given you the lives of all the people in the ship with you.' So keep up your courage, gentlemen! For I have faith in God, that it will be just as I was told. But we are to be stranded on some island."

On the fourteenth night, as they were driven up and down in the raging sea, the sailors thought that they were drawing toward some land. They sounded—that is, let down their measuring line—and found the water growing more and more shallow. So they cast four anchors out of the stern, and wished for the day.

The seamen let down the little boat into the sea and were about to leave the ship when Paul said to the officer, "You cannot be saved unless these men stay on board." Then the soldiers cut the ropes and let the boat drift away.

Paul kept urging them to take food. "Now for fourteen days," he said, "you have eaten nothing. You must eat to have some strength. And I assure you that no one of you will lose even a hair of his head." Then he took some bread, and giving thanks to God, he broke it and began to eat. This raised their spirits, and they all began to eat. There were about seventy-six men on board.

When they had regained some strength and spirit, daylight came; and though they could not tell what land it was, they saw a bay with a beach and decided to run their ship ashore there if possible. But they struck a shoal and ran the ship aground. The bow stuck fast, and the stern began to break up under the pounding of the waves. The soldiers proposed to kill the prisoners for fear some of them might escape, but the officer wanted to save Paul and stopped them. He ordered all who could swim to jump into the water, and the others to ride in on planks and other pieces of wreckage. So they all got safely to land. They found the island was Malta.

The natives received them kindly and made a fire on the beach, because they were soaked and it was cold. Paul gathered a bundle of sticks and put them on the fire; but a snake, a deadly viper, crawled out and fastened on his hand. When the natives saw this poisonous snake hanging from his hand, they said, "This man is without doubt a murderer. And though he has been saved from the sea, justice will not let him live."

But he only shook the snake off into the fire, and was unharmed. They looked to see him swell up or fall dead, but when nothing happened, they changed their minds and said that he was a god.

Near there was the estate of the governor of the island, Publius. He welcomed them and entertained them hospitably. His father happened to be sick in bed of a fever and dysentery. Paul went in to see him, and after praying, laid his hands on him and cured him. After that, the other sick people on the island came and were healed. They made Paul and his company many presents, and when they sailed, three months later, gave them everything they needed.

Tossed on the waves of a raging sea;
    Captain, what now?
Euroclydon bloweth on port and on lee;
The heavens are black with the ominous cloud;
And the captain, he prayeth, unshamed and aloud
    "Jupiter, hear me!
A garlanded bullock for rescue I vow
    From this furious sea!"

Lost in the tempest of violent gloom;
    Centurion, say!
Do you remember the prophesied doom
Of the prisoner-prophet who counseled to stay
In the landlocked harbor, out of harm's way?
    "Jove! What a tomb!
I'll give you my sword and my shield to allay
    This terrible doom!"

Wrapped in the arms of the devilish storm;
    Apostle, speak!
See you on billow and breaker the form
Of the Master who walks on the ocean's wave,
With hand outstretched to rescue and save?
    "Jesus, Thine arm!"
And, behold, on the deep where the demon drave,
    The Master's form!

Paul in Rome

Acts 28:11-31; Colossians; Ephesians; Philippians; Hebrews;
1 Timothy; Titus; Philemon; 2 Timothy

IN THE spring the shipwrecked party left Malta in another ship of Alexandria, named the Dioscuri. They soon put in at the port of Syracuse, the chief city in the island of Sicily. After three days spent there, they weighed anchor and soon reached Puteoli, on the north shore of the Bay of Naples. There they found brother Christians, and were permitted to stay with them for a week. Then they took up the journey by land to Rome.

When the brethren in Rome heard of their coming, they came out to meet them as far as a town named Three Taverns, about thirty-five miles from Rome, and some went on ten miles farther to a town called Appii Forum. When they met Paul, they greeted him with deep affection, and he thanked God and was greatly encouraged.

The centurion, or captain, who had charge of Paul, had the most kindly and affectionate feeling for him, and he gave permission for him to live by himself, with a soldier to guard him. Three days later he invited the leading Jews to come to see him.

He told them, "Brothers, I have done nothing against our people, yet I was turned over to the Romans as a prisoner in Jerusalem. But I wished to see you and talk with you."

They said, "We have heard nothing against you, but we do know that this sect is everywhere spoken against. So we would like to hear you state your views."

So they set a day, and they came in great numbers to the house where he was staying. And from morning to night he studied with them from the law of Moses and from the prophets, to convince them that Jesus was the Christ. Some of them believed, but not all of them. Then Paul said this last word to those who refused to believe: "Understand, therefore, that this message of God's salvation has been sent to the Gentiles. They will listen to it."

Paul stayed for two years in a rented house of his own and welcomed everybody who came to see him, preaching the kingdom of God to them and teaching them about the Lord Jesus Christ openly and unhindered.

Here ends the Bible account of Paul in the Book of Acts, written by Luke. As Luke was with Paul in Rome, it is supposed that he used this time partly to write the book, and closed it at the time he tells of. But through some of Paul's epistles and through other writings, we learn something of his after experience.

He was waiting for his trial before Nero, but that tyrant was busy with his pleasures and his vices. And also, for many months, the Jews of Palestine did not come to bear testimony against Paul.

He received reports from different workers and messengers of the churches he had had to leave behind; and several fellow workers stayed with him, some part of the time and some all through. There was Luke, the good physician. Timothy also, and Tychicus, were with him at first, but he sent them on missions to the churches back East. Aristarchus and Epaphras he called his "fellow prisoners," though they probably were with him by choice and not by arrest. He sent Epaphras on a mission to the churches. But Titus does not seem to have visited him, being kept at work in the churches of the East.

But one who gave him as much comfort and help as even Timothy, his "own son in the faith," was John Mark. Long before, at the beginning of his work, Paul had rejected Mark because he seemed too soft. But Mark had come up, and was now a good soldier of Jesus Christ. He shared Paul's lot, he chose the hard part of a follower of Christ. Long before, at the arrest of Jesus in Gethsemane, Mark had been there. When Jesus and His disciples left Mark's mother's home, Mark had followed, after hastily wrapping himself in a loose linen coat. And when Jesus was taken by the mob, they also set upon the young man, and pulled the linen coat away from him, and he fled. But he came back. And that was typical of his course in after years. He was not naturally brave, but he learned to be brave and enduring, and Paul loved him.

These companions, or some of them, he used as penmen to write the letters he dictated to them. The two years of his imprisonment were well filled with good instruction, which we ourselves have in certain of his epistles. Among them were epistles to the churches, such as Colossians, Ephesians, and Philippians, and the general Epistle to the Hebrews. He also wrote his First Epistle to Timothy, and his Epistle to Titus.

And there is one very gentle and tender letter he wrote in behalf of a convert. This was a slave named Onesimus, a pagan who had run away from his Christian master, Philemon, in Colosse. Paul found him in Rome, poor and wretched. He befriended him and taught him the

love of Jesus. Then he persuaded the converted servant to go back to his master, and he sent with him such a letter, if you will read it, as will make the tears come. It is reported that Philemon set Onesimus free when he went back to his master in Colosse, and Onesimus became a good Christian worker.

The Bible does not tell us, but the traditions of the church say that Paul was finally tried before Nero. It might be supposed that the emperor would condemn him to death; for Paul was everything that Nero was not. But his noble bearing and his fearless words so awed that wretched tyrant that, unexpectedly, he set Paul free. So for some time, perhaps a year or two, Paul traveled again to at least some of his beloved churches, and strengthened them in Christ.

Then he was arrested, falsely charged with dreadful crimes. For after his first imprisonment, the city of Rome had a terrible fire, which raged for many days, killed many people, and robbed multitudes of their homes and all they had. It was suspected that Nero had it set on fire himself; for while it burned, he sat up on the portico of his palace and played on his harp a song of the burning of Troy, a legendary city of the Greeks, while he watched the flames. But when the people began to cry out against him, he turned the blame on the Christians, and said they did it. So he put hundreds of them to death, crucifying them, burning them alive as human torches, and sacrificing many of them in the brutal games of the theater.

Paul was arrested and charged with inciting this crime, though everyone knew he was innocent. But Nero not only wanted a scapegoat for his own crime, he was also angry because some of his own household servants had accepted the Christian faith. Paul was imprisoned again in Rome. And it was during this imprisonment that he wrote his last letter, the Second Epistle to Timothy, who was then in the East. Great was his final word to the younger man:

"I am now ready to be offered, and the time of my departure is at hand. I have fought a good fight, I have finished my course, I have kept the faith: henceforth there is laid up for me a crown of righteousness, which the Lord, the righteous Judge, shall give me at that day: and not to me only, but unto all them also that love His appearing."

Before Nero again, he had short shrift. The tyrant condemned him to death by beheading, since as a Roman citizen he might not be crucified. Nero did not dare make it a public execution, for fear Paul's appearance would make many new converts. He was taken to a quiet place, and there, in solitude, he gave up his life, which he had devoted for so many years to the Lord Jesus.

486

Alone With God

1 John; 2 John; 3 John; Revelation 1

JOHN, son of Zebedee, brother of James, beloved disciple of Jesus, lived to be very old, longer than any of the other apostles. He died when about a hundred years old. He wrote the Gospel according to John, and he wrote three epistles filled with love—First John, Second John, and Third John.

He suffered persecution with all the other disciples of Jesus, and he labored and taught and bore the burdens of an apostle to the day of his death. His last years were spent at Ephesus, the church which Paul had first raised up. And it is said that when he was too old to walk to church or to preach or to teach, he used to be carried in by his friends and disciples, and that his message was always, "Little children, love one another."

In his youthful days, when he was a disciple of Jesus, he was greatly beloved by the Master. He was a fiery young fellow, as was also his brother James; and Jesus called them "the sons of thunder." But by living with Jesus, he was changed into a gentle, patient, faithful follower of the Lamb. His brother James was the first of the twelve apostles to suffer martyrdom; but John, though he too suffered great persecution, lived to be the last.

Before he grew so old, he came under the persecution of the Roman emperor—not Nero, who was long dead, as were also five emperors after him, but the Emperor Domitian, who staged a fierce persecution of all Christians. Thousands were crucified and burned alive and thrown to the wild beasts in the amphitheater; but it was said that "the blood of the martyrs is the seed of the church." For from their death sprang up many believers in their places.

John was arrested and taken to Rome, where one account says he was thrown into a caldron of boiling oil, but that, like the three friends of Daniel, he was miraculously saved from it. And then Domitian banished him to the lonely isle of Patmos. Certainly it is true that he was banished there, until Domitian was dead and the persecution was over, when he was released.

Patmos is a small island in the sea between Greece and Asia. It is barren of trees, but it has many flowering plants and shrubs. It was

used by the Romans as a place to keep some of their criminals whom they banished. And when the last book of the Bible, called "The Revelation of Jesus Christ," was to be given, John "was in the isle called Patmos, for the word of God, and for the testimony of Jesus Christ." There he was alone, without any Christian friends, without anyone to teach, perhaps without any books; and the emperor thought he had stilled John's voice forever. But John was not alone; for God was with him. And from that lonely island came forth a voice of prophecy that calls and echoes to the last days of time.

On a Sabbath, the Lord's day, John was thinking and meditating upon the message of Jesus. He fell into a trance in the power of the Holy Spirit. And he heard a loud Voice behind him, like the sound of a trumpet, saying: "I am the Alpha and the Omega [Greek for "the A to Z"], the first and the last." And, "What you see, write in a book, and send it to the seven churches which are in Asia." The seven churches were named in order: Ephesus, Smyrna, Pergamos, Thyatira, Sardis, Philadelphia, and Laodicea. There were these seven churches in Asia, among many others, and no doubt each one of them needed the message that was sent to it. But Christian teachers since then have believed that they see in these seven the symbols of seven ages of the Christian church, from John's day down to our own. And the message that was given to each of the seven fits the age and the condition of the church in that time. These messages are found in the second and third chapters of Revelation.

Then, like Isaiah and Ezekiel before him, John saw a vision of the throne of God, and some things that took place in the presence of God on the throne. This account is found in the fourth and fifth chapters.

Also in the body of the Book of Revelation comes a series of events shown under various symbols—of seals, and trumpets, and beasts, and angels, much like the visions of Daniel and Ezekiel and Isaiah. They set forth the history of the church and of the world down to the end of time.

And finally are told the scenes of the last days, and the second coming of Christ, and the judgment day, and the destruction of the devil and all evil, and the setting up of the kingdom of glory of our Lord Jesus Christ in the new earth and the New Jerusalem.

This is the Book of Revelation, which John was commanded to write, and which he did write. And out of this grand television program of the Bible we will take two scenes to close our story of the Word of God.

Saint John on Lonely Patmos

Patmos was not a prison to John, but the veritable
gate of heaven. Here God pulled aside for him the
curtain of the future and allowed him to see the out-
line of the closing scenes of earth's history. Here he
set these revelations upon the scrolls of prophecy.

ROBERT TEMPLE AYRES, ARTIST

The Throne of God

Revelation 4; 5

LIKE Isaiah and Ezekiel, John was given a vision of the throne of God, and of Him who sat upon the throne, and of His attendants and ministers, men and angels. If we put what John saw with what Isaiah and Ezekiel saw, we shall get a little idea of the majesty and glory of God, though never human eye nor ear nor mind can take in the King of glory nor the things which He has prepared for them that love Him. John writes:

*   *   *

After this I had another vision. There was a door standing open in the heavens. And the first Voice like a trumpet that I had heard before speak to me, said: "Come up here, and I will show you what must take place."

Immediately after this I was in a trance in the Spirit, and there stood a throne in heaven, with a Being seated on it. And He who was seated on it looked like jasper and sardius [green and red]; and about the throne was a rainbow of the color of emerald.

Ringed around the throne were twenty-four smaller thrones, with twenty-four elders seated on them, clothed in white, and with gold crowns on their heads.

And out of the throne came flashes of lightning, rumblings, and peals of thunder. In front of the throne seven blazing lamps were burning; they are the seven spirits of God. In front of the throne was what looked like a sea of glass, like crystal.

Around the throne, in the middle of each side, were four living creatures, having eyes all around, before and behind. The first living creature was like a lion. The second was like an ox. The third had a face like a man. And the fourth was like a flying eagle. The four living creatures had each of them six wings covered with eyes all over and under their wings. And day and night they never cease to say:

"Holy, holy, holy,
Lord God Almighty,
Which was, and is, and is to come!"

489

And whenever those four living creatures give glory and honor and praise to Him who is seated on the throne, the twenty-four elders fall down before Him, and throw their crowns down before the throne, and say:

"You are worthy, our Lord and God,
To receive glory, honor, and power;
For You created all things;
By Your will they are and were created."

Then in my vision I heard the voices of many angels, surrounding the throne and the living creatures and the elders. They numbered ten thousand times ten thousand, and thousands of thousands, all of them saying in a loud voice:

"Worthy, worthy is the Lamb
That was slain,
To receive power and riches
And wisdom and strength
And glory and blessing!"

Then I heard every creature in heaven, on earth, underneath the earth, and on the sea, and all that are in them, saying:

"Blessing and honor and glory and power
To Him who is seated on the throne,
And to the Lamb, forever and ever!"

And the four living creatures said, "Amen!"

And the elders fell down and worshiped Him that lives forever and ever.

* * *

That was a little glimpse of the glory of God, given to His beloved disciple John, alone with God on the isle of Patmos.

Paradise of God

Revelation 21; 22

FAIR was the earth that God made for man in the beginning of creation, wondrously beautiful the garden that God planted for Adam and Eve. Dark was the blight that fell upon it when sin entered into the lives of men. The gates of their garden home were closed, and the bright sword of the cherubim guarded it from all entrance of man.

But grand was the plan of salvation that God the Father and the Son laid for the redemption of man and all the creation of God. Brightly blazed the star over the fields of the shepherds and the far plains of the wise men of the East. The Babe that was born that night in the stable of Bethlehem became the Man who lived among men, the Sinless One among the sinful, the Healer of the sick, the Comforter of the sorrowing, the Teacher of the ignorant, the Lamb of God who died to take away the sin of the world.

He was crucified on Calvary, but He rose from the tomb in the glory of God. He comforted His disciples, and He ascended to heaven, there in the sanctuary of God to minister as His people's High Priest until time should be no more, and the books of God should unfold in the judgment day.

O glorious day of a new heaven and a new earth, when the first heaven and the first earth are passed away, and the sea shall be no more; when the earth shall bloom anew as Eden of old, and the Paradise home, with its river and tree of life, shall be renewed in the City of God.

There is heard a great Voice out of heaven, saying: "Behold, the tabernacle of God is with men, and He will dwell with them, and they shall be His people. And God Himself will be with them, and He will wipe every tear from their eyes. There shall be no more death, neither sorrow, nor crying, nor pain." John says:

*   *   *

And I, John, saw the Holy City come down from God out of heaven, adorned as a bride to meet her husband. For my angel guide carried me away in a vision to a great and high mountain, and showed me the New Jerusalem coming down from God out of heaven, in

491

all the glory of God. It shone with a radiance like that of some precious stone, like jasper, clear as crystal. It had a great high wall, with twelve gates in it, and twelve angels at the gates. And engraved on the gates were the names of the twelve tribes of Israel. Three gates there were on every one of the four sides of the city.

The wall of the city had twelve foundations, as there were twelve gates. And each section of the foundation, which was of a separate precious stone, had on it inscribed the name of one of the twelve apostles of the Lamb.

The city was a square, its length as great as its breadth. Measuring it around all four sides, the angel found it to be twelve thousand furlongs, or fifteen hundred miles, three hundred and seventy-five miles through the city in either direction. A great city it was, a garden city; for it was the garden of God.

Its gates were each one of pearl, and they were never shut. The pavements of the streets were of shining gold. And the city had no need of the sun or of the moon to give it light; for the glory of God lighted it, and the center of the glory was the Lamb of God.

Then He showed me the throne of God in the center. And out from under it flowed a pure river of water of life, clear as crystal, which ran through the midst of the street. And on either side of the river was there the tree of life, which bore twelve kinds of fruit, yielding a different kind every month; and its leaves were for the healing of the nations.

There shall be no more curse; but the throne of God and of the Lamb shall be in it, and His servants will serve Him. And they shall see His face, and His name will be on their foreheads.

There shall be no night there, and they have no need of lamplight or sunlight; for the Lord God will shine on them, and they shall reign forever and ever.

And He said to me, "These sayings are faithful and true. And the Lord God of the holy prophets sent His angel to show to His servant the things which must shortly be done. Behold, I come quickly! Blessed is he who heeds the words of the prophecy in this Book."

"Come!" say the Spirit and the bride.
Let everyone who hears this say, "Come!"
Let everyone who is thirsty come.
Let anyone who wants it come and take the water of life freely.
He who testifies to all these things says, "Surely I come quickly!"
Amen! Even so, come, Lord Jesus!

492

Glory Song of the Advent

Our eyes shall see the glory of the coming of the Lord!
He is riding on the wings of them that make His glorious guard,
The seraphim and cherubim who answer to His word:
Our Lord is riding on!

CHORUS: Glory! Glory! Hallelujah!
Glory! Glory! Hallelujah!
Glory! Glory! Hallelujah!
Our God, our Christ, will come!

The rumble of His chariot wheels resounds from Holy Writ;
The elements are warring, and their troubles echo it;
The nations blanch with terror, and the captains nerveless sit!
Our King is marching on!

His earthly legions answer to the drum's incessant roll;
They are charging up the heights of Time, and heaven is their goal.
Oh, be ye swift, my marching feet! Be jubilant, my soul!
For Christ will quickly come.

His trumpets sound the summons over land and sea and sky;
The banners of His host are seen, advancing from on high.
Lift up your heads, ye faithful; for the kingdom draweth nigh,
And we are almost home!